*Names in this book
have been changed to
protect the innocent*

FOREWORD

My daughter, Jamie, is a drug addict. In 1992 her young soncame into my care and I kept a diary of events for the custody court hearing.

Two further children were born, and placed in care for adoption. I began to realise how important my records will be for them in the future, detailing their roots and background. Most important of all, they would explain why their mother has abandoned them for her first love, CRACK.

Jamie's life is constantly at risk from her dangerous acquaintances. There is also a prostitute killer on the loose, and I log details should she disappear.

There have been many failures in the system: social services, probation, prison, health service, drug agencies. I tell how we as a family, and not just Jamie, have suffered from the effects of her drug abuse.

Many parents are living a nightmare, whether their children are using soft or hard drugs; not only in deprived cities but rural towns and villages throughout the land. Everyone must be made aware – DRUGS ARE EVERYWHERE AROUND US AND HERE TO STAY, leaving in their path a toll of destruction and devastation on all aspects of society – especially the family.

Contents

Jamie

Jamie acknowledges my arrival in the Crown Court waiting room. There is a tense sadness as we sit opposite each other. Our eyes do not meet. In her pale face I see a lost soul and long to put my arms around her. We have been such good friends in the past but are now total strangers.

It is May 1992. We are attending the directions hearing for custody of Jamie's son Max, aged 27 months. He has been a temporary ward of court, in my care, for the past year.

The recent words of the court welfare officer keep echoing in my mind, "It's so tragic." I wonder why the life of a previously happy and ambitious girl has turned out this way, at the tender age of nineteen?

In March 1973, my husband Bill and I, together with our young son Jonathan, collected six week old Jamie from a Catholic children's home in Norfolk. Our home was near Newmarket. At the time my husband was a manufacturers' agent and I was his secretary.

Two years later we moved to a village near Stratford-upon-Avon and lived in a picturesque seventeenth century cottage. A loving, middle-class upbringing provided Jamie with all the security and happiness any child could wish for. She attended the village nursery, followed by Catholic junior school. In her teen years she was privately educated and also attended the local high school. Jamie, who was very artistic and bright, participated in extra school activities, including music and sport. She loved Brownies, Guides, horseriding, youth club, playing the clarinet in the wind band, drama and modern dance.

In general, Jamie was an easy child and of reasonably good health. Only one unusual characteristic comes to mind – her 'stare'. She would look right through people as if to say, "I know exactly what you are thinking."

At fifteen Jamie had everything going for her; but her world began to fall apart when she was arrested for possession of *cannabis*. At sixteen she gave birth to her first child.

I reflect on my teen years. My character and lifestyle were so different from that of Jamie's at the same age. Extremely shy and quiet, I found it hard to socialise. My upbringing by my parents, together with my brother and sister, was middle-class. During my early years we lived in London, where I was convent educated. We moved to Birmingham when I was eleven, and I attended grammar school followed by secretarial college.

In 1964, aged 19, my life was so exciting; three months working as a nanny in Paris for a wealthy family; modelling for the World Hair Championships in Switzerland; and secretary for a market research company.

The sixties saw the beginning of a sexual revolution, but not in our family. We had a strict moral upbringing, respecting our parents, often with fear. Sexually naive, we lived at home until marriage.

In 1987, I had a successful kidney transplant. During my seven years on haemodialysis, I struggled to give Jamie as normal a childhood as possible.

Four years later I was divorced, after having endeavoured to keep the family together until Jamie left home.

Now, at the age of forty-seven, I ask myself why Jamie and I are so dissimilar, often poles apart? What has influenced her to choose such a dangerous and violent lifestyle?

Nature versus Nurture? Does the answer lie in the fact that Jamie is adopted? Many leading authorities suggest adopted children take on characteristics from their environment.

I would argue, however, that in Jamie's case they are inherent, although her upbringing has had some influence.

Relaxing in the comfortable surroundings of our terraced Victorian home in Stratford, I wonder what future lies ahead for Max, my grandson? Those fearful events, which led to Max's arrival into my safekeeping, are so clear in my mind...

Cover designed by
Gareth Austin.

Printed by
Antony Rowe Ltd
2 Whittle Drive, Eastbourne BN23 6QT

Life – 1989

January

The phone rings. "This is Stratford Police. Your daughter has been arr ested. Can you come down to the station?" He passes the phone to Jamie. "Mum, I didn't do anything, honestly," she says, convincingly.

I am stunned. Confused. What on earth is going on? Only an hour earlier, at 8.00 p.m., I had dropped Jamie off in the town to meet friends.

My heart pounding, I rush immediately to the station.
The police tell me, "Jamie has been arrested for possession of cannabis. She bought it from a dealer outside the Cross Keys pub."
Down in the cells, it breaks my heart to see my daughter curled up on a bench, pale and sobbing. Jamie tells me, "Plain clothes drug squad officers pounced, rounded us up, and shoved us in a riot van." As Jamie has her fingerprints and photos taken, I feel sick and faint. Surely, this is what they do to criminals, not to my fifteen-year-old daughter?
Eventually she is released from custody at 4.00 a.m.

I am frightened, exhausted and lonely, never dreaming this could happen to me, an ordinary middle-class mum. MY DAUGHTER IS TAKING DRUGS! Jamie says light heartedly, *"Anyway, I only took cannabis. It's no worse than smoking or drinking."*
Although not charged because of her age, Jamie appears in court as witness against the dealer. His girlfriend threatens her. Scared out of her wits, Jamie says, *"MUM, I'LL NEVER EVER TAKE DRUGS AGAIN."*

February/August

Jamie talks about Mikey, a nineteen-year-old known to be 'dealing'. With prominent devilish blue green eyes and ponytail, he is popular with

1

young schoolgirls hanging around McDonald's.
She introduces me to him and we smile acknowledging each other. He later remarks to Jamie, "Most mothers wouldn't have wanted to know."

A few weeks later I worry because Jamie is mixing with youngsters involved in drugs and decide to tackle her.
"Are you still seeing Mikey?" I ask.
"No," she says stubbornly.
But next day I discover Jamie has lied. As I peer out from the top of a bus, I see Mikey wearing the grey beret that Jamie had beautifully embroidered. There is no doubt about it. Jamie is seeing Mikey.

Jamie's G.C.S.E. exam results are a disaster – two passes instead of the expected seven. Why has a bright girl with such potential done so badly? Unexpectedly, Jamie gains a place at Leamington Art College. Although artistic, she is not brilliant and submits her schoolfriend's pictures instead of her own at the interview.

13th September – Wednesday

Jamie has decided to study General Design and is ambitious, wanting to be a dress designer – not just any designer but working in one of London's top fashion houses.

I am very worried. For the past two days Jamie has been pale and unwell, nearly passing out twice at college. She cuts the welts off her new jumpers. I am very angry – all that money down the drain. Why?

16th September – Saturday

We travel to Birmingham on a shopping trip. Jamie looks pale and exhausted and is desperate to sit in a cafe. I am beginning to wonder if she has a serious illness.

18th October – Wednesday

Evening: Jamie sits on the kitchen unit, wearing a pretty brightly coloured cotton dress. Jokingly I say, "Jamie, you look pregnant," and touch her tummy.
Her stomach is hard and solid...she is pregnant!

In disbelief I think, I must not panic – keep calm.

Immediately Jamie screams, "You're going to throw me out of the house."

"Of course not," I say giving her a big hug. "How far gone are you?"

"About seven months, I suppose," she says.

In my panic I think, my God – she could go into labour tonight and she hasn't had any antenatal care.

Suddenly, it dawns on me why Jamie was so ill during her mock exams and under achieved in her GCSEs; why she always looks so pale; why she fainted at college; the reason for cutting welts off her jumpers. Now it all adds up.

"Who's the father?" I ask, dreading her reply.

"Who do you think? Mikey of course," she says with a glint in her eye. I should have known.

Jamie tells me, "Four months ago the doctor referred me to hospital for an abortion but it was too late."

"What are you going to do?" I ask, feeling quite sick. "Will you have the baby adopted?"

She nods. "Probably".

19th October – Thursday

I am out of my mind. Who can I talk to? I decide to contact Life, the Catholic organisation. After listening to my concerns, they reveal that Jamie called to see them some months ago. Because of confidentiality, they were unable to contact me. When the counsellor advised Jamie to tell me she was pregnant she said, 'I can't 'cos my mum's in Ireland. She's looking after her mother who has got cancer.'

I can't believe the lies.

Jamie wants to change to a different doctor, thus keeping the pregnancy hidden from neighbours and friends. Her new doctor books her in to Banbury Hospital, outside our area.

Thirty-one weeks pregnant, and with her baby due early January, none of Jamie's friends are aware of her predicament.

21st October – Saturday

While relaxing by the log fire, we pluck up courage to tell her dad that she is pregnant. He takes it very calmly, much to our surprise, and Jamie tells him, "I'll probably have the baby adopted."

Her brother, Jonathan, is very annoyed, saying, "She's got herself into this mess – the baby must be adopted."
I shall never forget his words, "Mother, you'll end up looking after that baby if you're not careful."
"I won't," I reassure him.

31st October – Tuesday

We arrange for the social worker from Father Hudson's Catholic Children's Society, near Sutton Coldfield, to call at our house. After discussing adoption, she assures us everything will be done to help Jamie if she decides to keep the baby.

I am left numb. Recuperating from my kidney transplant, it would be impossible for Jamie to live at home with the baby. She loves time for herself: makeup, hairdo's, T.V. and partying. If she lives with me, I know the baby will become my responsibility.

"Jamie, have you considered looking for your natural mother?" asks Jane, the social worker.
"Yes, but I'd like to stand on the other side of the road to view first," replies Jamie. Jane smiles. "Everyone would like to do that," she says, "but I'm afraid it's not possible."

Jamie insists, "Mum, don't tell Mikey I'm pregnant, will you?"
Mikey, with his fashionable clothes and smart short pony tail, has an air of the pop star 'Boy George' about him. He was a very bright lad at school but later in his teens became wayward, got involved with drugs, and spent a short spell in prison.

November

The social worker requires personal details from Mikey for the baby's adoption. Eventually Jamie contacts him and they arrange to meet.
I drop her off at the Windmill pub and, after waiting for just five minutes, Jamie returns to the car.
"Did you see Mikey? What did he say?" I ask anxiously.
"Nothing really," she replies shrugging her shoulders. "I told him the baby was being adopted and he was surprised because he thought I'd keep it."

I can't believe how casual and irresponsible they both are.
Jamie appears half-soaked, always in a dream, and I am very worried.

27th November – Monday

Jamie finishes college, with assessments showing her work is up-to-date. Fellow students think she has glandular fever. Her trendy clothes and baggy jumpers conceal her pregnancy. Jamie, looking radiant, meets up with friends for a meal. Although she is very big, they still haven't cottoned on. Her Dad has given her a woollen cloak which helps hide the bump.

To prevent boredom, we try to keep busy. Jamie is keen on dressmaking which helps to while away the time. Waiting for the birth and spending so much time together has brought us very close.

December

We enjoy a very relaxing traditional Christmas as a family.

Jamie and I spend New Year's Eve alone at home. A heavy frost clings outside as we sit warmed by a roaring log fire and watch TV. We feast on prawn cocktail, party dips and salad; a very memorable evening.
A friend phones Jamie saying she knows about the expected baby, date due, and that it is to be adopted. Jamie denies everything saying, "It's just rumours." I honestly wonder how she gets away with it? We decide Mikey must have gone to the pub and told everybody.

1990

10th January – Wednesday

I persuade Jamie not to conceal the pregnancy from friends any longer. Her social worker phones to say she will be visiting the head office of the adoption society to look through Jamie's records. It is necessary to get background information in case Jamie decides to have her baby adopted. She obtains details of Jamie's natural parents. In 1973, her mother was rushed to hospital with a hidden pregnancy, and gave birth to Jamie. She had another daughter in foster care, whom she had kept.

20th January – Saturday 5.00 p.m.

We set off for hospital. The baby is to be induced.

Jamie wells up in tears. "Mum, can you stay with me?" She is very scared, just like a young child.

There is a spare bed on the empty ward and I stay to keep her company overnight.

21st January – Sunday 3.00 p.m.

Jamie gives birth to a healthy son, 8lb. 7 oz. As the nurse takes the baby over to her, Jamie turns her head away.

His birth was a wonderful experience for me, my children having been adopted. Peering into the cot I can see a beautiful bonny baby with thick dark hair.

Emotionally drained, I look at the tightly wrapped bundle and think how lovely he is, but what will he be like when he is sixteen?

Evening: Jamie asks to see her baby in the nursery. Pale and tired, she sits staring at him, holding his hand. "Max – that's what I'll call him," she announces.

That night I sigh a sigh of relief. At long last it is all over...so I think.

22nd January – Monday

Jamie has her own room and TV for privacy. She is very anaemic, tired and depressed. Max is in the special baby unit, to be cared for until foster parents collect him.

She sends a letter and photo of the baby to Mikey, which I drop in the pub on my way home.

23rd January – Tuesday

Late morning at hospital, I arrive to find Jamie cuddling her baby. In the afternoon Jamie is discharged: she is upset at having to leave Max in the hospital.

24th January – Wednesday

I am very depressed. At Banbury Hospital we meet the social worker and foster mum. They take Jamie with Max to the foster home at Sutton Coldfield. Feeling heavy hearted, I call at the hospital Resource Centre in Stratford, for a chat – the only way I can keep myself sane. I want to crawl into a corner and sleep forever. I feel much better after talking to them.

Calling at McDonald's afterwards, I see Mikey who joins me for coffee.

He appears to be a cheerful, chatty lad, but I notice that he is very thin and shakes nervously. Could it be the effect of drugs?

We talk about his work as a barman, his family, and Max. I take to Mikey straight away, regardless of his drug involvement, and feel much happier now that I have spoken to him.

5th February – Monday

Jamie's seventeenth birthday and she returns to college. She is pleased to have the company of her friends once more.

I am still trying to assess Jamie's emotions. She won't talk and express her feelings.

10th February – Saturday

On our way to see Max, Jamie and I discuss options including adoption. She says that she feels adoption would be best.

I am so confused. One minute I want her to keep Max, the next let him go. It is so hard.

I feel all the responsibility and weight is on my shoulders. What would be best for Max?

Jamie is so vague and hasn't got a clue.

14th February – Wednesday

I am very annoyed when the social worker wants Max to come to our house for the night. I say firmly, "No, I can't cope. I just don't feel well enough." Jamie stays at the foster parents overnight instead, to bath and feed the baby. Pressure is being put on Jamie to keep her son and she is finding it hard to make a decision. She appears confused, and tells me, "I think I'll keep him after all."

15th February – Thursday

When visiting Max, Jamie is very moody and doesn't speak in the car. I am so tired. How much longer can I keep going?

The social worker phones – she has found accommodation for Jamie and Max in Leamington. After discussion, we agree that Max will stay with Jamie during the week and with me at weekends. I will look after him with the help of a child minder while Jamie attends college.

Tonight Jamie admits she is starting to miss Max and at long last is expressing her feelings.

7

4th March – Sunday

My husband makes the comment, "Now Jamie has decided to keep Max, she should learn to dress like a mother."

I ask – how should a mother dress?

Jamie and I set off excitedly to collect Max from Sutton Coldfield. I am relieved that he isn't going for adoption after all.

In the car on the way home Jamie goes very quiet. Breaking the silence she says, "Mum, now that I've decided to keep Max can I still have a sewing machine for my eighteenth Birthday?"

"Of course you can. You'll be needing it now," I reply.

12th March – Monday

Today Jamie moves to Leamington. A housing Trust has offered her accommodation in a four bed roomed terraced house with three other single mums. Her room is very small with grotty decor and tatty stained carpet. There is just enough space for a single bed, cot, chest of drawers and little else.

Whilst Jamie pops out with friends, I paint the walls in the bedroom, and baby sit. It gives me a chance to get acquainted with other young mums in the house, including a girl called Claire and her baby daughter.

14th March – Wednesday

The child minder phones to tell me that Jamie hasn't turned up with Max. I am annoyed, paying out money when he is not being looked after. Jamie tells me later that she took Max to college to show him to her friends.

30th March – Friday

We have been looking for Mikey for days, so that he can meet the social worker, but without success. Jamie is hurt that he hasn't been in contact. She hears he is living rough but no one knows where.

Jamie is so excited when I call to collect Max this morning. She can't wait to tell me her news. "Last night I phoned Mikey's mum and told her about the baby. I felt sorry for her because she didn't know she has a grandson," she says.

"What was her reaction? Was she shocked?" I ask.

"She was very good about it, but is surprised that Mikey hasn't told her," says Jamie.

We agree I will write to Mikey's parents enclosing photos, giving details of Max's birth date, and name.

31st March – Saturday

Mikey's mother, Jackie, phones. She is very embarrassed at Mikey's non-involvement with the baby. Jackie has fallen in love with the photo and wants to see her grandson as soon as possible. We arrange this Sunday and she is hoping Mikey will come along also.

1st April – Sunday

Tom and Jackie Harper arrive at the cottage, looking so young in denim jeans and jackets. After an emotional introduction, they apologise for Mikey not turning up. He didn't arrive at their house in time.

The proud grandparents are very excited and think Max is a lovely bonny baby.

Half an hour later Mikey phones – he has overslept. His dad agrees to collect him, and when he arrives the atmosphere is happy and relaxed. The proud father cradles his son on his knee, hands cupped under his head. A special moment I shall never forget.

Jackie says, "I always wanted to be a grandma but didn't expect this!"

Eventually Jamie moves into a more spacious room in her house at Leamington. Over the months I grow concerned about Max's welfare. Very loud music blares from speakers by his cot and I worry about his hearing. When I tackle Jamie she says defiantly, "He's my child and I'll do what I want."

Because Jamie isn't bothered about Max's diet, I provide food, juice and nappies. Often there is little or no food in the cupboard – one week Max eats nothing but tinned spaghetti.

Jamie is more interested in spending money on Max's designer clothes – a new outfit every week, including L.A. Gear trainers. They look huge on his wee feet.

July

We congregate at the small Catholic Church for Max's christening. Jamie chooses three school friends as Godmothers and Jonathan, her brother, is Godfather. She always has to be different – normally there would be one Godmother and two Godfathers for a boy.

In our cottage garden, under the scorching hot sun, the happy group of

friends and relatives celebrate. During the afternoon Jamie goes missing. I find her weeping, and acting very strangely in her bedroom. "I'm sorry Mum," she says, "I'm just happy and want to thank you."
After the christening Jamie stays with friends overnight in Stratford. The next day I learn that she left her friends to spend the night in Leamington, telling them, "I must get my 'speed'."
It dawns on me – this explains her recent aggressive behaviour. When I tackle Jamie later she denies everything.

Jamie passes her art exams; much to my surprise because she missed a month of studies around the time of Max's birth. The Spring, she spent messing about and not attending the course.

September
Jamie returns to Leamington Art College to do a basic foundation course, furthering her ambition to be a dress designer.
As time goes by I become very concerned at the company she is keeping. While collecting Max, early one morning, I am horrified when I bump into a young man coming out of Jamie's room. He grins at me politely, half his teeth missing. He is black and bald, and is the first black man I have seen her with.
I try tactfully to point out to Jamie, "It isn't good for Max if you have lads in your room at night – particularly when he gets older."
Aggressively she turns her back on me and shouts me down.
Another black visitor to the flat worries me, a man who is much older than Jamie.
Something is amiss but I can't put my finger on it.

December
Jamie insists on buying Max very expensive Christmas presents and clothes. I wonder how she can afford it, being at college and on income support. Jamie is so materialistic; I fear this could be her downfall.

Running Wild – 1991

January

Almost every night since September, Max has been awake with a bad cough. I am so exhausted, having spent a couple of nights with him in hospital.

5th February – Tuesday. Jamie's 18th birthday

Jamie parties at home in Leamington with friends. She is thrilled with my present, the second-hand sewing machine she longed for. Her dad buys her a microwave and Jamie treats herself to a new fridge with birthday money. The bed sit is looking very homely, well equipped, and she appears happy.

6th February – Wednesday

Jamie phones sounding very fed up, "Mum, I've been given two days' notice to quit the house."
I am shocked and feel sick. "But why, Jamie?" I ask.
"The Trust have been told that I had a rowdy party and claim there was a lot of damage," she tells me.
When I call at the Trust offices the chap insists, "Jamie is no longer at college," with a wry smile on his face. But I am convinced he is wrong because Jamie's work is up to date according to her assessments. As guarantor for Jamie, I am responsible for the payment of £120 damages and I am livid.
What on earth has Jamie been up to? She won't discuss things with me. I am becoming very worried about the baby's welfare but try not to interfere.

Immediately, the Council re house Jamie and Max in bed & breakfast; a newly refurbished house in Leamington. The room has beautiful Laura Ashley style curtains and new carpet.
Jamie and Max are the only people in the house. She complains the place

is cold, particularly for Max with his asthma, and tells me that the chap who owns the house makes as much money as he can from social security tenants.

I continue to have Max to stay at weekends and the creche is now in operation at college during the week.

As the months go by, my concerns grow every time I see Jamie.

One evening, a brick is thrown through the window of her ground floor bedroom, shattering glass over Max's cot. Fortunately he wasn't in it, but Jamie is left stunned and shaking. "He could have ended up in hospital...or even dead," she says.

Jamie reports the incident to the police who tell her, "It's likely to be an associate who has a grudge against you."

Why, I wonder? What on earth has she been up to?

Once, when I collect Max at about 6.0 p.m., Jamie laughs saying, "You'll never guess what time I woke up this afternoon: three o'clock!"

I am mad. Max is only thirteen months old and has had to fend for himself all day. I am worried because he is getting an inadequate diet for such a young baby and Jamie never has any money.

I notice letters from the health visitor lying around her room, stating that Max has not been immunised. When I question Jamie she tells me sharply, "He was done three months ago."

Jamie continually seeks my approval of her friends and introduces me to Tammy – a pretty girl, who looks about nineteen years of age, with fair hair piled on the top of her head. Jamie informs me she stays at Tammy's house in Leicester sometimes.

One Sunday morning I return Max to Jamie in Leamington after his stay with me. But Jamie isn't there. Anxiously I wait outside her house. Eventually she appears, running along the road and gasping for breath. She looks dreadful, wearing a long dark green raincoat, tatty white high-heeled shoes and her fair curly hair is matted.

Very upset and angry to see her in such a state, I declare, "Jamie, you look like a prostitute." I feel awful afterwards for having said this.

"Sorry I'm late mum," she says. "I overslept at Leicester. I met this black guy, Winston, at a night club in Coventry, and he is really lovely. He has two flats and a super car. I stayed with him last night and he's taking me to London soon."

A guy with dreadlocks shouts and runs over from the opposite side of the road to join us. Jamie introduces him, "Mum, this is Steve."

He stares at me. "Whatever you do, you must stop Jamie going to London," he says. "I'm warning you...she's in great danger."

I feel uncomfortable. Steve's bloodshot eyes frighten me. He talks with a slur and I think he's probably on drugs. I don't want to get involved.

"That was Steve Dred," says Jamie. "He's only jealous 'cause I'm going out with Winston".

However, I am shortly to discover I should have heeded Steve's warnings. *JAMIE IS IN TERRIBLE DANGER.*

20th March – Wednesday

My divorce goes through today. I hope to start a new life once I have sold my house and moved to Stratford. Max continues to stay with me occasionally, during the week and at weekends. I enjoy having a little child around and it keeps me feeling young.

28th April – Sunday

My heart is pounding. I wonder where Jamie is? I had arranged to meet her lunchtime at Leamington as usual, to return Max. I panic when there is no sign of her. Time ticks on and I must get back to Stratford for work, as a telephone response operator, this afternoon.

In desperation I try to get hold of Max's grandparents, the Harpers, who agree to baby sit. Harassed, I arrive at work to be given a message, "Jamie says she has overslept over at Leicester and will get to Stratford by taxi as quickly as possible."

I am furious because she is getting so unreliable.

16th May – Thursday

It is two weeks since I last saw Jamie and Max, and I am very concerned. Last night she phoned; we arranged to meet at the Priors shopping precinct, Leamington, this morning.

I am relieved, when Jamie arrives. She appears happy, and Max seems fine. "I've been staying at Tammy's house at Leicester," she says. "Do you remember I introduced her to you at my B & B? Max has his own room and he is much better off now than in that small cold room at Leamington."

She laughs. "Tammy and I spent all Saturday night at a Blues club and didn't get home until 7.00 in the morning."
Alarm bells start ringing. "Who looked after Max all night?" I enquire, very concerned. "Winston and his friend," she replies.
Knowing how unreliable Jamie's friends are, I am horrified. Max is fifteen months old and I tell her I am concerned for his safety.
Jamie gets agitated. "He's okay. He's my child and I'll do what I want. I'm going back to Leicester." She promptly storms off with the baby in the pushchair.

18th May – Saturday

"I'm contacting the housing department about getting better accommodation because of Max's poor health," Jamie tells me. She promises to phone tonight to let me know how she gets on, but doesn't. I try to phone her at Leicester but Tammy informs me she isn't there. I haven't got a clue where Jamie is and worry if Max is okay.

23rd May – Thursday

Very worried, I call at Jamie's Bed & Breakfast in Leamington to speak to her friend, Julie. "I'm very relieved to see you," she says. "Jamie has spent most of the last three weeks at Leicester. She called with an awful crowd yesterday – two white girls and a black guy. She gave me an address on a scrap of paper with strict instructions not to give it to anyone. But because I'm concerned for Max's safety, I'll give you her address at Hinckley, Leicester.
Are you aware Jamie's friend Tammy is only fifteen?" she asks.
"But Jamie says Tammy has her own house." I say panicking.
"All I know," says the girl, "is that Tammy has run away from a children's home."
Thoughts rush through my mind. Where is Max? Is he all right? What is Jamie up to? I am desperate and don't know which way to turn.

I hurriedly scribble down Jamie's address, and rush over to see Max's health visitor to voice my concerns: that Jamie is moving out of her accommodation; Max has not had his injections; Jamie sleeps during the day not looking after Max; and my worries over his diet.

I say to the health visitor, "Jamie tells me you called to look at her accommodation, which is cold and smokey and badly affecting Max's asthma. She says you are contacting the council to rehouse them."

The health visitor looks at me strangely and says, "No, I haven't called to see her."

Jamie has told lie upon lie. How I hate her for it. "Now I am really getting worried," I tell her.

She tries to reassure me, "There's no need to worry. After all, Jamie is eighteen, young and carefree. Everything will be okay. We mustn't judge Jamie by our standards. Her way is probably equally as good."

So often social workers and health visitors say this but, as Jamie's mother, I know I have a right to be alarmed.

I AM DESPERATE – SOMETHING IS WRONG BUT NOBODY WILL LISTEN TO ME.

I fear for Max's safety so have decided to keep a full diary.

24th May – Friday

Jamie rings twice from Leicester, leaving messages with my neighbours and asking them to inform me that everything is okay.

But I sense things are very wrong and decide once again to pop over to Jamie's B & B.

Her friend tells me the housing department have written asking Jamie to contact them by tomorrow or get out. Worried, I phone the council and they promise I can remove Jamie's property if she doesn't make immediate contact.

I ring the social worker at Father Hudson's Homes saying, "I'm worried about Jamie and Max."

"Jamie is eighteen, don't worry," she says trying to allay my fears. "I am sure Max is safe. She is just a normal lively teenager."

By now I am tearing my hair out.

29th May – Wednesday

My gut feeling tells me something is very wrong. It is two weeks since we last heard from Jamie.

Agencies always seem to think they know best. After all, they have the qualifications. But what about my experience and gut feeling? Doesn't that count? To them I'm just another fussing mother.

My ex-husband, Bill, and I are out of our minds worrying whether Max is safe so I phone the health visitor. I give her Jamie's address and enquire anxiously, "Would a health visitor at Hinckley be able to check things out?" She tells me, "Any health visitor would say that Jamie is eighteen. She has a right to get on with her life in a manner she sees fit. After all, we may not agree with the way Jamie wants to carry on, but it's her choice."

Exasperated, I come off the phone in tears. Bill, says anxiously, "Right, I'll go straight away to Hinckley with Jonathan, our son, and see if we can find Jamie and Max."
Anxiously I wait for news- but there is nothing.

Hours later my husband returns, his face ashen and drawn. Looking straight at me, he says, "This has been the worst day of my life. We found a run down house where Jamie has been for the past ten days. The youngsters thought we were police or social workers and refused to talk. Eventually, we convinced them who we were and they let us in the house. They said Jamie disappeared with Max yesterday, taking a taxi and telling them, 'I'm going home to Mum'."
But Jamie and Max haven't come home. Where on earth are they?

Bill, tells me that they said, 'Max is in grave danger. Jamie is *evil*. Whatever you do, you *must* get him from her.'

As the youngsters told their story of horror, Bill and Jonathan were stunned. "Jamie has been working as a prostitute all over the country – London, Norwich, Sheffield, Swindon and Luton since February. Max is looked after weekly by childminders who charge £200. When Jamie works locally she sleeps all day, neglecting Max. She doesn't feed him or change his nappies...you must do everything you can to get Max to safety."
Their story revealed that for the past couple of weeks Jamie has been hiding from her pimp, Winston: the man she met at a night club who said he was a bank manager. He had been threatening Jamie with a gun and beating her with a baseball bat.
The youngsters admitted they were on the coke scene (taking the drug cocaine). Does this mean Jamie is also using? I hope and pray she isn't.

A guy introduced himself to Bill as Leroy. He said, "I looked after Max whilst Jamie slept all day." We learn later that Leroy is 27, mixed-race from London, and has spent four years in Pentonville Prison for GBH.

Bill said he would search for Jamie, but they warned him, "Don't go near the red light district – you'll get your legs shot off. Jamie is likely to get stabbed in the back in an alley before too long."

He changed his mind and visited the vice squad instead.
"We know Jamie well," said the police. "She is one of the worst cases we have ever known. We thought she was only thirteen, possibly a runaway from a children's home. Jamie always refuses to reveal the whereabouts of her baby.
She is one of the hardest prostitutes we have dealt with. We had to keep her in the cells overnight because of her temper and let her cool down. The other working girls were in and out in an hour.
Often, a new pimp steps into the shoes of an old one. Keep an eye on Leroy," they warn Bill.

This must be every parent's nightmare. Is this really happening to us? I had always worried about Jamie and her wayward ways. In the back of my mind I often thought of prostitution. Why? Did I have a premonition I wonder?

Stunned by the news, I ring Jamie's health visitor. She is speechless and agrees my intuition was right after all. If only she had listened to me in the first place.
Our social worker is on holiday so I speak to her superior who admits, "Only a few days ago, when I read reports, I was alarmed at the signs." Immediately I report Max missing to the police. Everyone is concerned for his safety. The police require descriptions and photos, and will release them to the press within 24 hours if we have not heard from Jamie.

30th May – Thursday

To our relief, Jamie phones this evening and I pretend I don't know what's going on. She asks, "Mum, will you be able to meet me at Coventry tomorrow? I'm moving there at the weekend."
Immediately I offer, "Can I have Max to stay for a few days?"
She is pleased at my suggestion, and sounds relieved.
"I'm staying at Tammy's," she says.
But I know Jamie is staying at the pimp's house.
I inform the police that Jamie has made contact. They are anxious for me to get Max into my safe keeping, immediately if possible.

31st May – Friday

I am relieved to see Jamie waiting with Max outside British Home Stores. The police thought she wouldn't turn up. Tammy is also with her and looks very smart – certainly more mature than her fifteen years. No wonder I thought she was nineteen when Jamie first introduced us.

While we lunch at a cafe, the girls chat, and whisper excitedly non-stop. I get a strange uncomfortable feeling that we are being watched – confirmed some weeks later by Jamie that Winston's 'minders' were there.

After I tell Jamie I would love to have Max for longer, she says, "Winston will be pleased. You can have him as long as you want."
Willingly, Jamie hands over her child benefit book and I hurriedly leave the store before she changes her mind.
As we part, Jamie and Tammy head down an alleyway laughing and giggling.

Max laughs nervously as we journey home in the car. On the verge of tears and very frightened I reflect, "That wasn't my daughter I met but a total stranger."
Bill is relieved to see us and says, "The Stratford police and social services are anxious you ring to confirm Max is safe."

But I feel let down. "There's nothing more we can do," the social worker informs me. I explain to her, "I feel so very much on my own."
"We can't apply for a 'place of safety' order because Max is considered to be safe in your care," she tells me firmly.
But somewhere out there is a pimp with a gun and baseball bat searching for Jamie. I feel extremely vulnerable. After all, he could try to use Max to blackmail Jamie to return to him. I don't think this social worker has any idea how frightened I am. Everyone is so naive in this small market town.
Max is weepy and frightened. He clings to my skirt and follows me everywhere, repeatedly calling, "ma" (grandma). At night he wakes up screaming, "No. No."

1st June – Saturday

Today I have to quit my weekend job in telephone sales at a minute's notice. Now I have to concentrate on looking after Max full-time.

During the week I work as a nanny to two children. Their mother has agreed for me to continue looking after them together with Max.

Letting myself into Jamie's B & B room, I am shocked to discover almost everything Jamie possesses has gone, including Max's cot and the microwave. A couple of black plastic bin liners lie amongst the rubbish and a few clothes are dumped in a corner.

Papers are strewn around everywhere: half-finished love letters, poems, pieces of diary, and sketches – all revealing a paranoid young woman's unhappy and lonely life involving drugs. Jamie describes her horrendous come downs on speed and writes of her confusion, depression, despair, and wanting to commit suicide.

"I wish Max had been adopted after all. I can't cope although I love him so much," she writes. Jamie tells of her confusion when she had to make the final decision to keep her baby. Also of the unbearable pressure put on her by the social worker who said, "It is in the baby's best interests to remain with its mother whenever possible."

There is a letter written by Jamie to the social worker. She asks for help in finding her natural mother that now she is eighteen. Some weeks ago Jamie had discussed the letter with me. "Trouble is," she said, "I'm scared to post it."

2nd June – Sunday

Max is quietening down and seems a lot happier.

He still wakes up at night shouting, "No, no," and I wonder why. The words hit me hard.

Late morning I receive an unexpected call from Tammy in Leicester. "Angela, have you seen or heard from Jamie...she has disappeared."

My heart races – where on earth is Jamie? Is she safe?

I am sure someone is listening on the phone, later confirmed by Jamie to be Winston, the pimp.

Tammy tells me, "Jamie has run away, saying she was popping to the phone box to ring you at eleven o'clock this morning, and hasn't returned."

I am relieved. At least she disappeared in daylight so is probably safe. "Can you collect Jamie's things from Leicester today?" she asks. "The landlord wants everything out by six o'clock."

My heart pounding, I agree to get over to Leicester and Tammy gives me directions to find the house. I phone Max's grandparents, the Harpers. Tom says he will come to Leicester while Jackie looks after Max.

I attach a roof-rack onto my small car, knowing Jamie has all Max's clothes, toys, portable cot and her clothes at Leicester.

We race up the M69. Tammy's directions lead us to a small street of modern terraced council houses. Cautiously, we creep up to the house. To our horror, blood is splattered over the front door. My mind is buzzing. Is it Jamie's blood? I take a deep breath. Realising the blood isn't fresh, I console myself that Jamie hasn't been involved in a stabbing or shooting.

I knock... eyes peer through the letter box at us.

"Can you come round the back 'cos the door has been locked by the landlord," says a girl's voice. The landlord, unbeknown to us, is Winston.

Tammy invites us in through the back door.

"That's strange, where are all Jamie's belongings?" I ask. Just three small carrier bags stand by Max's portable cot. No sign of his toys, or clothes.

"Winston has them," replies Tammy.

In a sweat, I feel a presence, as if we are being watched. We don't realise the guy is upstairs.

We grab the stuff and run. My heart beats ten-to-the-dozen.

Tammy slips an envelope in my hand as we leave. "Please make sure Jamie gets it," she whispers.

I put my foot down on the motorway, desperate to get away. Tom agrees with me something is very wrong.

Has Jamie run away from Winston? Is she safe? Is she still alive?

Tonight Leroy (Jamie's friend from Hinckley) phones. After making sure he is speaking to me, he passes the phone to Jamie.

Is he now in control? Is he her pimp now? The vice-squad had warned my husband this would probably happen.

Jamie assures us she is fine. But I am not convinced by the tone of her voice. She sounds in a state of shock.

"Mum, I'm hiding from Winston but will keep in touch." She doesn't let on where she is but at least she has phoned and I know she is safe.

3rd June – Monday

Tammy's letter is worrying me. Perhaps it could throw light on the situation? Bill persuades me to open it.

A horrific picture is revealed... Tammy writes she is cold and lonely in the unfurnished house and says, "I am writing this letter while waiting for your mum. Jamie be careful. You have a good brain – use it. By the time you receive this, you know what will probably happen to me. I could even be dead."

Immediately Bill faxes the letter to Leicester vice squad who are keen to receive the information.

Tammy is in great danger, being so young.

Tonight Tammy phones. "Have you heard from Jamie yet? Do you know where she is?" Again I sense someone is listening in and tread warily, for the safety of both Max and me. "No," I reply.

This evening Jamie makes contact, again via Leroy. She says, "I'm phoning Winston to get my things back – he wants £95 for them."

I warn her that she is mad if she contacts him.

We still have no idea where Jamie is staying.

4th June – Tuesday

Tammy rings again – "Any news from Jamie?"

"No, nothing," I reply, very scared and trying not to give anything away.

"What about her sister, Kate? The one married to the pop star?" asks Tammy. "Surely she will know where she is?"

Suddenly it dawns on me. Jamie has been fantasizing about her sister. Her natural mother had kept Kate, who was two years older than her. "Jamie is adopted," I explain to Tammy. "Now she is eighteen, maybe she has contacted her sister without me being aware of it."

"But Jamie is only sixteen, isn't she?" questions Tammy.

She is shocked when I confirm, "No, Jamie is eighteen."

5th June – Wednesday

I desperately need help. I feel isolated, and so alone.

Here I am with Jamie's son and she is on the run from an armed pimp. There are Tammy's calls trying to trace Jamie, with the pimp listening in.

I speak to the social worker again but she is most unsympathetic saying, "We can't help. Max is safe in your care. I advise you to go to a solicitor. We can only do something if Jamie tries to take Max from you."

I have no support whatsoever. This woman hasn't got a clue what I am going through.

A friend gives me the name of a solicitor experienced in child custody. I make an appointment immediately. The solicitor recommends I apply for a Ward of Court to protect Max. The cost could be prohibitive, but fortunately I get legal aid, being divorced and a single parent on a low income. My affidavit is drawn up and a date for the court hearing applied for.

What will Jamie do when she finds out what I have done? She will be mad and I am really scared.

Jamie phones to confirm that she is okay but I dare not mention my application for a ward of court.

6th June – Thursday

I am very surprised when a private detective rings. "I'm acting on behalf of your solicitors and it is necessary to serve papers on Jamie. But I want to discuss the matter first and need to see you urgently."

"Do you really want to go ahead with a Ward of Court?" he asks. "Do you realise the risk you're putting yourself in? There could be backlash from Jamie's dangerous and unsavoury friends and it could go on for years."

After discussing the pros and cons I tell him, "My gut feeling is to go ahead."

7th June – Friday

Jamie phones early morning. "Mum, can you pick me up from Hinckley and take me to the Leamington housing department? It also means I can see Max."

I never deny Jamie access to Max, believing that one day, when she has sorted her life out, he will return to her.

Jamie is waiting when we arrive at Hinckley. She and Max are so pleased to see each other. There seems to be an inexplicable bond between them. She introduces Leroy, her boyfriend. He seems a nice guy with a friendly smile and a broad London accent. He is dressed in blue denim jacket and jeans.

I drop them off at the housing department with Max, arranging to collect them in an hour.

Back at home, I phone the housing officer. She enquires, "Is Leroy Max's father? Are they having Max back in a day or two, as they claim?"

I confirm there is no way they are having Max at present and Leroy is definitely not Max's father.

"I thought it strange – Max is so fair and Leroy so black," says the woman. "Jamie has just told me this weird and wonderful story – that she has been forced to leave Leamington by a man who put a gun to her head."

"Actually, it's true," I tell the housing officer.

Aghast she says, "I'll do what I can for Jamie. But Leroy isn't eligible for accommodation because he's not a resident in the area."

As I drive them back to Hinckley, Jamie is very emotional, jumpy, and close to tears.

She talks of the pimp, the gun threats, the beatings and the loss of everything she owns.

I tell her, "Social services say Max must remain with me for the time being, for his own safety."

Hysterically she cries, "No one can ever take Max away from me."

I don't mention the wardship, fearing Jamie might get even more upset.

"Will you continue working on the streets?" I ask her.

"It's more than my life is worth," she replies. "Winston would find me and smash my head in."

We drive up to their hideaway in Hinckley, a neat modern semi. They live with a young single mum who is a prostitute.

Jamie continues to take dangerous risks. She has been shopping in town and I voice my concern, "Winston or one of his girls might see you." Jamie laughs at me and appears completely out of her head.

11th June – Tuesday

The private detective phones again. "Have you an address where Jamie can be found?" he asks.

I tell him she has an appointment at the housing department in Leamington tomorrow.

12th June – Wednesday

There is a knock at my front door. Jamie storms through the cottage with Leroy and a girl. They are fuming.

"What's this about a Ward of Court?" they shout. "Nobody's going to take Max away. You've got no right to interfere. We'll take Max into hiding and you'll never find him again."

Jamie sobs. "Why have you done this to me?"

I'm shaking, speechless and very frightened.

Then strangely, the situation calms down almost immediately and Jamie asks, "Mum, can I help myself to a biscuit?" as the smell of home-made biscuits wafts in the air. Maybe this will touch her heart and bring her down to earth.

When they leave the cottage I feel threatened and ring the police, giving their car registration and description. "What shall I do?" I ask, shaking and petrified.

The police suggest, "You must put Max's interests first. If he's at risk of being kidnapped, you must get him out of the house immediately.

A friend has offered help if ever I need it. I phone her and hurriedly pack a suitcase with the bare essentials and drive to her place.

In the safety of her home I am able to unwind and relax from the tensions of the day, and see things in perspective. Max is completely oblivious to what is going on and continues to be his happy placid self.

It isn't easy in hiding. I wonder if it will be safe to go back to the cottage. Eventually I pluck up courage to pop home.

Liz, my neighbour, greets me, "Jamie and Leroy called and left a note on your back door saying, 'Called to see Max, will call again later'."

What shall I do?

I decide that I must be strong and stand up to them, but it won't be easy.

16th June – Sunday

Mike, a friend, agrees to be with me for moral support when Jamie calls. We haven't got a clue what to expect.

Jamie and Leroy arrive late, just as Max is going to bed. Jamie gives Max lots of hugs and kisses. It is unbelievable. The atmosphere is relaxed and happy, just as if the threats a few days earlier had not taken place.

Mike sits observing- not saying a word.

Jamie is dressed in an elegant black lace, cotton short-sleeved suit, black stockings and gold/black very high heeled shoes. Her hair falls below the shoulders, blonde, curly and very pretty.

A mature sophisticated woman sits before me – no longer the young girl in designer trainers, cut-off jeans or leggings, and big baggy jumpers.

Leroy produces a black duffle bag. Delving inside, he throws onto the carpet toys, clothes, books and china ornaments for Max – just like Christmas. Not one item has a receipt or bag and my suspicions are aroused. They are probably shoplifted and their value must be at least £50. Max is delighted with his goodies.

Talk is of a criminal nature: driving cars without insurance, licence or tax, fiddling income support, friends in prison, theft and prostitution.

Jamie tells me, "I intend going to the police and have Winston up for assault. I've lost all my possessions but I'll get them back eventually," she says sadly. "Winston says he'll return them if I go and see him. It's worth risking. So long as the police know where I am."

"Don't be stupid," I tell her.

Why does Jamie put herself in such danger?

"At least Winston didn't hurt Max," I remark.

Leroy jumps in. "No, but he saw everything that went on."

I shudder to think what Max has witnessed – beatings, sex and drug taking. No wonder he shouts out, "No," every night.

Jamie recalls briefly the beatings with the baseball bat, the dreadful pain, and all-over bruising, but is overcome with emotion and cannot continue. She quickly changes the subject. "I'm thinking of coming home and going to college." I am pleased – maybe there is hope after all.

In a friendly, happy mood they depart saying, "We'll be back soon to see Max."

Phew – I sigh a sigh of relief. Things have gone much better than expected and Leroy doesn't seem such a bad guy after all. Hopefully, sooner or later, Jamie will sort herself out. Mike and I agree, "She just needs time."

23rd June – Sunday

"You'll never guess what has happened?" says Jamie on the phone. "The housing department gave me bed and breakfast in Coventry last night. I nearly died when I was told two black guys came looking for me and, from the description of the pattern cut in the hair of one, it was Winston." She sounds frightened. "I packed my bags and got out as quickly as I could. How do you think they found out I was there?" she enquires, puzzled.

"The Housing Department can't give me anywhere else," she says. "They suggested I try the local women's refuge, but I'm not going there. It's full of lesbians," she declares.

27th June – Thursday

Unexpectedly, Jamie and Leroy turn up at my cottage with Pete who shares their flat. As they enter the living room I sense something is wrong. The atmosphere is heavy, electric and tense.

Pete is about 26, short with blond hair, very effeminate and undoubtedly gay. Jamie calls me upstairs. I ignore her, not wanting to leave Pete and Leroy alone. I don't trust them.

I am so relieved when they eventually leave.

28th June – Friday

The vice squad phone me. "Does Jamie know where Tammy is? She has gone missing. Because of her age and the danger she's in, we have been asked to trace her."

I tell them Jamie is staying at her friend's tonight and I will have a word with her.

I pop over to Claire's and we grab the chance to talk while Jamie is out of the room.

Claire tells me, "Jamie arrived at the house teetering along in high heels, tight mini-skirt, and bust revealing blouse. She's not the old Jamie I once knew, in trainers and leggings. She's so different now. I'm fond of her but worry more about Max's welfare. He must be protected."

Claire talks of when she and Jamie lived together with the other young mums. "Jamie was completely mad. She pretended to take an overdose or slash her wrists, and took drugs. I even remember Jamie running along the road in her nightie in the dark. Because Jamie is so unstable, I consider Max is at great risk," says Claire, very concerned.

As we journey back to Coventry I ask Jamie to phone the vice squad at Leicester.

I wait in the phone box as she gives police the addresses where Tammy might be found. To my horror I overhear her say, "Yes, she's on coke."

I suspect Jamie has been on coke recently. She is very aggressive, but denies using when I ask her.

The private detective contacts me again and tries to persuade me to cancel the wardship proceedings. "Jamie's friends will hassle you in months or years to come," he warns repeatedly. "And we must consider that perhaps Jamie will return to college and sort her life out."

Under the circumstances I agree to withdraw the wardship, not wanting to aggravate her.

1st July – Monday

Despite my decision to withdraw the wardship, I still have to attend court. To my surprise the Judge is adamant – he will not consider withdrawal. After reading my affidavit he gives me immediate custody of Max for a further month.

Jamie and I remain the best of friends as she continues living in Hinckley. She has visited Max occasionally, always late evening just when he has gone to bed. Quite often she doesn't bother to turn up.
Max is eighteen months old, a happy lively toddler. I continue to work as a nanny which enables Max to be with children of his own age.

Jamie phones very upset. "I'm finishing with Leroy and will be coming home in a day or two."
Relieved I ask, "What has happened?"
"Have you noticed anything about him, Mum? He's so effeminate and keeps disappearing for days on end."
Chances are he's bisexual, I think to myself. Even so, I have the feeling she will continue their relationship.

2nd July – Tuesday

I make contact with Max's father, Mikey. He is named co-defendant in the wardship so it is important he knows what is going on. He has received my affidavit from the solicitor.
We meet at the pub where Mikey works and he proudly shows Max off to his mates. As we chat over lunch, Mikey is tense and shaking; his face pale, drawn and thin from his heroin use. He is extremely concerned about Jamie's situation and says Max is far safer with me.
Evening: Mikey phones Jamie at Hinckley. Afterwards, he turns to me saying, "I'm convinced, from the way Jamie speaks, she is being controlled by Leroy. And I'm certain she's on drugs."

3rd July – Wednesday

Jamie comes home for her usual few hours to see Max – not my daughter, Jamie, but a stranger. I catch her teaching Max to head butt saying, "Hit mummy, kick mummy. Kick mummy in the head," and she puts her head down towards his feet.

Later as we sit on the carpet in the sitting room, Jamie relaxes and is more her old self. We go through my original affidavit.
She confirms, "Yes, Leicester police kept me in the cells all night. I hit the bars of the cell with my shoes and wore down the high heels," she giggles. I drove the police mad.
Leroy is twenty-seven really, not twenty-three," she says. "He entered Britain as an illegal immigrant with his parents, and his false birth certificate shows him four years younger."

In the afternoon I take Jamie to see Mikey and leave them to chat for an hour in the park, while I play with Max on the swings. As we drive back home, Jamie tells me, "We talked about drugs and his use of methadone. He has offered me accommodation and I'll keep it in mind."

Jamie chats openly about working on the game and the life she is leading. "I have worked all over the country, often spending a week in one place while a child minder looked after Max." she says. "I worked in Park Lane London, earning at least £600 a night with rich, prominent men. Minders ensured the girls didn't run off with the earnings. Most of my work was via an escort agency and I had my own portable phone. Winston arranged designer clothes for me.
Jamie shows no shame for what she is doing. "It's just a profession and nothing more," she assures me.

"How did you get involved in the first place?" I enquire – although I know from her diaries, which I found recently.
"It started at college when I got involved with Steve Dred," she recalls. When Jamie introduced me to Steve last year, he frightened me with his bloodshot eyes and matted dreadlock hair. I remind Jamie he warned me, "Don't let Jamie go to London because she's in great danger."
"He was right," she says. "Winston intended to take me to London, to 'disappear me'. No one would have ever seen me again, including my family."
As she talks, my heart hits my stomach to think what might have been.

"Last Christmas Steve put me on the streets," she says. "I needed the money for Max's Christmas presents. After that, he blackmailed me all the time saying he would tell my parents, and everyone else, if I refused. I worked on the streets of Coventry earning about £200 a night. Much of this I pocketed inside my shoe.

While working there, I met Winston at a nightclub. He said he was a bank manager and wined and dined me at expensive hotels. Then he forced me to work on the game even though I was his girlfriend."
"Surely Jamie, you and Max could have escaped from him? But you chose to stay with your pimp, thus putting Max in danger. Why?"
Jamie goes quiet and doesn't answer.

Then she continues, "I was living at Winston's house, where Tammy rented a room. Tammy is very 'hot' because she is under age," says

Jamie. "She work*ed* mainly in saunas in other cities because of this. She comes from a good family but her parents have no control.
Most of the time we didn't receive any money for our work. It was all pocketed by Winston. We had to stash away anything we could in our shoes when the opportunity presented itself."

"Why did you tell them you were sixteen?" I ask.
"Winston treated me better because he thought I was very young," she replies."
"Why fantasize about Kate, your sister?"
Jamie laughs, "Yes, I told them Kate is married to a pop star; also, dad is a famous racing driver; and that you are a magistrate."
I'm dumbfounded.
Then she giggles, "I told them I'm due to inherit a fortune when I'm twenty-one." With only three years to Jamie's twenty-first birthday, no wonder Winston wants to hang on to her.
Many of my questions have been answered, but I still can't understand why Max's safety is not her first priority.

Jamie talks positively about returning to college in September. We call on the housing department in Stratford and they tell her that there is no possibility of being housed as a single person. Jamie hurls verbal abuse at the housing officer and calls her an 'old cow'. Stunned and embarrassed, I hurriedly escort her out of the council offices. I can't believe it. Is this really my daughter?

5th July – Friday

Just as I predicted, Jamie rings. "Mum, I'm not leaving Leroy after all. He's told me not to tell anyone, but he has cancer of the stomach and hasn't more than 12 months to live."
I warn her, "Jamie, don't believe him. Perhaps he's not ill, just looking for sympathy – or maybe he has AIDS?"
Reassuring me, Jamie says, "I'll insist on going to hospital with him. I'm sure he is ill. He says the scars on his stomach are burn marks from laser treatment."
I caution Jamie – "My friend says the marks could be needle marks from drugs abuse."
She says, "We are moving to a flat in Coventry and will be over soon."

I tell Bill that it doesn't sound too promising and there is little chance Jamie will return home after all.

29

He is speechless and then calming down he says, "The flat is in a notorious area for crime, prostitution and drugs. Whatever you do, don't let Max near the place."

9th July – Tuesday

Jamie rings, very tearful. "Mum, I'm coming home. Can you collect me from Leamington?"

At the rail station Jamie heaves along a large heavy suitcase, looking very dejected and unhappy. Her face is heavily bruised and swollen. She says, "I've fallen down the stairs at the flats," but I suspect she has been beaten (later, she confirms I was right).

She tells me, "I left Leroy a note explaining that I don't think he's ill, and that's why I left."

I warn her, "I'm convinced Pete is Leroy's boyfriend."

"No he isn't," she snaps.

12th July – Friday

Pete phones and tells Jamie, "Leroy read your note, stormed out of the flat last night and hasn't returned. Leroy is genuinely ill and I'm very concerned for his safety."

Frantically Jamie rings around the hospitals, and the police, to see if Leroy has been admitted, but has no luck.

Worried, out of her mind, Jamie packs her suitcase and returns to Coventry. She cannot let Leroy go. He has such a strong hold on her.

Another Court hearing is looming to extend care and control under the wardship. I hand papers to Jamie so she won't be harassed by the private detective.

How can she leave her son once more? Surely he is more important than Leroy who beats her, and who has another lover. I feel so sad for Max.

15th July – Monday

Jamie doesn't turn up at court for the second time for the wardship. The judge is angry at her apparent non-interest in Max's welfare, and gives me continued care and control of Max for a further eight months.

She phones and apologises for not attending Court. "I arrived late and had no idea which court it was in," she says.

I suspect she overslept but won't admit it.

Jamie demands, "I want Max to stay with me."

30

I am not happy, and check with my solicitor who reminds me, "We have agreed reasonable access. You must show willing and let Max go."

16th July – Tuesday

"Leroy has returned to the flat and I've decided to stay," Jamie says on the phone. "I'm not coming home."

This morning I receive notification Jamie has passed her college course. I am surprised with all those traumas during her studies. At least she has a qualification that could help her in any future career – that is, if there is ever to be one.

Crackhead

Nature versus Nurture –1991

17th July – Wednesday

My good friend Liz listens to the latest 'Jamie' saga. There is a new episode every day – a real life soap opera.
"Have you thought of looking for Jamie's natural mother?" she enquires. "It may answer so many questions as to why Jamie's life is in such a mess.
"It has crossed my mind," I say, "especially since Jamie has been fantasizing about her sister Kate."
Finding Jamie's mother is a daunting prospect but also exciting. Jamie often expressed her desire to find her mother. She wrote a letter to the social worker on her eighteenth birthday but could not pluck up courage to post it.

I call on my friend Cathy, who recently found *her* natural mother, to discuss finding Jamie's mother. "Go on," she says. "It may be the one thing Jamie needs to bring her to her senses. I will help you."

We have Jamie's original surname. The family lived up north and Jamie's grandmother, Ellen, divorced and moved with her children down south. Her daughter Tina, then seventeen, already had a two-year old daughter, Kate. She decided to have her second daughter Jamie adopted, and placed her in a children's home. Jamie came to live with us at six weeks old.

Cathy and I drive to the library and search excitedly through telephone directories. But, alas, great disappointment – almost sixty of that surname! Arriving home, armed with the first ten numbers, we dial frantically. "Do you know of Ellen who moved south with her children 18 years ago?" we ask.
"No," the broad northern accents say.
"We could try the town, down south, that they moved to," I suggest to Cathy. There is just one of that surname in the directory. The number is now ex-directory but we have an address from old library records.

I pluck up courage and write to the address hoping Jamie's grandmother, or one of her children, live there. A friend agrees to be an intermediary, and I expect it will take months to trace Tina.

27th July – Saturday

My friend phones, "I've received a letter and phone call about Jamie's mother's whereabouts. Can you come over?"

As we sit in the evening sun on her patio, I open the letter nervously.
It reads, "I was married to one of Ellen's sons. Not knowing why you want to trace the family, I am passing the letter to one of Ellen's other children – Tina."
This must be Jamie's mother. I have found her, not in months as I expected, but in one week!
The letter explains, "Tina is on holiday and will be home on Saturday."
The writer gives a telephone number in London. Tina's current name is 'Brown' – how lucky I traced her so quickly with such a common name.

"I received a call from Tina last night," says my friend. "She was anxious to know who Angela is? I didn't say too much but said I would pass the message on to you."

28th July – Sunday

One of the most treasured days of my life: emotions are running high and I make the decision to phone Jamie's mother.
Tina, who has been in my thoughts continually over the past eighteen years, will finally become a reality.

I take a deep breath and dial the London number...
"Tina?" I enquire
"Yes." The voice is much deeper than I'd imagined and sounds emotional.
"This is Angela. Did you have a daughter, Jamie?" I enquire.
"Yes," replies Tina.
I explain, "This is Jamie's mum, not Jamie speaking. Jamie is okay," I reassure her, "but her life is in a mess. That is why I am contacting you."

The next 45 minutes we chat, laugh, shed a few tears and exchange glimpses of the lost eighteen years. Tina is delighted to learn she has a grandson and wants to see him as soon as possible. She fills me in on her past and present.

When she was fifteen she gave birth to Kate, the daughter she kept. Proudly she tells me, "Kate had a daughter five weeks ago and lives with her boyfriend here in London.
Did you keep the name Jamie?" she asks. And did she always know she was adopted?"
"Yes," I reply.
Tina sounds really pleased.

"Are you good with a needle?" I enquire. "Jamie is very talented with a sewing machine. She would buy an outfit from a charity shop, and by evening had redesigned it to wear for a party."
"Yes, when I was young I was the same," says Tina. "I would buy clothes at a jumble sale and remake them – but by hand because I didn't have a sewing machine. And I used to love embroidery."
"What a coincidence." I tell her, "Jamie recently embroidered a beret which is quite unusual. Very few youngsters embroider these days."

Tina tells me she is married to Stuart and they have a pub.
Then I am hit by a bombshell...
Tina tells me, "I was hoping to find Jamie through social workers because my family have a hereditary illness. Jamie and her children may be at risk. It is a condition which results in a massive heart attack at approximately thirty and, more often than not, kills."
Tina's sister died last month and her brother three years ago. Another brother and sister have had serious heart attacks in their early thirties, but these are not believed to be associated with the disease.

I explain to Tina, "I don't feel the time is right for Jamie to know I have found you. She has gone completely off the rails." I decide not to reveal the full story, including prostitution, at this early stage.
Finally I say I will send Tina photos of Jamie during her childhood and teenage years; and agree to go to London to meet her soon.

30th July – Tuesday

I meet Jamie and Leroy at Coventry. They borrow my car to pop over to Hinckley to collect their income support, while I amble around shops with Max.
When they return Jamie says, "We can't hire transport because Leroy hasn't got a driving licence."
"Do you drive without tax or insurance?" I ask.

They laugh, "Of course, all the time," and I am horrified.
We walk over to the housing department. After their interview Jamie says, "We told the woman that we had lived in the area nine months, even though it's just been a few weeks. She believed Max is Leroy's son and that we're getting married," laughs Jamie.

Lunch-time we picnic in the Memorial Park under a huge oak tree, while Max runs around playing 'tig' with his Mummy. There is an inexplicable bond between them and he loves his mummy so much. As I sit and watch, I hope it won't be too long before Jamie gets her act together and Max lives with her once more.

We return to the flats, pulling up in the car park.
Suddenly Jamie panics.
"Mum, quick, park round the front".
Leroy tries to calm Jamie down. "Jamie, don't be silly."
Nearby is a parked red car. Four denim-dressed youths hang out of the windows.
"They are plain clothes police from the vice squad," explains Jamie. "They have been harassing me by the shops. This morning they kept knocking on the flat door asking where the 'business' is, implying prostitution is going on up there."
Jamie denies she is involved in anything, but I am learning less and less to believe her.

She steps out of the car, bawling a mouthful of abuse across the car park. The car revs up and speeds away, tyres screeching and burning.
Is this really me? I must be dreaming. I cannot believe what I am seeing. It is just like an American movie.

When I drop them off, I am confronted by Jamie, demanding aggressively, "I want Max to stay here tomorrow."
So unexpected, I am stuck for words. I don't want Max staying in this run-down area and I don't trust Jamie and her friends. Unhappily I agree, remembering my solicitor had told me to show willing by letting him stay for one night only.

1st August – Thursday
I take Max over to Jamie's flat. We drive past metal shuttered shops,

many closed, and litter is strewn everywhere. Young West Indian men hang around street corners in small groups, lazing on grass verges or leaning against pub doorways in the burning heat of the sun. A black youth sways in and out of the gutter – under the influence of drugs? An elderly drunken West Indian staggers past.

Popping into the shop for sweets, I note how different it is from my local shop. Everything, including newspapers, sweets and canned drinks, is covered with glass to prevent theft.

Max and I proceed to the high-rise flats and wait in the car park for Jamie. In front of us is tall wire fencing and, on the other side, happy little black faces peer through smiling. Jamie comes bouncing over to the car, very pleased to see us, and jumps in. Max is delighted to see his mummy.

"That's the local nursery school. Isn't it lovely!" exclaims Jamie. "I've put Max's name down."

Sudden panic. But then I think, keep calm, it may never happen. It never does.

Jamie continually talks of having Max back. But there is no way he can return unless she changes her lifestyle.

We amble across litter-strewn grassed areas surrounding the flats. Reggae music blares out full blast from balconies. As the hot sun pours down, it is hard to believe this is England. We could easily be in balmy Jamaica.

The flats, with newly painted corridors, are much better than I imagined. Jamie's flat is surprisingly clean, neat and tidy, with hardly any furniture.

Reluctantly saying goodbye and kissing Max, I keep my fingers crossed, knowing that it is for just one night only.

2nd August – Friday

I call at the flat during the afternoon to collect Max. The door is opened by a girl introducing herself as Annabel. She tells me she is keeping an eye on Max while Jamie sleeps. She shouts up to the bedroom, "Jamie, your mum's here."

Jamie enters the room, bleary eyed and very pale. She is irritable with Max and snaps. "He's been uncontrollable and naughty." This is so unlike Max because he is such an easy child.

"Jamie, he has been stifled in this high-rise flat," I point out. "After all, he is used to a large cottage and garden. You have no toys for him to play with. No wonder he's frustrated," I tell her crossly.

Relieved to see me, Max runs over shouting, "Mum" and greets me with a big hug.
We have established that he calls me 'mum' and Jamie 'mummy'. I maintain mum is the person who cares for and brings up a child, as I did with both my adopted children.
Thank goodness I have got Max away from that awful atmosphere and back to the security of our home.

3rd August – Saturday

A few days ago I sent a photo album to Tina, showing Jamie's childhood and teen years. Tina rings. "Can you come to London tomorrow?"
We arrange for me to meet Jamie's sister, Kate, at Victoria Coach Station.

4th August – Sunday

As I travel on the coach to London, I wonder if my questions will be answered: why did Jamie turn out this way? Will Tina understand the turmoil in Jamie's life?
Are there similarities between mother and daughter? After all, we have discovered coincidences on the phone already: Jamie and Tina had hidden pregnancies, weights of both babies were identical and labour the same number of hours: Tina's and Jamie's first babies went into foster care to be adopted, but they changed their minds at the last minute and kept them.

Nervously I walk down the steps at Victoria to meet Jamie's sister. Her back is facing me. But there is no mistaking it is Kate...she looks just like Jamie standing there, perhaps an inch or so taller. Kate is wearing similar clothes to Jamie's – a white cotton trouser suit, and brogue style brown suede shoes.
She turns around and smiles. Kate's blonde curly hair is below the shoulders, looking like Jamie's did recently. Although her face is different, the make-up is absolutely perfect; and the shape of arms, ankles, feet, and the walk are all just like Jamie's.

Immediately we are relaxed, and it is as if we have always known each other. Crossing the city by underground, we chat, comparing the sisters' likes and dislikes. Kate tells me that her mum is on her third marriage, to Steve, and had her daughters by two further relationships.

"I don't know much about Jamie's birth," says Kate. "Mum won't talk about the past. The family all know about Jamie and had hoped to find her one day," she says.

We arrive at the pub. As I enter, I take a deep breath...
Tina, looking very different from what I imagined, sits in the corner cuddling her grand daughter. I thought she would be tall, dark-haired and thin. There is a slight facial resemblance to Jamie and similar figure, although she is a couple of inches taller. Her hair is dyed blonde and short. She is very smartly dressed and, again, the perfect make-up. How I had battled with young Jamie about the make-up, when I myself wore so little. My first question has been answered.

Tina's husband, Stuart, serves us welcome sandwiches and drinks as we chat for six hours non-stop. Tina wants me to fill her in on Jamie's childhood and we compare notes. Does Jamie have good teeth; what food does she like; her interests, hobbies and schooling? Similarities soon become very apparent.

I tell Tina, "During Jamie's teen years, I had terrible problems with her changing hair colour and styles. Only last week Jamie had a disaster. She went from mousy fair to white blonde, finishing up auburn."
Tina smiles. "I also had a disaster last week – my hair turned a terrible blonde. I'm always at the hairdressers altering my appearance."

We discuss Jamie's lifestyle and reluctantly I explain, "Jamie is working on the streets."
Tina seems to understand and suggests perhaps she could help. "As long as she's not on drugs," she says. "It can cause such awful problems."
"I don't think so," I say, "but who knows?"

Sadly, Tina tells me, "My sister died from a massive heart attack recently and she was only in her late twenties. We are worried Jamie might inherit the disease. The family are going for tests shortly."

The pub appears to be very successful and Tina tells me they hope to leave London soon and get a pub on the coast.
Tina and Kate have written letters, including photos, for me to hand to Jamie when the time is right.

What a wonderful day – I am exhausted. I never dreamed this day would happen...the meeting with Jamie's natural mother.
Travelling back to Stratford, I ponder over the day's events.
When shall I tell Jamie? Will she be angry with me?

5th August – Monday

Perhaps Jamie will change her lifestyle if she knows her roots? I am dying to tell her but the time isn't right.
I offer to buy her new clothes and shoes. "I'll pay to sort out your bleached hair at the hairdressers," I tell her, smiling quietly to myself. If only she knew!

9th August – Friday

Jamie sounds much more relaxed over the phone. Time is right to tell her the breathtaking news, but first she must improve her scruffy appearance. "Get your hair done by next weekend and come over to stay," I announce.
Half-heartedly Jamie agrees to go to the hairdressers. A week later she rings me, "My hair is a much better colour and I'm coming over."

13th August – Tuesday

The big day arrives – there is no turning back. Am I doing the right thing? Baby sitter organised, we set off for a pub meal. As we drive to our venue Jamie is very excited, and gently pushes for information. "Have you got a new boyfriend?" she giggles.
"Are you moving house at long last?" She obviously has no idea of the news that will soon completely alter her life.
Sitting on a bench in the warm evening sunshine Jamie says, "Well, come on then, what's the news?"

Taking a deep breath, I look at her.
"Jamie, you'll never guess...I've found your mother Tina, and sister Kate".
Astounded, she looks at me and smiles. Then her eyes well up with tears. Composing herself, Jamie's first question is, "Does she smoke?"
"Yes," I reply.
Jamie can't believe it and declares, "I hate smoking."
I show her the photos from Tina. As she sits quietly taking it all in I tell her, "There are letters from Tina and Kate back at home. They want to make contact as quickly as possible, but it must be your decision when the time is right."

We return to the cottage and I hand Jamie the letters. She reads them with tears in her eyes and choked with emotion. After handing me the letters to read, she quietly retires with them to her bedroom.

Next day Jamie says excitedly, "Mum, I want to meet Tina and Kate as soon as possible."
I phone Tina with the news and she says, "We are all ready and on standby for this weekend – Stuart and myself, Kate, her boyfriend Marcus, and the baby"

17th August – Saturday

This is one of the most important days of Jamie's life – meeting her natural mother and sister. They are visiting us here because we feel Jamie will be happier on her own territory.
Jamie looks lovely and has made a special effort. Her soft curly hair, now a pretty auburn shade, falls just below the shoulder. Wearing a white, cotton, short sleeved two-piece suit, she looks the daughter any mother can feel proud of.

Immediately, when they arrive, the atmosphere is relaxed. Jamie proudly introduces Max to her new family. Kate in turn introduces Jamie to her daughter Polly, five weeks old. Kate is dressed in a similar outfit to Jamie. Tina's blonde bouffant hairstyle is reminiscent of the 60's. She is wearing a short length flowered cotton dress and white high heeled shoes.

There is so much to talk about and coincidences keep cropping up.
Kate says, "I don't like tattoos."
Jamie replies, "Well I've got one here," revealing a small rose on the top of her left breast.
Tina laughs as she lifts up her skirt, "I've also got one on the top of my leg."
I exclaim, "Now I understand everything. I have always disapproved of tattoos." Like mother, like daughter, I smile to myself.

Kate and Jamie compare their likes and dislikes of food. Neither of them drinks milk or hot drinks, and their favourite vegetables are cabbage and brussel sprouts, an unusual combination we all agree.

All three women had their first babies by men who had been in prison. Jamie and Kate's boyfriends, although of different mixed race, have broad London accents and are of similar build and skin colour.

After lunch I show Tina around the 17th century cottage where Jamie has spent her childhood since the age of two. Over the past eighteen years Tina thought Jamie was living in the Newmarket area, where we lived when she was adopted. We were unaware Tina's in-laws lived in Stratford and they often visited the town. Did our paths ever cross I wonder?
As we enter Jamie's bedroom, Tina whispers, "I'd love to give her a hug but perhaps she would think I'm silly."

Before the family leave for home, Tina turns to Jamie saying, "You must come and see us soon in London." Kate says she is keen to introduce Jamie to the rest of the family, including their grandmother.
We laugh as Max tries to get in the back seat of the car to go home with them. He is usually very difficult with strangers. There must be some chemical bond – it is as if he has always been part of their family.

After such an emotional afternoon Jamie looks contented, relaxed and very happy. She has taken to her new family – after eighteen years she has at long last found her roots.

26th August – Monday

Jamie has decided to leave Leroy and return home. She says she intends to go back to college in a few days to do a hair and beauty course at Leamington College. Perhaps Jamie's new family has given her the incentive she needs. Maybe, at long last, there is hope.

5th September – Thursday

Jamie took Max to London last weekend, to stay with her new family. When they returned she seemed very happy and announced, "We had a really good time."

A fresh start at college will hopefully set Jamie on the straight and narrow. She is full of enthusiasm and raring to go.
Jamie tells me Leroy has moved to Sheffield but they intend to keep in contact.

7th September – Saturday

Unexpectedly I receive a call from Jamie. "Mum, I'm on my way to London to take Leroy to meet Tina and Kate."

My heart sinks. Is Jamie doing the right thing? Leroy is a real rough diamond and has been in prison for four years.

A few hours later, the phone rings. Jamie is so excited she can hardly speak. "Mum, you'll never guess what's happened? When we walked into the pub, Kate was with her boyfriend Marcus. It was amazing... Marcus and Leroy knew each other – they did time in Pentonville prison together."
I can't believe what I am hearing. It's such an extraordinary coincidence. The sisters have chosen lads who were in Pentonville together. And yet Jamie met Leroy in Leicester, and Kate met Marcus in London. "Everyone found it highly amusing," giggles Jamie.

10th September – Tuesday

The custody court hearing today and Jamie has told me that she is unable to attend due to a special assignment at college.
She seems to be getting her act together at long last. I believe it is time for her to take responsibility for Max again.
At my request, the Judge awards Jamie 'care and control' of Max but states, "Jamie and her son must reside at her mother's address for the time-being." He orders a court welfare officer be appointed for reports.
I hand back the child benefit book to Jamie, expecting her to clothe and feed Max, and pay housekeeping.

14th/15th September

Jamie goes with Kate and Tina, for the weekend, to visit relatives on the coast. They have a wonderful time. Jamie meets her grandmother, uncles, aunts and cousins She seems very happy and contented.

Kate has told her friends over the years, "I have a sister," but no one believed her. This was an opportunity not to be missed. The sisters headed for Kate's old haunts.
Jamie laughs as she recounts, "We looked so much alike, and everyone was astounded when Kate introduced me as her sister."

End of September

With my blessing, Tina tries to persuade Jamie to stay in London, get a flat and attend a local college. Jamie says, "I'll consider it."

She maintains contact with Leroy, travelling to Sheffield by train most weekends. She is drawing closer to him, could pack up college, and join him any minute. I don't trust her an inch and instinct tells me there is little chance of her settling in London. Jamie is a northerner at heart.

Search and Find – 1991

October

Tension mounts between us now Jamie is back at home. She has custody of Max but shows little interest in him. All she is bothered about is her hair, make-up and watching T.V. Her relationship with Max is that of a big sister. She never plays with her child, prepares his food, or takes him out  of the house. I am left to do everything. When I remind her of the court order, she shrugs her shoulders and storms out of the room. She is getting very aggressive.

During this time Max has very bad asthma. I find it hard getting up night after night to nebulize him. When I ask Jamie to do it, she either falls asleep or can't remember how to work the nebulizer. I get very cross and end up doing it myself. Max is getting worse. I am exhausted and very concerned at Jamie's attitude.

My health visitor is wonderful. She listens to my concerns and calls around to assess the situation and chat with Jamie. It becomes evident Jamie has not got a clue about asthma and the nebulizer.
Agitated, Jamie announces, "I'm off to college," and storms off aggressively out of the house, not bothering to say goodbye or kiss her son. Having witnessed Jamie's attitude, the health visitor says, "I'm extremely concerned."

Jamie demands that she be allowed to take Max up to Sheffield to stay with Leroy for the weekend. I am not happy but my solicitor says, "Jamie has care and control. You must show you are giving her freedom and full access." Reluctantly I let Max go.

31st October – Thursday

The court welfare officer, Mr. Williams, visits me for the first time. I tell him of Jamie's lack of involvement with Max, and my worries for his safety should she get full care and control of him.

45

He insists, "Max should, and probably will, return to Jamie in the near future. It will be in his best interests."

I am very upset. This man doesn't believe me or understand the situation. How can he judge what is really going on, not having been involved until now? He hasn't got a clue what Jamie is about.

I sign off our interview near to tears and warn, "I believe Jamie will run off with him".
He probably thinks 'another neurotic grandmother'. It is general policy of social services and other agencies to state that a child is *always* better off with its natural mother, no matter how much of a threat is posed to that child. The new Children's Act is supposed to put the interests of the child first. Max is in grave danger as long as he is with Jamie. I am very angry!

8th November – Friday

The atmosphere is tense this morning as Jamie prepares to go to college and take Max to the creche. I can't understand why. This weekend they will travel to Sheffield to stay with Leroy.

I enter Jamie's bedroom and sense something is wrong. The room has an empty air about it...I rush to the wardrobe.
Horror strikes me. Almost all Jamie's clothes are gone.
I fly into Max's bedroom – his clothes are gone too.
JAMIE HAS RUN AWAY WITH MAX !

The police say they can't help, even though the court order states, 'Jamie must reside with Max at her mother's address.' Jamie has care and control, and their hands are tied.
There is nobody I can speak to over the weekend. I am desperate and there is nothing I can do for the next few days. Once again I feel so helpless.

9th November – Saturday

I phone Claire, Jamie's friend, voicing my fears.
She is extremely worried, and says, "Jamie confided in me, but I feel you should know what's been going on.

Leroy is living in Sheffield with his new boyfriend, Alan. When Jamie took Max up a couple of weeks ago, Leroy wouldn't let Jamie in the flat and insisted she leave Max with them. They told Jamie she must stay with a lesbian girl nearby. Fortunately, Jamie didn't leave Max with them and left in a hurry. Also, Jamie went with Max to a gay pub that weekend and was thrown out."

By now frantic, and fearful for Max's safety, I ring Jamie's mother and sister. Kate tells me, "When I saw Jamie recently she was badly bruised. Leroy had been hitting her."

I have to act quickly. My doctor suggests I contact emergency social services, in view of the probable danger Max is in. A social worker visits me to take details and suggests I contact the police first thing on Monday.

10th November – Sunday

Perhaps I have got it all wrong? I must be imagining things.

But by this evening, when Jamie said she would be home, there is no sign of her.

9.00p.m. Leroy phones from Sheffield asking, "Can I speak to Jamie?"

"She hasn't arrived home yet," I tell him.

I am beginning to feel really sick. Leroy sounds puzzled.

"I can't understand it," he says. "I saw Jamie and Max off at Sheffield station and they were coming straight home to you. I'll phone again tomorrow."

11th November – Monday

I am very worried and speak to the Samaritans for over an hour during the night, but they don't seem to understand, especially where drugs are concerned.

Once my solicitor hears of Max's disappearance, she arranges for a court hearing tomorrow.

Leroy phones again, "Can I speak to Jamie?"

"She didn't come home," I tell him. "Are you sure she caught the Birmingham train yesterday?"

He assures me Jamie and Max caught the train.

12th November – Tuesday

The Judge is horrified when he reads my original affidavit and hears of the latest details about Leroy and his boyfriend. Immediately he issues a 'Search & Find' order for Max, and gives full custody and control to me upon his return.

13th November – Wednesday

Where can Jamie and Max be?
I speak to Leroy once more but he says he hasn't a clue. From the tone of his voice I suspect he knows where Jamie is.
Over the past few days I have kept in touch with Tina in London. Between us we try to think where Jamie and Max can be.

On the order of the court, the police call at the Sheffield flat but Jamie and Max aren't there. Even if found, there is little the police can do – the Order is to 'search and find' and not 'return.'

Eventually, Tina decides enough is enough. "I'm sure Jamie is at Leroy's flat," she says and goes immediately up to Sheffield to look for them.

15th November – Friday

Mid-morning I receive a call from Tina. She called at Leroy's flat very early and he answered the door. "I demanded to see Jamie and she was there," says Tina.
Tina immediately returns to London with Jamie and Max. Bill and I travel to collect Max later in the evening.
In Tina's lounge we find Jamie huddled up in the corner of the settee, pale and weepy. She looks dreadful and refuses to speak. I kiss her on the cheek and say, "I'll be in touch," as we hurriedly collect Max's things together and depart.
I am exhausted from the week's events but now I can rest in the knowledge that Max is home and safe.

Tina is hopeful Jamie will stay a while in London and sort her life out. However, high hopes are short lived and within a few days Jamie returns to Leroy in Sheffield.

22nd November – Friday

I am applying for the return of custody of Max to myself, today.
My solicitor and I sit anxiously in the court waiting room for Jamie and Leroy.

They arrive and storm around the waiting area shouting in a frenzy. Jamie then sits herself down nearby, pale, withdrawn and not speaking. Leroy threatens violently, "No way will you get that child. We are getting married soon.

Max is *my* son and my parents will move heaven and earth to get him."
Strange, I think to myself. He recently told me his parents were dead.

He shouts in front of the waiting crowd, "I'll get a gun to you."
I shake from head to toe, knowing he could well mean it.
My solicitor and I feel threatened. As we enter the courtroom, Leroy is
stopped by a court officer. "But I'm getting married to Jamie," he shouts.
He is ignored, pushed aside, and we are ushered in.

Jamie, a total stranger, hurls abuse across the courtroom. Pointing at me
she shouts, "She's not a fit mother to have Max. She's not my natural
mother and has no rights."
Jamie rattles on saying, "My father hit me, drank heavily, and hurled a
whisky bottle around when I was a child."
Such lies. I can't believe my ears.

The Judge orders Jamie, "Shut-up."
Eventually, following a lot of verbal abuse, Jamie quietens down. After
hearing the solicitor's evidence, the judge returns Max into my safe
custody once more. Court welfare reports are called for, with a further
hearing in the New Year. I agree to Jamie's supervised access of Max at
Tina's pub in London.
Jamie furiously storms out of the court, bawling at the judge, "Get
stuffed".

Quaking at the knees, my solicitor and I are ushered out of the rear
entrance by a court official. As we hastily run to the car park, we jump out
of our skin at every black man we see. There is no sign of Leroy and Jamie.
My solicitor phones Stratford police to arrange an escort home.
I fear Jamie will turn up with Leroy at the cottage. I phone my baby sitter
and warn her, "Get Max out of the house as quickly as possible."
Police are at the cottage when I arrive. My heart is pounding, I am tense
and scared.

Jamie and Leroy arrive shortly afterwards. But they are so very
different...calm, relaxed and putting on the charm. Had I dreamed the
courtroom incident? Am I crazy? Nothing makes sense. So strange –
how can they change at the flick of a finger into two normal happy
people, laughing and playing with Max, and so friendly with me after
having hurled such abuse in court just an hour ago?

I phone my solicitor to tell her they have arrived, and of their sudden change in behaviour. I question, "What else could account for this odd behaviour – except possibly drugs?"

December

My solicitor confirms Jamie can only have access to Max at Tina's in London.
Tina and I meet at a bus stop at Oxford, thus sharing the journey. On one occasion I did the return journey, taking Max across London, in one day. I am exhausted and can't keep this pace up much longer.

Jamie demands, "I want Max to stay with me in Sheffield over Christmas."
"No chance," I tell her.
My solicitor and I agree Max can stay with Jamie in London, the weekend before Christmas.

20th December – Wednesday

Max and I arrive at the pub. Tina assures me she will keep an eye on things.
For Christmas, she has bought Jamie a portable CD player. I advise, "Don't let Jamie take it back to Sheffield, otherwise it will get lost or stolen."

When Jamie arrives with Leroy from Sheffield he is sweating badly and seems unwell. Maybe he is terminally ill after all?
Jamie unexpectedly announces, "I'm marrying Leroy in the New Year and I'm going to have his baby as soon as possible."
I feel so sick.

Reluctantly, I leave Max with them at Tina's for a couple of days.
When I meet Tina at Oxford to collect Max, she tells me Jamie and Leroy have returned to Sheffield with the C.D. player. I am disappointed Tina ignored my warning.

25th December – Wednesday. Christmas Day

5.00 p.m. I receive call from Jamie in Sheffield. "We have just woken up and I've left Leroy to cook the turkey."

Upon Jamie's return to the flat, Leroy forces her to give him all her jewellery (my mother's) and the C.D. player. He goes out and exchanges it for heroin.

Jamie is devastated to lose her first-ever present from her natural mother. When she complains Leroy beats her up badly.

26th/29th December – Thursday/Sunday

Jamie is distraught and takes an overdose, ending up in hospital. Tina travels up to Sheffield and brings her back down to London.

I have had no idea what has been going on. Tina has kept events of the last few days from me to save worry, because my father has been seriously ill and Max has spent a night in hospital with asthma.

31st December – Tuesday

Jamie phone, "I'm spending New Year's Eve at Tina's pub," she tells me.
"Are you going back to Sheffield?" I ask.
"I'll have to wait and see," she replies. But I know Jamie will return to Leroy as soon as possible.

Crackhead

Northern Lights – 1992

1st January – Wednesday

New Year's Day: Jamie phones from Tina's and sounds very bright but after chatting to her, I am convinced she will go back to Sheffield.

3rd January – Friday

Tina phones to tell me, "Jamie has gone to Sheffield to collect some clothes."

I am not at all surprised and my intuition has proven right once again. "Leroy isn't well, on a come down from heroin," says Tina. "Jamie says she intends to look after him for a few days before coming back to London. She has registered here with Social Security for income support and I think she will stay in London."
"I doubt it," I tell her. "Jamie has every intention of staying in Sheffield."

Tina then gives me the news of Jamie's overdose, explains about the C.D. being stolen on Christmas day, and the terrible beatings.

5th January – Sunday

Early morning I receive a distressed call from Tina telling me, "Jamie has just phoned from Sheffield Police Station. She, Leroy and his friend Alan, are in custody for armed robbery. Leroy threatened someone with a knife and he has also been charged with possession of heroin. I have only got a few details and suggest you phone Sheffield police."

The police are very helpful when I ring and tell me Jamie has been held overnight. It is alleged Jamie took clients back to the flat; Leroy and Alan forced the client at knifepoint to go to the bank cash dispensing machine.
"Is Jamie pregnant?" enquires the sergeant.
"I don't think so." I reply.
He goes on, "Jamie claims she's having a miscarriage. She went to hospital during the night but wouldn't allow them to examine her and is returning to hospital this afternoon."

I phone Tina to give her further details and she says, "I will go straight up to Sheffield."

I am so grateful to her for her support and concern. It puts my mind at rest and I can get on with the job of looking after Max.

This afternoon I phone the hospital and they tell me, "Jamie is comfortable after her operation but we cannot give further information." I believe Jamie has had a miscarriage.

8th January – Wednesday

Jamie is released on bail and Tina returns with her to London. In the meantime Leroy is remanded in custody.

21st January – Tuesday

Jamie comes home for few days to be with Max on his second birthday. A birthday card arrives for Max from Leroy in prison and he writes "To my son". How I hate him for that.

25th January – Saturday

"Tina has asked me to call her 'mum' and Max to call her 'grandma' but I don't want to," says Jamie.

Obviously Tina is not sure what to think after the awful things Jamie has told her about me. I don't blame Tina for trying to do her best for Jamie. Today Jamie visits hospital for x-rays and E.C.G. to check her heart. Tests are negative, but a scan is required for the all clear.

3rd February – Monday

After a few days in London Jamie rings unexpectedly, "Mum, can you collect me from the coach at Oxford? I've had enough," she says downheartedly, and I agree to collect her.

We arrive back home to be greeted by Bill who is livid. He has received a call from Tina saying, "I never want to see Jamie again. She's evil and I don't know how you have put up with her this long."

Tina told Bill that Kate had read Jamie's letters and diaries which indicated she was working at King's Cross and Tottenham Court Road. In the letters Jamie said, "Tina's not interested in me."

What a load of rubbish, for I know Tina has done everything she possibly can to try and help her.

Jamie boldly denies everything Tina has said.

I demand, "Jamie, what is it you want out of life?"
"To marry Leroy," she replies. "We're getting married on Valentine's Day."
"Right," I tell her. "Go to Sheffield and get on with your life and leave us all alone."
Staring right through me she shouts, "I will then," and storms off to pack her things.
I manage to persuade her to stay tonight because she is due to have a scan at the hospital in the morning.

Anxiously, Jamie awaits her trial, date unknown, and announces, "I'm pleading not guilty to the charge of robbery and will definitely get off." Leroy remains on remand while his friend, Alan, is released on bail.

4th February – Tuesday

Jamie fails to attend the hospital for the scan.
As she leaves my house to return to Sheffield, I breathe a huge sigh of relief and am glad to see the back of her.

14th February – Friday

Jamie is due to marry Leroy today and has bought a new Laura Ashley dress for the occasion. However, to my relief, it is cancelled at the last minute when the prison authorities refuse to release Leroy to attend the registry office.

Tina tells me, "I called at Leroy's flat, after Jamie's miscarriage in January, and was horrified at needles on the floor and in drawers. Imagine the risk to Max had he gone up there as Jamie demanded." We agree, Leroy is A1 risk for AIDS – a bisexual heroin addict. I tremble at the thought.

Mid February

I pop down to London to collect Jamie's clothes from the pub. Once home, as I unpack Jamie's possessions, I discover revealing and very informative letters.
There is a letter from Leroy to Alan his boyfriend. It confirms they were lovers and have now ended their relationship. Alan writes of when he hid Max from the authorities, and that he would move heaven and earth to do it again if he had to.

Crackhead

The lesbian woman in Sheffield had written to Jamie. She mentions Leroy and Alan's love for each other and that they wanted to keep Max. It proves to me that Claire was right after all and I was justified to be concerned when Jamie ran away with Max. Jamie writes of that fatal weekend, when she had been forced to leave Sheffield because Leroy and Alan wanted Max.

Afterwards, she and Max travelled to Wolverhampton to stay with a friend. "Max sat on the train watching me cry," writes Jamie, "and he wiped away the tears from my cheeks."

My heart aches for Max who was only eighteen months old at the time. I had no idea Jamie was in Wolverhampton and not Sheffield that weekend. Max had been entangled in a web of deceit and danger. Jamie showed no regard for his safety and welfare.

Jamie's diary talks of her continued work . She had written to a friend, mentioning a national newspaper, in which she had featured in an article, on a sex show up north.

It is essential I keep these letters as proof for the courts when I go for final custody of Max.

Arrangements have been made at my request, via the court welfare officer, for Jamie to have supervised access, over a three month period, at a church hall in Coventry run by volunteers.

March/April

Jamie travels by train to Coventry to see Max on Saturdays at the access centre and returns to Sheffield the same day.

Quite often she doesn't turn up. Max is old enough to understand and feels very let down.

At our first meeting, I am aghast when Jamie arrives wearing a low necked blouse revealing, nestled in her cleavage, a thick gold chain supporting six heavy glittering gold sovereign rings.

"Jamie, you'll be mugged and have those ripped off," I exclaim.

Unconcerned, she says, "They are Leroy's. I'm looking after them while he's in prison."

56

Jamie brings along her prostitute friend. She is twenty-two, very skinny and has five children in care. She thinks the access centre is awful and tells Jamie she shouldn't have to see Max there. Her remarks cause friction between us but, as far as I'm concerned, there is no alternative. The only way I can cope, and be sure Jamie won't run away with Max again, is to meet her at the centre.

One day, after her access visit, Jamie rings me. "Mum, while I was with you today, the police raided my flat, breaking down the door and looking for stolen goods."
The arrangements at Coventry access centre continue for ten weeks but we are forced to give up; Jamie only turned up five of those weeks.

While waiting trial at Sheffield Crown Court, Jamie remains on bail. She claims that she is working at a hairdressers and continues to live in Leroy's flat in Sheffield.
There is no further contact with Tina, but Jamie receives news of the family from a friend in London. Tina and her husband have moved from their pub in London.

Jamie regularly insists, "I want Max to stay with me," but I refuse, knowing she is still associating with dangerous criminals. The Court agrees with me.

24th/26th April – Friday/Sunday

I am preparing to move house, and feel unwell. Jamie rings, offering to stay and look after Max while I pack. I gladly take up her offer because it is hard to cope moving on my own, especially with a little one.

Jamie returns to Sheffield Sunday evening. Midnight, I discover that she has been through my things and stolen my papers.
Over the past eighteen months I have collected evidence for final custody of Max in August. Papers include love letters between Leroy and Alan; a letter from Jamie's lesbian friend; together with Jamie's letters and diaries from the time she was at college, showing how unstable she is.

Police follow up with a visit to Sheffield. Jamie admits she has stolen my papers and will return them in the post, but they never show up.
The police said she looked a real mess at the interview, wearing a mini skirt, which revealed stockings and suspenders.

Jamie broke bail conditions by leaving Sheffield and staying with me. Now she has to report up there three times a week.

Sheffield Council evict Jamie from Leroy's flat and she fears being rehoused in Sheffield's ghetto area. Often she talks of Max living with her and I dread it. But I know there is no sign of stability in her life, and the prospect seems further away than ever. Jamie says the D.S.S. have put her in modern hotel accommodation in Doncaster.

Meanwhile Leroy remains in prison. He writes to Max, "I'm learning kick-boxing and when I come out I'll teach you. Love from Daddy." How I dread Leroy's release.
A number of hearings for the robbery at Crown Court are cancelled and Jamie appears nervous, now convinced prison is on the cards.

Aggression – 1992

1st May – Friday

We move to our new home in Stratford. I know I will be very happy here with Max and the house has a wonderful atmosphere – my haven from all my problems with Jamie.

11th May – Monday

Today is the Court Hearing, the beginning of my book (see section 'Jamie'). Jamie refuses to speak to me in court, looking withdrawn and pale. The Judge agrees to access in Birmingham, to be agreed between myself and Jamie. I am happy to meet Jamie there, which will also mean less travelling by train for her from Sheffield.

16th May – Saturday

We arrange to meet at McDonald's, Birmingham. I am tense, dreading our first meeting since that awful court hearing.
Jamie is waiting when we arrive and Max runs excitedly to her. To my astonishment, she is happy and chatty as if nothing happened at court the other day.
Jamie must have a split personality. What on earth is going on in that mind of hers?

23rd May – Saturday

We wait for Jamie at our regular McDonald's spot. As she runs across the road towards us, I can't believe my eyes. She is dressed in a grubby white figure-hugging mini dress, straps hanging off the shoulders, revealing the rose tattoo on her left breast. Her rather full bust disguises the fact she is very thin and losing weight.
A large tattoo on her arm spells out the word, 'Leroy'. The rose is small and tasteful but this new tattoo is awful.

Jamie is due to travel to London to stay with a friend after our meeting. I can't bear to see her looking so scruffy and tarty, so I decide to treat her to a new blouse and black leggings. She is so thrilled, hugging and thanking me over and over again.

Before we say goodbye we pop into the Pavillions for a snack. I have had a glimpse of my 'old' Jamie this afternoon. Our meeting has turned out to be a surprisingly happy one.

30th May – Saturday

Max and I wait an hour in Birmingham – but Jamie doesn't turn up. She has been unreliable so many times and I am getting used to it now. Max is upset so I tell him, "Mummy's train has broken down."

Upon my return home, I receive a call from Bill to say Jamie has left a message that her money has been stolen, and she can't afford to get to Birmingham.

1st June – Monday

I am shocked to see Jamie standing on my doorstep when I return from town.

My heart races and adrenalin rushes through my body. What shall I do? I told her not to come here, but I can't turn her away after her long journey from Sheffield.

I have no choice but to invite her in.

Jamie is impressed with our new home and thrilled to see Max's bedroom. She comes with me to collect Max from nursery school and he is delighted to see his mummy.

The bus is due to leave Stratford early this evening for Coventry. From there she will get a train to Sheffield. Jamie gets on the bus in tears and Max starts to cry. It is so sad that an innocent child must go through so much.

6th June – Saturday

Jamie says she will be with us at mid-day but hasn't turned up. Eventually she arrives from Sheffield at 5.00 p.m. saying, "Sorry, I overslept".

As usual Jamie chats non-stop pouring her heart out.

She misses the last train from Stratford to Birmingham early evening, and I drive her to Leamington to catch the 8.00 p.m. train. I am determined I shall get her off my hands tonight.

10.00 p.m: the phone rings. My heart sinks when I hear Jamie's voice. "Mum, I've missed the connecting train to Sheffield so I've returned to Leamington. I'm coming back home."
I just can't win, no matter how hard I try.

12th June – Friday

Jamie has applied to my solicitor for Max to stay with her in Doncaster. We refuse, fearing for his safety.

July

Jamie shares a house with three girls at Doncaster paid for by Social Security and she appears happy. "Life is a lot easier without Leroy although I still visit him in prison," she says.
"Looks as if I'm right again, Jamie. There's no sign of Leroy having a terminal illness after all?"
"No, probably a figment of his imagination," she replies.

20th July – Monday

At the fourth hearing at Crown Court, for robbery, Leroy pleads guilty, is convicted, and transferred to another prison.
Jamie tells me on the phone that the police tried to persuade her to plead guilty but she refused. Her hearing is once again cancelled, "Because the police witness was injured falling off his bike," says Jamie giggling.

From now on Jamie will only be allowed to visit Leroy fortnightly, so maybe now she can get on with her life.
As we say goodbye Jamie sounds very dejected, leaving me feeling unsure of what lies ahead.

25th July – Saturday

Jamie arrives to stay with a bandage on her arm. "I burnt it with hot wax at the hairdressers," she says. I later learn that the bandage was really hiding the awful mess on her arm from injecting the drug speed.

28th July – Tuesday

Last week Jamie asked, "Mum, can you bring Max up to Doncaster?" I am curious to see where she is living so decide to drive up there today. Her home is a Victorian terraced, very similar to mine.

We call at Alan's flat in Sheffield (Leroy's friend) to collect Jamie's sewing machine, but Alan isn't there. I am determined Jamie should not lose her 18th birthday present, having lost almost everything else she owns. Maybe, one day, she will use her sewing talents once more.

Jamie points out modern flats nearby. "That's where Leroy and I used to live." I am quite impressed and she tells me they were refurbished for the Student Olympics.

31st July – Friday

Liz my neighbour gives me some welcome news. "I've got a message from Jamie's mother. She's been trying to find out where you moved to and wants to make contact."

Jamie is very pleased to see Max when she comes home and I tell her Tina has been trying to contact us.

Jamie says she sent Tina a Mothers Day card. "I haven't heard anything and hoped I would," she says sounding choked.

September

Max has been in my care for fifteen months and it is unlikely he will return to Jamie. There is her outstanding charge of robbery and it is anticipated she will get a prison sentence.

At the beginning of September Jamie stays with us for the weekend. She insists she must return to Doncaster on Sunday to register on a hairdressing course on Monday. Over the last six months I have had doubts whether Jamie has been hairdressing, although it seems genuine this time. I often wonder if she is working.

Jamie fails to make contact many times, as promised. Things must be bad for her at the moment. I am getting anxious and hope she will ring soon.

Tina phones and we arrange that Max and I should meet her and Kate's family at McDonald's, Marble Arch.

At first, when we arrive, I don't recognise Tina. Last time we met her hair was blonde and short. Now it is black and up in a French plait. I understand more than ever why Jamie, throughout her life, has changed hair colour and styles.

We amble through Hyde Park while the children have fun chasing the pigeons. Tina seems upset and enquires, "Is Jamie okay? I received a mother's day card from her," she tells me.

Tina says that the family have had results of the tests regarding the hereditary heart disease. To my relief, she is not a carrier and Jamie, Kate, and their children, are safe.

As I travel back on the coach, I reflect: I am pleased that I have kept in touch with the family. Perhaps one day, when Jamie has matured, she will see her mother again – after all they are so much alike.

And there is her sister Kate, a hard-working girl, with a beautiful home and family. She is very different from Jamie in so many ways, although there are similarities. Kate is always keen to know how Jamie is. It is is sad they can't get to know each other more but perhaps one day they will. In the meantime, I continue to maintain contact with her.

October

Jamie has moved and now rents a room in a private modern house on a new estate in Doncaster. It is warm, comfortable, and her landlady sounds very pleasant on the phone.

She comes to stay for the weekend of my birthday but is not at all well and sleeps most of the time.

"I've finished with Leroy, so he'll be after me when he gets out of prison," she says, sounding scared.

Crackhead

Justice – 1992

1st November – Sunday

"I don't agree with hard drugs – cocaine and heroin," Jamie tells me, trying to make believe she is not using

She is looking very pale and tired all the time and doesn't get up until mid-day. Chances are she is not telling me the truth.

5th November – Thursday

At long last, when I phone the court, they inform me Jamie's trial for robbery has commenced. I wait with baited breath to hear from her.

Jamie is very upset when she phones because she honestly didn't think the trial would go ahead. She turned up at the court unprepared, leaving all her clothes at her friend Jackie's house where she was staying.

She tells me, "I'm being kept in custody over the weekend for final sentencing on Monday.

Mum, Can you get up? I'd like to see you before I go to jail."

9th November – Monday

My friend Jane travels up to Sheffield with me to attend Jamie's sentencing. It is great to have some support.

Jamie stands in the dock facing the jury while the judge sums up. He recounts events leading up to her arrest last January, and her miscarriage while in custody.

"The police woman ignored my pleas," shouted out Jamie in court. "I was miscarrying with blood pouring down my legs." Continually Jamie interrupts, projecting her voice loudly and confidently to the jury. The irate judge tells her to, "Shut up."

Lunch-time, the jury retire. Jamie asks if we can get her some clothes from the market because she has worn the same clothes for five days. We manage to find her a pair of leggings and jumper.

Returning to court, we see an elderly gentleman and his wife sitting in the waiting area, looking very anxious.

A small black guy, with gold chains bedecking his neck, prances around restlessly, grinning at us. Jane glances at me dubiously. He appears to know who I am, so I assume he must be one of Jamie's friends.

Jane leans over and whispers, "I bet he's on cocaine. I saw a programme on TV and he has the signs, very agitated and can't sit still." We look at each other and find it hard not to laugh – he looks so funny.

In the courtroom Leroy, Alan, and Jamie stand in the dock awaiting sentence. Sitting on the bench next to us, grinning in our direction, is the little black guy.

The jury return a verdict of guilty on Jamie. The judge sends her to Newhall prison for four weeks and calls for reports for final sentencing. He is concerned Jamie is under twenty-one and has been influenced to a great extent by Leroy, who receives fifteen months and his partner seven.

As we leave the courtroom, we notice the elderly couple, who I assume are Alan's parents, appear upset. The woman wipes the tears from her eyes, and I approach them to say how sorry I am. I ask if they can let me know if the sewing machine is at Alan's flat and, if so, I will collect it.

We proceed downstairs to see Jamie before she is taken to prison. It is daunting, as we follow the guard with his dangling bunch of keys, and he unlocks the heavy door leading to the cells.

Jamie appears in her new pink jumper and leggings, looking refreshed. She is shocked at the prospect of being sent down but seeing us makes her smile. Jamie has left a bag of clothes at her friend Jackie's house, including a long dark green trench raincoat and trainers. She is keen we try to get them for her.

"Did you see Sam, mum?" she asks "I wouldn't have got up this morning if it hadn't been for him. He came to protect me, should Leroy be released."

"Was he the little guy with, with dreadlocks, wearing lots of gold jewellery, sitting by us?" I ask.

"Yes, that's right. He's called Sam Yardie because he's one of the main Yardies around here.

"Yardie? What's a Yardie?" I enquire.

66

"Oh, they are the guys who bring in cocaine from Jamaica. They are very dangerous and have guns.

Mum, can you get some of my clothes to Newhall Prison?" Jamie asks. "I'm desperate. I've got nothing."
"I'll do what I can," I tell her.
It is hard seeing Jamie sitting there behind a glass screen. We are unable to say our usual farewell with a hug. As we part we both have tears in our eyes.

At the court entrance we bump into Sam Yardie. He says he will return with Jamie's clothes in forty minutes, so we decide to wait.
Jane and I chat excitedly and can hardly believe we have spoken to a Yardie with a gun – not the sort of thing middle-class mums from Stratford do.
An hour passes and there is no sign of Sam returning, so we decide to get on our way.

We have to collect Jamie's things from her digs in Doncaster, and face the long journey home. It is 4.30 p.m. and already dark.
Jamie's landlady Lily, a middle-aged woman, invites us in and offers welcome refreshments.
"Have you seen Jamie?" asks Lily.
"I'm relieved to see you. We are concerned because we haven't seen Jamie for days and wonder if something serious has happened? We looked in her room for your telephone number but there was nothing."

It dawns on me Lily isn't aware Jamie has been in court.
"Unfortunately, she's in custody," I explain.
I look straight at Lily. "Jamie tells me she's at Hairdressing College but I don't believe her," I say, dreading her reply.
"Well," says Lily, "Jamie is certainly not at college."
"Oh no, not again" I say, glancing at Jane.
She knows exactly what I am thinking...Jamie must be back on the game.
Lily continues, "I don't know if I should say what we think Jamie is up to..."
Quickly, I put Lily at ease. "Chances are, Jamie is working as a prostitute."
Lily looks relieved. "You have confirmed my worst fears," she says.
I tell her Jamie's story and the reason for her going to prison. I am surprised she receives the news so calmly.

"Jamie has such strange eating habits," says Lily. "Mainly cereal with loads of sugar. She often gets a taxi to pop to McDonald's just around the corner to get some chips. In fact, Jamie uses taxis to go everywhere, everyday." This is quite normal when Jamie works.

It is getting late so we must pack up Jamie's things quickly and get on our way.
Jamie's bedroom is disgusting! I can't believe my eyes – cigarette stubbs and ash everywhere, and there is a used condom down the side of the bed; clothes are strewn all over the place: black thigh length high-heeled boots, a red Basque, see-through blouses and mini skirts, all confirming she is still a working girl.
As Jane and I open the drawers we discover dozens of unused condoms – all shapes, sizes, flavours, and styles: pina colada, fudge brownie, strawberry, raisin and vanilla, coca cola, ribbed, allergy – and many more. We glance at each other and giggle as we shove them into a carrier bag.
There are wads of letters, diaries, and court papers for soliciting charges. We quickly put everything in black bin liners, laughing nervously. If we didn't laugh we would cry. Jane is brilliant and tries to keep my spirits up after such a gruelling day in court.
Leaving the room reasonably tidy, and trying to hide what we have found from Lily, we hurriedly depart. Driving away, I think 'deja-vu'. This is third time I have cleared Jamie's possessions out of her accommodation.

About 9.00 p.m. I arrive home, weary and exhausted from such an emotional day.
As I unpack the black sacks, letters and diaries fall upon the carpet. One by one, I warily open and read them...a horror story unfolds.

The letters tell of her desperation, addiction, and craving for rocks (crack) and her working on the streets. One letter, from a drug agency, indicates Jamie has been on crack for at least twelve months.
As I read, I feel more and more sick inside. Now I understand why, for so long, there have been the lies, aggression, unreliability and shortage of money.
Then I stumble upon the word 'pregnant' in one of her letters to Leroy which she had not posted to him.
Surely not. She can't possibly be!
But Jamie has been very pale and sick lately. There is no mention how far gone she is. Suddenly I realise, and panic – this is going to be a crack baby.

I discover a piece Jamie has written:

SUMMER 1992

Next rock, next lick – midnight time, this is what I think.
Yes I have 'nuff money. In reality I don't.
When I awaken from my short buzz I'll want to kill myself
I'm a crack addict. I'm also pregnant.
The urgency to take that lick, to hear it crackle, burning into my
lungs.
I hold the smoke in...and then release.

I must know the truth. Immediately I write to Jamie asking, "Are you pregnant?"

28th November – Saturday

A long chatty letter arrives from Jamie and at the bottom, almost as an after-thought, she confirms, "Yes, I'm $5^1/2$ months pregnant."
I have contacted the prison to ask what I should tell Max, age two and a half, where his mummy is and why she cannot come home. They suggest I tell him she is in hospital.

Newhall prison is set in the green moorland countryside of Yorkshire. This, my first ever visit to prison, is very emotional. Tall iron gates are firmly locked behind us and we head for the modern prison block.

A lump comes to my throat. I am nervous and near to tears. Jamie is sitting at a table, looking happy under the circumstances, and very pleased to see us. The room is similar to a staff canteen where refreshments can be purchased.
The four families present are constantly watched by three warders sitting at a head table, heavy keys dangling from their belts.
Max is happy to see his mummy and after a cuddle plays in the toy corner.

I ask Jamie about her use of crack and the expected baby. For the first time ever, she talks openly about drugs and we have at long last broken down the barrier.
She tells me, "The baby's father is a Yardie and I can't stand him any longer."

"How long have you been on crack?" I ask.

Jamie screws up her nose. "Oh, about a year I suppose."

She goes on to tell me, "A piece of crack the size of a ten pence, costs about £50."

"Is this why you continue on the game, to pay for it?" I ask.

"Yes," she nods.

"Do you think I was good in court mum?" she asks perkily. "Even the screw thought I wasn't guilty – but I was." She giggles, "At least those drama lessons I had when I was eleven, paid off. I wonder what my teacher would think today if she knew!

I'm not bothering to contact Leroy any longer," she tells me.

"Jamie he'll be mad – you have sold all his jewellery and possessions, and are having another man's baby."

She casually shrugs her shoulders, but looks scared as she does so.

"You'll never guess what mum," she says with a broad smile on her face. "My friend, Jackie, was brought into jail the other day wearing my green trench raincoat and trainers. I was staying with Jackie when I went to court," she reminds me.

As we say an emotional farewell, I pray I shall never have to go through this experience ever again.

I have arranged to meet Alan's father at his son's flat in Sheffield, to collect the sewing machine. He is such a nice quiet gentleman.

As we sit chatting in the lobby of the flats he tells me, "I took an immediate dislike to Leroy, and distrusts Jamie because she lies all the time. I can't believe she is twenty because she only looks fourteen. Jamie is evil and together with Leroy has been the downfall of my son. I think she deserves a long, hard sentence."

Time to depart, with the sewing machine safely in my car. I am glad to return to normality back home.

23rd December – Wednesday

Jamie appears at Hull Crown Court for final sentencing, and I await anxiously to hear from her.

Out of the blue, she rings me from the rail station on a high – but not from drugs.

"Mum, I've been released. I'm on my way to a probation hostel in Birmingham. I'm over the moon. I am free for Christmas."

Max's behaviour is becoming very difficult and he is too young to understand what is happening. Telling him his mummy was in hospital has backfired. Jamie sat at the table, during our prison visit, for two hours without getting up; he thinks she is very ill and can't walk.
Max is very distressed, waking up at night crying, "I can see my mummy on the wall."
I vow I shall always tell him the truth in future.

24th December – Thursday

Max and I travel by train to the probation hostel in Birmingham. Immediately we enter the building everyone is friendly, especially the inmates. Their young children run around excitedly at the thought of Father Christmas's visit tonight.

The large comfortable spacious sitting room, with a large decorated Christmas tree, is just like home from home. In the kitchen is a small self-catering area to prepare inmates for their return to the community. Other facilities, apart from accommodation, include offices and a nursery.

Jamie is keen to go shopping so we head for Northfield, Birmingham. She is so excited. "I can't believe I'm free and all the space around me," she says repeatedly as we browse around. It is amazing, in just six weeks, how the 'closed in' effect of prison has affected her so much.

Back at the hostel I enquire, "Can Jamie spend Christmas Day with us at home?"
"Okay," the woman replies, "providing she is back by 11.00 p.m.."
Fog is setting in and I tell them I am worried Jamie may not get back in time tomorrow.
"Why don't you and Max join us for Christmas dinner?" they suggest.
I am dubious. I have never spent Christmas away from home before and say, "I'll make a decision in the morning depending on the weather."

Jamie has made a couple of presents for Max in jail – a small white fluffy toy cat and a hand-painted wooden picture with his name on. "I enjoyed the artwork there," she says and shows me a pair of earrings she made.

"There was a good library and I learned word processing. It could come in useful for my own business one day," she jokes.

25th December – Friday. Christmas Day

Fog is as thick as pea soup this morning. If we are to see Jamie we will have to go to Birmingham for just a few hours and get back before dark.

As Max and I enter the hostel we are greeted with the smell of home-cooking. There is a warm, cosy, Christmas atmosphere as children happily play with their new push-along toys and bicycles in the corridor. Inmates sit relaxing and watching TV, surrounded by a warm glow from the lights and tinsel on the tree.

"Dinner's ready," someone calls.
Max and I join eight families together with a couple of staff around the table. Before us a wonderful feast of turkey with all the trimmings, rounded off with wine, Christmas pudding and mince pies.

As we sit laughing and joking I learn more about the inmates; one is in for stabbing and killing her husband; another charged with drug-trafficking; and the girl sitting opposite is a habitual shoplifter. Most of the young women are in their early twenties, dressed in denim jeans and have crude self inflicted tattoos on their arms and hands. Am I dreaming? This is so unreal – another world.

After lunch, the gloomy fog hangs heavy over the hostel and I decide we should head home without further delay. I am elated after such a wonderful day. Having always believed one must take every opportunity in life, I am pleased I did so today. My Christmas Day has been just as enjoyable as any of those in the past.

30th December – Wednesday

We meet Jamie in Birmingham and buy her a wool coat in the sales. "It will see me through until the baby is born," she says. "Jackie has still got my green trench-coat and trainers in jail."
Max is pale and unwell. On our train journey home he keeps crying, "I want my mummy." What must the passengers be thinking? I am so embarrassed as I try to quieten him down.

1993
January

The weather is very foggy. Jamie visits Stratford occasionally, and afterwards I return her to the hostel early evening.

My health visitor refers Max and I to the Family Advisory Services Team because of the strain Jamie is putting us under.

I am tired of the Court welfare officer who is adamant, "Max should live with Jamie," which doesn't help the situation. He has absolutely no idea how Jamie poisons Max's mind when she gets the chance and I don't trust her an inch. She gives little time to Max when she sees him and acts like a big sister.

Concerned, I contact social services in Birmingham about Jamie's expected baby but they aren't interested. Very angry, I warn them, "This baby will end up in care. Jamie is totally incapable of mothering," and slam down the phone.

On the 21st January Jamie arrives for Max's third birthday party, and is unwell with 'flu-like symptoms.

Max declares, "I've seen Mummy on my bedroom wall again." He is confused and worries about her.

Jamie constantly tells him, "You're going to live with mummy soon," and talks about the baby.

We travel regularly by train to Birmingham to see Jamie and occasionally she comes to us. She is putting on lots of weight and looking fit, although very pale. The hospital gives the expected birth date as mid-March.

13th February - Saturday

We meet at Birmingham and Jamie is upset, agitated and unwell. Max picks up vibes, clings to me and refuses to hold her hand.

Jamie asks, "Why is he like this?"

She asks him a dozen times, "Are you going back to grandma's home or to the hostel with mummy?"

Head bowed, he doesn't reply but clings to my hand more tightly.

21st February – Sunday

Today Max and I are invited to lunch with inmates at the hostel.

Jamie talks of Max staying with her but I firmly say, "No". Most of the kids there are very rough. When I return home, I write to Jamie expressing my concern that she is upsetting Max and jeopardising her regular access.

23rd February – Tuesday

Furious, Jamie phones and shouts, "There's no way you can stop me seeing Max."
I point out, "Jamie, you know that's not my intention but I may have to change access to supervised."
She is very aggressive and I suspect she's been using. Probably her friends have got her wound up saying, 'We have our children here, so why shouldn't you have Max?'

24th February – Wednesday

Quite unbelievable...after yesterday's aggravated phone call, Jamie is happy and we spend a relaxed day here at home.

"Mum, I've received a letter from Annabelle in Wolverhampton."
I'm sure they don't have each others' address. Something is amiss.
What is she up to this time I wonder?

25th February – Thursday

Jamie phones me at teatime saying, "I'm on my way to Wolverhampton."
An odd time of the day to be travelling, I think to myself. It is very cold and dark and she is so close to having the baby.

27th/28th February – Sat/Sunday

Jamie stays with us for the night.
"How did you get on at Wolverhampton?" I ask, not letting on that I suspect she didn't go there.
"Oh Annabelle is fine and her little girl is gorgeous," she tells me convincingly.

5th March – Friday

My intuition is proved right when Annabelle phones out-of-the-blue from Wolverhampton, enquiring, "How is Jamie? Is she still in prison?"
She clearly has no idea where Jamie is or that she now lives in Birmingham.

Shocked, I phone the probation hostel asking, "Do you know where Jamie is?"

"Yes," they reply, "Wolverhampton."

"I understand Jamie hasn't gone there. I suspect she's gone to Sheffield," I tell them. "She's on probation at the hostel and I consider it's your responsibility to know where she is. The baby is due any day now and tracks should be kept on her."

After a couple of days Jamie returns to Birmingham.

During March I take Jamie a number of times to Cannon Hill Park in Birmingham, to break the monotony of the hostel. She is getting very tired and says, "I've been to hospital for a blood test because of itching and they wanted me to stay in, but I refused. I haven't booked in at the hospital yet."

With only a few weeks left to the birth, and the fact that Jamie is possibly on I am concerned for her unborn child.

Crackhead

Love is Forever – 1993

5th April – Monday

"Jamie is in labour," says the hostel warden on the phone. "Are you going to the hospital?"

"No," I tell her. "I don't want to get too emotionally involved."

It is early afternoon and she agrees to phone if there is any further news.

Suddenly Max cries out, "Ow, my tummy hurts," and he rolls and wriths in pain on the kitchen floor.

Half an hour later I phone the hostel to find out what is happening.

"Jamie gave birth to a little boy half an hour ago," they tell me.

What a coincidence that Max was writhing in pain then. I feel a chill down my spine at the thought.

Four hours after the birth I arrive at the hospital, surprised to see Jamie smiling and sitting up cuddling her baby. "I didn't have any painkillers," she announces proudly.

"Mum, I've decided to call him Ben," she tells me, looking down lovingly at her son.

Across her nightie are the words, 'Love is forever', and I wonder what future lies ahead for little Ben.

6th April – Tuesday

Jamie is discharged from hospital and I take Max over to see his new brother at the hostel. She looks very tired and in some discomfort.

15th April – Thursday

I arrange for Kate to meet Jamie in Stratford, so she can see the new baby. Jamie arrives from Birmingham by train, very excited and happy. We walk down by the river feeding the ducks in the warm spring sunshine, and the sisters catch up on all their news.

Max is unhappy to leave Jamie and Ben when I take them back to the hostel. Tears roll down his cheeks. It hurts me to see him so sad. Trying to calm him down, Jamie suggests, "You can stay when Mummy gets her new house."

16th April – Friday

Concern over Max's unhappiness prompts me to phone my health visitor for help. Her advice is, "Show Max he is loved, give him lots of cuddles, and let him cry." Great words of wisdom I shall never forget.

27th April – Tuesday

Max has nightmares. He wakes a number of times crying for his mummy, saying, "I can see ladies on the wall. I saw a lady, she was big and real, by the bed."
I tremble at his words...Jamie had exactly the same vision during a nightmare at three years old when we lived at the cottage.

3rd May – Monday

I pop over with Jamie for an interview with the court welfare officer and social worker regarding Max.
Jamie agrees to my having temporary custody but makes it clear, "I'm going to get Max back and I want a social worker."

Jamie has taken her bag of condoms out of my attic. Her baby is only four weeks old and it would appear she is back on the game.

11th May – Tuesday

In the court waiting room: Jamie looks very tired and tells me, "I baby sat until 5.30 this morning at the hostel. I'm exhausted."
She giggles, telling me the girls climb in and out of the windows during the night.

The final hearing only takes a couple of minutes. Jamie agrees to the 'Place of Residence Order', giving me permanent custody of Max. We are to work with the Family Advisory Services Team.

When I return Jamie to the hostel, she tells me "I've got £300 of fines to pay by next Tuesday. But I may choose to hand myself in, go to prison, and put the baby in care."
She tells me a friend at the hostel has been seriously injured while

working – a punter reversed his car over her. I find it hard to believe that these girls are allowed to go out working as prostitutes while in the care of the probation hostel.

Jamie tells me a couple of the girls started working while they were there.

12th May – Wednesday

When I speak to Jamie this evening she sounds very distressed about a bruise mark on Ben's back.

I reassure her, "Don't worry, I noticed it the other day. At my child minding course, we were told about 'Mongolian Blue Spot'. It is a very common marking on black or mixed raced children, on any part of the body.

"Thank goodness," she says relieved. "The hostel staff are querying what it is, as if they don't trust me."

I ring the hostel to confirm that Ben has a Mongolian Blue Spot and they seem happy with my explanation.

14th May – Friday

"I'm off to visit Long Lartin (maximum security prison) tomorrow with my shoplifter friend, Marti," says Jamie. "We're leaving the children in the hostel crèche."

Taxpayers' money down the drain again, I think to myself as I put down the phone.

17th May – Monday

Jamie arrives lunchtime. She is mad with the hostel staff because they have complained that she leaves baby's bottles out of the fridge.

I am not surprised, knowing Jamie of old.

Sleeping for two hours during her short visit, Jamie sees little of Max.

26th May – Wednesday

I invite Jamie to come over to see her aunt from America.

As we sit having our meal, Jamie says, "I was in Coventry yesterday. You know the young lad on the news who was murdered last night? I always got my gear from him. I saw him just before he was shot on the front line."

Her aunt stares in disbelief as she listens to Jamie chatting casually about such an horrendous event.

Ben is only eight weeks old, and I catch Jamie making up a bottle for him without sterilising it, using water from the tap to make up the feed. To my horror she proceeds to give him some pie saying, "He loves it, mum."

30th May – Sunday

Jamie arrives at Stratford midday and returns to Birmingham at 5.30 p.m. She sleeps for over two hours this afternoon and hardly sees anything of her son.

"I've been to Long Lartin again," she tells me, "and another prison as well."

As I listen to her, I am appalled that the nursery staff look after her baby while she visits hardened criminals.

Life has returned to normal for Jamie: sleeping all the time, she is aggressive, short of money, tells lies, and is unreliable. ***This confirms she is definitely back on drugs!***

Jamie admits to working and assures me she is using condoms. "Mum, for goodness sake stop worrying," she says. "I'm also on the pill."

But I do worry because Jamie will probably forget to take it.

Cheques – 1993

1st June – Tuesday

Max is quiet today and says unexpectedly, "I don't want to live with you anymore. I'm going to live with mummy. Mummy said so," and he bows his head sadly.

I am very upset and angry that Jamie is playing with his emotions. I try to contact her but the hostel warden tells me, "She's gone out and should be back later."

By mid-evening Jamie has not returned and I voice my concern to them that she is using again, and neglecting her baby.

7th June – Monday

Jamie returns to Birmingham after a few days in Sheffield and phones me. "I went to a nightclub last night. Ben's father was there and got a friend to hold me down while he beat me in the face with a bottle. My jaw still aches and I can't eat."

I try to persuade her to get x-rayed at the hospital but she ignores me.

Over and over again, Jamie returns to her dangerous pimps.

10th June – Thursday

We are off to Weston-Super-Mare for a holiday on Monday – Jamie, Ben, Max and myself. I suggest to Jamie, "Perhaps you could roast a chicken to take with us?"

"You must be joking," she says. "You know I can't cook."

12th June – Saturday

I take Jamie shopping and notice how much pain she is in all over her body. She is taking loads of pain killers.

We stop for lunch and she turns pale. "My ribs and breastbone hurt from when I was kicked last weekend in Sheffield," she says.

Turning grey with pain, she complains an ulcer in her mouth is painful and her knee is playing up.

14th/18th June – Mon/Friday

Jamie is in a happy mood as we pack the car and head for Weston-Super-Mare. Apart from her saying stupid things to Max, we have a relaxing holiday. There are times when Ben irritates her with his constant crying, and he appears to be an unhappy child.

Returning from Weston we drop Jamie off at the hostel. Max keeps asking, "Why can't my mummy live with us?"
I explain she has to live in a special place because she has done something wrong. With this explanation he now seems much happier.

20th June – Sunday

I phone the hostel at 8.30 p.m. and they inform me Jamie has been out all day. Eventually, at 10.00 p.m. she returns my call. Why does she always get back so late? Has she been working in Birmingham's notorious red light district of Balsall Heath?

Jamie rings to tell me her child benefit book has been stolen at the hostel. She is always losing her book and I assume she sells it on the black market. She says her Giro cheque hasn't arrived either. It is just one thing after another.

8th July – Thursday

During her visit, Jamie aggressively announces, "Max is staying with me at the hostel on Sunday night. I'm taking him to the West Midland Safari Park with the other children."
The atmosphere can be cut with a knife, which I assume is the result of her using crack. I am finding it so hard to cope.

18th July – Sunday

Birmingham City Council offer Jamie a flat in Rubery and she is due to leave the hostel on the 1st August. We pop over to view.
The flat is in a dreadful state, with huge holes and plaster hanging off the walls. There is no way Jamie can move in there with a three-month-old baby. It is appalling and Jamie is reduced to tears. I try to keep her spirits up, telling her I can sort it out. Having lived in an old cottage I am used to tackling anything.

Max and I are starving, and I hope we can get something to eat back at the hostel. Jamie is now self-catering, but all that she has in her food cupboard is a tin of baked beans, so reminiscent of when she lived in Leamington with Max – no bread, margarine, absolutely nothing.

Jamie talks excitedly about her new job. "I'm working doing gift vouchers (purchasing gift vouchers with stolen cheques) all over the country now," she says. "I've got £400 in the bank."

27th July – Tuesday

Phoning from Sheffield, Jamie says, "I'm on my way to see Ben's father. When he saw the baby yesterday he loved him. He bought Ben a super jacket and me some gold earrings."
I find it unbelievable she has seen this guy again after the beating he gave her recently.

28th July – Wednesday

"It's going to take up to fifty days for us to plaster the flat," the council tell Jamie, even though she insists the conditions are appalling for a new baby. It should be available by the end of August, so the hostel agrees Jamie can stay for a further two weeks.
A number of times Jamie sounds fed up and complains, "Ben is unhappy, waking and crying at night. Mum, he scares me. He's got a haunting stare – as if he knows exactly what I'm thinking."
How extraordinary – exactly the same as Jamie's stare when she was a baby.

1st August – Sunday

Jamie officially signs off at the hostel today and remains on probation for a further six months. They offer to let her stay there for another two weeks until her flat is sorted out.
Ben kept Jamie awake last night and he doesn't look well. She arrives in Stratford extremely tired and, as usual, sleeps most of the afternoon.

3rd August – Tuesday

I take an old white chest of drawers over to the flat and meet Jamie. The flat is an awful mess. I offer to plaster and decorate the hall and bedroom for her. Jamie is due to get a £600 social security grant, which will set her up with furniture and carpets.

7th August – Saturday

Jamie didn't phone last night as arranged and I am getting worried. When I ring the hostel they inform me she has been arrested in Preston, Lancashire, for credit card and cheque fraud. They suggest I contact the police for further information. "
Where's Ben?" I ask, very worried.
"No one knows," the warden tells me. "We believe Jamie's friend here, Marti, knows his whereabouts but won't say."
I am adamant. "There's no way I can look after Ben if she goes to prison."
The Preston police inform me, "Jamie appeared in court this morning and is in custody until Monday."

9th August – Monday

I contact the hostel early morning to be told Jamie has been unexpectedly released.
"What about Ben?" I enquire anxiously.
"Oh, he's here with Jamie," they reply. "She went to Preston court early this morning. Much to everyone's surprise, Jamie has been released with a two year conditional discharge."

I am mad with the hostel for allowing Jamie the opportunity to start such serious crime while under their supervision, and I inform them I intend to complain to my MP and the Home Office.
Anxiously, I wait to hear from Jamie.

10th August – Tuesday

Jamie phones early evening hysterical and mad with me. "Why didn't you contact Marti about Ben?" she shouts angrily. "They wanted to put him in care. I spent £200 to £300 in taxi fares to Coventry and paid for two baby sitters."
"I warned the hostel I couldn't have him," I tell Jamie. "They told me that if you were kept in custody you would have had to disclose where he is."

I am desperate after this call but there is no one I can turn to for help.

12th August – Thursday

Jamie talks of her arrest in Preston for possession of a cheque book, and stolen goods purchased with vouchers. "The day I was caught, the guy who drove me had intended we go on to Wigan and another town to do more cheques."

Jamie's friend, Claire, calls over to my house. This evening she phones. "Jamie told me a guy called Spencer had looked after Ben when she was arrested. I noticed she was very agitated with Ben while we were out and warned her that Ben could end up in care.
But Jamie replied, 'No way.'"

Claire continues, "I asked Jamie if she was pleased she had found her natural mother?"
'Mum found her, not me,' says Jamie. 'But, yes, I'm pleased I know who I am'."
My mind is put at rest. It appears I did the right thing finding Tina.

Max is very unhappy seeing Jamie off at the station and starts to stammer badly. I persuade him to wave goodbye to her. He says in the car on the way home, "My mummy made me upset".

I am under so much strain and must speak to someone. I visit my local drug agency and pour out my heart. Afterwards I feel so much better and more able to cope.

13th August – Friday
We call at Selly Oak Police Station, in Birmingham, to collect Jamie's keys. The police used the keys to search her flat when she was arrested in Preston.

I dread our meeting at my local probation office today, which is called for as part of the court order. Jamie is cheerful and can't understand why I am so down and want to cry.
"Are we seeing *that* woman again?" Jamie enquires, meaning the probation social worker.
When I reply, "Yes,"
she says, "Then I'll walk out. I'm not seeing that old bag."

During the meeting Jamie is very tense. I mention our problems of access and that Jamie wants Max to stay with her. In view of past events, I am not happy about the situation.
Jamie states categorically, "Ben will *not* go into care."
She says I must have her permission to take Max on holiday abroad, but the social worker tells her I have care and control. After a lot of argument, Jamie storms out of the room in a blaze of fury.

As I leave the probation office I find Jamie sitting at the bottom of probation office stairs with Ben. "I haven't got any money," she says. She has no alternative but to return home with me.

When I take Jamie back to the hostel she looks more relaxed. I suggest we visit her next week but she says sharply, "No, it's okay. I'll be busy painting the flat."
I suspect she intends to go out working, doing cheque fraud.

16th August – Monday

Jamie phones in tears, "The police have been. My Giro grant cheque was stolen while someone was baby sitting for me during the night.
I have to be out of the hostel by Friday," she says. "Because I haven't got any money I've decided to stay at Spencer's flat in Coventry – the guy who looked after Ben when I was arrested."

I offer to help her sort out her flat tomorrow morning. but Jamie isn't keen to move to Rubery, saying the Giro will take three months to be reprocessed.
I'm exhausted. If it wasn't for Max, I think I would crack up all together.

19th August – Thursday

After consulting my health visitor, local drug agency, and hostel staff, I decide to support Jamie with my credit card until she gets another Giro. Jamie has received two cheques – one she claims has been stolen, and the other she says she has used to purchase a bed.
We pop into Northfield to buy some pretty bed linen and cheap carpets, a new Baby Belling hob and oven, and a white plastic garden table with two chairs.

20th August – Friday

After decorating, and fitting some carpet in the living room, Jamie's flat is beginning to look very homely.

In the evening, I take Jamie to Coventry, and she shows me the street corners where she works.
"My key worker at the hostel thinks I'll end up murdered," she says quite flippantly.
I agree, and remind her, "I predicted some time ago that you'll be dead by twenty-five."

Jamie, why didn't you contact me when you were arrested in Preston?"
I ask.
"Because I was frightened what you'd say."
We have always agreed, if arrested, Jamie would use her one phone call to contact me. It was unusual for her not to do so this time.

Chatting about the cheque fraud, she jokes, "Mum, do you want a driving job for £200 per day? They're short of get-away drivers. We do 20 shops and I get £10 a time," she says.
"I prefer this to going on the game because I'm protected, and my fines are paid by the people I work for.
As I drop her off Jamie says, "Thank you Mum for everything. I'll remember this and look after you in your old age."

24th August – Tuesday

Afternoon: Jamie helps me to emulsion the large living room of the flat.
"Do you think you will ever move in?" I ask.
Screwing up her nose she says, "I don't know. I'd be lonely without a TV and must get one."

27th August – Friday

I phone Spencer's flat but he says Jamie has left and he doesn't know where she is.

A social worker phones, "We have received a letter from Jamie's probation hostel stating you are concerned about the baby. The letter says Jamie is a good mother when she's not using."
The social worker has now confirmed to me that Jamie is on drugs, as I suspected.
The woman asks if I know where Jamie is, and requests that I report to her if Jamie contacts me.

28th August – Saturday

Jamie phones on a mobile asking, "Mum, can I come over tomorrow?"
"Jamie, have you forgotten, Max and I are off to Holland today?"
"Oh yes," she says...and the phone goes dead.

At the airport, Max and I enter passport control and customs. Suddenly it dawns on me,
"We are free...free from Jamie...and free from drugs."

On the plane, as I belt up and relax, I am determined to forget my never-ending nightmare – at least for the next week. Holland here we come.

1st September – Wednesday

In Holland, as the week progresses, I feel heavy and uneasy within myself. I am convinced something is very wrong with Jamie.

6th September – Monday

We arrive at Birmingham Airport, and I am sure there has been a crisis.

I am pleased when Jamie phones. "Mum, can I come over?" she asks sounding bright and cheerful. Can't be much wrong after all, I console myself.

As usual, Jamie arrives late.
I've been having driving lessons," she says. "The guy is very strict and I should be proficient by the end of the week. There's no need to take my test. I'm driving a Mini now but am having a BMW next week."
"What about tax and insurance?" I enquire.
"Oh, I won't bother with that," she replies.

"Jamie," I ask, "was something wrong when I was in Holland? I sensed it was."
"Nothing I can think of," she replies and, after pausing for a second, continues, "There was the bad argument on Wednesday."
"It was Wednesday when I felt ill," I tell her.

As we talk I notice her arm. "How on earth did you get those awful bruises?" I ask. "Don't know," she replies and goes quiet.
"Jamie, where were you staying before we went away?"
"I had to move out of Spencer's," she says but doesn't volunteer any further information.

"Mum, have you got the video of 'Pretty Woman'?" she asks.
It reminds me of those early days of the film's release during Jamie's teens, when she thought the film was wonderful. I often wonder if the story of a prostitute, together with her favourite pop idol Madonna, inspired and influenced Jamie.

I have been curious to learn more about the time Jamie was in London early last year. "Tell me, Jamie, about the designer clothes you wore when you worked Park Lane."

She recalls with a glint in her eye, "I had a black velvet dress with a red line running through the fabric, just above knee-length, and collared across the shoulders, 1950's style. Another dress was in green crushed velvet with shoestring straps. I had outfits for all occasions and they were beautiful."

9th September – Thursday

Jamie didn't phone on Tuesday as promised and I have heard nothing since.

I have just received a sad call from Jamie's friend, Candy, who lives up north. "Can you let Jamie know that my sister Jackie died on Tuesday? She was a crackhead working in London. I was worried because I'd heard nothing from her for some time.

Jackie was found heavily beaten, with crushed-up drugs in her stomach," she says. "We are waiting to hear more – they suspect murder. She looked so bad that they had to identify her by her fingerprints.

I want Jamie to come to the funeral if possible," says Candy.

Jamie is shocked and dumbfounded when I break the news of Jackie's death. "I'll go straight up to Candy's tomorrow," she says.

"Jackie was the girl who turned up at the prison wearing my clothes. I was in digs with her before I went to jail. (see 28th November 1992).

Tell me about Jackie," she says. Jamie is keen to know who and when – and then says, "she was with the yardies in London."

"Tell me about the yardies," I ask, keen to know more.

"They are in London, Sheffield, and Birmingham – in fact they are everywhere. I feel bad because I introduced Jackie to them. I was staying with Sam and another yardie, Lloyd, at Jackie's house – up to going to prison."

She pauses for a moment and then continues, sounding scared, "Knowing the people Jackie was involved with, I could have been beaten up as well. One of them always said, "Jamie, you'll end up dead."

Jamie sounds frightened and asks lots of questions. "You never think it's going to happen to someone you know.

I'm dreading the funeral," she says, "I will go up there tomorrow but will call and see you first."

11th September – Saturday

Jamie hasn't turned up here to see us.

I have just received a call from Candy, and she wants Jamie to see the state her sister is in before the funeral. "It might shock Jamie into changing her ways. I'm worried Jamie will end up the same way," she says.

We both agree, Jamie is living on a knife edge, just as Jackie did.

12th September – Sunday

"Sorry I couldn't get over yesterday but the car broke down. I'm hopefully going up to Sheffield this afternoon," says Jamie on the phone. "Mum, I'll *never* take drugs again, after Jackie dying."

How often have I heard this before? I think to myself.

16th September – Thursday

The health visitor at Rubery phones, "Do you know where Jamie is?"

"I haven't seen her for nearly two weeks," I tell her, "although she phoned last Sunday. I have given her address to a health visitor in Coventry who has reported her missing to social services and probation."

Jamie eventually contacts me. "Mum, don't worry. I'm okay. I'll explain tomorrow when I come over. I didn't get to the funeral in the end."

17th September – Friday

Jamie turns up here at lunchtime. She chats non-stop about Jackie's death; and how she, Jackie, Lloyd, and Sam Yardie used to pool money to buy rock cheap.

Late in the afternoon I take Jamie over to her Rubery flat. Plasterers have been in and the place is more habitable.

"I've got a friend, called Clinton, who is going to paint my flat and put up curtain rails," she says. "He's really nice."

"Who is Clinton?" I enquire.

"Oh, some guy I've got to know. Actually, he's Steve Dred's brother," she replies.

Jamie is concerned about the £300 Giro cheque, and the money she owes me. She says the D.S.S. say it will be about three months before she gets it. "Everyone says I seem so much happier now I'm away from the hostel," says Jamie. "They tried to break my personality and make me what they wanted me to be."

We call at a chip shop in Balsall Heath and she tells me, "Mum, this is the drug front line." The small side road is jammed with big flashy cars driven by West Indians adorned in gold jewellery, chatting from wound down windows.

Suddenly Jamie ducks below the dashboard "I don't like him," she says, appearing very frightened.

As we drive away she says, "Mum I couldn't go to Jackie's funeral in the end. Her parents blame me for what happened to their daughter. Jackie was big and strong and wouldn't let anyone touch her. I'm sure she was forced into some dangerous situation."

As we drive along the Coventry Road, Jamie unashamedly says, "I did cheques along here at the ASDA and Safeway supermarkets, and garages," pointing them out as we pass.

"There's lots left to do to make quick money," says Jamie. "I'm the best worker they have for vouchers and cards and do ten cheques in half an hour. But I don't like getting caught."

She tells me more about Clinton, "He's good looking, has dredlocks and makes his money selling grass."

"Who looks after Ben for you when you work?" I ask.

"Dionne, his sister," she replies.

24th September – Friday

Social Services ring, very concerned. "Do you know where Jamie and Ben are? She has given us false addresses, including those of two friends."
I tell them that Jamie is due to visit me today. They ask that I ring them back to confirm Ben is alright.

Jamie is in a good mood when she arrives. I tell her, "Social Services have been in touch because they are concerned you have given false addresses." She is livid because of social services' involvement but I ignore her.

I ring social services to assure them Ben is okay and Jamie says she will be seeing the health visitor. They say they will monitor the situation and phone me once a week.

"I'm getting on well with my driving," Jamie tells me. "I've been to Birmingham and around Coventry and am getting lots of practice."
"How are you going to make money now?" I ask.
"I'm starting an escort agency with Clinton," she says. "But I intend to run it, not work in it," she says positively.

Crackhead

I have always maintained Jamie will end up a madame one day.

She says, "I intend to prove myself by putting Max and Ben through private education."

You'll need a nanny," I joke.

Jamie laughs, "Will you do it?"

I smile to myself, having visions of me opening a grand mansion door to her clients.

Jamie phones Clinton to collect her in Stratford. "Mum, will you come and meet him?" she asks. "But don't go by appearances will you?"

What strange sight will greet me, I wonder anxiously?

Clinton is already waiting with a friend. He is in his late twenties – black, tall, slim, very fit looking, and with a lovely smile. His hair is in locks, tied on top of his head in a pineapple style. He is wearing a white designer patchwork, baggy denim suit. Jamie introduces us and as we chat she mentions, "I've told mum about the escort agency." He just smiles.

Since Jamie has been with Clinton her aggression appears to have ceased. Perhaps she isn't using crack any longer.

30th September – Thursday

Today I write in anger to Michael Howard, Home Secretary, about the running of the probation hostel.

I complain the inmates have total freedom, with the condition they return back at 11.00 p.m. at night. During the day they continue crimes and involve new inmates, while the crèche looks after the girls' babies. At night they work as prostitutes in Balsall Heath.

Because of the enormous cost of running the hostel, and the lack of facilities to occupy the inmates, I state the girls could continue this same lifestyle in their own homes – thus saving the taxpayer huge sums of money. They gain absolutely nothing while being there and are bored, which encourages heavy drug-taking.

I appeal to Michael Howard to consider improving the running of probation hostels when he carries out his prison review.

Jamie shouts above the noise in the background, "I'm at the hostel. Can you meet me in Birmingham. I move into my flat tomorrow?"

"Shall I meet you at the flat?" I ask.

"No," she snaps abruptly.

Strange, I think to myself. What is she up to now?

Missing – 1993

1st October – Friday

Jamie has gone missing!
Max and I go to Birmingham as arranged but
Jamie doesn't show up. I telephone the hostel.
"We are extremely concerned," they tell me. "We
don't know where Jamie is. She went to work in
Balsall Heath last night, leaving her bag with
Marti. Twenty four hours later she still hasn't returned. Her bag only
contains make-up and flat keys."

I'm in a panic!
"Where's Ben?" I ask.
"No-one knows," they tell me.
"Shall I phone social services in the morning?" I ask.
"It could be too late then," replies the hostel warden, worried for Ben's safety.

Immediately I contact social services; they give me an emergency
number should I need it.
I phone Marti at the hostel and she is desperately worried. I decide to
drive over to the hostel to find out exactly what is going on.
Before leaving I contact Balsall Heath police. "Jamie has not been
arrested," they tell me.

I call on Pat, an understanding friend I met at our local drug support
group, and tell her my distressing news. She insists, "I'll come with you
immediately,"
We collect Marti from the hostel and go to look for Jamie. She recalls,
"When we worked the streets last night, Jamie left her bag with me. She
didn't return and has been missing for 24 hours. I was furious because
Jamie ditched me without any money to get back to the hostel."
She hands me the bag. Inside are just a few condoms, nothing else.

Marti directs us to Balsall Heath saying, "I think my friend might have
seen Jamie or have Clinton's mobile number. Last night my friend was

beaten up by a punter. I'm worried Jamie might have been involved with the same guy."
She directs us to a house in the red light district. Marti knocks on the door and an old man answers. He tells Marti her friend is out working, even though she was so badly beaten last night.

As Pat and I wait in the car, we become aware of drug dealing going on around us. "We're being watched," says Pat. Feeling extremely vulnerable and in danger, we quickly push the car door locks down. We laugh nervously, "Perhaps the drug squad are keeping an eye on us!"

Marti returns to the car and directs us to Coventry. She talks of her shoplifting, which is her main line of work. "When I was a child," she tells us, "my mother gave me the weekly list to shoplift. If I returned empty handed I was beaten. I'm now using heroin and I badly want to go to rehab for the children's sake."

On the journey she talks about Jamie. "She bought the baby walker from me which I shoplifted. Jamie spent the two social Giro cheques on drugs, and she owes quite a bit of money to a girl at the hostel."
Jamie's version to me the other day had been very different – she told me she had bought the baby walker from an addict outside a chip shop.

Then, Marti drops a bombshell out of the blue...
"Are you aware Jamie is two months pregnant."
"Oh no," I gasp, "not so soon after Ben. I can't believe it."

Marti tells us that Jamie was invited to stay with a friend, in a cottage within the hostel grounds, on Monday night. But she left with Ben at four in the morning, in the pouring rain.
"The hostel staff are very concerned about Clinton," she says. "They offered Jamie a room but she declined. He is extremely violent and Jamie is very frightened of him. He takes all her money – she has made him hundreds of pounds. While she is out every night, Ben stays with Clinton's sister -- for which Jamie pays her £80 per week.
The girls and staff at the hostel are so concerned for Ben's safety that they have offered to look after him, but Jamie refuses.

On Wednesday night, Jamie stayed at the hostel without Ben," says Marti. "Staff wanted to call in the police to get him to a place of safety and put Jamie in a refuge. But Jamie refused to divulge Ben's where-abouts. When Jamie rang Clinton, the next day, he told her to come and get Ben or else the baby would end up in care.

Jamie went over to see Winston at Leicester, one of her first pimps, a couple of weeks ago and stayed for the pipe," (for smoking crack) she says. Marti recalls, "Jamie told us Winston was pleased to see her and they had a really good night together."

I can't understand, why does she return to these guys?

"Spencer chucked Jamie out because she was taking all sorts of weird friends back to the flat for a smoke," says Marti.

"Last month she had crack, and then again a fortnight ago at Winston's. Clinton won't let her smoke crack because it costs too much."

There is no sign of anyone in Clinton's flat in Coventry, which is in total darkness. Dogs bark and howl from flats around the large estate, echoing through the chill winter air. Frightened, we decide not to hang around.

Along the road, we pull up for Marti to ask any black person in sight, "Have you seen Jamie?" but we have no luck. Eventually I leave a message at Clinton's flat for Jamie to phone me.

2nd October – Saturday

2.00 a.m. I have just got to bed and Clinton phones, "Angela, I've got your message. Jamie's fine."

"Can I speak to her," I ask.

"Sorry, she's asleep," he replies. "She will see you tomorrow."

At lunchtime, I decide on the spur of the moment to pop over to Coventry. Jamie looks as white as a ghost when she answers the door. She leads the way into the living room.

Ben is lying tummy down on a duvet, screaming his heart out. Jamie pats him heavily on his back. He is pale and chesty. Lifting his head, he smiles sadly as our eyes meet.

I am choked and wipe away the tears. He desperately needs a cuddle and love.

"Can I pick him up?" I ask her.

"No," she snaps. "I'm trying to get him to sleep."

I am alarmed. He is now seven months old and there are only two small rattles in the room – not a toy to be seen. Eventually Jamie lets me give him a quick cuddle and he stops crying.

Shoving a bottle of milk into his mouth, Jamie puts Ben back on the floor and continues to bang his back, trying to get him to sleep. I have seen this before on a number of occasions at the hostel.

Obviously, after working on the streets all night, Jamie needs to catch up on her sleep during the day. Her baby is an inconvenience.

Marti mentioned to us last night, "Jamie shoves a bottle or dummy in Ben's mouth all the time."

"Jamie, why did you disappear?" I ask.

Her explanation is simple. "I was arrested under the false name of Annie Ford."

No wonder the police knew nothing of her arrest when I enquired at the station.

"Eventually, I was released at three in the morning," she says. "I had nowhere to go so contacted Clinton to collect me.

"By the way, I've seen the health visitor," she says, but I hesitate to believe her.

4th October – Monday

I speak to a member of the hostel staff who expresses her concern for Ben's safety, saying, "Clinton is a very violent man."

Immediately I contact the social worker telling her of everyone's concern, including that of the hostel staff. She says she'll pass information on to the team manager.

"Can you contact me if there is any news?" I ask anxiously.

6th October – Wednesday

This morning I receive a letter from one of Jamie's prostitute friends. She writes,

> "I wish I could give you good news about Jamie, but I'm afraid I can't. About three weeks ago we were talking when a black man ran up, grabbed her, and started dragging her across the grass.
>
> He took the money she had earned that night, slapped her across the face, then left. There is nothing you, me, or anybody else can do to help her. She just wants a man who can abuse her.
>
> I feel she is a very lonely and insecure person and that she plays the dangerous game of playing one black man against another."

I am furious with the social worker; she is very vague when I contact her. I remind her of our very recent conversation about Jamie's false addresses. She doesn't recall a thing and says she will speak to the team manager.

I am very unhappy and frustrated at the lack of interest and concern for the baby's welfare and safety.

Jamie's new health visitor tells me on the phone, "I'm thinking of asking Jamie to bring Ben to see me."

I point out, "Everyone is very concerned, including the hostel, and things must be checked out."

"I'll contact social services immediately," she says, assuring me she will phone back – but she doesn't.

I meet Jamie as arranged at Coventry. Every store we go into, Jamie says, "The security guards know me here because I go around with Marti when she's shoplifting."

As we amble through C & A's a guard observes our every move. "I once ran out of here with clothes and the alarm bells started ringing," says Jamie. "Fortunately, I managed to get away."

Making our way back to her flat she tells me the health visitor called this morning but Ben was at Dionne's house.

Jamie talks of a recent shooting, "My friend's son did it. I arrived there a few minutes after. The taxi driver warned me but I went through and saw the body." As we drive along, the black dealers supplying crack stand on the street corners.

"Mum, what sort of job can I do?" Jamie asks.

Knowing she will never change I say, "You could work for an escort agency. It would be much safer." Jamie laughs and agrees.

"Why do you go with violent men?" I ask.

She makes excuses. "They aren't really violent," she says, "Clinton just caught me the wrong way. I fell and banged my head."

She doesn't convince me.

"And what about the baby? Will you have an abortion?" I ask her.

"Yes," she says." I took antibiotics, so the pill didn't work."

"Are you sure you are only two months gone?" I enquire.

"The doctor told me," she says. "I took the 'morning after' pill because I felt sick but it had no effect."

Jamie talks about her Methadone prescription. "It's so easy to get one and I sell it for £10 for 20ml," she says.

10th October – Sunday

"Clinton has moved out of the flat," says Jamie. "I'm not working for him, anymore. I've got so much money now."

"When are you moving into the Rubery flat?" I enquire.

"I want it perfect, so I must now get on with earning the money to do it up," she says.

"Jamie, when it was raining the other day, I thought of you. How awful it must be working in bad weather."

She replies, "I don't get wet because I just don't bother to go out then."

14th October – Thursday

Jamie phones about 5.00 p.m. "I'm in Doncaster and it's bitterly cold. Ben is with me and I'm going to Candy's place."

"What if she's not there?" I ask, concerned.

"It'll be okay," she replies.

15th October – Friday

Jamie phones from Coventry. "I wasn't able to stay at Candy's and I only had £10 on me. A taxi driver gave me a free lift to look for someone to mind Ben while I worked.

I tried Ben's father but he had moved. Finally I found a friend to baby sit. Eventually Ben and I got a taxi home in the middle of the night and it cost me £50.

I'll be leaving Ben with Dionne tonight while I return to Sheffield," says Jamie. "I quite fancy moving back up there."

16th October – Saturday

Jamie missed my birthday today. She has never forgotten before, even when things have been really bad.

It leaves me feeling very unhappy – crack has taken over her mind.

20th October – Wednesday

Jamie was due to phone yesterday, to make arrangements to meet in Coventry, but she didn't make contact. I am worried Clinton might have beaten her.

But this evening she phones sounding bright and her usual self.

"I've been in hospital with a septic eye and poison went into the blood stream," she tells me. "I was taken into hospital unconscious and my eye is a bit of a mess."

I sleep very badly and wake up suddenly. Thoughts of Ben and Jamie buzz through my mind. I am very frightened.

24th October – Sunday

8.45 p.m: "This is Clinton," says the voice on the phone.
He sounds worried. "Jamie is on crack. There is nothing more I can do for her."
"Where's Ben?" I ask, worried.
"He's with my sister," replies Clinton, "and he's okay."
"But if Jamie is bad on crack she won't be able to look after the baby," I say.
"That's what my sister says."
"Can your sister phone me?" I ask him. "We must call in Social Services."
I phone social services, urgently enquiring, "Do you know Dionne? Is she a registered child minder? I'm registered and have to meet strict criteria," I tell them.
The social worker admits they don't appear to have any record of Dionne, and I am horrified because she appears totally disinterested.

25th October – Monday

I leave a message for social services to phone me – but once again they don't bother to reply.
The health visitor calls at the flat and Clinton tells her that Jamie is out shopping. She doesn't see Ben after all. It appears Clinton may have moved back in with Jamie.

26th October – Tuesday

In desperation I go over to the probation hostel in Birmingham. Staff voice concerns over Ben's safety, in view of Clinton's threats and Jamie's lack of home and mothering skills.
"Why don't you phone probation?" they suggest.

In the afternoon I phone Jamie's probation officer, who says she is pleased to hear from me and we have a long chat.
She says, "The housing department are chasing Jamie. An eviction order has been served because she owes £400 in rent on the Rubery flat.

Jamie appeared to have two female minders when she called here the other day," she tells me. "She didn't turn up at the last meeting arranged by us. If Jamie doesn't attend on the 28th, I'll request a warrant for her arrest. I have just spoken to social services. I'd phone them, if I were you."

Immediately I phone. At last, the social worker I speak to is very helpful, saying she has spoken to probation and understands the urgency of the situation. "I have no idea what happened at the weekend," she says, "because your information wasn't passed on."

I put her in the picture: that Jamie is on crack and Clinton is worried about the baby.
"I'm trying to get hold of the health visitor, to get her to call on Jamie," she says.
I tell her, "I can't possibly cope looking after the baby, if asked to do so."

The social worker actually calls me back this time saying, "The health visitor called at Jamie's yesterday. Clinton was there but he said Jamie was out shopping and Ben was with his sister."
I tell her firmly, "It isn't satisfactory that Clinton's sister is paid to mind the baby, when we have no idea who she is.

She says, "I asked Clinton to get Jamie to visit the clinic with Ben this morning, but she didn't bother to turn up."
Social services now appear to be taking me more seriously thank goodness – about time. They say they will phone back if there is any more news.

Rubery housing department confirm, "Jamie has been served an eviction order. Can you try to get her key and collect her things?"

27th October – Wednesday
No news on Jamie. I am very anxious.

I call this evening at the drug agency parent support group and feel much better afterwards. It is good to talk to other parents who have been through it and really understand.

I phone the social worker and she says, "I'll get probation to let me know if Jamie turns up at their office tomorrow. If she doesn't, I understand Jamie will be arrested."

28th October – Thursday

I wait anxiously all afternoon, but hear nothing from probation. Eventually I phone them. Jamie hasn't turned up and the probation officer says, "A warrant is to be issued for her arrest.
I think a 'child protection' order should be taken out on Ben because he appears to be in such a lot of danger."

The local radio announces that there has been a police raid on flats where machetes, guns and crack have been found. Was Jamie involved, I wonder?

29th October – Friday

I speak to the health visitor who reports, "I called and saw Jamie, Ben, and met Dionne yesterday. Everything is okay and the baby looks fine." I learn later she didn't undress Ben to note how scrawny he is.

The social worker rings and informs me, "There is no question of a 'child protection order' because Ben looks okay. We will check Dionne, interview her and Jamie, and see what can be sorted out.
Can you tell Jamie she has until mid-week to report to probation and let me know how you get on, please?" she asks.

She sounds so sorry for Jamie. As far as I am concerned it's pathetic. I can't believe the ignorance of this social worker as to what is really going on.
"I am very angry," I tell her. "Jamie has conned you all. She is very, very clever."
In three weeks there has been no word from Jamie. After fighting for the safety of her two children I am so drained and worn out. Throwing up my arms in despair, I decide to let everyone get on with it.

The hostel are concerned, probation are concerned

SO WHY WON'T ANYONE LISTEN TO ME?

The system is letting us all down.

I write to the Chief Probation Officer in Birmingham telling him there has been a gross failure in the system. Jamie is totally out of control. No one knows where she, who she is with, or the crime she is committing. The probation order will run out and nothing be achieved whatsoever.

Crackhead

Abandoned – 1993

5th November – Friday

Jamie is due to report to probation at midday. Otherwise, once again they say, "A warrant will be out for her arrest." They said that seven days ago.

Clinton phones saying, "Jamie has disappeared again. Have you got social service's number?" When he phones back later, I am very concerned and ask, "Is Ben with Dionne?"

"Jamie and Ben are with me," he says. "Jamie is leaving and hasn't anywhere to stay."
I am out of my mind with worry so decide to ring probation.
The probation officer says, "If we can get hold of Jamie, maybe another probation office could take over. I'll contact social services immediately."

I'm very angry. Things are desperate.
Jamie is spaced out and the baby is in danger. Everyone treats me like a 'fussing grandmother', as if I don't know what I am talking about.

7th November – Sunday

1.45 p.m. A very distressed Jamie rings, reversing the charges. I haven't seen her for five weeks.
She sobs...and sounds suicidal.
"I'll come straight over," I reassure her. I must also find the baby. Rushing down the by-pass to Coventry I am scared what I shall find? As I drive up to a shuttered fish and chip shop, I see three figures silhouetted against the building.

Jamie sits on a concrete post, head in hands -- a ghostly figure of her former self, grey and gaunt, with red eyes. There is an enormous yellow-black bruise on her face.
Her scraggy blonde hair is scraped back into a pony tail with a grubby head band; her thin scrawny body is clad in a black leather jacket, a dirty greyish white low-cut top, black leggings and scruffy trainers.

103

Crackhead

It is hard to believe this is my daughter. She looks a stranger, so down-and-out. I walk over and give her a big, warm hug.

"There's nothing more I can do with her," says Clinton, throwing his arms up in the air.
"Where's Ben?" I ask, worried out of my mind.
"At my sister's," he replies. "Jamie knows where that is."

Jamie turns around sobbing, black mascara streaked down her cheeks.
"I don't want Ben any more," she says.
I am sickened inside and want to cry, ''Help!''
Only a few days ago the health visitor assured me, "Everything is okay and the baby is fine."

"Have you got anything else, apart from three carrier bags?" I ask Jamie, but she doesn't reply.
"She's thrown most of it in the dustbin and left a few things at my brother, Steve's," says Clinton.
"When did you last have crack?" I ask Jamie, realising she must be on a comedown.
"About four hours ago," she replies.

A young mixed-race girl, aged about 15 and very pregnant, stands by Jamie. She looks totally lost.
Jamie asks, "Mum, can Collette come with us?"
"I'll drop her off in the city centre," I say reluctantly.

I must quickly find a phone box. I am desperate for help and phone Sue, the drug agency family worker, at home.
"There's no one available on Sundays," she says. "The agencies are only open weekdays, in office hours. Does Jamie need medical help?"
"I don't know," I reply, feeling so helpless, knowing nothing about drugs and their effects.

In the car I ask, "Jamie, what about the baby you're expecting?"
"I shan't have it," she says. "I'm only $2^1/2$ months. I'll get an abortion."
"You must be nearer $3^1/2$ months, because Marti told me a month ago," I tell her. "If you intend having an abortion, you'll have to get on with it."
Jamie is totally disorientated.

I stop at a garage to buy the girls cigarettes and chocolate. They shove the food down as if they haven't eaten for days. Jamie puffs away. It seems strange – this is the first time I've seen Jamie smoking.

Next stop: to phone emergency social services. I tell the social worker, "There's no way I can look after Jamie's baby."
He says he is African and finds it hard to understand me, and visa versa. I have to spell out every word, which is so frustrating. He suggests I contact social services in the morning.
I am frustrated and angry. My daughter is extremely ill, there is a baby I can't look after and I need urgent help – NOW.

After we drop Collette off at the rail station, Jamie explains, "Collette is only fifteen and pregnant, with nowhere to go."
I feel so guilty leaving her but I have got enough problems on my hands and can't take on any more.
I must concentrate on finding Ben. Dionne isn't at home and her husband is baby sitting. Ben is lying happily on the floor and looks up, giving me a big grin. He certainly seems very well cared for by Dionne.

Once we are back in Stratford, Pat kindly offers to have Jamie for the night. I need my space at home to keep my sanity although Ben stays with me overnight.
Jamie says, "I'm exhausted. I've only slept for a few hours the past fortnight. Clinton wouldn't let me sleep. He punished me for taking crack."

I call over to Pat's to see Jamie. She has totally transformed – batteries recharged after a good hot bath, and tucks into a welcome roast chicken dinner.
She looks so pretty, her old self once more, hair washed, make-up on, and clean clothes. The dimples in her cheeks return, giving that cheeky youthful look when she smiles.
"The doctor called," says Jamie. "He was absolutely useless. He didn't want to know about my drug problem, even though I told him I'm pregnant."

Pat and I are cross at his attitude, and agree most doctors haven't got a clue about drug addiction and how to handle the abuser. A ridiculous situation, especially since drug use is rapidly on the increase.

"Another of my friends was murdered up north two weeks ago," says Jamie. "Clinton and I were questioned by police. They've got the chap who did it. I know four people who have been murdered in the last few months," she says quite casually.
"How do you feel about that?" asks Pat.
"I'm getting used to it, I suppose," she replies.
Max and Jamie hug and kiss goodbye. Pat remarks, "You can see there is such a bond between them – look how close they are."

I am shattered. Ben is pale and has a constant piercing cry. Back at home he crawls and gets into everything and, after such an exhausting day, I find it so hard. When I try to bath him his body goes as stiff as a board.

Immediately I realise he will have to go into care. Already I find it difficult looking after one child and can't possibly cope with another. Ben has hardly any clothes: just one vest, a couple of odd socks and two tatty outfits. Slowly it dawns on me just how bad things are. Jamie's priority had always been beautiful clothes for her children.

I phone Sue, who suggests, "Call at the office with Jamie in the morning. If she wishes, perhaps we can get her into hospital for detox."

Next, I speak to emergency social services and they inform me, "There's no guarantee you'll be seen in the morning. We are so busy with child protection cases."
By now I'm fuming and tell them angrily, "But Ben is a child protection case."

My friend, Gill, phones and, after hearing of my problems, offers to come around this evening to help me with Ben.
At 9.00 p.m. I receive a phone call from Collette, distressed, saying, "I want to speak to Jamie."
I tell her Jamie isn't here. It is important I stall Collette while I convince her to seek help. I say, "Sit tight and I'll meet you at the phone box as soon as possible."
I manage to contact emergency social services who say they can find a foster home for her tonight.

Gill offers to baby sit while I rush to Coventry to meet Collette. She is waiting by the phone box, cold and frightened. I give her a big hug and then drive her over to the police station.

The woman officer at the reception desk is abrupt telling Collette, "You'll probably end up in a grotty place tonight." I feel really sorry for the poor kid.

Collette says, "I've not eaten all day apart from some chocolate." It is 11.45p.m. She is tired, hungry, and pregnant. The police only offer her a cup of tea so I pop to the garage to get rolls, chocolate and a drink. Would she have had anything to eat if I wasn't there, I wonder?

I leave Collette with the social worker, give her a big hug and wish her all the best. "Let me know how you get on." I ask. I am much happier knowing this vulnerable young girl is safe off the streets – at least for tonight.

Ben is sound asleep when I get home but my friend is exhausted. We agree our problems seem small in comparison with these kids on drugs and working. Gill says, "It's strange, Angela. I knew I had to contact you this evening – I sensed you needed help."

I sleep just two hours tonight. Ben tosses, turns, and cries. Eventually I give in and put him in bed with me.

8th November – Monday

Jamie asks me to take her to the drug agency, where she discusses detox and rehab Sue makes an appointment for her to see a doctor tomorrow to discuss having methadone. I notice Jamie is sniffing and wiping her hand across nose, a habit common in addicts. She is so very pale and ghost-like.

"I've been doing drug runs between Coventry and Birmingham four or five times a night, to re-supply dealers who run out," Jamie tells me". I buy on their behalf."

"Did you know anything about the recent police raid?" I ask Jamie.

"I know the couple involved, where crack and machine guns were found." she says. Then pointing to her legs, she laughs, "In fact I've got the girl's leggings on now."

After counselling Jamie, Sue tells me, "She's on a real come-down from crack and in a very confused state."

I phone social services to tell them, "We are coming in. Ben will have to go into care. There's no way I can look after him."

"I can't promise anything," says the social worker. After a lot of hassle, and my threatening to go to my M.P., she agrees to see us.

12.30 p.m: we are interviewed by a very young, and clearly inexperienced, social worker.

Jamie makes it plain to her, "I can't look after Ben. I want him to go into temporary care while I sort myself out. I want to go for detox at hospital and rehab with the baby in London," says Jamie.

But I know, from past experience, ninety per cent of what Jamie says doesn't happen.

"Maybe Ben could stay with Dionne?" suggests the social worker.

I am horrified. Social Services haven't got a clue who Dionne is and she isn't registered.

"Jamie, if you hand your Child Benefit book over and we paid extra money, would Dionne look after the baby?" enquires the social worker. There's little reaction from Jamie.

The social worker tries another suggestion. "Jamie, if we offer you and Ben a flat near here, would that help?"

"That's not what I want," snaps Jamie. "I need time to sort myself out."

I am fuming. This young inexperienced social worker hasn't got a clue. She clearly knows nothing about crack and it's side effects.

I interrupt. "Jamie says she can't cope looking after her baby. You are offering to put her back into exactly the same situation. She has had a flat in Birmingham since the middle of July which she never moved into and owes £400 rent."

Reluctantly, the social worker agrees to arrange foster care for Ben. While she is out of the room, Jamie falls asleep snoring from her comedown.

Why on earth aren't drugs and their effects on the family' included in the training of social workers? It is essential.

Jamie agrees with the social worker that Ben should be placed in care for six weeks. She will visit him three times a week, and is told transport can be provided if she requires it."

As we leave the office Jamie laughs, "Fancy suggesting a flat here," she says. "It's crazy.

They might as well give me crack to go with it."

We find a phone box to phone the probation officer. I tell her, "I've found Jamie and she's in a dreadful state."

The officer says, "I'm keen to get Jamie into her Rubery flat and want to support her." I am totally exasperated with everyone.

She speaks to Jamie, asking her to come into the office on Wednesday. Jamie laughs as she puts down the phone. "The fools. Don't they realise I don't want to live in Birmingham – it's even worse than Coventry."

We call at Dionne's house to collect Ben's pushchair and I meet her at long last. She is a pretty, slim built Jamaican woman in her thirties, with long thin braided plaits all over her head. Certainly I need not have worried about her child minding Ben. She has a lovely personality, a very comfortable clean home, and well looked after children. If only social services had checked up, I would have been a lot happier.

Dionne offers to take Jamie back to social services later. Jamie changes into a mini-skirt, and leaves all her clothes and make-up in my car.
"Can you ring me from the foster parents please Jamie?" I ask. "I can collect you later."
She agrees to ring, since the foster family are placed outside the area and transport is difficult.

During the evening, I wait anxiously to hear from Jamie. I feel very uneasy and sense things are wrong when Jamie hasn't made contact by 8.00 p.m.

Dionne phones, "Angela, I can't believe it. Jamie has been seen back in Coventry and she has called on Clinton, pleading with him to have her back. She's mad."
As time ticks by, I become very worried and phone Social Services. They tell me, "Jamie was taken back by a social worker."

10th November – Wednesday

The team leader, at social services, finds it hard to believe me when I say, "I know for certain Jamie will only make contact with the foster mother once or twice – if that."
I phone Linda, the foster mother, to see if Ben is okay. She says Jamie has not made contact.

Jamie doesn't keep her appointment with the doctor, at the drug agency. She isn't really interested in getting methadone. There is only one drug Jamie is interested in-- and that is crack.
I hear nothing, and exhausted, I drag myself to bed at 7.30 p.m.

Crackhead

11th November – Thursday

Dionne rings. "Jamie's moved in with friends and is doing cheques again."
"She's crazy," I tell her. "What if she gets caught?"
Jamie told me she'll be more careful this time," says Dionne. "She says she has been to probation, and has spoken to you."
"I haven't spoken to Jamie," I tell her.

12th November – Friday

The probation officer is very wary and abrupt with me when I phone.
"Did Jamie contact you on Wednesday?" I ask.
"No," she replies. "I'm waiting to see Jamie, to put her in the flat and give her help," she says.
A bit late for help now, I think to myself.
I am livid. "You must be joking. Jamie says she doesn't want the flat in Rubery."
The probation officer sharply tries to put me in my place saying, "As far as everyone is concerned, Ben is healthy and well."
Of course, like everyone else, she thinks she knows best.
"Do you realise Jamie is heavily involved in crime and desperate on crack?" I ask her.
"If you have a complaint speak to my senior," she says angrily.
"There has been mention of eviction from the flat," she says, and is annoyed with me for speaking to the housing department.
I tell her Jamie says she doesn't want to go to Birmingham, because it is worse than Coventry.
The officer is annoyed having read my letter to social services, and says, "You have no right to tell them I am concerned about Ben."
"I have every right to tell them that you and everyone else are concerned for Ben's safety," I tell her. It is amazing how her attitude has suddenly changed. All she is worried about now is Jamie.

After four days, Jamie still hasn't contacted the foster mum to find out how Ben is.

13th November – Saturday

Dionne phones this evening asking, "Is Jamie there?
She's been on the rocks. She turned up at Clinton's at six this morning, but he sent her away.
Jamie tried to jump from a window," says Dionne. "Fortunately my friend managed to save her."

110

Dionne agrees to see social services to tell them Ben is at risk. She says, "My friend saw Ben left on bed a number of times and roll off, banging his head. Jamie fed Ben on chocolate which went right through him; and never gave him solid food – just milk.
She left Ben with my husband when I wasn't there. He would tell Jamie, 'I'm not the baby sitter,' but she would reply, 'Oh well Dionne will be back soon,' dumped the baby and went off.

When I tell Dionne of probation's handling of things, she is in total disbelief.

14th November – Sunday

I call to see Ben today at the foster home. He is settling in very well. Upon his arrival he was pale, thin, crying, with his body stiffening all the time. Now he is relaxed, sleeping better, and not appearing so frightened. Jamie still makes no contact.

Dionne phones to tell me, "Clinton received a call from Jamie about ten p.m. She asked him to meet her and he says she appeared really strange." I arrange to meet Dionne tomorrow at social services when she hopes to tell them of her concerns about Ben.

15th November – Monday

I phone social services first thing, insisting I speak to the team leader. "I *must* see you today," I tell him. "You must get an order to prevent Jamie removing Ben from the foster home. Ben's child minder, Dionne, has evidence indicating it would be unsafe for Ben to return to Jamie at present."
The Team leader says, "No one can see you until tomorrow."
"But that will be too late," I tell him.

I have had enough and say angrily, "I will send you a copy of my letter complaining to the director of social services, and I shall also send a copy to my M.P."
"There will be a planning meeting later in the week," he tells me.
I demand, "But something must done today. It must not be left," and immediately I deliver my letter to the director of social services.

Afterwards, I call to see Dionne who is keen to tell me her latest news. "I can't believe it. Jamie is now with one of the most dangerous men around, called Vernon," says Dionne sounding horrified.

"Last night I saw her shouting across the street to Clinton saying, 'I love Vernon and I'm going with him now.'

She went to work for Vernon last night," continues Dionne. "He's one of the main crack dealers. Jamie will get into a lot of trouble with him. She must be totally out of her head."

Dionne goes immediately to social services' office to voice her concerns about Ben.

Sounding very despondent and furious, she phones me. "The social worker made me feel as though I'd wasted her time. She told me it appears Jamie doesn't have a drug problem and the baby is okay in my care. Their attitude is that nothing can be done until the baby is harmed!"

16th November – Tuesday

I write to the chief probation officer in Birmingham, putting in an official complaint and tell him, "Probation have no idea where Jamie is, what she is doing, and the crimes she is committing. She is completely out of control."

18th November – Thursday

The probation office phone to tell me Rubery housing department have had to break into Jamie's flat. Water was seeping through to downstairs. I tell probation, "Sorry, I can't tell Jamie because I don't know where she is. She is missing."

Social services inform me today that Jamie is demanding to see Ben. They have invited her to a planning meeting at the foster home today.

The foster mum tells me this evening, "Jamie arrived half an hour late and Clinton dropped her off. She only stayed 10 minutes, appeared very sleepy and has a bad cough. She wasn't interested in Ben and found him difficult to handle. She tried to give him some food but said he didn't want it. Eventually, she left in a hurry with the social worker.

I ended up giving Ben his food without any problem," says Linda. "He is putting on weight in his face and on his bottom, loves cuddles, sleeps better, is much more relaxed, and his body no longer goes stiff."

Jamie has been informed there will be case conference early December. Police, NSPCC, probation, and social services will be represented. I am sure she won't bother to attend.

19th November – Friday

Pat and I visit Ben at the foster home. How he has changed, now such a happy baby – into everything and laughing. He has put on weight and is starting to look plump.

On our way home, we call to see Pat's new age traveller friends, living in caravans on a disused railway line. It is a cold November afternoon, the autumn mist hangs over the site as the sun sets. Smoke from the chimneys of the vans drifts back down. Pat's traveller friend, Aileen, invites us into her snug neat van for a welcome cup of tea. A log fire burns fiercely in the corner in a converted calor gas canister. Enveloped by the warm glow of the fire, and with a piping hot mug of tea, I feel so much happier – Ben is safe at last.

24th November – Wednesday

Dreadful news on Midland's TV this morning: "An unidentified man has been found shot dead in Birmingham with bullet wounds to his head and chest. He is black, with dreadlocks in a pony tail. The shooting is believed to be drugs related."
Six o'clock news. The murdered man has been identified. He is called 'Vernon Wells'.
That name sounds familiar, I think to myself. Is this the same Vernon that Dionne said Jamie was with 10 days ago? Immediately I pick up the phone. "Dionne, have you heard? There's been a murder – a guy called Vernon." But she has heard nothing.

The housing department ring. "Jamie is being evicted today. Can you clear her things out?"

25th November – Thursday

Bill drives me to Rubery in a van to clear out Jamie's unoccupied flat. Opening the door, I can't believe my eyes. Everything of any value has gone! Has it been stolen or did Jamie take it?
As I look around it breaks my heart. All my hard work has been undone. Jamie's photos, Ben's birth tag and birth certificate, lie on top of a pile of rubbish in the middle of floor.

A further radio announcement: "The murdered man was believed to have been abducted from his flat. Police want to interview a fair haired woman seen nearby."

Is that Jamie, I wonder?

Dionne rings saying, "The guy murdered was definitely Jamie's friend Vernon.

I've just seen Jamie working and drove up to speak to her," says Dionne. "She's very upset. I told Jamie I'm worried and asked her to ring you."

The police are looking for her as a witness," says Dionne. "They've been to my house enquiring. Jamie told me she gave Vernon money for drugs and then he went down in the lift. She went back to his flat and waited, but he didn't return.

Jamie says it will be her next," says Dionne. "She has promised she will phone you tonight."

I wait anxiously but hear nothing.

27th November – Saturday

Jamie sounds very scared on the phone. "I'm alright Mum," she says. My heart beats fast as I decide what to do. "You must get protection Jamie. Shall I get the police to collect you?"

"Yes," she replies.

"Have you had any crack?" I ask.

"Yes, four hours ago."

The police assure me they will collect Jamie in ten minutes.

I ring back and talk to Jamie, to keep her at the phone box.

"I've lost a really good friend," she says. "The last time I saw him was at the lift."

Suddenly I realise I am talking to myself...the phone is dead. I phone back but there is no answer.

The police contact me. "Jamie wasn't there. Maybe she has been abducted, but chances are she hasn't. Perhaps she saw someone passing by who could give her a lift," they suggest.

Jamie later contacts the police who interview her for six hours.

A social worker enquires, "Do you know where Jamie is? The address she gave us was boarded up some time ago."

"I haven't a clue," I tell her.

Out of Control – 1993

2nd December – Thursday

7.30 a.m: Jamie sounds desperate.

"Jamie, why have you phoned?" I ask

"Don't know."

"Do you want medical help?"

"No."

"Where have you been all night?"

"Don't know."

"Have you had Crack?"

"Yes."

"Have you been on the streets all night?"

"Yes."

"Have you got anywhere to go?"

"No."

Jamie hangs up...the phone is dead.

I phone Sue telling her, "Jamie says she doesn't know what she's doing. When I ask questions, she just replies 'yes' or 'no'. What should I do?" She points out, "Jamie could be on a come-down now, and be totally different later."

There seems so much I have to learn about drugs.

I seek help from the 'Solace' help line, our local nigh time listening service, for those distressed or depressed. They suggest, "Talk to Jamie rather than ask questions, and make a list of things to talk about beforehand."

This evening as I get into bed, list at the ready, Jamie phones. "I'm fine and sorted out now," she says cheerfully.

It is unbelievable how she has changed. Sue was right after all.

Jamie informs me, "I've been doing cheques again, as I did at the hostel." We talk about Ben. "His first tooth appeared this week," I tell her.

"I'll be visiting him soon," says Jamie. But I know the longer she leaves it the less she is likely to do so.

4th December – Saturday

7.45 a.m: Jamie calls. She is very low, but perks up when I tell her that I will meet her later in the Coventry Precinct."
Jamie runs towards me, we hug, and then take ourselves off to a cafe for a hearty cooked breakfast. "I'm starving," she says, and appears not to have eaten for days.

Chatting non-stop and hardly finding time to eat, Jamie tells me about her latest friend. "He's the biggest drug dealer in the area," she says.
"I have recently acquired some very expensive clothes with stolen cheques," she tells me. "And I went to Toxteth in Liverpool the other day."

As she pauses for breath, I ask, "Jamie, where on earth did you get that awful black eye?"
"I was in a fight up north," she says. "A girl tried to take my money."
"Have you had any crack lately?" I enquire.
"Not since Thursday," she says. "I take it when Clinton does me head in."
I note the way she speaks. This is not my Jamie. She often speaks these days with a 'Rasta' lilt, obviously influenced by her associates.

Talking of her relationship with Clinton she says, "It's very bad. I've got the chance of three-bed house so I can be away from him."
"Jamie," I warn, "Clinton will shoot you if you go with these other guys."
"More likely I'll shoot him," she jokes.
"Someone gave me a gun the other day. Trouble is, I put it down somewhere and don't know where." "Was it loaded?" I ask.
"Of course," she replies.
"You are putting your life at risk," I warn her.
"I've already been threatened," she says. I sense fear and panic in her voice.

"Do you think I've lost weight?" Jamie asks, as she does every time I see her.
"I haven't got anywhere to stay tonight," she says as she fumbles through her bag.
Suddenly, she panics. "I hope I haven't lost them," she says. Then relief as she pulls out little scraps of paper with different guys' phone

numbers on. To save any further panics, I give her my diary to put the numbers in.

We part with a big hug and kiss, and I tell her, "Take care, Jamie, and keep in contact."

"Don't worry, I will," she replies.

I give her change for a phone call and she skips off, nourished and happy, to phone her dealer friend to see if she can stay with him. There is little more I can do.

She turns around and shouts, "Thanks Mum, for everything."

6th December – Monday

4.00 a.m: Jamie phones in the middle of the night, very weepy.

"I've nowhere to go, I'm frozen and hungry," she says, hardly able to speak. We talk for almost an hour.

On this bitter winter's night I can't bear to think of Jamie in such a state. "I'll come and collect you," I tell her and arrive at Coventry about 5.30 a.m., with Max asleep in the back of the car.

Everywhere is deserted this crisp, dark night; street lamps glow, the only bit of comfort around. We arranged to meet by the courts but there is no sign of her. Suddenly, she pops up cautiously from bushes saying, "I'm sorry I rang you but I was desperate with nowhere to go."

On our way home Jamie recalls her teenage years, what she got up to when I thought she was elsewhere, doing other things. Laughing, she says, "I even spent a night in a horsebox."

"Why did you do the things you did?" I ask her. "Were you bored? Were you unhappy, or what?"

She replies, "If I fancied doing something, I just did it"

Jamie keeps asking, "Do you think I look thin?" and I agree she certainly does.

Back at home she has a steaming hot bath to refresh herself. Starving, she tucks into hot porridge and toast, then washes her clothes and sorts out bags of old clothes in the attic.

"Last week I had a private abortion," she says. "I only stayed in four hours although they wanted me to stay longer." She is weepy and I feel sad for her.

"I had a large amount of crack yesterday, about £200 worth. The guy gave it to me because I buy such a lot from him.

117

I've got a stolen cheque card on me. I've decided to leave Coventry and should be able to use the card for travel and a hotel."

Jamie's eye is black and swollen. "I was hit again last night," she says. "Someone tried to stab me. They had a knife at my throat but I managed to get away, jumping over a balcony. My legs really hurt because I was hit with a baseball bat."
9.15 a.m: we take Max to playschool. Jamie kisses him, saying sadly, "Bye, Max. You may never see me again".

I take Jamie back to the house where she is now staying. She collects a few things in a bin bag from the house, and a friend of hers asks for a lift to town. He and Jamie chat about Vernon's murder, and Jamie recalls the threats made to her yesterday.
We leave the bag of clothes and make-up vanity case in a station locker. "The locker's only a £1 per day," she says, "and at least I know it's safe." I drop her off at social security to collect her money and she asks, "Would you like to take a photo – it might be the last one you get."

When I call at my library this afternoon the librarian says, "There's such a lot to think about at this time of the year, isn't there?"
More than you'd ever know, I think to myself, as I smile at her.
7.00 p.m: on the radio – a reward for £5,000 is being offered for information regarding the killing of Vernon Wells.

Jamie phones, "Mum, I've been arrested by police and then released again," she says. "They were kind and gave me a photo of Vernon from their poster."
She sounds much happier. " I'm staying with a friend tonight and hope to get away tomorrow," she says.

7th December – Tuesday
I attend a social services planning meeting on Ben's future.
They state, "Jamie is a known drug addict," and it hits me hard. For the first time I have heard it said that my daughter is an addict. Tears come to my eyes and I feel really choked.

Probation haven't got a clue as to where Jamie is, what crime she is committing, or when her probation runs out – which is in a month's time. To put them all in the picture, I read my report on Jamie's background and recent history. Everyone, including social services, are dumb-founded. They know nothing about Jamie's dangerous lifestyle. An immediate Court Child Protection Order is to be applied for, to run parallel with the care order. At last I am happy. Something positive is being done, and I am now being taken seriously.

8th December – Wednesday

Jamie rings early morning saying, "Mum, I don't know what to do. I've got no money to get away from here."

She rings again an hour later, very low, "Mum, I'm desperate to leave Coventry." I agree to meet her at the rail station.

Jamie appears in the distance, hair bedraggled from the rain, wearing a black leather jacket, bust revealing cotton top, and jeans. As we sit in the car and chat, she pulls out the folded photo of Vernon from her bag which the police gave her.

"I knew him for three months," she says sadly.

I tell Jamie the result of the case conference yesterday. She is annoyed saying, "I'll have Ben back for Christmas when I've sorted myself out."

"You won't be able to," I tell her.

"I'll get him," she replies. "If not, I'll take him out for a few hours."

I say, "You can't because of the 'Protection Order'."

"Why?" Jamie asks crossly.

"In view of the dangerous people you are associating with," I tell her, "Ben has to be protected."

"I suppose so," she agrees, as she tries to hold back the tears.

It is obvious she loves and wants her baby so much but drugs and men come first, and control her life.

"Be careful Jamie," I warn her, "For goodness sake, don't get involved with the yardies again."

"But they're good and look after me," she says.

"Yardies would have no sentiment as far as your children are concerned. At least Max and Ben are safe now."

Jamie nods in agreement, "I suppose so."

Once again she asks, "Do you think I'm thinner? I haven't eaten for two days."

Jamie is paranoid about her weight. I wonder if she is anorexic?

Weepy and emotional, she turns to me saying, "The person who
threatened me on Sunday had a gun."
"Jamie, promise me you'll phone and let me know you're okay," I ask
her. "But please don't phone at night. I'm so tired."
Jamie agrees she won't bother me. "I'll stay in a hotel tonight," she says,
as I cuddle her and give her photos of the children and me. As she walks
away in the distance I wonder what crisis will happen next...or if I will
ever see her again?

9th December – Thursday

At teatime. Jamie phones, sounding very happy.
"I slept well," she says. "I hope to go to Sheffield tonight. I'll come back
in a week to see Ben."

16th December – Thursday

"Hi Mum, it's Jamie. I'm ringing from Cheltenham and am on my way
back from Sheffield to Coventry. I've just bought loads of toys for the
children."
Purchased with stolen cheques, I think to myself.
"Can you collect me at Leamington station tomorrow, so I can take Ben
his presents?"

17th December – Friday

No sign of Jamie at the station so Max and I go alone to see Ben. I hear
nothing from her and by evening decide to phone Clinton.
He says, "Jamie slept until 1.15 p.m. When I tackled her about seeing the
children, she told me you are taking her tomorrow instead."
"That's rubbish," I inform him. "I haven't spoken to Jamie. She will now
have to contact social services direct if she wants to see Ben."

19th December – Sunday

There has been another prostitute found murdered, this time up in
Doncaster. Jamie says she knew her, having spent a lot of time in Sheffield
and Doncaster over the past two years. There have been so many girls
murdered who have worked with Jamie...it could well be her next!

20th December – Monday

Evening: The doorbell rings. It is Jamie, clutching a torn black bin liner full of toys. I am surprised, and at the same time sad. She looks so thin and haggard standing in the doorway puffing her cigarette.

"I've brought Max's presents," she says as Max runs to her in the hallway. "Open them," she says, excitedly.

Much to his delight there is a transporter plane, lorry kit, and model racing car. Not one present is wrapped and I'm convinced they have been shoplifted.

As they part with a kiss Jamie says, "I have to go to see Ben now," and hurriedly leaves. I phone Linda the foster mum to warn her Jamie is on way over, but she doesn't turn up.

23rd December – Friday

Early evening I receive a surprise call, "Happy Christmas mum," says Jamie chirpily.

"Where will you be Christmas Day?" I ask.

"At a hotel in Coventry," she says.

"Will you be having Christmas dinner?" I enquire.

"Don't know," she replies...the phone goes dead.

24th December – Friday. Christmas Eve.

8.30 p.m: I get a call from Jamie. "I'm with Dionne and we're on our way to see Ben."

"But you won't be able to see him," I tell her. "You have to give plenty of notice. Anyway he'll be asleep at this time of night."

"Well, I'll leave the presents at the door then," she says.

While Jamie is on the phone, I arrange to collect her at 4.00 p.m. tomorrow so she can have her Christmas dinner here at home.

After Jamie's call, I ring and warn the foster parents, "Jamie is on her way over."

Later, Linda phones, "Jamie insisted on seeing Ben but John told her he was asleep. The presents Jamie left for Ben were in a ripped black poly bag and the gift tags have no messages on. It's so sad isn't it?"

25th December – Saturday. Christmas Day

3.30 p.m: I collect Jamie, leaving Max with a baby sitter. I can't tell him his mummy is coming, just in case she doesn't turn up. We meet at the deserted railway station.

In the car Jamie recalls her childhood memories of Christmas, speaking like the daughter I used to know. "I remember when Jonathan and I

opened the presents," she says. "It was nice to have someone to open them with."
As we walk through the door, Max is thrilled to see his mummy and his face is a picture of delight.

Jamie dives into the freshly baked mince pies, saying, "These are my first this year."
Mum, can I take the rest of the mince pies back with me?" she asks.
It is wonderful to see her tuck into her turkey dinner and, as she eats, she chats.

"I spent the night in the police station on the 22nd, for not attending court for possession of an offensive weapon – a knife," she says. "The police were awful to me; spitting, calling me a black man's whore and nigger lover. I put in a complaint to the policeman on the desk, and he made them apologise.
Next morning I went to Court and got a two year conditional discharge.

I'm not working on the streets any longer. It's too dangerous and too many people are getting murdered. Recently, I worked cheques in Islington," says Jamie quite openly. "I'm with the same guy all the time now working on the cheques. I've decided to stay at a hotel," she says. "I don't have to answer to anyone and can get a bit of peace. It's comfortable, with bed, shower and TV. I'm going to the 'social' next week to get them to pay."

Out of the blue, Jamie holds up some stolen travellers cheques and asks, "Mum, do you know where I can get these cashed? Would you like them?" I'm speechless!

Jamie tells me, "I intend to go to rehab with Ben." As I look at her I think – Jamie you're in another world; you don't even bother to visit you child or find out how he is.
The subject changes to the probation hostel in Birmingham. "Do you know," she says, "they won't allow drug users there anymore. The rules were changed after Marti and I left."
Jamie laughs, "All the money I got from working, hundreds of pounds, was in the office safe there, right under the noses of the staff."
"Are you still being threatened over Vernon's murder?" I ask.
"No," she replies, "everyone's on my side now."

After a couple of hours it is time for Jamie to return home. No transport is running over Christmas, so I offer to take her back.

29th December – Wednesday

This morning I receive a letter from the Deputy Chief Probation Officer of West Midland's Probation Service, in reply to my recent letter, in which I complained that probation have no idea where my daughter is, the danger she is in, or what crime she is committing. Although they threaten to issue a warrant for her arrest they have done nothing.
As usual they have all the answers saying:

> "The case has been considered carefully by the officer and supervising senior probation officer, and the need to balance work aimed to support your daughter in her resettlement with the need to enforce the requirements of the probation order has been very much in the minds of the Service in working with this case."

Everyone I speak to, including agency workers who know Jamie, agree with me. Probation has not acted firmly and make it obvious they are totally disinterested. It is appalling that this should be allowed to continue.

Jamie's probation officer has no idea of Jamie's history or circumstances. She is only interested in whether the authorities are meeting the ethnic needs of Jamie's two children – proving she hasn't got a clue...because Max is white!
There is too much concern by everyone on black cultural issues. What about 'white'? Doesn't it count anymore, especially in this case where Ben is three-quarters white?
Jamie is only one of many thousands of criminals on probation who get away with everything.
I write back saying I am very angry.

30th December – Thursday

I receive a reply from the Home Office to my letter of September in which I made complaints about the running of the Birmingham probation hostel. As expected, they always have an answer:

> "The purpose of approved probation hostels is to provide an enhanced level of supervision that allows certain offenders and

bailees, based on the judgement of the courts, to remain in the community. During their period of residence, hostel residents are expected either to be in employment or to attend projects, training courses or treatment facilities.

Approved hostels are reserved for those who require this level of supervision and are not meant simply as accommodation. They provide a supportive and structured environment within which effective supervision is possible. Residents are required to be present in the hostel between specified times, usually 11.00 p.m. until 6.00 p.m. The nursery is seen as an important feature, playing a vital role for both mothers and children. The staff are able to observe and support the residents and their children. The nursery allows the residents to attend appointments outside the hostel, with solicitors, social services or court.

It is important to realise that these facilities, staff time and commitment can be made available to hostel residents but the decision to make the most effective use of a period of residence in the hostel rests solely with each individual."

I am furious and reply to the Probation Service Division of the Home Office, telling them,
"You are sticking your heads in the sand. During Jamie's period under hostel supervision:
She took up employment – that of cheque fraud.
Yes, Jamie attended interviews – in maximum security prisons.
Yes, she did have training – for her new crime.
She smoked crack in the presence of hostel staff.
Jamie travelled all over the country committing fraud.
The curfew was non-existent. The girls were allowed out from very early morning until 11.00 at night (7.00 p.m. after the birth of her baby)."

When I spoke to the inmates, they told me their time in the hostel was a waste of money. They were totally bored, and continued to commit crime, prostitution and take drugs to fill in their time and have excitement. Many took up new crime, or worked on the streets for the first time.
They felt compulsory education or training would have given them less time for criminal activity. Maybe, then, they would have the incentive to

improve their future and that of their children – many of whom will end up back in care once the mother leaves the hostel.

31st December – Friday. New Year's Eve

"I'm going to see Ben on Monday," I tell Jamie on the phone.

"Can I come with you?" she asks eagerly.

I make it clear, "No Jamie. You probably won't bother to turn up. We will see you at the foster home between 1.00 and 2.00 p.m."

"Okay, I'll be there," says Jamie.

She tells me, "Mum, my friends thought your mince pies were great. That's all they ate on Christmas day."

How sad, I think to myself – at least I'm relieved Jamie had a proper meal with us that day.

The end of another year and things don't seem to get any better. Jamie still owes me the £300 I lent her when she had her Giro stolen at the hostel. The DSS haven't paid another cheque, so it's unlikely I will ever see the money.

Her crises continue without a break and, as we enter 1994, I wonder what the future has in store for us?

Crackhead

Flying Socks – 1994

1st January – Saturday

"Happy New Year mum." Jamie sounds very bright. "I'm leaving Clinton tonight. If he phones, can you say you don't know where I am? I'm leaving the area with my friend Dexter, who I met a few weeks ago. I will still come and see Ben on Monday though."

Today, on the news, another prostitute has been found murdered – a girl who worked in Balsall Heath. I wonder if Jamie knows her?

3rd January – Monday

Will Jamie turn up to see Ben at the foster parents at 1.00 p.m. as arranged?
No sign of her...eventually she arrives. Clinton drops her off at 1.50 p.m.
Ben smiles at Jamie, but then seems confused and cries. Tears come to her eyes.
After a short while Max and I depart, leaving Jamie waiting for Clinton to collect her.

6th January – Thursday

Our local radio wants to interview Jamie and myself. I drive over, having arranged to meet at 9.30 a.m.
As I wait in my car, Jamie arrives looking very pale and tired. "I didn't get to bed until five this morning," she says wearily.
"Are you still working?" I enquire.
"Yes," she says, "but at least I have money," and produces about £50 from her bag.
"Clinton hit me this morning to wake me up," she says. "I tried to stab him last week but he managed to stop me."

The reporter arrives and records his interview with Jamie in my car.
He asks Jamie, "What drugs are you on?"
"Crack and heroin," she replies.

"Can you confirm most drug dealers in the area are young?" he asks. "There are the big men but the fifteen year olds run around for them," she tells him.

"Do you think your mother was informed enough to talk to you about drugs when you were young?" he questions.

"Even if she had been better informed, I would still have done it," says Jamie. "I think it is up to the authorities to inform kids properly."

"What would you do if you didn't take drugs?" he asks.

"I'd still work on the streets but have more money for other things," she replies.

Jamie does a brilliant interview considering she is almost asleep. But the sudden realisation, as I listen to her, that she is on both crack and heroin makes me sick inside.

11th January – Tuesday

"Would Max like a Scalelectrix for his birthday?" enquires Jamie on the phone.

"He would just as much appreciate something small," I tell her.

She insists – but I know he will probably get nothing in the end.

Jamie mentions, "I've got some new clothes; a pair of black shorts for evening wear, a blouse and a long green denim dress."

As Jamie runs out of money she says, "I'll phone back," but doesn't.

I speak to the social worker and voice my fears, "I'm frightened of getting too emotionally involved with Ben because I won't see him when he's adopted."

She reassures me, "Open adoption is very new, but the court will consider Max and yourself having regular contact, possibly twice a year."

12th January – Wednesday

I go to bed early tonight – shattered emotionally and physically.

At eleven o'clock I am woken up by the phone.

"This is Sheffield Police," they say, and pass the phone to Jamie.

"Mum, I'm in custody."

"Nothing surprises me any more, Jamie," I say, half asleep. We had always agreed she ring me if in custody. At least I know where she is.

"What are you in for this time?" I ask.

"Cheques," she replies. "Could you phone Clinton please, and he'll

arrange for someone to collect me? They will know where."
Jamie returns to Coventry and later phones to say she is spending the night in custody.

18th January – Tuesday

7.30 a.m: Jamie sounds very low, is cold, and has been out all night.
"I'm freezing here in the phone box," she says. "Clinton has got all my things and I don't want to go back because he'll beat me up."
"Why don't you get a police escort to get your clothes from his flat?" I suggest. But she is too frightened.
"I'll be over in a couple of hours," I tell her.

Jamie appears at the car park in her new green denim dress, with a soft beige check cloth jacket. She doesn't look bad, considering she has been up all night, although she yawns constantly.
She phones Clinton, "Mum and I are on our way to your flat to collect my stuff."
Once there, she is reluctant to get out of the car saying, "I'm can't."
Now we are here, we must get her things. Warily I tread up the steps and bang on the flat door.

Clinton appears, fuming and very angry – so different from the elegant guy I had met a few months earlier. He is wearing a heavy net over his locks and looks quite scruffy. As I enter the entrance hall he quickly closes the interior hall doors, not wanting me to see any further.
He snaps, "I haven't got Jamie's things. Some are at the launderette."

I hurriedly leave and drive in haste to the launderette...but Clinton gets there before us. Heart thumping, I park on double yellow lines right by the traffic lights and fly into the launderette to get hold of Jamie's things before he does.
He searches through two black plastic bags for his underwear, shirts, and socks.
The launderette girl demands, "£7.50 please." Clinton has already disappeared so I end up paying.
As I run to the car Jamie shouts, "Quick mum, drive off."

I am cautious, not wanting to aggravate Clinton. He is in a blazing mood and I don't fancy him turning on me.
Suddenly, he gets out of his car, storms over and demands items left in

the bags.

As I throw socks and underpants to him, people in cars at the traffic lights watch aghast. Once Clinton has what he wants, I speed off as fast as I can.

"Gosh, Jamie, he's in a violent mood. I wonder why? He looked as if he was ready to shoot us."

Jamie looks puzzled. "I can't understand it," she says. He only takes cannabis."

As we drive along Jamie says, "I've nowhere to go until my hearing on Thursday," (for stolen cheques).

I state firmly, "Jamie, that's probation's problem – not mine," and promptly phone probation to see if someone can see her. No one is available.

I decide to take her home for an hour or so, give her a good meal, hot bath and let her see Max in case she is kept in custody in Sheffield on his birthday.

Jamie rambles on as usual. "Clinton is vegetarian. He won't even let me eat cheese and chive crisps, and throws them in the bin. I get them out when he's not there." she says.

I give her turkey in a white sauce – how she tucks in, enjoying every mouthful.

"Clinton wouldn't allow me to have meat," she says as she delights in scraping the sauce from the side of the casserole.

She then tells me, "I was up north a couple of times last week on drug deals but wasn't paid for doing it.

Last night I stayed with the chap who recently chased me with a gun to my head," she says quite nonplus.

January 21st – Friday Max's fourth birthday.

2.00 p.m: Jamie phones from Leamington station. "Can you collect myself and a friend?"

I am annoyed but agree to collect her for Max's sake, and he is very pleased to see her.

After she had said recently, "I'm buying him a Scalelectrix for his birthday," she hasn't bought him a present at all, not even a card.

Jamie's friend, Lisa, tells me she is sixteen. "I ran away from home at fifteen, lived with a dangerous black crowd, and met Steve Dred at a club.

He used to say, "Come back with us – it's great and you won't want to leave."
Lisa and Jamie are so alike in looks, hair, clothes and make-up, and have
similar personalities.
Jamie tells me, "I rescued Lisa this morning – we fled across the grass
while Clinton was out."

Towards evening, while the girls tuck into their meal, I observe Jamie
has difficulty in eating. She explains, "I was found unconscious last
night and woke up in hospital. When I got back from Sheffield I was
badly beaten. I had to have the inside of my cheek stitched." Bad scratch
marks are visible across her cheek.

Lisa says, "It's the first time for ages I've felt full. I haven't had meat at
Clinton's. We live mostly on sweetcorn, rice and tuna. I didn't even have
a proper meal at Christmas," she says.

Turning to Jamie, I hear Lisa remark, "Isn't it wonderful to sit and have
a meal without any hassle. Clinton criticised everything. He made us
wash up – sterilize first, put boiling water in the bowl, throw away and
refill, wash glass, plates, cups and then pans. Everything had to be rinsed
and dried naturally."
"Clinton is beating us up all the time now and things are getting worse,"
says Jamie.
"Why?" I ask.
But they don't have an answer.
Lisa says, "I've tried hard to stop Jamie going out for drugs but it's very
difficult."
The girls have left all their clothes at Clinton's. "We'll get them back
somehow," they say.
They are very frightened and want to get out of the area. Lisa phones
home and arranges for relatives in Leicester to collect her and Jamie.

Pat has a quiet word with Jamie, telling her I am unwell and to give me a break.

22nd January – Saturday

I receive a call from Lisa's mother, an articulate and educated woman.
She sounds an ordinary mum like me. "Do you think they'll go back?"
she enquires.
"Yes," I reply, "probably within a few days."
"Are they with yardies?" she asks concerned.

"As far as I know they aren't," I reply.

Lisa's mother speaks with the voice of experience. "I'm aware Lisa has been taking drugs but I'm not sure what, and she's sex mad. These girls obviously know the danger they put themselves in but it doesn't seem to make any difference."

Max's paternal grandfather, Tom Harper, calls and is longing to tell us his good news.

"Mikey phoned on Christmas morning, after not being in touch for over 18 months. We have been down to the West Country to visit him. He is looking really well, has been off drugs 12 months now, and lives in a hostel.

We showed Mikey photos of Max, and he thought he was lovely. Maybe we could take Max to see Mikey in the summer?" suggests Tom. Delighted to hear his good news, I agree.

23rd January – Sunday

Jamie rings.

"Where are you Jamie?" I ask.

"Back in Coventry," she replies.

"Jamie, I don't believe it. Only three days ago you ran away and you are back already? I predicted you would be," I tell her.

Jamie's call is brief and she promises to keep in contact. She sounds very cheerful and giggles as friends pass by the phone box.

I feel so much better having spoken to her. I am not sure whether I prefer to know where Jamie is and what she is doing, or to know absolutely nothing. Either way, it is hard. But as I write this, I am happy to know she is okay.

30th January – Sunday

Jamie rings very excited, "I've applied for an 'Employment Training' typing course.

I'm going to the homeless hostel tomorrow and hope to get council accommodation within a month."

I invite Jamie to come over next Saturday, on her 21st Birthday, and offer to cook her a roast beef dinner, her favourite. She is pleased and says, "I can't wait."

"There is nothing I can give you in the way of a present," I tell her. "It

would only get lost, sold, or stolen."
Jamie agrees saying, "The best thing you can give me is a memory."

I tell her the good news about Mikey. Jamie is very happy that he acknowledges his son.
"I haven't had drugs for about a fortnight," Jamie states proudly.
Honestly, I wonder?

31st January – Monday

Jamie has only seen Ben for a total of $1^1/2$ hours since he went into care three months ago. One hour of this she sat waiting for Clinton to collect her.
Ben is very happy and settled, and I find it hard to accept he will probably be adopted. Thank goodness he is now safe and his future looks secure.

Crackhead

Visions – 1994

Jamie arrives here mid-afternoon. "Sorry I'm late." she says "I went to bed at eight o'clock this morning after being out all night."

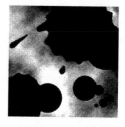

Pat joins us and we have a lovely meal – prawn cocktail, roast beef, Yorkshire pud, finishing with white chocolate gateaux decorated with 21 candles. Max thinks it is great fun.

As Jamie tucks in, she has problems with her jaw and mouth. "I walked into a lamp post," she explains.

Pat jokes, "That can't be good for business." We glance at each other, suspecting Jamie is probably putting on an act and has been hit.

My present for Jamie's 21st is simple bath accessories, and Pat's gift is a small bottle of perfume. At least we know they probably won't get stolen. Jamie is delighted with them. How many youngsters would be grateful for such presents on their twenty-first I wonder?

"I'm off to a party with Dexter tonight at three o'clock," she says excitedly.

"Three in the morning?" I ask.

"Of course," she giggles.

I am curious, and ask Jamie about her drug use. "Jamie, when did you first have cocaine?"

"Oh, Winston asked me if I wanted some white powder and I thought I might as well try it. That was three years ago."

"Clinton seems very aggressive these days," I remark. "Do you think he's on hard drugs?"

"Well, I know cannabis can be laced with cocaine, so perhaps that's why," she says.

"I'm not with Clinton any longer. There's another guy who loves me and gives me crack for nothing," she says, appearing a lot happier and

135

relaxed. "The guy I'm going out with now is very wealthy and in his 40's.
Don't worry mum, I'm not in danger any more."
We joke with her, "It's about time you got someone rich to look after you."
I am amazed Jamie talks so openly. She says she has sold her social book and has to collect her money personally over the counter these days.

I tell her I saw two girls looking for punters on a street corner in Stratford the other day, and she seems surprised. There is no getting away from it. Drugs, prostitution, and crime to pay for drugs, exist in city, town or country. Everyone is affected but so many bury their heads in the sand not wanting to know.

"By the way, I want to visit Ben next week when you go over," she says.
I give her the social worker's number to arrange a lift, and refuse to be involved.
Before taking her home, we read the playing cards, using a fortune telling book to guide us through. It is not good news – they tell of a fair-haired woman, sadness, loss and separation. I have a feeling they are right and we are heading for disaster, but Pat says she feels there is hope.

After a memorable afternoon, I take Jamie back, late evening. She chats, hardly pausing for breath. "My clothes are at the station in two lockers," she says. "I must go and get them," although I doubt she ever will.

I drive Jamie along the deserted road and she points out the streets where she works. As one of the punters drives slowly past, she says, "I know him."
"Are there many dangerous punters around?" I ask, knowing there have been a number of local prostitutes murdered recently.
"Not many," she replies.

10th February – Thursday
Max and I visit Ben and, as expected, Jamie doesn't turn up.
Returning home, I find a message on the answer machine, "This is Jamie speaking, I'll phone back."
But she doesn't. I am getting anxious because I have heard nothing. For days my gut feeling tells me there is something very wrong.

17th February – Thursday

Jamie phones, unusually lively.

"For the past couple of days I've been in Sheffield and hope to go to Doncaster tonight," she says, "and I've seen Ben's father.

Sorry I haven't been in touch," she says. "I've been in trouble and arrested twice in Birmingham for not attending court, and possession of an offensive weapon.

I've not had drugs for quite a while." She certainly sounds much brighter.

"By the way, the guy you met at Sheffield Court, Sam Yardie, sends his regards to you," she laughs.

18th February – Friday

"I'm not dead yet," Jamie says on the answer phone. "I won't be at court on Monday, so I'll try to pop over to see you then."

A friend and I discuss the plight of parents in our area whose children are involved in drugs. There seems little information available, as to who to go to when there is a crisis. We decide to fulfil the need by putting together an information pack for parents, schools, police and the health authority, and financing this with a car boot sale.

23rd February – Wednesday

We hold our first parents support meeting with two other parents at my house.

Sue, the drug family worker is keen to help. She will refer parents who need support once they have received counselling from her.

25th February – Friday

Max and I visit Jamie's sister, Kate, and her family in London. There is great excitement with preparations for Kate's wedding at the end of May. The invitation is addressed to myself, Max and Jamie.

"Things are really bad and Jamie hasn't made contact," I tell Kate.

"If she can't come, bring a friend to the wedding," she says.

Kate tells me that their uncle has a pub. "He has grand ideas about what he's going to do and the money he's going to make, but never does it. He's always on the move and can't settle."

Just like Jamie, I think to myself. Must be why she and her uncle get on so well.

Crackhead

26th February – Saturday

Dionne anxiously breaks the news to me:"Jamie has tried to commit suicide."
"I'm not sure which hospital she is in, Angela.
Clinton left Jamie in the flat last night and when he returned she had slashed both her arms – from elbow to wrist."
In a panic I phone round, finding Jamie eventually in her local hospital. They tell me, "She is in a pretty bad way and needs lots of stitching."
"Should I come straight over?" I ask.
"Not at present. We will ring you back," says the nurse.

The Nurse phones back late afternoon. "Jamie is being collected by a guy called Clinton and she insists on discharging herself. Jamie has seen a psychiatrist but she refuses to go to our psychiatric unit."
"She should have seen a psychiatrist ages ago," I tell the nurse. "Jamie desperately needs help."
"I'll put details in her records in case anything happens in future," says the nurse.

27th February – Sunday

Jamie sounds very subdued on the phone.
"I expect you had a bad night, and are in a lot of pain?" I ask.
"Yes," she says. "There are three layers of stitching on one arm and I cut both arms."
"Why did you do it?"
"Clinton did my head in," she says repeatedly
"Where will you stay tonight?" I ask.
"Clinton's," she says.
I can't believe she is going back to him.

I phone the ward sister and she informs me, "Jamie has an appointment in the morning to have the stitches checked and dressings changed."
I warn her Jamie is very unreliable so the sister asks if I can take her in personally.
"Clinton, can you get a message to Jamie?" I ask on the phone.
"She is very bad now," he says.
"She has left me for another guy and had a lot of crack. His conversation is confused. He isn't sure when Jamie left his place, the day, or week – and I wonder why?
I anxiously wait...but there is no call from Jamie.

28th February – Monday

Clinton phones. "Jamie will meet you by the shops at ten this morning.

Jamie arrives accompanied by a very thin pale youth. She introduces him, "Mum, this is Terry."
She looks dreadful, having tried to disguise a badly bruised eye with lots of make-up. She shivers, being inappropriately dressed for the bitter cold – wearing an unbuttoned thin cotton shirt, with a low fronted top, and jeans. Her greasy hair is pulled up in a scruffy pony tail.
Obviously in tremendous pain, Jamie supports one arm with her other hand, the wounds protected by thick bandaging.
"Mum, can Terry come with us to hospital?" she asks and I nod in agreement.
"How on earth did you get that black eye?" I ask.
"Oh, I got that and a grazed knee falling out of a moving car." she says. "We had a Blues party, which started on Thursday and ended Monday. I was totally drunk all weekend.
Terry chats from the back seat and tells me he is nineteen. "I'm on all drugs imaginable and I've also been a car thief," he tells me. "I've spent years in care."

As we drive along Jamie says, "Mum, it's really weird. Clinton's mother dreamed about Clinton and saw blood everywhere. She warned him to be careful of a girl called Jamie, even though she doesn't know me."

We arrive at the accident department, where Terry escorts Jamie into the cubicle to have her stitches checked. I manage to have a quiet word with the Sister about Jamie and tell her, "She forgot this appointment, and wouldn't be here if I hadn't brought her."
Once the wounds have been checked and dressed, I am invited to join them in the cubicle. The nurse is very kind and asks, "Jamie, would you like to see the Doctor?"
"I would, but must phone Clinton first because he said he'd look after me."
The nurse talks to her about the bruising and says compassionately, "Jamie, no one deserves to be hit like that."
While the nurse pops out for a minute, Terry speedily shoves handfuls of swabs, plasters and bandages into his pockets, ignoring my presence.

She returns to shows us photos taken of Jamie's slashed arms. I am horrified to see half a dozen slits crosswise on each arm. Jamie has an appointment on Wednesday and as we depart the nurse asks, "Jamie, make sure you attend. It is very important."

Driving her back to Clinton's I ask, "How is Lisa these days?"
"You can see her if you like," she replies, and directs me to the flat where Lisa lives with Steve Dred.
We arrive at the flat and Jamie calls on the intercom, "Mum has come to see Lisa."
Steve replies, "The place is a mess. I have just got out of the bath and I'm not dressed."
Lisa comes outside with wet hair, wearing a 'T' shirt, leggings and trainers. It is freezing and she waits in the car for five minutes. He waves, smiling, from the upstairs window. The girls get out of the car and beckon to me shouting, "Steve wants to have a chat with you."

Warily, I enter the flat. He ushers me into the kitchen, orders the girls to the living room and closes the door.
Steve looks very different from our previous meetings when he was scruffy, with bloodshot eyes. Before me today stands a fit looking guy, with thin dreadlocks to the shoulders, and dressed in designer blue baggy denims. Three heavy gold chains adorn his neck and four large gold rings gleam on his fingers, one with half a dozen diamonds set on top.
He asks, "Has Jamie had ever told you anything about me or confided in you?"
"No," I tell him cautiously.
"Why do you think Jamie slashed her wrists?" he asks.
"She was furious with Clinton," I reply.
"Do you think she loves him?" he asks.
"Yes, but she gets very hurt when he goes with other girls."
"I'm worried for Jamie's safety," says Steve.
I voice my concern, "I'm frightened she'll end up dead – either committing suicide or be murdered."
He agrees. "It's inevitable something is going to happen."
At times I find it hard to understand Steve's strong Jamaican accent.
He talks of a crackhead he knows. "Her mother can't cope with the awful lies," he says. Sounds familiar, I think to myself.

Jamie enters the kitchen and we talk about Ben. "Why haven't you bothered to visit him?" I ask. "You have the chance to get him back but, unless you prove yourself, he will be adopted."

She shouts aggressively, "No child of mine is going to be adopted."
Steve tells her, "You are arguing with your mum without stopping to
think what she is saying. Maybe she's right?"
Annoyed she says, "I'm going to rehab with my baby soon."
"Why have you only seen Ben for an hour in four months?" I ask.
"Originally you said you were leaving him in care for six weeks, visiting
him three times a week. You've been offered transport by social services
so there's no excuse."
Jamie glares at me, not replying.
Steve asks, "What did you think when you were expecting Ben?"
"I just blanked it out of my mind," she replies.
"I agree with your mum," he says. "Jamie, you'll end up with lots of
babies with different fathers. There's a girl in a flat nearby who has six
children, all with different fathers."
Jamie snaps, "I won't let that happen."

Steve sends Jamie out of the room and we discuss her drug problem.
"Jamie and I have been good friends over the past four years," he tells
me. "No matter where she lives we keep in contact and talk to each
other. I always went to Jamie as a friend, but can't talk to her any longer.

Did you know Jamie tried to take her stitches out last night?" he asks.
"She must be mad. Is there anything I can do to help her?"
"Steve, I have done everything possible and I'm worn out," I tell him.
"We have to tackle each day as it comes. She has been given an
appointment to attend the psychiatric outpatients on Wednesday. You
can help by reminding Jamie and offering to take her," I suggest. "That's
all we can do."

The intercom rings through from downstairs. It is the guy for whom
Jamie 'does cheques' wanting to know how she is. "Come on, I'll
introduce you if you like," she says, and I follow her downstairs.
I can't believe what I see. The guy is middle-aged with the air of a
behind-the-desk insurance clerk, sitting behind the steering wheel of a
really dilapidated car. He doesn't look the big-time dangerous criminal
he actually is – it is incredible.

Returning upstairs, we continue our discussion. "Jamie," Steve asks,
"Why are you still working on cheques?"
"Because I need the money," she replies.

"Why?" he enquires.

"I earn about £250 per day. I give Clinton £150, and take £100 for myself which I spend on drink and drugs," she says.

Steve asks Jamie about her attempted suicide. "Did you feel anything?"

"Not at the time," she replies, "although it hurts a lot now.

I locked myself in Clinton's flat and knew I had the only keys, but some friends broke the window and got in."

It is getting late and I have to say good-bye to Jamie.

I arrive in Stratford in time to collect the children I child mind from school. As I wait in the playground, mothers stand huddled in small groups. I listen to their chat – holidays, injections, coffee mornings and their little ones' progress in school. If only they knew, I think to myself.

I want to stand on a soap box and shout out, 'Hey, all you mother's out there...this is what is going on in the real world. My daughter went to this little Catholic school, I cared for and nurtured her, giving her my full support throughout.

Listen – this is happening to me, an ordinary Mum. This could be you in a few years' time.'

But I doubt they would believe me (See 'Reflections' 1997).

6th March – Sunday

10.50 p.m: "Mum. Quick. Put the TV on. I'm on my way over with Steve. Stay up...I can't talk." Jamie hangs up.

There is no news on TV at this time of night.

Desperate to talk to someone, I phone a local all night help line, and explain to the volunteer, "I've received a call from Jamie. I'm convinced she's stabbed or murdered someone."

The woman sounds shocked – must think I am mad. "I am sure she's alright," she says trying to allay my fears. "Maybe she has just decided to come home."

"No." I tell her, "I know Jamie better than that."

Midnight – I am restless and can't sleep. Phone rings and makes me jump. Jamie, on a mobile, cautiously says, "Just confirming I'm on my way. Can't talk."

2.00 a.m: I try to get some sleep.

3.00 a.m: Phone rings – my adrenalin rushes. "We are out of the area," says Jamie. "We aren't coming to Stratford now. Can't say much. It's Clinton...you can guess what he's done? Have you heard from anyone?" she asks, panicking and weepy. "Have you seen the news?"

"Nothing," I tell her.

Clinton has probably murdered someone, or been involved in a shooting, I think to myself. Jamie is very worried someone is listening on the line.

I try and get some sleep but Jamie wakes me at 4.50 a.m. just to say, "Mum, don't worry. I'm okay."

"I warned you, Jamie. I predicted something awful was going to happen soon."

Jamie continues..."Clinton will probably get life. I was with Dionne when it happened."

"Did you see it happen?" I enquire.

"I don't know who's been shot," she says.

I now have confirmation there has been a shooting. Jamie gives me her mobile number and I can hear voices in the background.

5.00 a.m: I listen to the news: details of a shooting, outside a pub, filters through. The youth has been seriously injured. Police are looking for two black men. One had a scarf around his face, and torn fashion trousers. After the shooting they sped off in a car.

I speak to Jamie late morning. She sounds brighter but very cautious.

Lunchtime news, "A man has been arrested and the search continues for the other." By 6.00 p.m. the second has been arrested.

9.30 p.m. Jamie reverses the charges. "Thought I'd let you know I'm okay, mum," she says. "Have you heard – they've got them."

I tell her, "The radio said one man is being charged with attempted murder." I ask, "Is it Clinton in custody?"

"Yes, I always knew he was mad!" she exclaims.

I relay the latest news to her.

"Yes, the description of the car is his," she says. "And the trousers, guess who bought those for him? I did!"

"Jamie, what about the stitches in your arm? Did you keep your appointment at the hospital today?" I ask.

"No. I took the stitches out myself," she replies. "I've got more important things on my mind".
My stomach turns over at the thought!

Jamie tells me her clothes are in a station locker, and some are safe in a boarded-up house where she has been staying.
As I put the phone down, I reflect over the past few weeks, including Clinton's terrible aggression.

9th March – Wednesday

7.00 a.m. news: Clinton has been charged with attempted murder and possession of firearms; he is due to appear in court today. The other person has been released.

Jamie rings to let me know she is staying away from the area.
"Have you got your things from the house?" I ask.
"Oh, I'll collect them in the morning. Don't worry, they are safe," she says.

10th March – Thursday

Announcement on breakfast TV news: "Last night a house was set alight..." and there before my eyes on the TV is the gutted, boarded-up house where Jamie left her clothes. Looks as if she has lost everything. If only she had listened to me and collected them.

10.50 p.m: Jamie phones asking, "Have you seen the TV?
Hold on a minute," she says. There's a pause..."Sorry about that. I had to hide. A police car went by."
Jamie is weepy. "Clinton is mad with life," she says, "He's now in prison on remand.
Everything's gone, including most of my stuff," she says, choked and finding it difficult to talk.
Jamie confirms she will be coming home for Sunday lunch (Mothering Sunday).
"The Council are giving me a flat tomorrow because of the fire, but I want to go to another area," she says.
"Are you in much danger?" I ask.
"I'm getting death threats, from the injured guy's friends, all the time," she says.

11th March – Friday

Max comes into the kitchen saying, "Mummy turned and smiled at me in the photo." He is so close to her – it is quite eerie. I tell him he will see mummy soon. He must be missing her after not having had contact for so long.

3.45 p.m: Phone call from Jamie – very distressed and weepy.
"Steve has been beating me, so I grabbed my bag and ran from his flat. He wants me to work for him, now his brother is in prison. He needs the money to buy guns."
Because she is so distressed, I say I will go over to collect her.

Back at home she tucks into any food she can lay her hands on. Pat comes round straight away.
Jamie tells us how she heard about the shooting. "I was tripping on acid, ready to have a good time out with Clinton. I phoned to arrange to meet him. He didn't let on about the shooting, and calmly told me not to join him but to get to the rail station and meet Steve.
I took a taxi, but at the station there was a mass of police. I phoned Steve on his mobile and he told me to meet him somewhere else immediately. When I got in Steve's car he said, "Duck down quick." He headed full pelt out of the city to an old girl friend's place; but then he changed his mind and headed in the opposite direction."

"On the TV news last night they were interviewing Clinton's neighbours," says Pat. "They said there was a prostitute in the flat – I presume it was you. There had been lots of trouble, including fraud."

Jamie tells us, "After the shooting, the dealers felt sorry for me and kept coming up and giving me crack. I made up to £200 one night selling it on." Tonight I arrange for her to stay in Bed & Breakfast up the road from me. It is vital I have a break from Jamie when I go to bed, and keep her away from the house.

12th March – Saturday

It is afternoon before I take Jamie back. "I'll see you tomorrow," she says as we part.
"Jamie, I am too tired to collect and take you back tomorrow."
"Don't worry," she says, "I'll hitch a lift."
I honestly don't think she will turn up.

13th March – Sunday. Mother's Day
To my astonishment Jamie arrives about noon. She is thrilled she has made the effort and got here by hitching a lift. "I stayed awake all night to make sure I got here on time," she says.
I am very proud of her and, for once, she has proven me wrong.

As always, Jamie is starving and, tucking into a roast pork meal, she says, "All I could think about was this dinner while hitching my lift. Can we have crumble for pud?" she asks.
After her meal she falls asleep on the settee, waking up just before I return her home.
I feel sorry for Max. He just gets the odd cuddle from her, otherwise she sleeps most of the time during her visits. Looking back over the years, this happens every time we see her.

Jamie shows me a gold bracelet saying, "I bought it after selling crack. It's embarrassing, all this rock people are giving me."
Her friend Gibbo phones here tonight. It is difficult to understand his strong Jamaican accent. I tell him Jamie is out and he says he will phone her back.
When I tell Jamie that Gibbo has phoned she says, "He's setting me up in business selling rock."

She asks, "Mum, when is Kate getting married?"
Will Jamie ever remember? "At the end of May," I tell her.
"How is Ben?" she enquires.
"He's almost walking, and Linda says he is very strong willed," I tell her.
"Well he would be, wouldn't he – just like his mother," she says.

I feel unwell and can't take Jamie back home tonight. Unfortunately she has missed the last bus which left at 5.30 p.m, so I decide to take her back in the morning. After being asleep on the settee all afternoon, she zonks out on the dining room floor, for the rest of the evening and night.

14th March – Monday
I drop Jamie off at the station so she can visit Clinton in prison in Birmingham. "You can come again at Easter," I tell her, which will give me a couple of week's breathing space and a chance to re-charge my batteries.

16th March – Wednesday

Midnight: Jamie rings. "Mum, can I come over and sleep on the floor overnight? I've nowhere else to go."
Reluctantly I agree, but tell her to get herself over here.
"I'll get a taxi and should get there in 20 minutes," she says.
Hearing her arrive, I call her up to my bedroom. She sits on the bed chatting for a few minutes, saying, "I tried the usual hotels but they are all full."
"Where did you get the money for the taxi fare: did you have to work?" I ask.
"It was very quiet tonight," she says, "and I only made £50 whereas it would usually be at least £100 – much more if I'd worked longer."

17th March – Thursday

Jamie gets up at 7.00 a.m.
Having only one set of clothes after the fire she creates a new outfit from the children's dressing-up box. Many items are from her teenage years. She pins up the wide brim of a dark green felt hat with a gold twisted brooch, in pirate fashion. "Can I have your old cricket jumper, mum," she asks and sorts out black leggings and knee length black suede boots from the box. To complete the outfit she wears her beautiful wool coat which I bought her while at the probation hostel. She looks so stylish, just as if she has walked out of a fashion magazine.

No one at Stratford rail station would ever imagine this attractive, young, fashionable woman is deeply involved in drugs, prostitution shootings, murders, and has two children in care.
"Keep in touch," I shout as the train pulls out of the station.

Afternoon, Jamie phones, very excited. "I saw the council at lunch time and they're giving me a flat tomorrow." Jamie has gone around in a full circle. Her flat is in the same high-rise block she lived in after Max came into my care. I never dreamed she would return to this downtrodden area once more.

18th March – Friday

Jamie phones saying, "I'm staying at the homeless hostel until Monday. I will get a decoration allowance, and I've bought a carpet. The flat isn't that bad – better than the Rubery one."
"Shall I see you on Tuesday?" I ask.
"Oh, yes," she says, "then I can show you my new place."

19th March – Saturday
Phone rings around 9.00 p.m. and wakes me up. "Mum, did you have a bad feeling about me tonight?" she asks.
"No. I went to bed early," I tell her. "Why?"

Jamie sounds in a state of shock. "I've been attacked by a punter. He held a knife to me and tried to put handcuffs on. The police believe he may be involved in the murder of two prostitutes recently," she says. "They have your name and number and may contact you, but I gave a false name because of warrants out for my arrest."

She chats about her flat. "I'll be able to find a home for my china dragons now," she says excitedly.
"Jamie, It will be ages before your life is stable enough to have them in your flat. They will stay here until I'm sure you won't lose, sell, or have them stolen."
Our conversation finishes abruptly. "Must go." she says. "My taxi has arrived. Bye."

21st March – Monday
Jamie tells me she is staying in a homeless hostel until she sorts the flat out. "I've had to buy a new bag because the other one was lost on Saturday night in the punter's car," she says. "There wasn't much in my bag – just telephone numbers on scraps of paper and an umbrella. The police have taken the money I earned, to test for fingerprints," she tells me.

22nd March – Tuesday
Max and I pop to see Jamie. She is waiting in the car park with Collette, the fifteen-year-old girl I helped in November. Collette has since had a miscarriage.
Jamie appears tired all the time. When she tells me Collette is moving in with her temporarily, I am relieved just in case she is ill or tries to commit suicide again. At least she will have company and someone to keep an eye on her.
"Jamie, your make-up is very orange," I remark. She has a fair complexion, and it is unusual for her make-up to look so awful.
"What do you expect," she replies, "I put in on at night."

I pop up to the flat with Jamie, while Collette sits in the car with Max. The flat is really grotty – wallpaper hanging off the walls; orange, blue, white, black and purple paint on the woodwork and floors. How Jamie will be able to do anything with this place is beyond me. She talks of spending her £180 allowance on carpet so nothing will be left for decorating.

"I won't need to do the kitchen because I don't cook," she says. This is the world of fast food and takeaways. In Steve's kitchen there was absolutely nothing, not even a kettle. No wonder Jamie has a good tuck-in when she comes home.

I have taken up a couple of bags of clothes up to her flat, some bedding, and old towels suitable only for jumble, which I am prepared never to see again.

Jamie points out the flats where murdered Vernon Wells used to lived. Noticing a policeman by the main entrance, she quickly ducks saying, "There are warrants out for my arrest."

As dealers stroll past, faces hidden under their anorak hoods, she gives them a fleeting glance.

Jamie says, "I'm fed up because I had £30 stolen from my room in the hostel last night. I forgot to lock the room while having a drink in the bar. I'm too frightened to go out on the streets after that episode with the punter, so I've got no money."

In the car Jamie and Collette discuss going clubbing tonight. Their day begins about four in the afternoon, when they get up. They work all night, and return to bed early morning. As we drive along I see girls working, even though it is only three in the afternoon. We arrive at the homeless hostel, which appears to be an old army camp situated in the middle of a residential area.

"Mum, can you lend me some money if I give you my social book?" asks Jamie.

"Sorry Jamie, I haven't got any." I have learned not to have money on me when seeing her.

She turns on me aggressively asking, "How can I get to town without money, having had it stolen. Haven't you got £15 or £20?"

"No." By now I'm really angry and tell her, "Use a bus instead of a taxis."

23rd March – Wednesday

Marie, a T.V. producer friend, rings to ask, "Can you mind my children after school?"

I explain, "I'm sorry, it's impossible. I am finding it hard to keep going with my daughter. Her story is horrendous and there is an ongoing crisis."

Marie shows interest as I tell her all about Jamie. "Sounds as if it would make a good film," she says, and I agree.

24th March – Thursday

Marie phones. "Angela, are you serious about making a film? I can have a chat with the TV film people if you are interested."

"Yes, I think it's a good idea," I tell her. "I want people to know what is really going on around us and the effects of drugs on the family.

4.30 p.m: Jamie calls, reversing the charge. I tell her I'm annoyed she wants to chat at my expense.

"Sorry, I had no change," she says cheerfully. "I'll phone you back."

Evening: there is a message "Mum, it's Jamie. I've been locked up." She is very down and her speech sounds very nasal. "I'll see you soon okay and I'll phone you tomorrow."

25th March – Friday

3.00 p.m. There is a call from the police station. "Mum, I've been here overnight and appeared in court this morning. I got bail for non-attendance at court on Wednesday for cheque fraud, and I also forgot a hearing today. A police escort has been arranged to take me to Sheffield, to appear in court tomorrow morning – again for cheque fraud.

Mum, can you collect some clothes from the flat for me please?" she asks. "I haven't had a change of clothing for 48 hours."

I can't get over until about eight tonight and after she confers with police officers, they say I can collect the flat keys from the station.

"I'm sure they will remand me in Sheffield," says Jamie. "I'll phone you again in the morning."

I ring Pat and she jumps at the chance to come to get Jamie's clothes. We arrive at the police station and the officer collects the keys together with a note from Jamie. "Can you get me a can of coke, cigarettes and some chocolate, please?" and lists a few clothes she needs.

By the time we arrive at the flat, it is dark. The streets are quiet and shops shuttered; a mini-skirted girl on the street corner tries to attract punters, and a couple of youths lark about along the pavement. The take-away is busy, different nationalities popping in and out. One black guy enters wearing a traditional African gown in white, edged with blue embroidery, with a flat round pill box hat to match.

A couple of young girls looking no more than sixteen, with babies in pushchairs, hang around the phone box. It is about 9.30 p.m, dark and bitterly cold. Sadly, as I watch them, I think, "This could have been Jamie with Ben."

Pat and I proceed through the entrance of the flats. Bad memories haunt me from two years ago – when Jamie lived in these same flats with Leroy. I constantly lived on a knife-edge then, when she threatened she was going to snatch Max back.

At the flat, as I had feared, there is no electricity. We step over the mountain of post by the front door. Beams of light shine through the large picture windows, casting shadows over the rooms. Downstairs is the bathroom and a bedroom. Upstairs leads to a living room, kitchen and another bedroom.

The only piece of carpet in the whole place is a remnant in the living room which doesn't fit. It is covered with black bags bursting open, clothes scattered everywhere. The kitchen is empty, apart from toothbrush and toothpaste on the draining board. Moonlight shines through the bedroom window onto the bare tiled floor. Wading through the bags, and tripping over in the dark, we find Jamie's income support books she has requested.

We sort out the clothes as quickly as possible, tipping everything out of the bags to make our search easier in the dark; hoping we can get to the police station before Jamie leaves for Sheffield. Lying amongst the heaps of clothing are two boxes of condoms, a hundred in each. Pat and I look at each other and laugh. We shove everything into a plastic bag, leaving the place in quite a state, lock up the flat, and enter the lift.

"Jamie's flat reminds me of the squats my son used to live in," says Pat. We dash to the off-licence and then fly round to the police station. But we arrive too late – Jamie left the police station for Sheffield five minutes ago.

Jamie has requested on her note, "Can you let Dionne know where I am?", so we head over to her house.

Dionne is pleased to see us. "Where's Jamie got to?" she asks anxiously.

"Collette is also very worried about her. Jamie told me yesterday she was seeing you"
I tell Dionne, "I didn't arrange to see Jamie."

We talk of Jamie's attempted suicide. Dionne says, "I think she meant it," and recalls, "I went with my brother early morning to the flat. When we entered the front door we found Jamie splayed out in a chair, with both arms cut, blood everywhere and unconscious. The gas fire was also switched on but not lit.
The ambulance men slapped Jamie on the face to bring her around.
Jamie said she didn't feel the cuts until they were being stitched up. Then she screamed.
She must be out of her mind," says Dionne.
"I think she has been for years," I tell her, "and desperately needs to see a psychiatrist."

"I counted nine girls in the courtroom during Clinton's hearing," says Dionne. I can't understand why Jamie keeps going back to him?"
"Has Clinton always been aggressive?" I ask, "Or has there been a recent change in his behaviour?"
"He has always lost his temper," she tells me. "It is only twelve months since Clinton was released from prison for armed robbery – and now this."

"My mum had these awful premonitions," says Dionne. "She hardly knew Jamie. But she contacted me to say she had dreamed that someone called Jamie was no good for Clinton. She told me Jamie was going to hurt herself.
Immediately I went around to Clinton's and found Jamie had just tried to commit suicide."

The second vision she had, was Clinton's picture in the papers, and blood everywhere. For two weeks she rang Clinton, having the same dream repeatedly. She asked, "Clinton, have you got a gun?" but every time he denied he had. Eventually, she and her husband went over to see Clinton and demanded once more, "Have you got a gun?"
Finally he said he had, but refused to hand it over. The next day it is alleged he shot the guy.
"Jamie recently tried to stab Clinton in the back with a knife," says Dionne. "Apparently, the people in the room managed to grab the knife just as Jamie was about to stab him."

Dionne's husband puts us in the picture about Vernon who was murdered. "He went to Birmingham, held pretty girls and dealers to ransom with a gun, and took their money," he says.

26th March – Saturday

11.00 a.m. Jamie contacts me from Sheffield very excited. "Mum, I appeared in court this morning and was released. Can you collect me from the Leamington rail station?" she asks. "I've got to go to a bail hostel at Reading later."

Jamie is waiting at the station when I arrive. There is a strong sickly odour as she gets into the car, not having changed her clothes for days. "Mum," she says, "Can we go back home? Can I have a bath – I hate being like this. And I'm starving."

I find an opportune moment to tell her she won't be able to see Ben on his birthday. Social services aren't working that day, which is Easter Tuesday, and Jamie's access must be supervised.
"I shall see him on his birthday and take him," she says angrily.
Knowing what a dangerous woman Jamie is, and that she and her friends have guns and knives, I don't trust her.
"Anyway, I've made an appointment with social services to get Ben back," she says.
"It's unlikely they will let you have him," I tell her. "His future would be bleak and dangerous, and he would spend his life in and out of care." She becomes agitated, "I'm not talking about it any further," and cuts me dead.

Back at home, Jamie ransacks the fridge. Starving, she tucks into shepherd's pie and chats between each mouthful.
After a bath she keeps repeating, "How wonderful I feel, it's so good." We have a large Victorian bathroom, with cast-iron bath and attractive fittings. She couldn't have wished for more luxurious surroundings. Such a contrast to her flat, with no electricity; and not having changed her clothes for three days. Jamie has always insisted on being clean although she doesn't bother when high on crack.

We sort through her clothes from the flat. I had picked up, by mistake, a number of Collette's clothes, including a very good black leather jacket. Jamie decides to put it on, with a pair of cream jeans, a black bodysuit, and her short heavy black leather boots, all from my attic.

"The court wanted to send me to the Birmingham probation hostel again," she says, "but they refused to have me, saying I was involved in drugs when I stayed there...and the rest," she jokes. "Then they wanted to send me to a hostel in Stratford," she says, "but I told them I didn't think you'd take too kindly to that," and we laugh.

Jamie chats about her male friends. "They are dying to meet you mum. I'm always telling them about you and your cooking. I promise I will only introduce you to the decent ones," she says.
I assume 'decent' means dangerous, rather than very dangerous friends.

"Have you had any crack lately," I enquire as I normally do when we meet.
"Not much, not as much as usual. It's getting scarce because there have been so many arrests. But I wouldn't mind selling crack again."
"Again," I question. "So you've done it before?"
"Well, you know," she says, smiling to herself.
"Jamie, your new flat will become a crackhouse if you aren't careful," I warn her.
"No way," she replies. She goes on to say, "I'm on bail for possession of a Class A Drug. Nothing was on me at the time but I admitted to having crack shortly before being arrested."

"Mum, Gibbo wants to meet you," she says. "He was the guy who phoned your house recently – the one with the strong Jamaican accent."

Jamie tells me, "My friends are keen to decorate my flat. I'll get a £1000 loan from the social."
Yet another loan from the D.S.S., I think to myself. And they never get paid back what is, in effect, taxpayer's money.
Suddenly Jamie panics, "My gold bracelet. I wonder what's happened to it? The one I swapped for coke the other day." Then it dawns on her, "Oh, it was in the bag I left in the punter's car – the one who attacked me."

We talk about the false names she uses. She is amused because the police don't believe her real name is Jamie.
"Why do you use the names of people you know Ashleigh, Laura, and Elenor?" I ask.

"When I get caught I don't have time to think," she says. "I just give the first name that enters my head – people I know, I suppose."
"Mum, when is Kate's Wedding?" she asks yet again. Jamie's memory is very bad.

By late afternoon it is time to start thinking about Jamie returning to Leamington station to catch the train to Reading. She wants some money, not having a penny on her. She gives me her income support book signed so I can cash it, and in exchange I give her £30.

In the car she says, "A guy wants to set me up selling for him – but I need to find someone reliable to sell the rock for me, otherwise I might be tempted to take it myself."
Leaving Jamie at the rail station, she agrees to keep in contact while at Reading,

27th March – Sunday

I go over to Jamie's flat this afternoon, with Pat and Max, to return Collette's clothes, worried that she might think someone has burgled the flat.
When we arrive at the car park of the flats, we are startled by a sudden loud tapping on the window.

I can't believe my eyes...it is Jamie! She laughs, knowing I think she is at the hostel at Reading. As we get out of the car she says, "I missed the train yesterday," but I don't believe her because I dropped her off ten minutes before the train was due. I should have realized she was up to something. Looking back, it seemed strange at the time Jamie had no clothes, only her bag...I have been conned again! Jamie says,

"There will be a warrant out for my arrest but I'll just keep a low profile. Don't worry. It will take six weeks for the system to find me. By then I'll have had another court appearance."
We make our way up to the flat. Jamie says, "Collette went back to the flats with a £50 client the night before last, only to find you had locked the bottom lock, for which she had no key. Needless to say, she lost her client. We were locked out all night and had to stay at Gibbo's place."

The flat is in an awful mess after our visit the other night. Collette sits herself in the middle of the floor, crossed-legged, putting her make-up on. She peers into a broken, jagged, piece of mirror about 9" square. Jamie changes into little white shorts over black leggings. She takes the mirror from Collette and puts her make-up on.

It is four o'clock in the afternoon, and they are both transformed, ready for work. Looking less tired than of late, and with fresh clothes and make-up, Jamie's day has just begun.

She and Collette talk of going to a blues party tonight. They have been preparing to venture into the seedy twilight world of drugs, guns and violence, but first they must work to pay for their habit. The girls whisper to each other. What are they up to I wonder?

I hear Jamie say, "Did you tell them my mum's here?" They chat about something in the kitchen. Perhaps it is coke, or another illegal substance? They appear to be on edge waiting for us to leave.

I begin to wonder – is Jamie's flat a crackhouse after all, as I predicted it would be? Jamie kisses Max, and we hug and say our goodbyes.

Heading for home, we feel secure in the knowledge that we are returning to the comfort and warmth of our homes in our quiet market town; where residents get on with their suburban lives, oblivious to the dangerous world which exists just a few miles down the road.

Crackhouse – 1994

1st April – Good Friday

Max comes into my bed this morning, hugging and kissing me. He is so gentle and kind.
"You are my angel from heaven," I tell him.
He knows I give him love and security; and is fully aware his mummy can't look after him, even though she loves him very much.

Only two months to Kate's wedding and there is little chance Jamie will be going. She was in such a state last Sunday when we dropped her off. I've still heard nothing from her – something is wrong and the balloon is about to burst.

3rd April – Easter Sunday

Jamie made contact last night and we are to meet her today. As I sit watching Max play with his toys, he is so happy and well adjusted, appearing to accept the situation.
I am pleased I have decided to be open with him. Should he hear anything, whether it be on the answer phone or other people talking, he already knows the truth.

I call in to see Dionne on my way to pick up Jamie. She is feeling very low and tells me her brother Steve has been arrested for attempted murder with Clinton, and is now on remand.

Max and I drive up to the car park and glance over to the block of flats. I can see Jamie waving from her balcony up on the third floor balcony. She comes down to join us, no coat on, even though there is a sharp bitter wind.
As we drive back home she says, "I haven't eaten for four days because I had no money.
I was working but got arrested. Fortunately, by using my false name I got away with it. But it's now too risky and I can't work until my court hearing is out of the way.
When I had a packet of crisps the other day," she says, "they made me sick."

My ears prick up and alarm bells ring. Is she genuinely not eating because of lack of money or is it because of drugs, anorexia, or pregnancy?

Excitedly she talks about her new boyfriend, "His name is Jay, a Yardie from Mosside. He's small, so I can handle him and won't let him hit me. He bought me a Getto Blaster and, as you can imagine, I'm not very popular with the neighbours. He lives in a world of guns – not just one, but many."

As I look across to Jamie, I notice the rolled-back cuffs of her shirt revealing the many red scars on her arms from the attempted suicide. I hope they fade, although she doesn't seem bothered. Jamie is far more concerned about losing weight.

"Someone has burnt a hole in my new carpet," she says. "When you have a place of your own, you realise other people don't respect your property." It is as if the old values she has been brought up with are shining through.
She tells me, "I've got electricity and hot water in the flat now."

Back at home Jamie is her usual self – diving into the fridge at the first opportunity and eating everything in sight. Shortly afterwards, she tucks into a meal of baked potatoes and juicy chicken in white sauce. A warm satisfied smile appears across her face.
"Mum, can I wash the things I'm wearing?" she enquires.
Jamie goes up to the bathroom to undress and as I enter the room I notice how thin she is, standing there in her black tights and bra. "I'm seven stone on your scales," she proudly declares.
Worried, I tell her, "Jamie, don't lose any more weight. You are slim enough."

"Did you tell the Council that you have Ben, to get the flat?" I ask.
"Why shouldn't I," she replies. "It's about time they gave me somewhere to live."
As the conversation continues, I nip in and out of the kitchen making notes as she talks. It is the only way I can stop my brain getting overloaded and remember everything. After the meal, Jamie complains of tummy pains and is sick. I am convinced she has an eating disorder.

Before going back home she searches through the dressing-up clothes box and comes up with another new look.

She is wearing the long black skinny rib sleeveless dress down to the ankles, which she arrived in, her heavy short laced black boots and brown fur muff. Her loose hair is topped with a black velvet pill box hat covered with green, red and gold beading. She finishes the total look with a red unbuttoned shirt worn as a jacket.

No longer, standing before me, is the youthful-looking girl who always tries to pass for fifteen. Here is a sophisticated woman, looking much older than her twenty-one years, more like thirty-something. The loss of weight in the face and the heavy use of drugs, are now beginning to tell on her.

As we leave the house I pop a bowl of homemade apple crumble into a carrier bag and a packet of assorted biscuits. At least, I console myself, she will have something to eat for the next twenty-four hours. "
I don't suppose you have any cutlery at the flat?" I ask.
"Oh, I'll pop down to the take-away and get a plastic spoon," she says. "We don't have anything in our kitchen."
Pat pops a bag of chocolates into Jamie's hand as we leave, and she tucks into them as I drive her back to Coventry.
"Have you had any crack lately?" I ask her.
"Of course," she replies. "Jay sells it, so I don't have to pay."
We go to the car park at the back of the flats because it is raining heavily which means she won't have to walk too far. As we drive around she points out, "Jay was in that taxi which just passed us." We pull up and she says uneasily, "I won't introduce you to him."
"Because he's dangerous?" I ask.
"You could say that," she says, hurriedly jumping out of the car.

During our journey I have been speaking to a hard, stubborn woman – very much on edge and very scared. There has been a strained atmosphere during the afternoon and Jamie will not talk. Usually she bubbles over with news; who she has been with, what she has been doing and where. There is no usual kiss on the cheek, hug, or proper goodbye. As she runs towards the entrance door to the flats, I get out of the car and call her back. "We need to confirm details about picking you up from Leamington station on Ben's birthday."
She is jumpy, restless, and obviously wants me to leave.

A couple of youths in anoraks, faces hidden under their hoods, walk through the door, and her eyes follow and survey them. She looks as if she intends to do a runner at any time.

We say goodbye. Reluctantly and awkwardly Jamie lets me kiss her on the cheek, then disappears quickly into the flats. For a moment I sit in the car and pause for thought. Those youths – perhaps she thought they were police, or maybe they are there to buy crack...from her flat. Heavy hearted, I return home knowing things are very bad and I am scared.

5th April – Tuesday. Ben's First Birthday

Will Jamie be there, I wonder, as I drive up to the station. Chances are she won't turn up...and she doesn't.

I told her I don't intend to hang around if she's not there.

Max and I head for the foster home. Ben is in good form and started to walk a couple of days ago. Linda says he is much more relaxed and happy these days. He loves Linda and John very much and calls them 'mum' and 'dad'.

I find it so sad that chances are he will leave them soon to start a new life with adoptive parents. But it must be better than anything Jamie can offer him. She hasn't turned up for his first birthday which proves how committed she is to her son.

It has been a very sad day for me. I remember last summer Jamie remarked how Jackie had gone to London on the game, spent all her money on crack and said, "Isn't it awful Mum. She didn't even bother to see her son on his birthday and give him a present".

I remarked to Jamie, at the time, that she herself was on the game and spent her money on crack.

"But at least I buy the children presents," she said, "and turn up for birthdays."

Things must be really awful for Jamie, not having turned up today. She had good intentions to buy Ben some toys saying, "At least I have a cheque book to get them with."

Leaving Linda's, I decide to head for Coventry, to cash Jamie's income support book at the named post office. She gave it with me in lieu of the £30 I had lent her when she left for the hostel at Reading.

The post office counter woman looks me up and down suspiciously, and informs me, "There's a stop on this book," and promptly takes it from me. Bang goes my £30. I won't see that again.

I feel guilty, believing everyone in the shop suspects I am the criminal. I am furious with Jamie.

Looking back over the past two weeks, I realise Jamie is drifting away from us and our contact is now by a very fine thread. Perhaps she knew, when I dropped her off on Sunday, that she wouldn't be seeing us again. Pat has remarked how strange Jamie was before I took her back. She didn't give me the normal kiss before getting out of the car. When she eventually makes contact, it will probably be as if nothing has happened.

This evening I receive a call – but the person hangs up. Was it Jamie?

6th April – Wednesday

Feeling very low, I call at the Resource Centre at Stratford Hospital. The events or crisis always hit me the next day, once the adrenalin wears off.

Yesterday I felt so sad for Ben that his mummy didn't turn up; am very angry about the income support book having a stop on it; I'm cross because I have lost £30; and I am unhappy that I am losing my daughter.

I tell the counsellor, "Losing a child through death, you can grieve. But you can't grieve a drug abuser – and yet I have lost the daughter I love so much."

After talking I feel much better and shed a tear. I am desperately tired and need to sleep. I believe sleep is one of the best healers.

8th April – Friday

I have been criticised for my handling of the situation these past four years, but have coped with it in a way that was right for me. I was once told to always use my gut feeling, regardless what others say, and this is what I have done.

The knowledge of what Jamie is doing, and where she is living, helps me. Not having contact, or knowing where she was, would be an even worse nightmare. I have grown accustomed to the dealers, drugs, crime and violence she has associated herself with and accept her chosen life, even though I disagree with it – and she knows.

Freedom of choice is what our society in this country is all about. She must go her way and I go mine. A spell in prison would give her respite and a chance to look at her life. She would probably return back to her friends and drugs.

Jamie may get counselling and medical attention, something she has never had much of. I suppose there is always a glimmer of hope.

I have found myself praying things will sort themselves out and that Jamie will find peace instead of torment – I know God will hear my prayers and something will happen one day.

At this moment, things are very wrong – I now wait for a call, or the police knocking on the door!

11th April – Monday

No news from Jamie. It seems strange – I feel free of her. Suddenly I realise this is the first time I am not worrying about the children and the danger they may be in. Ben is safe and happy with Linda and John, while Max continues to be settled and happy with me.

15th April – Friday

Still I hear nothing from Jamie.

A canvassing councillor, for the local elections, turns up on my doorstep today and states, "It's about time parents took responsibility for their children's actions. They are too often to blame."

I am upset with her remark and tell her my story. I speak of the failures in probation, the legal system, and social services. "I know I've done everything I can to support Jamie and have been a good Mum," I tell her firmly.

After listening to what I say, she sympathizes and says, "You must take it further. Write to your M.P. Alan Howarth."

20th April – Wednesday

It is nearly three weeks since I last heard from Jamie. Over the past two weeks I have been relaxed and feel much better.

Suddenly, today, things have changed. I am weepy and have that awful feeling that things are very wrong. I wait and anticipate – I'm frightened – what news or crisis is looming? Is Jamie ill, or even alive? Dionne hasn't had any contact with Jamie but says she will let me know if something is wrong. If she is kidnapped or disappears, there is no way I would know.

We hold our support meeting this evening. Sue, the family drug worker, brings along two male fellow workers who are very suspicious of our motives for starting up the group. They make it clear we should not talk to pupils in schools about the effects of drugs on our families because they say, "We don't believe in horror tactics."

We are annoyed and tell them, "The kids have to know the truth of how drugs have devastated our lives, and that of our children. If it means we have to tell the truth, even if it is a horror story, then we must, and insist, "We are not counsellors, but can support parents because we have first hand experience."

24th April – Sunday

2.45 a.m: The phone has just rung – I jump out of bed, my heart pounding. It must be Jamie...but no one is there. I disconnect the phone to get some sleep.

A Head Teacher on T.V. states, "Children who fail are often those whose parents have shown little or no interest in school life."
I am mad. I certainly gave time, energy and interest to Jamie in her school life, more so than many parents, and couldn't have done anything more. It is so easy for others who haven't been through it to criticise.

27th April – Wednesday

I ring the police who tell me, "Jamie was last seen nine days ago and, under the circumstances, she appears okay."
Today I have felt really bad, and tense when the phone rings. As time goes by there is less and less chance she will make contact.

28th April – Thursday

The answer phone is flashing – Jamie has left a message. "Mum, I've written you a letter and you'll get it in the post. See you later."

My heart beats fast. Why is she writing? Will the letter give an explanation for her silence? Is she in hospital? Maybe she is in prison?

Her voice and diction sound rough – no longer my bouncy, bubbly Jamie, which is normally a sign she has been using heavily. My happy relaxed day is no more. I get into bed wondering where is Jamie? Fortunately, exhausted, I drop off to sleep immediately.

29th April – Friday

Midnight: The phone rings...but no one is there. Since I last saw Jamie I have received three such phone calls. I go to bed and turn the phone off – I must have a break from this awful world of drugs.

The weather is beautiful today and I do some gardening. My garden is my haven of peace and sanity.

1st May – Sunday

It is over four weeks since I last saw Jamie. I doubt there will be a letter in the post tomorrow, as her telephone message indicated. Some would ask why I don't go looking for her? But I know she is in a very dangerous situation, and it would be crazy for me to go anywhere near her flat.

3rd May – Tuesday

9.30 p.m: Thank goodness, Jamie phones tonight from the police station. She has been locked up for loitering, so at least I know she is safe.
"Are you okay?" I ask. "We haven't heard from you for so long."
"I've been in trouble lately and been staying with friends," she replies.
"Are you aware it's over four weeks since we spoke?" I ask.
Quite casually, she says, "I realised that the other day."
"What about the letter you said was in the post?" I ask.
"I lost the stamp," she laughs.
"I may be remanded tomorrow, in Sheffield, and they say 'bail on warrant'. She promises to keep in touch and I have peace of mind she is safe tonight.

4th May – Wednesday

I receive a call from probation, mid-day. "We understand from your daughter, Jamie, that you may be able to accommodate her?"
Horrified, I immediately say "No," which is so hard to do. But probation are looking for an easy option and I am sure Jamie doesn't expect it. I am very angry.
Later, Jamie leaves a message. "Can you come over, and get the keys from my flat and some clothes please? I'm going to Sheffield with a police escort. Don't worry if you can't get over."
Maybe I'll go in the morning.

6.15 p.m. Another call from Jamie: "I'm appearing in Court tomorrow morning. Can you ring my friend and let him know I'm alright?"

The Jamaican sounds very friendly on the phone. He is extremely worried, wondering what has happened to Jamie, and is relieved when I tell him she is in custody.

He says, "Angela, she's in grave danger."

I am curious, and ask, "Who am I speaking to?"

"Dexter," he says.

5th May – Thursday

Jamie rings, very happy. "Mum, I've been released from Sheffield. See you later."

7th May – Saturday

"Can I come over on Monday?" asks Jamie.

I don't want her here and am taken aback. My mind races. What should I say?

"I'd rather come to see you," I tell her. I need to know she is okay, and arrange to meet her on Tuesday.

News announcement on T.V. this evening – "Another prostitute found murdered in the Midland's." Is there no end to all these murders? It could be Jamie next.

10th May – Tuesday

I arrive 1.00 p.m. in Coventry – no Jamie as arranged. Is she in custody? I wait back at home for a call from her – but nothing.

Evening: Jamie rings, "I've been at the pub drinking," she says. "Don't be cross with me for not being there. I tried to phone you last night but you were engaged. I've been in custody.

I'll have the £30 for you tomorrow. I'll get £890 from Income Support as a loan and as soon as I have it, I'll give up my flat."

"I don't suppose I will ever see my money," I tell her.

Jamie says, "I'm having to keep away from my flat and the area around – it's too dangerous." I am pleased she sounds bright and her old self.

15th May – Sunday

I hear nothing from Jamie. It is six weeks today since we last saw her, and the only contact has been an occasional phone call. She must be in real trouble.

Two weeks to Kate's wedding. I hope and pray nothing will happen to Jamie to spoil things.
I go out with friends for a meal and skittles tonight, but can't relax – too many reminders of Jamie. The Juke Box plays the music she loves. A young girl, about her age, laughs with her mum – this could have been Jamie and I had things not gone so wrong.

25th May – Wednesday

Seven weeks since we last saw Jamie. As the days go by I worry more and more about her and decide to contact the police. I need to know if she has been seen.
"Jamie was arrested last night," says the officer. "If I see her tonight I'll phone back to let you know she's okay."
I am so relieved to know she has been seen around.
Message on the phone, "Mum, this is Jamie. You know I don't like speaking on the phone. Just to let you know I'm okay. I'll ring you back."
But she doesn't.

29th May – Sunday
Kate's Wedding

We are very excited. Max, Pat and myself set off for London for Kate and Marcus's wedding. As we arrive at the church I wonder who Jamie's relatives are, trying to place faces to names. Kate looks beautiful and radiant, Marcus very handsome.
Family photos are taken on the green by the church. Photographer calls, "Brothers and sisters please on Kate's side." Sadly there are none. Max and I are invited on the photo to represent Jamie. I feel very honoured to be asked.
At the reception Tina, Jamie's mother, says sadly, "I had hoped Jamie could have come to the wedding."
Reluctantly I tell her, "I haven't seen Jamie for 8 weeks and don't know how to contact her."
Music rings out, children chase balloons across the floor and Max, looking super in his little sailor suit, has a wonderful time. Tina glances at him and, although sad at not seeing Jamie, she must be happy to see her grandson.

I am introduced to Jamie's aunts and uncles from up north, who generally agree that Jamie has probably inherited the genes of her grandfather who is an alcoholic. I have read that alcohol and drug addiction are closely linked, the theory being that addictive genes pass from one generation to another.

I chat to Jamie's grandmother Ellen, a lovely lady. "I hope Jamie understands that she was adopted because of family circumstances at the time," she says.
Ellen tells me she left her husband and moved away with her children. While Tina was expecting Jamie, her two-year-old daughter, Kate, was in care. "There is no way, living in such cramped conditions, was I able to take on another baby," says Ellen.

"I know exactly what you mean," I say to her. "I am in your shoes now with the pending adoption of Ben. I expect he will blame me, his grandmother, for not keeping him." It is plain Ellen and I have so much in common.

Tina smokes nervously and stares at the dance floor. "Can you pass a message to Jamie?" she asks. "Please tell her she was missed here today."
"If she makes contact, I will pass the message on," I assure her.
Tired and happy after such a wonderful day, we journey back home. As we chat on the train Pat remarks, "It's amazing how alike Tina and Jamie are – they are identical."

30th May – Monday

A West Indian guy phones asking, "Is Jamie there? She said she was coming over to see you today."
"I know nothing about that," I tell him. "She phoned and left a message on the answer phone, saying she's okay."
"She was fine when I saw her yesterday," he says. I am relieved to have this news.

Jamie rings this evening as if nothing is wrong. "I've started a new job," she says. "I went into Debenhams today and took a pair of short dungarees, denim trousers, bodysuits, and socks. I just walked through doors and nothing was tagged. I took the lot home and decided to do it again. Next time I'll try Marks & Spencers."

"Jamie, we went to Kate's wedding yesterday," I tell her. "Tina asked me to tell you that you were missed there."

Jamie becomes weepy, asking, "Why didn't you let me know when it was?"

"I give up, Jamie. How many times have I told you? And I sensed you were in dreadful danger so I didn't dare go to your flat."

"Yes," says Jamie, "I was, but not anymore. I've left my flat and am at Dexter's now. He's been good and is getting me sorted out. I have a new hairstyle, streaked and shoulder length. I look sixteen again."

We arrange to meet tomorrow and she promises, "I'll be there. Don't worry about the picnic. I will bring something along."

31st May – Tuesday

Max and I meet Jamie outside British Home Stores.

How painfully thin she looks, her collarbone sticking out and her top half so scrawny. She is dressed in her newly acquired white short dungarees, skimpy pale blue top, and trainers.

We set off for the Memorial park where we spread our blanket under the large oak tree. It is a perfect warm sunny day with bright blue skies. As we tuck into prawn sandwiches, plump chicken breasts and tuna pate provided by Jamie, she declares, "These are courtesy of Marks & Spencers. I just took them and openly walked out of the shop without being stopped."

I feel a pang of conscience – but decide to go ahead and enjoy the sumptuous feast before me.

Jamie talks of her shoplifting activities over the past couple of days. "It's so easy," she says, "Yesterday I stole two silk shirts from M & S at £35 each, and then sold them on for half price. I've got an order for two NEXT suits for a funeral.

Do you think I look better with extra weight on?" she goes on. "I've actually put on weight after having been six stone. Dexter makes me have breakfast before I get up in the morning.

I'm his bit of stuff on the side, since he's got a steady girlfriend. He's in his forties, an old style Yardie," she says.

"The young Yardies from Jamaica are awful, threatening with guns all the time, and they threatened me. They wanted the sole right to sell drugs from my flat, which is now a crackhouse. Lester and Dexter stepped in to protect me and Dexter said he would use a gun if he had to."

I am horrified and ask, "Are you still on crack?"

"Yes," she replies.

I show Jamie the video and photos of Kate's wedding and tell her, "The family rushed out of church at the end of the service to have a smoke." She smiles. "If I had been there, I would have sat at the back of the church 'chasing the drago.'

All Jamie talks about is shoplifting, drugs, and yardies. It is a good thing she didn't attend the wedding. It would have been so embarrassing.

She points to a huge yellow bruise on her shoulder saying, "Dexter did it – almost as a game, with the base of a glass. I had to see how long I could put up with him hitting me. I won," she chuckles.

I am horrified.

Jamie is wearing a small gold necklace and I enquire, "Where did you get that from?"

"Someone robbed a house," she says, "and gave me a load of jewellery including a diamond ring."

At the end our happy picnic Jamie stands astride, hands on hips, shouting, "Hurry up mum, I've got my shoplifting to do."

"You'll get caught," I warn her.

"Mum, do I really look like a shoplifter!" she exclaims.

As we drive into the city centre Jamie points at the police station saying, "That's where I'll probably be in an hour's time."

We drop Jamie off and she skips into the distance, looking very much a lively fourteen year old – very different from nine week's ago when she looked thirty odd."

Crackhead

Caribbean Dreams – 1994

1st June – Wednesday

"I've been in custody for shoplifting," says Jamie, phoning from the police station. "I was caught an hour after leaving you yesterday.

This morning I appeared in court for cheque fraud and I've been convicted, but will be sentenced in three weeks' time. They are sending me off to Risley prison tomorrow.
Could you collect some clothes for me from my flat?" she asks. "It's so hot and sticky, and I've only got what I stand up in. Also, any chance you could pop some cigarettes, coke and chocolate into the station please?"

Cautiously, I knock on Jamie's flat door. Someone shouts out, "Who is it?"
As Jamie instructed, I reply, "Jamie's Mum."
Suki, lets me in. She is about twenty, pale, spotty and very thin; wearing dungaree shorts and T shirt. I look at her with sadness in my heart – a mum is probably out there worrying herself sick about her daughter, just as I am.
"Jamie is off to Risley and I've come to collect her things," I explain.
Suki introduces me to Lester who enquires, "How's Jamie? I'll go and see her in Risley" (it is very unlikely he will). His hair sticks up, with one long Rasta lock hanging down his back.
I am curious and ask, "Can I touch it?"
"It's real," he laughs. It feels like a coarse sheep's fleece.
I learn later that Lester is one of the most dangerous guys around!
After collecting up five sacks of Jamie's dirty washing, I thank them and head for home.

3rd June – Friday

Unable to get the clothes to Jamie yesterday, because she was escorted up to Risley early, I decide to take them up to her.
I arrive at the high walled prison and make my way to the visitor's reception, feeling like a fish out of water. Everyone looks very

171

streetwise. Doors are locked behind us and we are ushered briskly to the office.

As I hand over Jamie's clothes they inform me, "We can't take them, and you won't be able to see Jamie. She is waiting to be transferred to Newhall prison." I try to persuade them to search the clothes and give them to Jamie's escort, but they refuse. I despair, having travelled four hours to get to Risley.

As I walk away my name is suddenly called out and Jamie enters the room. They allow us a few minutes together. We sit either side of a long line of tables.

She is wearing the same clothes I saw her in five days earlier. Pleased to see me, Jamie smiles, but is very disappointed she can't have her clothes. The bag sits by my side, a foot from Jamie...it is absolutely ridiculous!

"What do you think the outcome of court will be?" I ask.

"Probation hopefully," she replies. I am astounded, especially after the previous probation fiasco. Jamie names the charges against her, which are: shoplifting, receiving stolen goods (cheques), cheque fraud, soliciting and possession of a Class A drug.

Her name is called out, to be transferred to Newhall prison, and we part with a kiss. I post the clothes to Newhall from a nearby village in the hope Jamie will get them by morning.

After an awful journey back along the motorway, I arrive home exhausted, physically and emotionally. For the next two weeks I can rest...Jamie is safe

7th June – Tuesday

I appear on a local radio programme with a recently retired drugs co-ordinator for schools. When I say we have a big drug problem with youngsters, he argues otherwise. On the programme he states, "We must keep it in perspective. Figures indicate three out of four young people never even touch a drug in their lives. Although drugs are more widely available, the figures have stayed fairly constant."

Our support group has interviewed youngsters and indications are that at least fifty per cent of youngsters are trying drugs, many as young as thirteen. I am very angry and write telling him, "You are not living in the real world."

22nd June – Wednesday

Jamie appears in court. I overhear her solicitor ask, "Jamie, is the magistrate a client of yours?"

"I turned him down once," she says. There is concern this could go against her.

After the case has been put before the magistrate, Jamie's solicitor makes a plea on her behalf. "She has lost her son to a care order and hopes to make contact with him. Also, she wishes to get assistance with her drug problem. I recommend probation for Jamie who desperately needs help."

The magistrates give their verdict, "Consideration has been given to the offences which are so serious, and we have decided on a custodial sentence.

Crime involving the use of stolen plastic cards is a blight upon society, and so serious it merits loss of liberty." Jamie is sentenced to eight months imprisonment.

Stunned and angry, she shouts across the courtroom, "I've lost my son, I've lost him forever now."

My heart aches and I have difficulty in keeping back the tears. These words will haunt me forever.

Later Jamie phones upset, but brightens up as we speak. She says, "I've got an £800 loan from social security. It's safe, and I intend to visit Jamaica for six months when I get out of here."

26th June – Sunday

There have been very precious memories these past few years – Max meeting his father and grandparents for the first time; Jamie meeting her natural mother and sister; Christmas dinner 1993; and Jamie's twenty-first birthday.

Today, we travel to the West Country to see Max's father. I warn Mikey beforehand, "Max is usually shy with strangers."

Surprisingly, when he meets his father, he is very relaxed, and immediately calls him "Daddy". It is amazing. There seems to be a chemical bond, just as if Max has always known him.

Mikey looks so well. I remember the nervous, shaking lad I met at the pub three years ago, when Max came into my care. The drugs and drink had taken their toll; for two years Mikey had no contact with his family. To see him so well today is a miracle, and I hug and congratulate him.

29th June – Wednesday

Jamie was transferred to Drake Hall open prison in Staffordshire two days ago. This morning I receive a call from her, "Mum, have you heard?"
"Heard what?" I ask.
"I'm in Manchester," she says.
"Manchester Prison or hospital?" I enquire, worried.
"No," she says. "I've escaped. I'm in hiding."
Am I hearing right...escaped?

Jamie recalls, "It was my idea. On Monday, a few hours after arriving from Risley, a cell mate and I climbed out the window. We ran past the offices, under the fence and over the fields. A passing taxi picked us up and took us to Manchester. I'm okay but thought you might be worried."

"I'm surprised the police haven't been in touch with me Jamie," I tell her and she agrees with me.
"Mum, I am okay and not on drugs, so don't worry.
I intend to put in a plea," she says, because I don't think I should be in prison, and that's why I escaped. Have to go, will keep in touch."

My heart beats fast -- no three month rest, no relaxing, no mental unwinding, as I thought. Jamie is back on the helter skelter of life once more and I wait with baited breath for the police to knock on my door.

30th June – Thursday

Jamie phones. "Dexter is looking after me and I'm bored. Mum I need to see you urgently. Can you get some photos together for me?" She sounds weepy. There is a pause and then she says, "I'm going to cry". She pulls herself together, "I'm in trouble and danger. I'm getting a passport this afternoon and leaving the country tomorrow." Crying she says, "You probably won't ever see me again."
We arrange to meet early tomorrow morning.

1st July – Friday

Middle of the night: the front door bell rings.
Two police officers stand before me. Heart pounding and bleary eyed, I invite them in. "Are you aware your daughter has absconded?" they ask.
I tell them, "Jamie rang yesterday, saying she is in Manchester."

"We would like to look around the house," they say and proceed to search the cellar, bedrooms, the attic, and finally Max's room. He sleeps peacefully, totally unaware of the two policemen searching his cupboards. Satisfied all is well, they quietly leave at 3.45 a.m.

There is little point in going back to bed. As dawn breaks and birds sing, I pray Jamie is safe and prepare myself for the expected stressful day ahead. I find photos depicting Jamie's life, and have written to her saying how much we love her. God give us both the strength to go on.
It is a scorching hot day with blue skies. Max and I set off early for the coach station where we are to meet Jamie. She arrives, looking very pale, and has put on quite a bit of weight. All she possesses in the world are the clothes she stands in – a pair of new Levi jeans, a lacy top, heavy black boots and a blue denim jacket.
Jamie is bubbly saying, "Mum, I've been off drugs for four weeks now." I believe she is telling the truth. This is my daughter Jamie, not the addict standing before me.

As we drive along she looks through the photos and talks about Jamaica. "I've got a false passport and it's quite a good likeness. Our tickets cost around £350 each, which I bought with my grant, and we fly from Heathrow tomorrow morning. If you don't hear from me by mid-day tomorrow, you will know I'm okay." At that point she gets weepy and puts the photos to one side.

"Dexter's family live near Montego Bay in Jamaica and that's where I'm going. His parents are old and wealthy," she says.
How naive of her. I suspect he comes from a very poor background because he can't read or write.
"People are chasing Dexter with guns because he owes lots of money," she says. "That's why he must leave for Jamaica, otherwise he'll be dead next."

Pat joins us and we head for the playground down by the river. While Max runs around, Jamie tells us, "I've been charged with fraud for three cheque books, whereas it's more likely I've done three hundred books."

We drive to Dover's Hill on the edge of the Cotswolds. It is a beautiful warm day, with magnificent views across to Wales. As we relax eating our picnic, Pat smiles, "I wonder what people around here would think if they knew we were with an absconder." We laugh.

Crackhead

Back at the car park we sort out clothes retrieved from my attic. Jamie holds them up to see if they fit. In the bottom of the bag, she finds the small precious bottle of perfume Pat gave her for her twenty-first birthday and, holding it up, we all smile.

As we make our way back to Coventry, Jamie talks of some of her clients over the years, including a chairman of one of Britain's top industries, magistrates, and two judges.
"We have to leave for London by 6.00 o'clock," says Jamie. If you don't hear anything by Sunday you can assume I've got to Jamaica okay."

Next we call at Gibbo's flat. Feeling sick, I turn to Pat, "What if Dexter lets Jamie down?"
After a couple of tense minutes waiting Jamie returns panicking, "Dexter's not there."
She is getting hot, agitated, and tearful.
The atmosphere is electric and we realise something is wrong and although Jamie paid for the air tickets, Dexter has them.
We look for a phone box and Jamie rings her friend Sindy.
We are all feeling the strain as time ticks by. It is getting close to 6.00 p.m., and we keep our fingers crossed that Dexter hasn't done the dirty on Jamie.
Returning from the phone-box she has a slight smile on her face – perhaps everything is okay after all?

Instructions are that we collect Sindy, her friend, outside the hospital. As we drive slowly along the road Sindy runs towards us, and quickly jumps into the car. "We have to be careful because of video cameras everywhere along the road," she says.
Jamie ducks down as a police car drives past, and then as a riot van crosses our path.

She introduces Sindy. "I'm hiding at Sindy's place," says Jamie. As we drive along, Sindy says that she uses heroin occasionally, but stresses she isn't a prostitute.
Outside the house, Jamie gives Max and myself a big hug. "Thank you mum for everything," she says. As we part, she looks back quickly over her shoulder with tears in her eyes, and then runs hurriedly into the house.
Sindy reassures me, "Don't worry, I'll look after her."

176

As the hours tick by we assume, because there is no news, Jamie must be on her way to the Caribbean.

4th July – Monday

We have heard nothing from Jamie and wonder if she is there by now. I phone Drake Hall prison and ask, "Can you keep Jamie's possessions safe. I believe she has gone to Jamaica."

"Lucky thing," says the officer. She makes no further enquiries as to when, or where I last saw Jamie and isn't interested in her escape. Surely someone at the prison must want to know where she is? I can't believe it.

This evening Dionne phones. I tell her Jamie has escaped from prison, and ask if she can check if Dexter and Jamie are still around.

7th July – Thursday

Dionne phones back, "My friend saw Jamie last night and today, but no one will say where she's staying."

If Jamie is not on her way to Jamaica, why hasn't she contacted me?

12th July –Tuesday

Middle of the night the phone rings. Heart pounding and half asleep, I answer. "It's the police phoning from the Walsgrave Hospital. Jamie is here."

"Is it an overdose?" I enquire.

"I believe so, but she seems okay. Have you got a message for her?" he asks.

"Yes, tell her I love her. I can't get over but will be in touch."

Early morning I phone the hospital and they tell me she has been discharged into police custody. I phone the station and they say Jamie has gone to prison, but they are not sure where.

Six o'clock in the evening Jamie calls and is very weepy. After a pause...she says, "Mum, I had an abortion a week and a half ago."

I feel really sorry for her. "I did wonder if you were pregnant Jamie. Are you okay? And what about Jamaica?"

"I meant to go but things went wrong. Dexter hasn't gone yet but intends to.

Can you visit me here at Drake Hall?" she asks.

"Yes, I'll come when I can." As I hang up, I feel a lot happier.

This afternoon Marie, the TV producer, asks if I am still interested in doing the documentary? I confirm I am.

Crackhead

17th July – Sunday

As we hand in our visiting order at Drake Hall, the officer smiles and asks if Jamie got back okay? She was the woman I spoke to on the phone when Jamie escaped.

I enquire, "Do girls run away often?"

She replies cheerfully, "Oh yes, all the time, especially on their day or weekend leave."

I can't believe it – what a joke!

As we enter the prison the atmosphere is very relaxed. A voice shouts out our name. Nervously, we enter a canteen-like room and our eyes scan the crowd for Jamie. There, over the far side, we can see her smiling, and sitting at a small square table. Jamie's hair is a mass of thin plaits all over her head. Admiring them, I say, "Someone's been busy."

"Yes," she says, "My cell mate did them. It's so boring in here."

Pat asks, "Well, what happened then Jamie?"

"Don't talk about it," she says. I can see she is choked and suggest we discuss it later.

"My clothes were stolen in prison while I was out," she says looking fed up. "They've provided me with this 'T' shirt and these denim shorts." Jamie doesn't seem too bothered, knowing that she has a few good quality clothes safe at Sindy's.

She laughs about her escape from prison, and points to the window. "It was easy, we lifted the fence just outside by the gate. I will do it again if I get half a chance."

I mention to Jamie the BBC film and she is keen to be involved.

The subject of Dexter, and Jamaica, crops up. "We definitely intended to go that Friday night. The tickets can't be used now," she says. "All that money, £700 odd, down the drain-- but I've still got my passport.

If I had gone to Jamaica I wouldn't have had an abortion. I would have kept the baby.

When I handed myself in last Monday night, I'd been drinking heavily. Someone laced my drink with ecstasy. I was hanging over my balcony and Sindy saved me by grabbing my legs. Then I went unconscious. Sindy was covered in awful bruises and we are both lucky to be alive.

The prison have organised a business course, which I can continue at college when I get out. The wardens joke about me putting it to good use on cheques," she laughs.

Jamie is pleased she still gets income support for Ben. I just don't understand it. The Department of Social Security spoke to me in February checking if Jamie still has her child – yet five months later they still pay her the money.

She tells us, "The Council are boarding my flat up. I'll go back on the housing list and will probably end up at the homeless hostel."

Time up, we say our goodbyes. Jamie smiles and the long-lost dimples have returned to her cheeks once more.

19th July

I receive a letter this morning from Jamie. She writes, "I have been interviewed by the police, and they are charging me with £12,000 worth of cheque fraud."

Jamie has written about her recent prison escape:

> *In the middle of the night I spotted a screw in the office. I grabbed my mate's hand and we ran for our lives across the grounds, lifted the wire fence up and rolled underneath. We got off the road, diving through the nearest hedge, scratching ourselves to pieces. We walked through brambles and stinging nettles, falling down every ditch in sight and got covered in mud and cow muck. After walking for about three miles, we spotted a phone box and called a taxi. He dropped my mate off and then took me back home. I blagged the driver I could pay him the other end – no chance and left him at the bottom of my block of flats.*

> *I knocked on the flat door and there were some very surprised faces. Rock was produced and I had my first pipe in about four weeks. God it felt good. I got paranoid but managed to hold it down. Had more rock – I was dead jumpy by now and was sure any car that passed was the police. I decided that week that life on the run was no fun, until I teamed up with Sindy. We met these blokes and they gave us all the drugs we wanted as long as we'd score for them.*

So Jamie didn't ring me from Manchester after all when she absconded. I suppose she told me this in case the police interviewed me. Jamie encloses another piece:

179

I met a man. At first he was charming and offered to help me get off drugs. The first night he arranged for an all night child minder. Since then I have only spent three nights with my son. Eventually I had to put him in care to get him away from danger. The baby was seen as a way of keeping me.

It was after a week when the guy started demanding money – if I didn't give it to him, I was on 'punishment' as he called it. This could be anything from not being allowed food, sleeping on the floor, or not seeing my son.

Later these punishments became worse. Regular beatings for not tidying up or, when I managed to escape and was eventually caught, being locked in a freezing cold flat, no furniture, no carpets, and just a night shirt on. I was kept there until he felt I had learned my lesson.

I never went a day without having a black eye or bruising to my body. I was terrified of him. I could not get away. He knew my family address and I did not want to bring my problems to my mother's doorstep.

In the end, being 'good' was the only way and to do everything he said. This included working the streets and cheque books, handing over everything to him, even my social money. I had to ask if I could get changed or for a glass of water. I could not even touch his food.

When I asked to see my baby he would refuse to take me, saying I shouldn't have put him in care. I had to. He was not being cared for properly and I feared for his life.

Towards the end, I felt there was no way out for me. One morning, locked in the punishment flat, I smashed a mirror and slit my wrists several times. All I wanted was to die. This was my only way out.

He took me to hospital where I had my arms stitched. They wanted me to stay, but he refused and took me back home where I was put under 24 hour supervision. A day later, with stitched arms, I was forced to go out on the streets. He had a phone bill to pay...

It is too painful for me to read on. Why did she ever get herself into such danger in the first place?

22nd July – Friday

Standing in the dock, for shoplifting and other charges, Jamie looks sixteen with hair loose and a small pony tail on top. She glances up and down as proceedings progress. Why is there so much evil in one looking so innocent? No one would believe her tragic life.

Appealing to the court, the barrister says, "Jamie needs help with her crack cocaine problem. She absconded from prison for two weeks to have an abortion and then gave herself up. After being in prison she is clear of drugs and wants to go to the homeless hostel."

We hold our breath as the magistrate announces his decision... "WE WILL ALLOW THE APPEAL," he says. Jamie looks aghast, mouth open wide...she is free.

He continues, "We believe a probation order could offer some help." Conditions are that – Jamie be given chance to prove herself – if this fails, she be resentenced:
She must attend an assessment group to decide a suitable programme
She shall live in a decent home
Jamie must be involved in a drug programme
Not continue offences
Keep in touch with her probation officer
And be of good behaviour."

The solicitor leads me to the cells. Jamie is so excited, expressing her gratitude that I have been there for her. She can't believe it and declares..."I'm free."
Before we leave the court, Jamie is approached by a probation officer who explains the conditions of her release.
I tell the officer, "Please ensure you get it right this time. Probation has proved a disaster in the past for Jamie." I hope she has listened.

181

Jamie tells me, "The police reckon I've done at least £100,000 of cheques. In real terms it's more likely £200,000. There's no way I'm hanging around to do three to five years. I'll be off."

Jamie has already forgotten to be at probation just two hours later – what hope is there for the probation order?
We head for the benefits office and after a short time she appears with a broad smile, waving a Giro cheque for £160.
Eventually, Jamie calls in to see the duty probation officer.
Throughout the afternoon she keeps saying, "I'm not going to do fraud anymore...if you can't do the time, don't do the crime."

23rd July – Saturday

Jamie is lovely, bubbly, and her old self. Over and over, she says, "Thank you for everything mum," and I know she means it. "I'm not on the brown stuff or crack anymore," she says repeatedly.

25th July – Monday

I ring Jamie and she tells me, "I spent the night out and didn't get to bed until nine this morning. I had a really good time. You'll never guess who I went to see yesterday?"
Curious, I ask, "Who?"
"Dionne took me to prison to see Steve. He was so pleased to see me.

I've decided not to go after men any more – they must come running after me. I have one in mind. It's about time I found someone to spend money on me for a change."
"It's about time you listened to me for a change Jamie," I tell her.
"Mum, there's only one person who can do it – and that's me."

28th July – Thursday

Will Jamie be ready when I arrive to collect her and Sindy I wonder? We have to be back in Stratford by 10.30 a.m. to meet Marie and the TV crew.

I knock on Sindy's door. Jamie is rushing around not quite ready. I nearly have heart failure as she pushes the iron plug into the socket with no top on it, and exposed wires. I am horrified. Eventually, I am convinced Jamie will leave this earth in the most unexpected way. As we head along the Warwick bypass back to Stratford, Sindy remarks, "Gosh, I'm relieved to leave the city behind and be in open countryside. We heard gunshots this morning back home."

The skies clear and sun appears – just perfect. Jamie is filmed outside Shakespeare's Birthplace. Afterwards, Max and I join her for filming at the recreation ground. As we picnic, Jamie shows us a big bruise on her arm. "Dexter bit me," she says.

Sindy turns to me saying, "I can't understand how Jamie can exchange this, beautiful Stratford for the run-down, inner-city area she lives in now." I voice my concern. "Jamie hasn't grown up. She is playing the dangerous game of one man against another. It's a game of fantasy which will kill her in the end."

After filming, early evening in the garden, Sindy and Jamie tuck into their meal as if they haven't eaten for weeks. "How quiet it is," remarks Sindy, "No police helicopters or sirens – we have them all the time back home."

"Occasionally, we hear sirens and helicopters here in Stratford," I tell her.

Jamie talks of her paranoia, caused by her heavy drug use, when her flat became a crackhouse. "They couldn't let anyone in because I was so out of my mind. I would have gone for them."

Early evening, as I drive them back home, Sindy remarks, "I'm dreading going back after such a wonderful day. Only last week my young daughter witnessed a stabbing outside school. It was quite frightening."

Jamie tells me, "There's a woman in the flats who takes so much crack that her little girl, who is five, is regularly high from the smoke. It's awful, mum. There are so many babies and children high on crack and heroin where we live."

I find it unbelievable a five year old should be abused in this way. And, to think, Max and Ben could have been high on drugs, as those children are, had they stayed with Jamie.

It is now 8.00 p.m., and as I drop the girls off, Sindy says, "You just don't walk around here at night. The only people hanging around are dealers. If I ever go out, I head straight for the shop or take-away, and then straight home again."

Jamie introduces me to a pleasant clean-shaven black guy and we shake hands.

As we walk around the flats there are cans, dirty nappies and broken glass strewn everywhere. How dead and derelict the place looks.

Crackhead

Back on the Rocks – 1994

6th August, Saturday

We arrive at Sindy's to collect Jamie for our arranged picnic, but no one is there and Max is very disappointed.

During the evening Sindy phones, "I went to look for Jamie this afternoon. She had lied to me and didn't return home last night. I found her sitting on the grass by the flats with her head in her hands. She was very down and tearful. I told her, 'Jamie, you are a pretty girl, and you must have the will to live.'

7th August – Sunday

"Jamie is very low," says Sindy. "I've just cooked a huge roast dinner and she ate the lot. I don't think she's eaten for the past couple of days and has probably had crack. She is a lovely kid underneath it all, with such potential."

"Yes, I agree. But sometimes she can be so evil," I tell her.

"Oh yes, I know – believe me," she says.

13th August – Saturday

Sindy says, "Jamie is no longer with me and I haven't seen her since Monday. I've been to her flat but there was no sign of her."

Where on earth is she, I wonder?

Eventually Jamie makes contact. "I'm sorry I didn't turn up for the picnic. I was trying to get off the drugs and was sick all day.

Mum, do you mind if I come over to your place? I don't want you coming here any more – it's too dangerous.

It's been an awful three weeks," she sighs.

20th August – Saturday

11.45 p.m: Suddenly the phone rings and wakes me up. Jamie sounds bright. "I'm alright mum, don't worry. Just to let you know I've burst my eardrum falling on concrete when I was drunk, and I've been to hospital."

Falling on concrete? More likely to have been beaten about the head, I think to myself.

21st August – Sunday

Max and I see Ben today. It looks as if he will definitely be adopted. He is such a loveable child. I feel so guilty I can't look after him, but there is no way I can cope with any more children at my age. I wish there was an answer.

Jamie rings complaining, "I may lose my hearing in one ear and it's very painful. I'm in agony and had to go to hospital today."
I tackle her. "Jamie, have you been hit?"
"No," she snaps...the phone goes dead.

A TV news item comes through: "Four police forces in the North and Midland's think they may have a serial killer on their hands. A number of prostitutes have been killed recently or disappeared."
This murderer could be one of Jamie's punters. The thought makes me shudder.

24th August – Wednesday

Mid-day I receive a call from Jamie. You're not in Jamaica yet?" I joke.
"No, but I am working on it," she replies laughing.
"You'll be pleased to know my ear is a lot better," she says, "although I can't hear properly." "Have you contacted probation Jamie?" I ask.
"Yes...It's boring."
It is four weeks since I last saw Jamie. I am exhausted and turn the phone off when I go to bed tonight so she can't bother me.

29th August – Monday

Max and I stay with friends in Lincoln this weekend, where I hope to recharge my batteries. As we drive home along the motorway the signposts for Doncaster, Sheffield, Leicester, Hinckley and Coventry loom up. Jamie has lived and worked in all these places over the past four years.
After the journey I feel quite depressed. Wherever I go, there is no escape from Jamie.
I get more tense with every phone call as I wait for news from her. I wonder if she will meet us on Friday as arranged?

1st September – Thursday

"Sorry I haven't phoned before," says Jamie. "I've been partying – drunk all night and every night."

"Are you taking drugs?" I ask.

"Hardly any, and I'm doing really well. I'm still with Dexter and I've been with him for five weeks now. We are sharing a lovely flat with another guy."

Jamie has probably been *stoned* out of her mind – this explains why she hasn't been in touch.

"Will you get up tomorrow to meet me?" I ask.

"Dexter will make sure I do. He'd like to meet you tomorrow, mum, but he's embarrassed and shy."

I smile, "I don't know why – I won't eat him. Here's a man, with a gun under his bed, and you say he's frightened of me!"

2nd September – Friday

Jamie greets us, as she sits on the pavement putting on a pair of socks outside British Home Stores. She is wearing a long dark blue denim dress and the cream socks go very well with new navy suede boots. She looks really good and is pleased to see us.

"Mum, can you help me with these carrier bags?" she asks as she struggles, heavily laden with shopping.

Walking through the precinct she casually remarks, "I've just shoplifted the stuff in the bags."

I want to run when it dawns on me -- the bags that I am carrying, are full of stolen goods!

Jamie shows no sign of shame or guilt as she tells me what she has acquired a tartan swag bag; full set of expensive make-up; a pair of Levi jeans; denim skirt; boxer shorts; and the socks and boots she is wearing. To crown it all, she has just shoplifted the denim dress she has on, from the shop opposite.

Jamie giggles, "I originally arrived in town wearing brown leggings and a cream jumper."

Max is pleased to see her and they pose for a photograph. Every time we meet I take a photo – just in case it is the last time I see her.

Excitedly, Jamie gives Max a Batman lunchbox; crayons; pencils; and shoe bag – all just acquired. "I have no alternative," she says. "I want to buy him presents but have no money."

As Max takes the goodies out the bag, Jamie panics telling him, "Quick, put them back in the bag and wait until we get to the park."
"Are you still working?" I enquire.
"Only sometimes if I need the money," she says.

She asks, "Mum, why didn't you take drugs in the 60's and why don't you try them now?"
"Jamie, in the 60's I had too many other things to do with my time," I tell her, "and my body is too precious to abuse now."
From the stupid way Jamie is talking, I know she is out of her mind. As Max chats to her, she is in a world of her own and doesn't hear him. Yawning all the time she says, "I've been up all night."

We amble over to our usual spot at the Memorial Park, under the big oak tree, and relax as the warm sun filters through the leaves. Jamie is ravenous and tucks into her sandwiches. In between mouthfuls she says, "Over the last few days I've got up at nine in the evening and gone to bed at nine in the morning. Yesterday afternoon (Thursday) I got up, and won't be going to sleep again until Sunday – that's if I'm lucky."
"Can't you sleep tomorrow, Saturday?"
"Oh, I've got something special on then," she says secretively.
"Drug running?" I enquire. She doesn't answer, so I am probably right.
"These Jamaican meals are getting a bit boring," she tells me. "What I'd give for fish and chips."
"How about roast beef and Yorkshire pud?" I ask.
"Oh, don't" she says.
"Is Jamaica still on the cards?" I ask.
"Yes. I've still got my false passport."

It is now four o'clock. Jamie is getting restless and needs her crack. As I drive home, my head pounds with disbelief at all I have seen and heard.

8th September – Thursday

"Can you take a reverse charge call from Jamie?" asks the operator. Something must be wrong.
"Are you okay Jamie?"
"Yes, I'm fine," she replies, but is weepy. "Dexter hit me last night. He bust my head, and my ribs are so badly bruised I can hardly breath. I'm on my way to probation to get accommodation. There's no way I'm putting up with it.

There was an argument over me wanting to do a runner. He told me, 'It had better be where I can't find you'. I want to leave the area as soon as I can."

I warn, "Jamie, be careful when you go back to the flat to get your clothes."

9th September – Friday

"I was turned away from probation," says Jamie. "They couldn't see me, so I went back to Dexter. He's okay with me now but I'm not stopping any longer than I have to."

"Is he heavy handed?" I enquire.

"Heavy footed, more like," she says. "He split my head – it's not really bad though.

Oh, by the way, I was knocked over by a bicycle on the way home. The bike hit my already bruised ribs. When I got up I couldn't breathe properly and thought I'd have to go to hospital. Fortunately I managed to walk home."

I can't believe it – Jamie is a walking disaster – and mad to keep returning to Dexter.

"I'm bored out of my mind and fed up," she says. "Once I get my income support, I shall leave him – it's the only thing that keeps me going."

12th September – Monday

"Quick, while I've sent the guy for change," says Jamie on the phone...
"Dexter's got a minder watching me. I can't say where I'm intending to go except the guy I'm with will help me."

"Shall I come over to see you Jamie before you go?" I ask. She is really pleased I have offered.

Marie wants to see Jamie regarding the film, and offers to drive me over. We collect Jamie and go to McDonald's.

She puts on a brave face saying, "Everything's fine," but we know it isn't. Her make-up is very heavy, partially disguising her badly swollen and bruised face.

"Dexter won't find me," she says. "I'm going to Sheffield."

"Are you using at the moment?" I ask.

"Not very often," she says. "Last week I disappeared for three days, and stayed at my flat with a guy. We had three great days on crack. I'd rather have it all in one go occasionally. He was pinching the drugs from the hiding places of others – they had loads.

The yardies want me to return to Dexter because they like us together. They are really bad – guns and everything," she says.

Turning to me, Jamie says, "I'm so bored. I want a job and purpose in life."

How many times have I heard this before? Jamie really believes what she says, but never sees it through because crack rules her life.

Marie drives us back to the flats. "Mum, did you see Dexter? He's hiding over there."

But I can't see him.

"Are you still working?" I enquire.

"Only very occasionally when I want clothes," she replies. We drop Jamie off – a very tense, unhappy and sad young woman. Where is it all going to end?

16th September – Friday

Another reverse charge call. Immediately I know something is wrong.

"Mum, I'm fed up. I'm pissed off."

"What's Dexter been up to this time?" I ask.

"Nothing – that's the problem," she replies.

"Why don't you go and see probation?" I suggest.

Jamie sounds so dejected. "Because it's Saturday."

I point out it is Friday. She is really pleased, and says she will see them straight away.

20th September – Tuesday

11.30 p.m: Jamie is bright and asks. "Did you get my message on the answer phone last night? I rang to let you know I'm okay. I didn't get to probation on Friday.

Oh, by the way, I've got a place in the Y.M.C.A. hostel."

23rd September – Friday

6.30 a.m: phone rings. "I'm bored. I can't take anymore. I've got to sort my life out. I must get out. I move into the hostel on Monday. Mum, can I come home for a few days?"

I agree to pick her up. Marie drives me over to collect Jamie, and we find her waiting with bags of clothes.

On the way home Jamie says, "Mum, I'm really upset. While I was at the phone box, two girls aged about fifteen asked me if I could buy them some coke. I just couldn't face it. It was awful. They were so young.

I'm hoping to go to Mosside this week to see a friend who is being deported. A number of guys from here are being deported soon.

Dexter is in terrible danger from the Mosside crowd," says Jamie. "He owes them thousands. They've already been flaunting their Brownings (guns) around and making threats. I reckon he'll be shot soon. One of the guys moved into my flat in the Spring when it became a crackhouse."

"Jamie, you'll get caught in crossfire."

"Oh don't worry mum, I'll be alright."

I point at the religious medallion around her neck. "It helps to keep evil away," she says. A friend gave it to me.

Thank goodness I'm out of that place," she sighs. "There are some new young girls on the patch, rumoured to be from Stratford."

How awful. There must be so many parents desperate, as I have been, and in need of support.

24th September – Saturday

Jamie spends most of the day in bed. "I'm bored, and need a place of my own to be independent," she says.

"You are very fond of Dexter, aren't you Jamie?"

"Yes, and he's fond of me. So far, he has phoned me five times in the last twenty-four hours.

Dexter spent £700 last weekend on crack," she says, "and after the buzz we used heroin in a spliff to get to sleep.

Since arriving home, Jamie has slept most of the time and eaten me out of house and home.

25th September – Sunday

"Will it be okay if I come to see Jamie?" asks Bill, my ex-husband. It is three and half years since he and Jamie have seen each other.

Jamie looks tarty before he arrives, so I make her change. She puts on her long black ribbed dress. Upon his arrival they hug, and chat for a moment or two. But gradually Jamie becomes distant and sits reading a book. As her dad leaves, they hug once more and I am happy the long gap has been bridged.

26th September – Monday

The housing department tell Jamie there is no accommodation at the hostel available. They say she has made herself purposely homeless, even though she has been forced out of her flat by the yardies. The council tell Jamie she must evict them.

When Jamie collects her income support I ask, "Why don't they make you get a job?"

"Because I'm claiming for Ben," she says. "It'll be bad if I'm caught."

"The money isn't much." I say.

"Well it pays for my crack," she jokes.

"How much is crack these days?" I ask.

"£100 a time," she says. "It's not worth buying in smaller amounts."

Jamie has not been attending probation. There is a warrant out for her arrest but I know nothing will be done.

6th October – Thursday

"You are still with us then?" I ask Jamie.

"I'm working on it. I'll get to Jamaica one day," she says. "I'm trying to get some money together – I really want to go. I'm bored. The whole place is boring." Jamie is so negative. I believe only a long spell in prison, or rehabilitation, will give her a chance to reflect on her life and possibly change things.

12th October – Wednesday

Jamie phones, "I'm tired. Dexter is making me get into proper hours. I now go to bed at three in the morning and get up at midday."

I recently followed up an article in the local press – a mother in Coventry whose three sons are involved in drugs. She has decided to set up a parents' drug support group, based on ours. I call to see her today and we seem to have so much in common and understand each other.

15th October – Saturday

11.20 p.m: "Happy 50th birthday for tomorrow," says Jamie on the phone.

"Gosh, I can't believe it. You forgot last year," I tell her.

"I remembered a month ago, and was determined not to miss it," says Jamie.

I am pleased to hear from her. We arrange to meet at ten on Monday morning.

"I'll go to bed tonight, about three o'clock for a short while, and then get a taxi to meet you," she says.

"I would like you to meet my friend Joy," I tell her. "The other day Joy said, 'You know, I'm very fond of Jamie after hearing about her, even though we have never met'."

16th October – Sunday. My 50th Birthday

My sister cooks a wonderful Indian meal and my son, Jonathan, and his partner join us. My happiness is complete when a bubbly Jamie phones during the meal to wish me a happy birthday.

17th October –Monday

10.00 a.m: Jamie doesn't turn up as arranged and I am disappointed. Later she phones, "Sorry I didn't turn up – Dexter was arrested.

Then changing the subject she tells me, "I lifted Dexter three new shirts in town today." She sounds very bright and I put the phone down feeling relaxed and at peace.

24th October – Monday

As arranged, Jamie waits for me by the phone box, with a suitcase and carrier bags. "I joked with my friends that I'm leaving Dexter – but it's only my washing," she says in very good spirit. "Dexter had to throw cold water on my face to wake me."

Jamie doesn't bother to put on any make-up and looks very tired.

Back at Stratford, as we sit on the canal lock, the BBC photographer asks me to put my arms around Jamie. But every time I touch her, she shouts out in dreadful pain. "I think I cracked my ribs in the fall a few weeks ago," she says.

"You mean when you were beaten," I insist as I put my head against her face.

"Ouch," she screams. "I've got cuts in my mouth from my brace," (the brace was put in 5 years ago, for a twelve month period). Jamie looks very pale and appears in bad shape.

"Dexter and I are in hiding from the Mosside guys. No one knows our address."

"Why does he owe so much money?" I ask.

"Because he smokes crack with any money he has," she replies. "We have an ounce of rock in one night between us. It is holding its price and

is very expensive. We buy ours cheap in large quantities.
Dexter doesn't pay for his. He gets it in deals but I don't ask where from.
I just smoke it with him. We make our own by boiling raw cocaine,
bicarbonate of soda and water.

Sometimes we invite friends to join us – usually a couple he can trust
who won't spill the beans. Occasionally I walk out in the middle of a
session and go to bed. He says I'm the only one he knows who can do
this.
Dexter talks such a lot of rubbish while 'freebasing' and drives me
mad," she laughs. "We do it in the kitchen, bathroom, wherever. Some
do it on the stairs of the flats but I don't."

During the afternoon, Jamie gets her hair cut into a shoulder length bob
– it looks lovely. She is keen to take the 'No Drugs' record, by Mikey Tuff
(reggae singer) to be played in the clubs. On the journey back Jamie is
shattered and nods off, not having slept for days.

When we arrive at Joy's, Jamie is only half awake and not with it.
However, she manages a smile as she chats. While Jamie pops out of the
room for a minute, Joy turns to me and says, "What a pretty daughter
you have."
As we leave Joy asks Jamie, "What does it feel like to take so much
crack?"
Jamie pauses for a second then says, "I can't describe it. It's wonderful.
You just need more and more."

We arrive back at the flats early evening. Jamie tells me to pull up by the
guy in the designer jeans and hooded parka and I assume he is her
dealer friend. He helps Jamie with her bags, not realising he has the 'No
Drugs' record under his arm. I wonder what his reaction would be if he
knew?
As I drive away, a couple of fifteen-year-old hooded youths hang
around as runners for the dealers.

Tonight, Jamie is going out. How will she keep going I wonder,
exhausted from lack of sleep? Her make-up looks really good; but inside
there is a shattered and very unhappy woman. God knows what state
her bones are in from the beatings – almost every bone in her body must
have been broken at some time or other.

As we say goodbye, Jamie hands me a belated birthday card that says:

> *"To my only Mom.*
> *Thank you for always being there – you are the best.*
> *Love you always,*
> *Jamie."*

It makes me glow and feel very happy.

Crackhead

Crack of Doom – 1994

5th November – Saturday

11.00 p.m: the phone rings. "Mrs. Harrison? It's the police. Jamie wants to have a word with you, I'll pass her over."

"Hi mum. I'm in custody until Monday – breach of something or other. Any chance you can get over tomorrow please and bring me a coke, cigarettes, and chocolate?"

I warn Jamie, "You may end up in prison if there's a warrant out for breach of probation."

"Probably not," she replies confidently.

7th November – Monday

I cannot attend court and Marie goes on my behalf. She rings me, "Angela, the solicitor has asked if Jamie can be bailed at your house for four days until her hearing on Wednesday?"

"No way," I tell her.

Jamie has made her mistakes and must take the consequences. Why should I put up with the hassle.

Jamie phones, sounding brighter, "I've been let out until Thursday when I have to appear in court. They may consider Community Service. Imagine it," she laughs.

I doubt she will bother to attend court on Thursday.

9th November – Wednesday

I contact Jamie via Dexter's mobile and warn her, "You must be prepared for prison tomorrow."

She is adamant, "It's not on the cards. But if it is, I will make sure I don't go."

"I refuse to traipse across country with your clothes," I warn her. "Make sure you have the essentials with you at court."

"Have you got my birth certificate and old passport?" she enquires.

"No," I reply.

I wonder what she is up to this time?

197

10th November – Thursday

Jamie tells me, "I've got my Hearing this afternoon. Would you like to have lunch with me beforehand? I've bought a Cumberland pie, and we could eat it at the flat."

"I would like that," I say, smiling to myself. Jamie never ever cooks and any meal must be ready-made.

As I drive up to the flats, it looks like little Jamaica – West Indians with Rasta locks and big baggy berets. Hooded-anorak dressed lads hang around, riding mountain bikes back and forth.

Max and I stroll over to the flats. Jamie calls out from a balcony and runs down to meet us. Delighted to see Max, she holds his hand tightly, looking so proud of him and introducing him to friends passing by.

Her make-up is very heavy and she looks good. But what, I wonder, is underneath? She is very heavy-eyed and informs me she has been up all night.

As we eat I say, "Jamie, if you go to prison...she interrupts,

"I'm not," she says.

However, in her bag are photos, a little underwear and deodorant; so she has listened to my advice, to be prepared. I drop Jamie off at court. Back at home, I wait for news all evening – she promised to phone as soon as the Hearing was over, but she doesn't make contact.

11th November – Friday

I ring the Court. "Jamie has been released on conditional bail and is due to return to court in a few days time," they tell me. I am annoyed she hasn't been in touch but know Jamie loses all concept of time when she is on crack.

Joy has offered to give Jamie dinner on Christmas Day, while we are on holiday in America. It is wonderful to know Jamie will have a family Christmas and not be on her own.

7.00 pm: "Sorry I didn't phone," says Jamie. I went home from court and fell asleep. I've just woken up – must go." She rushes off the phone.

14th November – Monday

I tell Jamie her birth certificate is at Joy's for collection.

Joy phones. "I met Jamie at a pub and gave her the certificate. She's fine but looks very tired. I insisted she contacts me if she needs a break," says Joy.

"Jamie remarked 'I could have done with one last night'."

Later Jamie contacts me, "Mum, I apologise for shouting during my earlier call. I'm going to Peterborough to get my passport at six o'clock tomorrow morning. I'll tell you about it later.

"I've been robbing today. I've got a green cord coat, wool skirt, suede 'A' line dress, and jumpers for Dexter. I also got some dressy shoes, a bag, and leggings in green crushed velvet."

15th November – Tuesday

5.00 a.m. – The phone wakes me up. Jamie sounds very frightened and is crying. "Mum, can I come to the house until next Monday?"

I tell her, "No, but you can come for the day."

She sounds very relieved. "I'll hitch over," she says.

I worry about her hitching. Stupid really – she is in greater danger working on the streets. Jamie arrives 5.45 a.m., hungry and very pale. She says she hasn't slept for days and looks shattered. As her story unfurls, Jamie tells me, "I was due to be collected this morning to go to Peterborough. Mum, I was so scared and knew I couldn't go through with it."

She says, "It was planned for me to go to Jamaica in the next few days, and to bring back drugs. I didn't want to do it.

A couple went with me yesterday to ensure I got my birth certificate from Joy. When Dexter saw Joy, he ducked down the back seat of the car. I realised then that he doesn't really care for me.

Dexter kept telling me what a lovely holiday I'd have in Jamaica. Another girl was going as well. The trip would have been financially very profitable. I was offered £5,000 up front, £450 to spend there, and £5,000 after the deal had been done."

Jamie is very scared. She tells me that she suddenly saw sense at the last minute, remembering the book 'Crack of Doom' by Jon Silverman, which tells of the Yardies and drug importation. "If I get caught drug running, I could get fifteen years in Holloway," she says, "and there's no way I'm doing that."

Jamie roots through the fridge for whatever she can find – and at six in the morning, garlic wafts through the house as she eats spaghetti bolognaise and chicken.

"Last night," she recalls, "I had a punter try to throttle me. Fortunately a nearby taxi driver heard and saved me.

My hearing is really bad now and Dexter is getting annoyed.
He's keeping me awake all the time, to work. I'm absolutely worn out.
He splits the money and spends every penny he can get his hands on.
But he always lets me have money that's left after buying two pieces of
brown. He's mad with me for spending money," she says. "I had £70 of
which I spent £10 on rent; £10 on food; £40 the brown stuff and had £10
left.
He says he'll have to start treating me as Clinton did. It frightens me he
may have a brainstorm.

Exhausted, Jamie retires to the comfort and safety of her bed. Thank
goodness she realises the danger she has put herself in. I can't believe
she is so naive. Probably because she is out of her mind from crack most
of the time.

At 7.00 p.m. I am due to take Jamie back to Coventry. She feels ill, looks
dreadful, and wells up in tears saying, "Mum, I can't face going back.
Can I stay the night?"
Because she is so poorly, my heart tells me I must let her stay. She
appears very frightened.

Jamie has slept all day and after I say she can stay the night, she returns
to bed. At 1.30 a.m. I hear her making her way downstairs, put on the
T.V. and, with the microwave working overtime, she eats everything in
sight. By seven o'clock Jamie is fast asleep, covered with a duvet on the
dining room floor and TV left on. Eventually she wakes up and takes
herself off to a comfortable bed upstairs.

Midday, I badger Jamie to get up so I can get her back to Coventry. She
looks awful, and admits her 'flu symptoms could well be cold turkey.
She has a shower, does her hair and make-up, and looks good once
again, dressed in the clothes she stole a couple of days ago.

We are just about to leave the house, when Jamie runs downstairs, very
excited, announcing, "Mum, I have phoned a hotel. It's £16 deposit and
the DSS will pay the rest."

As we dash along the by-pass she says, "I can earn the £16 deposit in
half an hour." Glancing at her, I see how ill she looks. There is no way
she can work on the streets this damp and bitterly cold night.

I offer, "Jamie, I will give you the £16." Her face lights up, and spirits are raised. She is so happy.

I sigh, "Oh well, you might as well have it now. I'll never be able to leave you money in my will – it would only go on drugs."

The receptionist leads us to a small dark wooden panelled bedroom on the outside of the building. It is damp, musty, and basically furnished with a single bed, dressing table, small table with TV, and a smoke-stained fan heater on the wall. The place is awful but Jamie is thrilled to bits.

"Can the room be aired and sprayed to hide the musty smell?" I ask the woman. "Has the bed linen been aired?

She assures me, "It's fine – the bed was made up a week ago."

A week ago! It must be very damp by now, with no heat on in the room during this cold, damp month of November. Reluctantly, I pay the £16 deposit.

Jamie is thrilled – just as if it is Christmas. "I have a place of my own – I can do what I want," she declares.

I put my arm around and give her a hug. I can't believe how happy she is to have just £16.

We drive to her flat and leave her there to collect her things. She tells me, "Dexter doesn't allow me any female friends, except one, because he claims they are a bad influence. I'm unhappy when I don't see them." Tonight she rings, so excited. "I got all my things from the flat in two journeys by taxi. Luckily Dexter wasn't there."

Now safely installed in her damp dingy room, absolutely over the moon, Jamie says, "Thank you Mum, for everything." As I put down the phone I am happy. Jamie now has a refuge, and no pimp to answer to. If she can't get the DSS to pay for the room she says she will gladly pay it herself with her earnings.

18th November – Friday

"Mum, I'm not taking rock anymore," says Jamie, sounding really pleased with herself. "Suki, the girl who stayed at my flat, is also staying in my hotel. I've decided I'm not going back to Dexter. He slapped me the night before last and I'm not getting involved with him any more.

It's wonderful. I made £30 last night and then went back to bed – it was so easy. I get up early every morning and have a full cooked breakfast."

Jamie sounds really happy at long last, and my mind is at rest...for a while at least.

We chat about Christmas, when Max, Pat, and I will be staying with my brother in California, and I tell her she has been invited to Joys for Christmas day.

Repeatedly Jamie says, "Thanks mum, for the £16. It has made such a difference to my life. I'm still in the same grotty room but it looks really good now. Must go and get your Christmas presents. Bye."

20th November – Sunday

Jamie proudly announces, "I've been off the brown since yesterday. Can I come over tomorrow mum? I need to occupy myself."

I agree she can come on the condition that she helps me. "But I don't want you sleeping all day and eating me out of house and home. Are you eating properly, Jamie?" I enquire.

"Of course," she replies. "I've got money now. I've just been to 'Kentucky Fry'. I'm really pleased I don't need drugs anymore."

I smile to myself – she has only been clean for twenty-four hours.

21st November – Monday

Jamie arrives, stylishly dressed in jodhpur trousers, a loose shirt, and a big black flat beret-style hat. Every time we meet she looks so different.

She tells me with a glint in her eye, "It's wonderful to have my own money. "Last night when I saw Dexter he didn't believe I had been staying with you. He was cross I didn't turn up to go to Peterborough for the passport."

Jamie finds a piece of Max's white cellular baby blanket. "Can I have this Mum," she says as she runs her fingers along the silk ribbon edge. She sits on the settee and I observe her caressing the blanket just as she did as a child – her comfort blanket. Is this a sign of insecurity, I wonder?

"I feel ill," she complains. "I'm on a come-down from the brown and have 'flu symptoms."

As I watch Jamie with the blanket, her eyes stare straight ahead in a glaze.

Coming down to earth Jamie says, "I'm worried I let my friend Suki down. I ignored her knock on my door during the night. This morning I discovered she went out to a dealer who tried to double cross her, and he knocked her two front teeth out. Her lip was so badly bruised and swollen. Mum, I realise it could so easily have been me," she says, her voice shaking.

"I think I'll treat myself to something, tomorrow," she says. "Perhaps some new clothes – I'll show you the jeans and boots I nicked today on my way here. There's also a big jumper for you for Christmas back at the hotel."
She produces a mug with Jamie written on. "I acquired this from the post office, and also a badge with the name Jamie." She takes it out of her bag and pins it to her shirt, just like a teenage kid of fifteen, not a twenty-one year old.

"Jamie, you'll end up in prison by Christmas if you are not careful."
She has a smirk on her face, "It's a habit I suppose. I just do it without thinking. I've got my winter wardrobe so it won't be necessary for me to get anything else for a while."
I don't believe her – next time we meet she will be dying to show me her newly acquired things. She must be very clever to get away with it, with such heavy security in the large city stores.
"I just puts the things over my arm and walk out," she says. "Some big stores don't have security tags, which makes it easy."

This afternoon Jamie is feeling quite poorly and falls asleep on the settee. She has missed the last bus to Coventry but I insist she goes to Leamington and sorts it out from there. Phew, relief as Jamie leaves us. Once more I can return to normality and relax.

23rd November –Wednesday

At 10.00 a.m. I collect Jamie from her hotel for her final meeting with the film crew. As I enter her bedroom I notice the musty smell has gone although little else has changed. On the wardrobe door are photos of Max and Ben. "Have you managed to keep off the rocks?" I enquire. "Yes" she says proudly, but immediately admits, "I had a small amount of brown last night."
It is late and I tell her to hurry up and get dressed. Jamie has been up all night and is tired out. I leave her with the film crew, and return home. In the afternoon, filming re-commences at my house. While I am interviewed in the kitchen, Jamie takes to her bed and falls into a deep sleep.

Off to Stratford police station next, where they film me walking down to the cells. Memories flood back of that first time Jamie was found in possession of cannabis – probably one of the worst moments of my life. When a parent discovers their child is taking drugs is absolutely devastating.

We return to the house to find Jamie is out to the world. Marie and the crew are anxious to film Jamie walking the streets. Reluctantly she gets up, is very aggressive and bad tempered. She insists on making them wait, while she eats an overflowing bowl of cereal, piled high with cornflakes, weetabix, and oats, sprinkled with loads of sugar and milk. There is peace and relief as Jamie leaves the house. Now I can get my thoughts together.

Tonight, our parent support group hold a 'No Drugs Disco' for under eighteens at a Stratford nightclub. Jamie arrives by taxi, wearing a skimpy sequined black top, black velvet hot pants, dark green suede boots, and natural tights – but no coat on this freezing November evening.
Our friends from the Drug Awareness Team, in Bristol, arrive to support us. The singer, Mikey Tuff, has long dreadlocks down past his waist and looks typical of the black guys Jamie mixes with. But his message is, "Do NOT Take Drugs", which he promotes with a recently released video, incorporating well known TV personalities, for European Drug Prevention Week. Pat and I greet these lovely guys with a big hug.
Jamie watches aghast. "Hey mum, how about introducing me," she laughs.
During the evening my friend's young daughter, Isobel, asks, "Angela, is Jamie alright?"
When I tackle Jamie she says, "I'm feeling very ill. I'll pop along to McDonald's." She must be mad going out dressed like that, I think to myself. It's freezing. During the evening Jamie is in a trance, eyes glazed – the result of using Temazepam I presume.

24th November – Thursday

This morning my friend Jane, who helped at the Disco tells me, "Last night I walked home with Jamie. She said she took five Temazepam yesterday.
Also, that Dexter will kill her if he gets the chance. He has already beaten her four times. But she says it wasn't as bad as when she was with Clinton.

Jamie said the worst ever beating with Dexter was when she was drunk."
"I bet that was when Jamie said she fell on concrete steps and burst her eardrum," I say to Jane. "I just knew she had been beaten."

Jamie stayed with me overnight and I ask, "Have you been to probation?"
"Yes, they're going to see me every week," she says. Mid-morning she goes to bed for the day and I take the opportunity to ring her probation officer.
"No, Jamie hasn't been in touch with me," says the woman. The officer asks, "And how are you. Are you okay?"
I feel rather choked. No professional, dealing with Jamie, has ever asked how I am. If only more would think of what the families of drug users go through. Those simple words, "How are you," mean so much to keep us going.
"Jamie thinks she may be sent to prison in a couple of days," I tell the officer.
"I have made an appointment for next Monday – to give Jamie a chance. I really want to help her," she says.

Late afternoon Jamie wakes, is very aggressive, and we argue which is very unusual. We hardly ever fall out. I put my arm around her to calm her down. After telling her I have spoken to probation, Jamie writes the appointment in her little book saying, "I'll definitely attend."

We walk into Stratford with Max to see the switching on of the Christmas lights. At five o'clock we hug, say our goodbyes and Jamie walks in the opposite direction to catch the bus home.

26th November – Saturday

6.45 a.m: The phone rings. I think, Oh no, what now?
It is Jamie, as bright as button, hardly pausing for breath as she chats.
"I've bought a padded patchwork quilt cover with the £50 TV money and I'm so excited.
I've seen Dexter and he's angry with me. But he says it's better to be friends than enemies. He's like a father to me," she says.

I am shocked and appalled to read a full-page article in this evening's press: 'My daughter is a Robber, Shoplifter and Thief'. I was not interviewed and these are not my words. They got the information from the BBC press release, and made up the heading.

I ring the editor and complain, but there is nothing I can do about it.

Jamie phones unexpectedly, "Mum, I've got to get out of my room."
"Was it the newspaper article?" I ask. "What do you think?" she says, sounding fed-up.
Suki, Jamie's friend, comes to the phone. "Angela, it's awful, when you think what Jamie has done for the community by making the film," she says.
I tell Jamie, "There's a bed here, if you want it." I feel partly responsible, having arranged the filming. But I wonder in my heart if she would have been given notice to quit anyway, having had her unsavoury friends around at all hours, using.

30th November – Wednesday
6.45 a.m: Jamie says, "I've got to be out of the hotel this morning."

I persuade her, "Come home for a few days, Jamie, until I go away." When I arrive at the hotel she is ready, everything packed. As we drive home, Jamie talks of trying to get a job in the next few days, in a Birmingham Sauna.

She tells me she went to a Rave in London last weekend with a crowd of friends on a coach. "Dexter was selling rock and, with the coach blinds down, we smoked our way to London. It was very strong stuff" recalls, Jamie.
"After I'd had some, Dexter put rock in my hand, about £400 worth. As I walked down the bus, I was swaying and couldn't stand up – thought I was going to drop the lot, and had to give it back to Dexter quickly. We got through £4000 that night."
During her conversation Jamie says, "I owe £10,000 at least for drugs. I'm one of the best at buying and can negotiate the best deals."

Nearing home, Jamie is very on edge. "I need to see a doctor urgently. I've slept for the past three days without drugs and desperately need methadone."
On the advice of our drug agency, I make an immediate appointment for Jamie to see a local doctor to whom drug addicts are referred. The counsellor says it is doubtful Jamie will get methadone immediately – the wait is two weeks. Jamie, on a very bad comedown at the surgery, goes as

white as a sheet, is irritable, and restless. Tension mounts. She looks as if she's going to go mad and snap. The receptionist, seeing Jamie's distress, ushers us into another room.

The doctor invites me into her room at Jamie's request. I introduce myself as joint coordinator of our local support group. By doing this, I hope she will take me seriously and not treat me with suspicion as most professionals do.

I put the doctor in the picture about Jamie and ask for a full check-up. She listens carefully, and then I leave the room.

After twenty minutes the doctor calls me in and explains she has prescribed Jamie methadone. The conditions agreed with Jamie are: not to sell the script, not to overdose, and to contact the drug agency for counselling.

Jamie is elated as we leave the surgery. "She's brilliant. The best doctor I've ever seen."

As we drive to the chemist for her methadone, Jamie contemplates her future. "I can't imagine life without drugs," she says.

Crackhead

Every Parents Nightmare – 1994

1st December – Thursday

Jamie sleeps through her first night on methadone. She would normally work all night as a prostitute, and sleep all day.

This morning I am due to appear on the Anne Diamond Show on BBC TV. I drive to the studios in Birmingham with Sue and Marie. During my interview with Anne, Tony Blair, the Labour Party leader, watches and listens nearby while waiting to appear in the next slot.

Afterwards, I worry what Jamie thought of my interview. Did I say the right thing? Will she speak to me when I get home? Mid-day I return to Stratford.
As Jamie opens the front door, I hold my breath..."Mum, you were brilliant," she says. "Absolutely brilliant. I'm dead proud of you."
I am amazed and so relieved. Jamie hugs me and we all laugh with relief.

Marie leaves a copy video of the documentary 'Every Parent's Nightmare', due to be shown on TV this evening. If there is to be any aggro with Jamie, or emotions get high, we can talk it through before the programme goes out. Marie has produced the documentary with great sensitivity and we are all very happy with the outcome.

At the end of the film, Jamie talks about taking crack. "It's a habit," she says, "like making a cup of tea in the morning. But instead of making tea, I'll have a point 2 rock for my breakfast (0.2 gram.)"
She continues: "Nobody can ever have crack under control. You think you have, but crack controls you. It's a very powerful drug."

Finally Jamie is asked, "Your mum is going to need a lot of convincing you can start again. Should she trust you this time?"

A moment's pause...and then Jamie replies, "No. I don't think you can ever trust a Crackhead."

Although Jamie is sick and itching from the methadone, she is becoming much brighter with clear blue eyes.

When she pops out to get some cigarettes I remind her, "Don't shoplift in town, Jamie," which I repeat every time she visits.

"I won't, don't worry mum," she says.

However, half an hour later she arrives home with a hardback book which she pinched from the local book store. Jamie is addicted to shoplifting, just a much as drugs, and can't stop herself.

This evening Sue and I go to a local radio station for a phone-in after the programme. Many callers ring in.

The final call comes as a shock...

"This is Angela's daughter, Jamie.

I agree with the caller who says my mum deserves a gold medal. She certainly does – thank you mum.

I'm trying to stop taking drugs. I don't know how long it will last. Drugs have killed my life.

I must admit, when I'm taking drugs I'm not a very nice person," agreeing with her brother's statement in the film. She appeals to him saying, "I'm trying to come off – but Rome wasn't built in a day."

As Jamie puts down the receiver, the interviewer remarks on my smile; but I am also choked because the call was so unexpected.

Jamie's eyes are beginning to sparkle and she is stable and happy. During the day she is cheerful, considering she is often sick and has bad itching. She is very helpful with Max and there isn't any aggression. This morning she sets off to the rail station to go to Birmingham seeking work, but half an hour later she returns home feeling sick.

During a phone call to her friend Dalton, I overhear Jamie, "I'm really happy to be with Max and Mum. I don't need crack when I'm away from it."

"Would you like to invite Dalton over for a meal?" I ask her.

She is thrilled. "Dalton is so nice," she says. "You'll like him, mum."

Jamie is happy during the day but by at teatime begins to get irritable, with heavy eyes. She takes her methadone and seems a lot better afterwards.

Tomorrow Jamie is off to get her social money. Worried, I ask, "Will you contact Dexter?"

"If I want to, I will," she snaps. I am sure she will go back to him if she gets half a chance.

6th December – Tuesday

During the evening I notice bad spots on the top of Jamie's legs and question her about them. Jamie says. "Oh, I've always had them. They're from my scratching due to the heroin."

I pay for Jamie to have her hair done as her Christmas present. She has it beautifully cut into a chin length bob and looks lovely.

Jon Silverman, author of 'Crack of Doom', calls at the house to record us for radio, on the effects of crack on the family.

Tonight, a friend calls at my house. When I introduce him to Jamie, I proudly announce, "She's on methadone and doing ever so well."

He appears unusually relaxed, considering this is the first time he has met Jamie – or so I think.

After he leaves the house, Jamie exclaims, "Mum, I can't believe it. He's one of my regular clients and I see him most weeks."

7th December – Wednesday

After ten days off drugs and taking methadone, Jamie is looking wonderful apart from a spotty face. I can't believe the change in such a short time.

She gets up early to catch the bus to go over to probation and discusses rehabilitation. But probation only knows a quarter of Jamie's story. She has been given so many chances. I am angry they feel sorry for her. Jamie gets away with far too much and they need to be harsh to be kind.

Late afternoon, Jamie returns home to show off her latest shoplifted goods, expensive chemist items and a long wool jumper and skirt, Doc Martin boots, pants, bras, and green over-the-knee socks.

Jamie knows I disapprove of her shoplifting activities and I am amazed she talks so freely without shame. But then her mind doesn't think like ours. I am convinced her brain is permanently damaged from using crack.

8th December – Thursday

In a few days' time I am off to America with Max and Pat. Joy has kindly offered to put Jamie up, while I am away, for the whole fortnight. I am happy knowing she will be with a family. Jamie is very pleased and says she loves Joy.

The police phone me, wishing to interview Jamie about cheque fraud. When I tell Jamie, she gets aggressive saying, "They'll remand me. No way will I let that happen."
I persuade Jamie to contact her solicitor, telling her of my concern on the effect on Max if the police search my home.

9th December – Friday

Jamie gets up early morning on her own initiative. Every day sees a vast improvement. She rings her solicitor and arranges to meet the police soon. Her friend Dalton is coming over and we also invite Pat to join us. She hoovers and tidies throughout the house, entering into the spirit of things by putting up a small Christmas tree.

Dalton arrives; a very well-spoken, slim, black guy wearing heavy rimmed glasses. Quite different from Jamie's usual guys. He seems straight – almost too good to be true.
As we eat, he talks of how he tries to persuade working girls to come off crack. He admits to having used crack for six months, but assures me he has it totally under control.
He glances at Jamie and asks, "Why Jamie, when you have all this and such a lot of support, do you prefer your life?"
She just shrugs her shoulders and smiles.

Pat and I cannot make Dalton out. After he leaves, Jamie says, "He's such a good friend – he buys the girls sandwiches, Cornish pasty or a drink when they are really down. There have been times when he's bought me a sandwich when I was starving."

As a teenager Jamie always had a book in her hand. I am pleased to see she is reading and using the library, which indicates she is returning to a life of normality.
Jamie looks lovely. I only wish she would stop the shoplifting and then things would be almost perfect.

A young friend of mine is taking Jamie to a local club tonight, and she is very excited. With her new hair-do, nail polish and make-up, I see before me my beautiful sophisticated daughter – not the rough addict.
When Jamie returns home she is very bubbly and can't wait to tell me, "I had a really good time. Old school friends came up and shook my hand, which meant a lot to me."

13th December – Tuesday

I am apprehensive as I drop Jamie off at Joy's. What will she get up to while I am away? What will I find upon my return? I dread to think. She has been off drugs for two weeks and is so lovely. I now have my daughter back. But will I see a stranger upon my return in three week's time?

Jamie looks very relaxed and happy with Joy as we say our goodbyes. I am so lucky to have such a friend who understands drug problems.

As we board the plane I think, America here we come – over a fortnight free of drugs, and constant crises.

While away, I phone home. Joy tells me that although Jamie is being very good, she is seeing Dexter again and he phones every day – bad news as far as I am concerned.

28th December – Wednesday

This evening we attend a drug support meeting at a hospital in San Diego. Both parents and their youngsters attend, which we find most interesting and informative. They talk together as families, about the use of drugs over the past week. They provide support for each other and then the group splits up – parents in one room and users in another. Each week the sessions take a different format.

Pat and I learned so much from that evening. We agree how beneficial it could be for everyone if we did the same back in England. Unfortunately, the general consensus, back at home, is that families and addicts should be treated separately and not as a whole. If it works in America, why can't it work here?

30th December – Friday

Early morning, as we return home from Heathrow and drive along the M40, I turn on the radio. "Someone was shot dead in Coventry last night," they announce. "The murder was believed to be drug related." Astounded, Pat and I look at each other.

"Oh no," I say, "I hope Jamie's not involved in this one."

Immediately I ring Joy and she tells me the police are trying to contact Jamie. Fortunately Jamie was with Joy at the time of the shooting.

"I will collect Jamie's things and she must leave your house immediately," I tell her. "There is no way you should have the police arriving at your house looking for Jamie." Joy tells me that Jamie is out at present.

Eventually, I manage to get hold of Jamie, but she isn't interested in speaking. It is as if I am talking to a total stranger – not the daughter I left behind when I went to the States. My heart sinks...Jamie must be back on crack.

Hurriedly, she says, "Dalton's waiting...must go."

I insist she listens. "Jamie, because you are back with Dexter, you must find somewhere else to live immediately."

Before she hangs up I say, "The police want to speak to you regarding the murder."

This evening I go over to Joy's to collect Jamie's things. We agree all the signs point to Jamie being back on crack. She is sleeping a lot, out at night, and spending money immediately she gets it. Joy also suspects Jamie is no longer collecting her methadone.

Jamie has continued to shoplift while staying with her. Some of the items are very expensive, including a black dress costing £160.

31st December – Saturday

Dexter phones Joy's home three times to speak to Jamie, even though she has left.

As I pack Jamie's clothes into bags, I find a letter from Jamie to Dexter, never posted, which states: "As you know, I'm pregnant and it's your baby."

I am stunned. Only yesterday I told Joy I suspect Jamie may be pregnant, because she is being sick, losing weight, (as she always does), and is constantly sleeping.

Jamie phones to say she is staying at Sindy's for a few days to give me a break and I tell her, "Jamie I know you are pregnant."

"I'm not," she says sharply.

"The letter here, to Dexter, proves it," I tell her.

"It's all been sorted out now," she says. Jamie quickly changes the subject. "I'm not on drugs any more."

"There's no way you can keep off them if you stay with Dexter and your crack friends," I say angrily.

Jamie doesn't challenge me, so I know she has had crack recently. When I mention yesterday's murder, she says, "I don't know anything. At least I'm not involved this time."

9.00 p.m: Jamie phones, very upset. "Can I come home tonight mum?" she says. "I'll try to get some money together by working. There's no transport at this time of night and it's far too cold to hitch a lift," she says.

I hesitate, and she says she will ring back.

Another call half a hour later: Jamie is much more upset and desperate to leave, saying she only has £15 and a taxi would cost £40. I say I will only collect her because it is New Year's Eve. She thanks me and is very grateful.

When I collect Jamie, I notice she still has bright eyes and smooth, spotless skin, even though she admits to having smoked a little crack.

Midnight: as we say goodbye to a horrendous 1994, and see in the New Year, Jamie and I agree things can only get better.

Crackhead

Never Trust a Crackhead – 1995

1st January – Sunday

Every New Year's day I hope things will get better but my crisis continues without a break. A month ago, at the end of filming, there was a glimmer of hope.

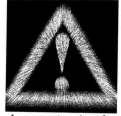

But I now suspect Jamie has returned to crack, after only three weeks on methadone, and sleeps most of the day. She has forgotten to get her methadone script for the New Year holiday period but doesn't have a bad come-down as I expect.

In the evening I ask her, "What hopes have you got for the future?"

"I want to return and get accommodation at a hostel," she says.

"Dexter wants me to go and live on a chicken farm in Jamaica. Can you imagine it?" Jamie laughs.

"Yes, I can – probably a yard with a few breeze blocks in the centre of Kingston," I warn her.

2nd January – Monday

Carrying only her handbag which contains underwear, Jamie prepares to return to her friends.

Her probation officer phones here, to enquire why Jamie hasn't been attending probation. Jamie speaks to the officer about rehabilitation and is told they can help. The officer isn't happy about Jamie returning to her previous situation and feels a move to another area is necessary. Jamie is ecstatic.

4th January –Wednesday

8.30 a.m: Jamie phones, "I've got a room at a hostel, and after two months I get my own flat." She is happy, but I doubt if it will come off.

She chats away and says, "I was recently looking for a carrier bag at Dexter's. I found what I thought were hair rollers and shook them out. She muses as she recalls, "Dexter asked what I was doing with the gun cartridges? I honestly had no idea what they were."

Jamie's clothes are still at my house and she only has underwear with her. She must be shoplifting for a change of clothing." I feel tight in my chest, am tired and tense.

7th January – Saturday

Mid-afternoon: Jamie rings, "Hi Mum. Just to let you know that I didn't like the hostel. We had to be in early at night and I couldn't handle that.

I'm now with Dexter and Hughie. But under no circumstances must you ring or let anyone know where we are."
I tell Jamie, "I expected you to come home to collect your things."
"Sorry. I didn't have time," she says.
"What have you been doing?" I ask.
"Watching TV."
"How are you managing for clothes, Jamie?"
"Oh, I've acquired some new jodhpurs and a lovely jumper."
She denies she is back on crack.
Later, however, I say, "It's obvious you are smoking."
"Well, I'm off the methadone and heroin, so it's got to be better. Anyway, I've only had a little bit," she says.

At teatime: Dalton phones "Do you know where Jamie is?" She has been lying to him and he seems confused.
Evening: a call from the police station, "Mrs. Harrison? Jamie's in custody for shoplifting. Is she using?" the officer asks. "She certainly looks better than I've ever seen her," he says. She was caught with a load of clothes.
I'm sure you'll be pleased to hear they will probably keep her in custody overnight." Obviously he's on my wavelength.
"Yes. I am relieved. At least I know she will be safe tonight," I tell him.

9th January – Monday

When Jamie appears in court, I am unable to attend. I phone the Magistrates Court this afternoon. She has been remanded until the 30th January when there will be a further hearing.
Five o'clock: Jamie phones from H.M.P. Risley, very shocked at being sent there, and is weepy. "I shouldn't be in custody for shoplifting," she says stubbornly. I try to reason with her but she won't listen.

13th January – Friday

Jamie's hearing at Crown Court today and she hopes to get bail.

Late afternoon: "Have you heard?" Jamie asks excitedly. "I'm at the station and been freed. I'll phone you later, must go."

Jamie's solicitor phones saying, "The conditions of Jamie's bail are, that she should stay with you and attend the police station on Mondays and Thursdays. Also she must attend probation."

I am fuming, and say, "Nobody consulted me."

The solicitor is aghast when I tell her, "Jamie probably won't come home."

"I now see and understand that other side of Jamie which you warned me about when we first met," she says.

Jamie doesn't make contact. She is definitely back with her friends and on crack.

14th January – Saturday

A call at 9.15 am: "Mum, can you meet me today please?" she asks.

"No. Your bail conditions state you must reside at my address, and yet you knew you couldn't come here. Why did you let the solicitor do it?"

"I know," she says. "Must go...pips gone...run out of money. Bye."

15th January –Sunday

9.00 a.m: An operator's voice, "I have Jamie on the line. Will you pay for the call?"

Here we go again, I think, what this time?

Jamie sobs and is desperate. "Mum, can I come home? I can't face things here, and I must get out."

"Jamie," I say, "You can't. I just can't take any more."

"Can I come just tonight, Mum?"

I have to be firm. "No, you can't. You would have been better staying in prison," I tell her.

"Tell me about it," she says.

"You agree with me then?"

"Yes," she replies.

I talk to her for a while. I am torn. What should I do? But Jamie sounds so desperate and frightened. Her life is in danger.

"I'll ring you back in ten minutes," I say. This will give me a breathing space to get my thoughts together and assess the situation.

I phone Pat. "What should I do? I can't possibly cope with her here."
Pat saves the day by offering to have Jamie to stay with her.
Relieved we can offer Jamie respite, I phone her back saying, "You can have a meal here, and then go to stay at Pat's. One condition I make is that you must make your own way over."
Jamie sounds so relieved saying, "Oh, thank you Mum – I really appreciate it."

Jamie arrives in less than half an hour. But where is the bright eyed, clear skinned Jamie I left a week earlier?
Her face is streaked with heavy orange make-up, which seems to be a chemical reaction from her use of crack. Her hair is unkempt, and she looks drawn from lack of sleep.
"It was so awful last night," she tells me. I stayed at a junkie's, and just had to get out," she says weeping.

Jamie has a bath, washes her hair, and once again looks my old Jamie. Her clothes are piled high in black bin liners in the lounge. I tell her, "You had better sort some out in case you go to prison."
Normally she would challenge the word 'prison' but doesn't argue and sorts through them.

Dexter phones to tell Jamie he has found somewhere new to live, and I am sure she will return to him.
"He's very different now," says Jamie. "He treats me well."
Who's kidding who, I wonder?
As she pigs out in the kitchen I say, "You are using again Jamie, aren't you?"
"Yes, just a little," she replies.
After our meal, I drive Jamie round to Pat's. Taking one look at her, Pat exclaims, "Jamie, what on earth have you been doing? You look awful. Not the Jamie I last saw."

16th January – Monday

I explain to Jamie's probation officer that I can't have her living here. She agrees to see Jamie and indicates they can help with accommodation. I drive Jamie over to meet with the officer.

17th January – Tuesday

The police phone me. "Do you know the latest on Jamie? We've heard she's out of prison."
I tell them, "She's back on crack and working."

If only someone would contain Jamie, for her own sake. It is never ending. She hurts herself, her family and society. No one seems to care. They say the law is an ass – I know it is.

18th January – Wednesday

Mid morning: While bagging-up Jamie's clothes I find a Christmas card from Jamie to Dexter. She speaks of her baby, due June/July, and she intends to keep it. Is she still pregnant I wonder? Where is she now?

I pluck up courage to ring Jamie's probation officer. Agencies will not generally speak to parents about their clients but this woman is brilliant. She says, "When I saw Jamie on Monday morning, I found her a probation hostel which would give her a new bail address. She is contacting the drug team regarding rehabilitation.

We had half an hour break for lunch, intending to continue afterwards. But Jamie failed to return. I have no option but to issue a warrant for her arrest," she says.
When I mention Jamie's pending cheque fraud charge, her probation officer knows nothing about the charge. She appears very kind and understanding and we agree to keep in touch.

Social services say they are having difficulty finding a mixed race family to adopt Ben. The system is crazy, absolutely crazy!
He is quarter-caste, and there may be a white family longing to adopt such a beautiful child. But, black is the dominating factor as far as social services are concerned.
There are white people from this country going abroad to adopt black babies. What is the sense in all this?
What about the best interests of the child, giving him a loving and caring home as soon as possible?

At teatime, Jamie phones and I am very annoyed with her. "Why didn't you go back to probation this afternoon?" I ask. "A warrant has been issued for your arrest."

221

"I thought there would be," she says. "I intend to give myself up after Max's birthday."

"Why on earth didn't you take the opportunities offered by probation?" I ask.

"It's my life," she says aggressively and slams down the phone.

Later Jamie phones and apologises, saying she was in a bad mood earlier – but I know she was desperate on a comedown.

I warn her, "If you come over here, the police are aware of the broken bail conditions and I don't want them turning up, for Max's sake."

She quickly changes the subject. "I shoplifted a £99 duvet and silk cardigan today." I can't believe her nerve.

"How on earth do you get a duvet out of the store?" I ask her.

"Oh, it's easy," says Jamie, "I just picked it up and walked out.

Must go, I'll be in touch"...the phone goes dead.

21st January – Saturday. Max's Birthday

6.15 a.m: I am half asleep in bed when the phone suddenly rings. Jamie is weepy. "Mum, can you pick me up? I've got all my stuff. I want to be with Max on his birthday."

"Jamie, you'll have to get a lift."

"I can't," she says.

Half asleep, I find it difficult to get my thoughts together. "I'll come over on the condition that you hand yourself in to the police on Monday."

"Okay," she replies, weeping. "I'll have to rob Max's present 'cause I haven't got any money."

Jamie is waiting for me, looking very tired and vacant, with plastic bags stood by her side.

On the journey home she says, "I've suddenly realised. I have got some sheets, which I shoplifted last week. I can return them and get gift vouchers for Max's present."

Jamie speaks of her shoplifting and says, "I put the clothes, complete with coat hangers, over my arm, and walk straight out through the door, behind someone else – so as not to be seen on the video.

When I was caught two weeks ago, I'd taken most of the labels off so they couldn't prove they were shoplifted." Jamie laughs, "I was able to keep all those items."

Jamie has a bad mark above her lip and says, "It's a bruise from a punter.

He wanted me to go to a certain place, but I insisted we went to a place I knew. He pulled my hair, got nasty and punched me in the face.

I thought, Jamie, you've got to look after yourself and get out of here – so I punched him in the private parts and got out quickly.

I always take clients to a pub car park or by the taxi rank. It's much safer. I can call for help if necessary. I planned my getaway from him, screamed for the taxi men, and the chap drove away."

After chatting for a short while back at home, Jamie retires to bed. She asks me to wake her at noon so she can get Max's present.

Jamie is costing me a fortune even though I don't physically give her money. When she is in prison she needs stamps and writing paper, I use petrol, and buy refreshments when we visit. Most times we meet, I treat her to a packet of cigarettes and sometimes a snack. When she is in custody at the station, I buy chocolate, drinks, cigarettes and sandwiches, with petrol costing £5 a time.

At noon, I shout at Jamie to get up out of bed but she takes no notice. It is four in the afternoon when she eventually rises, halfway through Max's birthday party. She appears looking pale and puffy, with her wet hair held back off the forehead by a band. Jamie isn't interested in what is going on around us. Her total state of lifelessness, and walking around like a zombie, indicates recent drug use.

My friend Jane asks, "Angela, is Jamie pregnant? She certainly looks it." "She constantly denies it," I reply. "But you now confirm my suspicions."

Jamie leaves to stay the night at Pat's house. There is no way I can cope with her here. On Monday morning I have every intention of driving her personally to the police station.

As I sit down and reflect on the day I feel so sad for Max...no card or present from his mummy. He is hopefully too young to bare a grudge against her – but next year, or the year after, he will be much more aware he has been let down.

22nd January – Sunday

Late afternoon, Jamie turns up at my house saying she slept until four o'clock.

Pale and very preoccupied, she sits on the settee watching T.V., taking no notice of Max. There is little conversation and she eventually falls asleep. I study her as she lies on the settee. Is she pregnant? She always denies it but I am convinced she is.

After tea, Jamie sorts out her clothes, putting aside a small bag of items for prison, expected tomorrow. She goes back to Pat's for the night.

23rd January – Monday

10.50 a.m. Jamie arrives from Pat's. While changing her cardigan, she purposely turns her back on me. Is she trying to hide her slightly bulging tummy from me?

I overhear Jamie on the phone to a friend, telling him, "I probably won't hand myself in."

As she puts the phone down, I tackle her. "Jamie, I'm only prepared to drive you back on the condition you go directly to the police.

Jamie shrugs her shoulders, "Why should I? Anyway, I haven't got a bail address."

"Why should you get bail?" I ask angrily. "You must pay for your crimes – you get away with everything."

Jamie stares right through me – eyes unblinking...the same stare she had as a child. I feel threatened. She looks as if she might stab me.

"I'm disgusted with the way you carry on." I tell her. "There's no way I'm taking you back. You can hitch a lift," I shout as Jamie continues to stare.

Who is this woman sitting before me? Certainly this is not my daughter. As Jamie storms out of the house, I hand her the bag of clothes; and sigh a sigh of relief as she slams the door.

24th January – Tuesday

Dexter phones this afternoon. He has to repeat himself a number of times because I can't understand his broad lingo. "Have you heard from Jamie?" he asks. "Do you know where she is?"

"I don't know," I tell him.

"Dexter, is Jamie pregnant?" I ask. "I have found a letter confirming she is, but Jamie is denying it."

"I think she may be," he says.

26th January – Thursday

8.00 p.m: The doorbell rings – two police officers stand on my doorstep. I invite them into the dining room, asking, "Is it about my daughter, Jamie." They confirm it is and enquire of her whereabouts. After hearing the full story they say they will send papers to court for Monday and contact the probation officer to see if the warrant has been issued.

30th January – Monday

Jamie's court hearing: I phone the court who inform me that a final decision will be made tomorrow morning.

This evening I contact one of Jamie's friends and he tells me, "As far as I know Jamie didn't turn up at court this afternoon."

I am not surprised. What has she got to lose? She won't be penalised. Jamie **never** is.

She hasn't contacted me and must be lying low.

31st January – Tuesday

Jamie sounds very down this evening. "You didn't turn up at court then," I say warily.

She retorts, "I'm not stupid."

"Where are you living Jamie, at a friend's?"

"Yes," she replies but doesn't divulge where. "Dexter and I aren't speaking.

The council have to give me a flat because I'm homeless – providing I accept a flat in a grotty area. I'll furnish it with the grant I'll get of £900."

"But you had a huge grant last year," I say horrified.

Jamie quickly changes the subject. "I'm organising it so I don't have to go on the streets. There's no way they're going to catch me! Even though I am in hiding, I will keep in touch with you."

Crackhead

Killing Me Softly – 1995

2nd February – Thursday

Today, Pat and I give our first talk to 400 pupils in assembly at a local high school. The children listen, stunned at our stories, and one is in tears. For half an hour they sit in total silence.

Previously, these children have only heard the good side of drugs and how to take them safely. It is time they hear the sadness, heartache and painful effects of drugs on abusers and their families.

3rd February – Friday

"This is the solicitor's secretary speaking," says the voice at the end of the phone. "Jamie is with her solicitor at the police station and has been caught shoplifting. She is rather high, on goodness knows what, and the police can't interview her. A solicitor will call and inform you what's happening."
Four hours later, Jamie phones. "I'll be appearing in court in the morning and prosecution aren't opposing bail."
She shouts above the constant noise of someone banging on the cells. "Mum, is it possible for you to bring a couple of big shirts and a cardigan tomorrow?"
Of course...she will need them big if she's pregnant.

4th February – Saturday

Jamie phones in the afternoon saying, "I've been released on bail until Tuesday. Can we meet?"
Why is it always *bail, bail, bail?* Where is the control on crime in this country? There appears to be none.
When I tell Bill I suspect Jamie is pregnant he says jokingly, "She'll probably give birth to a load of Marks & Spencer clothes."

5th February – Sunday
Jamie's birthday.

I feel so sorry for Joy when I pop in to see her. With three sons on drugs,

227

she is so depressed. It must be horrendous for her and I honestly don't know how she keeps going.

Mid-day, no sign of Jamie as arranged, and Max is very disappointed. After waiting twenty minutes, I pull away from the car park. Looking over my shoulder, I see Jamie racing towards us. She tries to catch her breath to speak, sounding very asthmatic and looking so pale and washed out.

"I'm sorry I'm late," she gasps. "I've only been awake two minutes. I didn't sleep at all last night, and fell asleep at 11.30 this morning."

Jamie's black cardigan is covered in dog hairs. She is dressed in leggings, short black leather heeled boots, a cardigan with a body suit under. In her hand she carries a black beret and gloves. She always seems to manage a totally new look.

As we drive to meet Joy, Jamie struggles to change her clothes in the back of the car. I glance in the mirror and she appears to be hiding herself as she changes. Is it because she is pregnant?"

While Jamie puts make-up on in the cloakroom of the pub, Joy arrives with her daughters. I tell her, "I'm sure Jamie is expecting. She's got such a big bust."

Jamie joins us, face freshly made-up, but she looks gaunt and pale. As we eat lunch and chat, Jamie talks of the past 24 hours.

"I knew the magistrate would let me off as soon as I saw him," she says. "He had that look about him.

When I was released from court, they put a ban on me entering the city centre. Immediately, I walked into town and shoplifted at Boots," she chuckles, proudly pointing to the bodysuit and black cotton blouse she is wearing.

"The alarms went off. I nearly died and just continued to calmly walk through the doors."

"Dexter lost £3000 worth (2 ozs) of crack last night," she says sounding very worried. "He was totally out of his mind, as he always is. He shoved the crack under the fence of an old peoples' home and couldn't remember where he'd put it.

While groping in the dark in the middle of the night, with a torch, we were tackled by a woman who asked what we were doing. We said we were looking for jewellery.

By this morning we hadn't found it and Dexter is panicking because he hasn't paid for it."

Jamie tucks in, enjoying her roast beef and Yorkshire pudding – my birthday present to her.
I glance over at Jamie and with horror notice her hands – then her collar bone. So thin and bony: she looks anorexic. But her breasts are so full. She must be expecting.
After the meal, Joy takes the children outside to play. I think...now is my chance I take a deep breath...
"Jamie, are you pregnant?" I ask.
She looks up, and snaps, "No."
Looking straight at her, I say, "You are, aren't you?"
A momentary silence then, "Yes," she admits, "I'm seven months. Honestly, mum, I couldn't believe it when they told me at the prison."
I can't believe it either. She looks barely four months, and still in size 8 clothes. At long last I know the truth. My suspicions have proved right.

"Jamie, I can't cope emotionally with being involved with another baby."
"Well, I don't want the baby," she says. "Anyway, Dexter says he'll have it."
"You must be joking," I say horrified.
"One of his 'baby mothers' will look after it," says Jamie. "She has a lovely home and at least the baby will stay in the family."
I am aghast at the thought. Chances are they could use the baby to blackmail Jamie.
"Are you getting any antenatal treatment?" I ask. "No," she says. "They've told me to book an appointment."

"Why don't you consider adoption, together with Ben," I say cautiously. Jamie looks up surprised, obviously not having considered it. Again, after some thought, she says, "It will go to Dexter's baby mother."
Jamie starts to look tired, and the blusher on her cheeks fails to hide how pale she is. We drive Joy home and she hugs Jamie warmly telling her, "Jamie, look after yourself."

7th February – Tuesday

I ring the court and they inform me, "Jamie hasn't turned up. A warrant for arrest, no bail, has been issued." But Jamie is NEVER arrested. Perhaps this time we will have results.

As I lie in bed, I am very worried and tense, haunted by how thin Jamie looks.

9th February – Thursday

Jamie's ex-boyfriend Clinton, and his brother Steve, appear on an attempted murder charge. The court public gallery is deserted and I am the first to arrive. The brothers peer through the door and, pleased to see me, glance over smiling and wave.

The jury consists of all men, with the exception of one woman. A black solicitor is the only black person in the room. I think to myself, how very unfair. Both guys have tatty dreadlocks: Clinton is dressed in a suit, his brother in casual attire.

The hearing proceeds and witnesses are called. They talk of Steve Dred, a name so familiar to me from the past. I recall when Jamie was in college and she introduced me to him, and how scared I was. Dionne arrives to support her brothers, with her mum.

The exhibit, a sawn-off shotgun, is passed around the courtroom. I never thought in my life I would ever see a real shot gun right before my eyes. I chat to Dionne's mother who confirms the premonitions she had before the shooting.

Tonight I am worried something is very wrong. Is Jamie in hospital I wonder?

17th February – Friday

The brothers are found not guilty. Clinton has been released. But Steve is held on a further charge.

I contact the police to ask if they have seen Jamie recently and voice my concerns. "She is pregnant and looking very ill, and should have contacted me, but I have heard nothing."

The officer tells me, "Jamie was certainly seen working last week although she didn't turn up in court for the cheque fraud. There is now a warrant out for her arrest."

It's a joke. Another warrant!

"I'm sure she will be on the run from the police and in hiding," he says,

I request that he informs his colleagues Jamie isn't here in Stratford. Hopefully they won't come looking for her in the middle of the night. I can't face it. He says he will phone with any further information as soon as possible.

10.40 p.m: At last, Jamie makes contact.
"Why haven't you been in touch, Jamie?" I ask.
She is very cagey, not wanting to say much or give me her number. "Speak to you later," she says.
I sense things are very wrong and tell her, "Jamie ring at any time. Joy is also asking you ring her because she's worried about you."
"I will," she replies and puts the phone down.

Jamie rings again. "Why haven't you been in touch for so long?" I ask her.
"Well, I've been busy. You know what it's like," she replies.
"On crack, you mean? Out of your head on crack?" I ask bluntly.
"Well I suppose so. Yes," she replies light heartedly.
"Are you alright? Is the baby alright?" I ask.
"Yes, everything's okay," she replies.
Jamie says she is getting a good grant for the flat she hopes to get soon. It's criminal. She gets grants or loans, one after another from the Department of Social Security and never pays them back.
"You didn't turn up for your cheque fraud court hearing then?" I ask.
"Yes, I know," says Jamie, becoming weepy and upset. "I must go. Bye," she says, quickly putting the phone down.

21st February – Tuesday

I write to Michael Howard MP, Home Secretary, saying I am appalled with the way things are being handled in Jamie's case. I am getting very angry, especially when everyone denies there is a problem.

23rd February – Thursday

Jamie sounds surprisingly well when she rings. "Mum, are you coming over?" she asks. "Can I see you? I'm staying at Sindy's, where I stayed before."
I arrange to go over tomorrow. At least I can see if she is okay.
"Mum, can you bring some vegetables, please? We have a chicken and I don't know what to do with it."
"Okay, I'll bring some," I tell her.

24th February – Friday

This morning I'm feeling very angry at the lack of the authorities' control of Jamie. For over a year there have been many warrants for her arrest but to no avail.

I am just one of many frustrated parents whose children are getting deeper and deeper into crime to pay for their habit – but they are never made to pay for their crime. Jamie represents thousands of youngsters and adults in this country who break the law without being penalised. Nobody seems interested.

I complain to the Chief Superintendent of police, telling him, "The last two years have been a fiasco. Jamie is totally out of control."
He agrees, but points out that this time Jamie is pregnant, which could pose a problem if she is arrested and tries to do a runner. This could possibly start early labour and loss of the baby, and she would then blame the police.
Under the circumstances, I totally agree with him.
Joy phones me tonight and reads a poem over the phone, which she wrote earlier this month, when Jamie confirmed to us that she was expecting her baby.

Killing me softly

It's warm in here and comforting,
Feels soft and so secure,
What wondrous thing is happening?
I'm changing more and more.

Yesterday I found my fingers,
Today I spotted toes,
And guess what funny thing I found?
I think it's called a nose.
I can hear my mummy's heartbeat,
And sounds, outside quite near,
Is that my daddy's voice now?
Oh, it's lovely growing here.

Mummy I don't feel too well,
What's happening out there?
I can't see things so clearly
Please help, it isn't fair.

I'm shaking and I'm frightened,
Why do I feel this way?
Mummy can't you hear me,
Please...not again today!

You keep talking about the crack,
And say how great the hit,
But you know it makes me poorly,
You must care just a bit.

What did you just say mummy?
You don't want me at all?
But I love you so much mummy
Please listen to my call.
I hardly feel a part of me,
What's happening in my head.
Stop it! Stop it mummy!
or I think that I'll be *dead*.

Joy Palmer

As I put down the phone, I am left with a lump in my throat.

Joy is keen to come with me to Sindy's to see Jamie. We bang on the door and Jamie appears smiling, inviting us in. She looks so ill, pale and very thin – her face covered in spots. It is difficult to assess how far gone she is but, as Jamie gets out of her armchair, she looks almost full-term.

"Dexter says, when I have had the baby, I must toe the line and behave myself" she tells Joy. "He says he will have the baby after it's born."

Jamie says she has to meet Dexter shortly, and looks much better after putting on her make-up. "It's wonderful to have some clean clothes again – Sindy has bought a washing machine especially," she says.

The terraced house is very warm and cosy and I am a lot happier now that I know Jamie is comfortable and relatively safe. As Sindy shows me around the house, I realise she knows nothing of the warrants out for

Jamie. "I'm worried about Jamie returning to the house with the baby afterwards," she says.

"Social Services will probably put the baby into care" I reassure her.

Sindy is very surprised, knowing little of Jamie's history.

"What if she goes into premature labour? They often do when they stop taking drugs," she says sounding frightened. "Jamie hasn't had any for a week now, and sleeps most of the time."

I suggest, "Get Jamie straight to hospital as soon as she starts, otherwise the baby could be born in the house. It could put you in an embarrassing situation because you are harbouring Jamie from the police."

Sindy shows me Jamie's bedroom, warm and well furnished. "I couldn't let Jamie sleep on a concrete floor, as she was in her previous place," she says, "especially being so heavily pregnant.

When Jamie came here she was smelly and her clothes filthy. That's why I had to get the washing machine. Jamie is giving me some money for food."

Back downstairs, I ask Jamie, "Did you have any crack last night?"

"No", she replies.

Sindy says, "Jamie looked really well until she stayed out last night. Chances are she had some."

We drive to the shops and park while Joy pops into a store. Jamie and I wait in the car and watch a couple of guys enter a supermarket. "Hey Jamie, is that Dexter over there?"

Peering through the window she says, "Oh yes."

I get a fleeting glance at Dexter who appears to be quite good looking.

Exhausted, as I get into bed tonight, I can relax knowing Jamie is warm, comfortable and well fed.

26th February – Sunday

Today I feel very stressed and can't put my mind to anything. I call at Solace, for support and a 'listening ear'. After a long chat I feel so much better. Batteries recharged, I am now ready to face heaven knows what in the next few days.

Max and I go to Irish Dancing – I hope the music and new people will do me good. We arrive early to see the young girls in their dancing class. It reminds me of Jamie when she was young and brings tears to my eyes.

I have written to Jamie today, to say I shall take a meal and groceries over once a week, and ask her to keep in touch. I am doing it mainly for the sake of her unborn child.

27th February – Monday

Jamie phones this afternoon, very excited. "Sindy has arranged for me to see the drug agency tomorrow about rehab. Maybe, if I can get my act together, I shall hand myself in. I need six weeks detox. I will be able to look after the baby at a rehab centre," she says.
My heart sinks. I have heard it all before and can't bear it anymore.
"Mum, I'm really doing well now and I'm not having hardly any crack."

"Jamie, if things carry on like this, I will be needing crack before long!" I say exasperated

28th February – Tuesday

Afternoon: Sindy phones, "Jamie has been to the drug agency and they hope to get her a place at rehab in Birmingham."

At at teatime, Jamie phones from a call box – very bubbly about the idea. "A drug counsellor will be coming to see me in the next 48 hours," she says.
"I'm thrilled, and have done it off my own bat," she says. "I'm in a phone box waiting for a taxi and I'm frozen. I haven't got a coat on, only a cardigan. I've been to visit a friend."
There is a bitter north wind tonight with lots of snow expected. I worry about Jamie, especially with her baby due at any time.
"What have you been doing?" I ask.
"A bit of drugs and that," she replies. "I can sit and relax at Sindy's. I don't have crack and don't even think about it. I only have £20 to £30 worth of heroin a night and I'm satisfied, whereas it used to be £300 to £400 of crack a night."
"But the baby is still a crack baby," I tell her. "Are you both okay?"
"Oh yes," she says, "I've put on loads of weight and I'm right chubby now."
I smile to myself as I detect the hint of a Yorkshire accent.
I can hear Jamie's teeth chattering as she shivers in the phone box.
"I've been waiting twenty minutes," she says.
"Mum, can you chase the taxi for me, please? It's booked in the name of Sophie – just in case I have to do a bunk and can't pay," she jokes.

If Jamie wasn't pregnant, I wouldn't phone the taxi firm. However, I am worried about her and the safety of the baby in such freezing conditions. When I ring back to say the taxi is on it's way she says, "Talk to me mum, until the taxi comes...bye, must go, taxi's here," and she hangs up.

Waiting for Angel – 1995

3rd March – Friday

I drive over to Sindy's armed with pork casserole, and rock cakes – though not the rock Jamie is used to. I knock warily on the door. Sindy answers followed by Jamie dressed in her silky white pyjamas.

Jamie says, "I had an appointment to see a doctor at 'All Saints drug rehab.' this morning but the trains weren't running because of the snow."

"Have you let them know you couldn't make the appointment?" I ask.

"No", she replies, appearing disinterested.

The girls are pleased with the food, and as we sit talking Jamie scoffs the cakes. She is looking a little better and, although pale and spotty, she has put on quite a bit of weight.

I am concerned when Jamie tells me she still hasn't had any antenatal care or seen a doctor. As I drive home I worry and decide I must seek help. The interests of the baby must come first.

7th March – Tuesday

I speak to a midwife on the phone. She is very concerned to learn of Jamie's situation and will call to see her. I write to Jamie to put her in the picture. "You are having a crack baby and *must* have medical attention," I insist.

9th March – Thursday

I knock on the door and Sindy hurriedly ushers Joy and myself in. She is keen to chat while Jamie is out.

"Has the midwife called?" I enquire.

"Yes, but Jamie wasn't here.

Earlier in the week there was a knock on the door and it was Gibbo, announcing he was suddenly off to Jamaica. Jamie was distraught and heartbroken," says Sindy. "She immediately went to Gibbo's where Dexter was staying. Jamie has been with Dexter ever since, returning here only for her meals in the evenings."

I give Sindy a leg of lamb and some vegetables. "I'll have a good meal ready for Jamie if she comes home tonight," she says. "Jamie is looking really good now and has a real round tummy. I make sure she eats and then I know she's okay. It worries me that Jamie is now with Dexter and smoking crack. She is losing weight again."

"Who is taking Jamie to hospital?" I ask.
"Dexter," says Sindy. "He says he will take Jamie. He's got ten kids already."
As we leave the house, numb from what we have heard, Joy turns to me, "I dread to think what state Dexter could be in when Jamie starts labour. Jamie told me at Christmas that Dexter is always high on crack. At times he is gone completely and Jamie would leave him for hours until he regained consciousness. Imagine if he is like that when she goes into labour."

It is comforting to have a friend like Joy who understands, without whose help I have couldn't have got through all this.

11th March – Saturday

10.45 p.m: The telephone wakes me up. "It's me Mum, I've been arrested," says Jamie. "I'm in terrible pain."
I ask to speak to the officer in charge. "Jamie is okay and has just seen a doctor," he tells me.
"Why were you arrested Jamie?" I ask.
"On warrant." She complains of pain once more. "I had to run when they tried to arrest me – and fell down some steps...Mum, the pain is really bad." Jamie is weepy but seems to be sound of mind.
"Have you had any crack tonight Jamie?" I ask.
"No," she replies.
"Mum, can you bring me in some clothes please? When will you be able to come? I'll be here 'till Monday."
Repeatedly she says, "I'm in terrible pain."
As I say goodbye I tell her, "Jamie, take care and let me know if you go into hospital."

Adrenalin rushes...at this rate I shall be an ideal candidate for a heart attack. One of my biggest fears was that Jamie would do a runner if the police tried to arrest her – and she did. On the other hand, I can go to bed tonight knowing Jamie and her unborn baby are safe.

12th March – Sunday

Jamie has been taken to the hospital for a check up and is now back at the police station. Sindy is upset when I tell her Jamie is in custody but I try to convince her it is for the best, both for Jamie and the baby. She agrees with me that long-term prison will probably be Jamie's saviour.

We sort out Jamie's clothes. Sindy says there are loads of condoms in Jamie's bag, but we find they are gone. She is convinced Jamie has been working, even though she is eight month's pregnant.
Sindy delves into the plastic bags and, as she draws out loads of black tights, says, "When they were dirty Jamie would just shoplift another pair."

I call at the police station to drop off the clothes for Jamie, together with requested items. The policewoman behind the desk passes me a message from Jamie, scribbled in red biro on a paper serviette. She asks me to pop to her friend Hughie's flat and leave a message for Dexter. Hughie turns out to be a good-looking man of mixed race with long black curly hair. He asks me into the house and enquires about Jamie saying, "She must get herself sorted out."

This evening Jamie rings. The hospital has told her that the baby is very small, 30 weeks in size, and if not born by 3 to 4 weeks, they will induce it.

13th March – Monday

At the Magistrates Court, Jamie's name is called. She looks pale and unwell as she stands in the dock, looking sixteen with her hair behind her ears. Her breasts are full and heavy under her large green shirt.
The nerve of it – Jamie gives my address when asked where she resides. I vow, never again.
She pleads guilty to charges of shoplifting, non-attendance of probation, failure to report for court hearings, and breaking bail conditions. While the magistrates are out deliberating, Jamie and I chat. She is annoyed the way things are going and says, "I should get off lightly."
"You have to come to terms with what you've done and pay for your crime," I tell her.
As we chat Jamie tells me, "Dexter kidnapped someone at gun point last week. He got the money owed to him but is now being hunted by a gang. The Mosside crowd are also after him."

The magistrate returns and declares, "We can only give a maximum sentence of twelve months, but we don't consider this long enough. It will have to go to Crown Court."

Jamie is shocked. She sways as if she is going to faint and the matron warder supports her by the arm. Jamie is taken off to Risley prison.

She rings very upset, telling me she is being transferred to the prison hospital, and asks, "When can you come up?"

"It will have to be when I'm ready and can face the long journey," I tell her. "Perhaps 2 to 3 weeks, or when the baby is born. In the meantime I will see you when you are brought down to appear in court soon."

14th March – Tuesday

I write to Jamie asking, "Have you decided what you are doing with the baby? You said you didn't want to keep it."

Dexter phones me and says he will write to Jamie. Very unlikely, though, because he can't read or write.

27th March – Monday

It is two weeks since Jamie went to prison and I am trying to unwind. This has all been too much for me. Jamie sends me a visiting order asking when I can get up to Risley? In her letter she writes a little piece, which touches my heart:

> *"I hope you like the mother's day card – made it today in education. Put all the kids names in – even the unborn, because I'm sure they are as grateful to you as I am for all you have done for us. Even though they are too young to understand – but one day they will.*

I answer reluctantly:

> *"Sorry I can't get up at present. I feel too ill but will definitely come up when the baby is born. I enclose a mother's day card from Max and £5 for a phone card. See you when you come down for the court hearing on Friday."*

31st March – Friday

Crown Court: Jamie stands in the dock, pale and stern faced, looking full-term. Her hair is shoulder-length with small pony tail on the top of her head and she wears no make-up on her spotless skin. She is wearing a jumper and leggings.

Pat and Joy come to support me in the public gallery.

The barrister presents his case to court, using the unborn child to get a lesser sentence. "Jamie is being induced on Tuesday," he says. "If she has a long sentence the baby will be put into care and be adopted."

Such a sad sob story: he fails to mention her two children already in care, one due to be adopted. I reach boiling point as the barrister points to me saying, "Her mother is very anxious for her."

I break down. It's all lies. I can't stand listening to such rubbish any longer and leave the courtroom. I am angry that Jamie's legal representatives are using an innocent unborn child as a pawn in their game.

Sentence is announced. Afterwards, Joy and Pat inform me Jamie has got eight months, and we go down to the court cells to chat to Jamie before she returns to Risley. Tearful, she asks, "Are you okay mum?" having observed my reaction in the courtroom.

Around her neck I notice a small silver medallion of the Virgin Mary and remark, "I haven't seen that before."

Jamie giggles, "A little nun gave it to me during her prison visit. Believe it or not, I went to church last Sunday."

"Have you heard from Dexter?" she asks.

I tell her I haven't, and she wells up in tears. Jamie feels very let down and upset that he hasn't contacted her.

Time for Jamie to return to HMP Risley and we say our goodbyes. "I'll see you when the baby is born," I say, hugging her.

"Oh, by the way, mum," she says with a wry smile on her face. "I'm not being induced on Tuesday – I was just lying to get off. The baby is actually due on the 17th April."

Pat and I make our way to Hughie's house. I knock and he comes out to my car to chat. "I saw Dexter last night," he says. "I bought these stamps to post his letter to Jamie. Dexter can't write so he dictated the letter to me.

"Jamie is amazing," says Hughie with a smile. "I knew her when she lived in Leamington. She even managed to find me in Swindon – Lord knows how. I can't understand why Jamie returns to such violent situations," he says. "I'm quite happy for her to stay with me, as she has done in the past. I'd prefer her to take crack in the bedroom rather than sneak out as she has done."

We discuss Jamie's potential. She can present such an air of elegance and style, and could work for an escort agency, or massage parlour. But she is now almost rock bottom, sinking further and further out of her depth. "In a letter to me, Jamie indicated she will 'get out' if transferred to Drake Hall," says Hughie. "Her letters appear to be written in such a strange mood."

"I think it's because she hasn't heard from anyone, including Dexter who is, after all, the father of her child." I tell him. "I feel quite sorry for her."

5th April – Wednesday

I call over to see Ben on his second birthday. He is very bright, and quite a handful. Before I leave he gives me a big hug and cuddle and I suddenly realise..."I'm his real grandma – this is my grandson going for adoption." I feel pain and sadness. This should never ever be.

I have written to Jamie today saying I can't tolerate her addiction, crime and neglect of her children. I tell her:

> *"I'm angry you are using your children as pawns in this dangerous game of life you play. I was upset you used the unborn baby to get a lesser sentence, and the sob story about inducement."*

Jamie will be mad with me but I don't care. She will have three months in prison to cool down

8th April – Friday

This morning a letter arrives from my M.P. regarding my complaint on the running of the probation hostel.

He encloses a letter from Baroness Blatch, of the Home Office stating:

> "While I share Mrs. Harrison's frustration that her daughter did not benefit from the community facilities, such as drug

rehabilitation, that will have been available to her when resident at the hostel, there are issues of personal responsibility here. It is not something for which the legal system, the probation service, or the approved hostel sector can justifiably be blamed."

I am fuming. Having spoken to the inmates regarding prostitution, drug taking, and continuing crime during their probationary period, they believe the hostel is a waste of time and taxpayers' money. But naturally there has to be denial by the authorities. Why, for a change, don't the government officials listen and then maybe there could be improvements in the system.

I feel so guilty I haven't been able to visit Jamie. She knows I can't until the baby is born. My doctor insists on giving me anti-depressants because I'm so weepy. Reluctantly I take them, for the first time in my life.

11th April – Tuesday
I receive a letter from Jamie saying she is totally bored with nothing to do but watch T.V.
Risley was mentioned on the news last week. Inspectors say it is one of the best prisons and men were shown working on computers. What about the women I wonder?

17th April – Monday
Jamie's baby is due today but there is no news. She is to appear in court on Wednesday for cheque fraud. I write to the magistrates today to warn them she will use the baby to try to get a lesser sentence.

Max is so happy and contented these days, showing very few signs of insecurity. It makes life much easier for me.

19th April – Wednesday
While waiting for Jamie to be brought into court, her solicitor comes over to me and explains, "Jamie may go to Drake Hall after the baby is born, or Styles baby unit."
"But she can't go to Styles," I say in a panic. "She is totally incapable of mothering." I am left speechless.

Jamie enters the room, glances up and smiles at me from the dock. She looks so pale. The baby is a good size now – she has been eating well in prison, and hopefully is drug free. The charges are listed, including cheques used in Northampton, Warwick, Lincoln, and Doncaster. This is a very small proportion of what Jamie maintains she has done – over £100,000. The police only have £12/13,000 proven against her. Magistrates agree the case should go to Crown Court.

Jamie's solicitor points out Jamie is already a serving prisoner, due to give birth on Monday, and requests she be remanded in custody. Jamie is led away from the dock.

20th April – Thursday

I speak to the social worker, voicing my concern over Jamie going to Styles mother & baby unit. She assures me, "Everything is in hand. Don't worry. The hospital say the baby will probably go into their special unit for a while to be monitored because of Jamie's drug use. Jamie is fully aware the baby will go into care when released from hospital."

I am very relieved.

21st April – Friday

I call at Joy's this morning and she is going out of her mind with her sons. Although the lads have their own accommodation, they doss around her place with their mates, eating her out of house and home.

She is desperate because there is nothing left in the larder to feed her little girls. I pop to a supermarket and purchase some food for them – bread, biscuits and margarine and other basics. Joy assures me she will keep the food in the boot of her car so the boys won't be able to touch it.

As we sit chatting, we look out of the window. We can't believe our eyes as Joy's son drives her car away with all the food in the boot. Poor Joy, she can't win. I don't know how she keeps going with three problem sons.

I take Max to see his brother, Ben, who is very warm, loving, energetic and full of fun, but shows signs of aggression. I wonder if this is related to Jamie's use of crack during her pregnancy or inherited? The brothers are getting very fond of each other and I am relieved they will be able to maintain contact with an 'open' adoption.

28th April – Friday

Early this morning I receive a call from Jamie, saying nervously, "Mum, I'm going into Warrington Hospital to be induced."

"I shall come up Sunday after the birth." I reassure her.
"Social Services will be collecting the baby on Monday," she tells me.

Linda, Ben's foster mum, informs me Angel will be going to her friend temporarily for six weeks, and she is quite sad. She had hoped to look after the baby straight away, but this has been arranged because she is due to go on holiday shortly.

Once the baby is born I will break the news to Max. I wonder what he will think about having a baby sister?

29th April – Saturday

4.00 p.m: The thought rushes through my mind of Jamie having a caesarean, even though it hasn't been on the cards.
5.15 p.m: A male prison officer phones to say, "Jamie has produced a 6lb. 4oz. daughter. She is fine but had to have a caesarean. I can't give you any further details except Jamie is very weak."
"Will you be guarding her?" I enquire.
"Yes, right through the night," he says.
How ridiculous, I think to myself. Jamie's not likely to do a runner immediately after a major operation, and she isn't classed as a dangerous criminal.
I am worried as to why Jamie had a caesarean? Was the baby distressed and weak because of crack? Was Jamie weak? I will know tomorrow.
This is one problem I hadn't anticipated. At least Jamie will be in prison for three months, enabling her body to heal before she works again.

I make regular contact with the hospital and speak to Jamie. Both she and the baby are progressing well.

30th April – Sunday

Warrington Hospital: Two prison officers, on guard, frisk Pat and myself, and then let us into the private room.
Jamie looks up from her bed and smiles. "Oh, hi mum," she says excitedly, very pleased and surprised to see us. Looking extremely pale, but quite healthy and chubby in the face, she lies on the bed in a white gown, trying not to move because of the pain. She is heavily dosed up with morphine.

A nurse by the door holds a small tightly wrapped bundle in a blanket. I peer at the baby – she has a mass of black hair, looks healthy and sleeps peacefully. I look at Jamie. "She's really beautiful."

Excited she says, "Mum, I've decided to name her after you – not Angela but Angel." Everyone in the room agrees they like the name and I am very touched.

Jamie explains, "The baby was transverse in the womb. It could have been a dangerous labour." Fortunately all is well, mother and baby are fine.
Pat and I have brought Jamie some toiletry items, food, note-lets, stamps and change for the phone. The warders give us the go-ahead to give them to her without a search.
An officer passes Angel to me. Jamie tells us that the new pink cardigan and babygrow have been provided and knitted by the prison staff.

I give Angel a big cuddle. She is warm, plump, and healthy. After all the crack and other drugs Jamie used constantly during her pregnancy, I am holding a little miracle. She sleeps peacefully, oblivious to the sad world surrounding her – her mother is guarded by two prison officers 24 hours a day and is due to return to prison; and she will go into the security of a loving foster home shortly.
As we take photos of the baby, the officers look on broodily.

Jamie is choked and very bitter when she talks about Dexter. He has only sent one letter in the past seven weeks and none of her so-called friends have been in contact. I am the only one to write and keep in touch. Maybe, having time to reflect will change Jamie – although I doubt it.

"I am thinking of going to a special mother and baby home with Angel," she says.
My heart sinks. I must not get too stressed up, I tell myself. It will never happen."
Jamie tries to make herself comfortable, painfully sliding into position to lovingly cuddle her baby.
I recall Ben's birth when her emotions were the same, but it eventually ended in tragedy.
Proudly looking down at Angel, she says, "I've always wanted a daughter."
I glance at the warders who observe Jamie – a loving mother, so they think – unaware of her past and the neglect of her two previous children.
How will Jamie feel when she and the baby are parted? This is the first time Jamie has no control over the situation and won't be able to say, "She's my baby and I'll do what I want."

Perhaps, if someone had taken things in hand a few years ago, we wouldn't be in this mess now.

We pop out of the room with the warders for a couple of minutes and, I turn to one saying, "I have seen all this before. Jamie's other children are now in care." The warder nods and I think she understands what I am saying.

I ask Jamie about her first days in Risley with no drugs. She says, "I went through cold turkey for about three weeks – it was dreadful. I'll never forget the pain of water touching my skin when I had a shower during custody. I also had electric shock sensations running down one side of my body."

Angel is returned to the special baby unit for observation of possible withdrawal symptoms. As we prepare to leave, Jamie smiles, thanking us once again for coming.

This evening I tell Max he has a new little sister. But he just shrugs his shoulders and continues to watch TV.

5th May – Friday

The ward Sister tells me Jamie is returning to prison this afternoon. Jamie comes to the phone crying and so unhappy, naturally upset at leaving her baby. "I think I'll be moved from Risley pretty soon," she says.

I tell Jamie a joke, she laughs, and seems a lot happier when I put the phone down.

9th May – Tuesday

Ben's foster mum tells me, "Social services are collecting Angel this morning." The baby has passed all the tests at the hospital and everything is fine.

Linda phones again in the evening, "Angel has arrived at her new foster home. She has a very piercing cry, just like Ben, believed to be the result of Jamie's prenatal drug use."

11th May – Thursday

I am very frightened and can't remember anything. I call at my doctors in desperation, only to be told, "Sorry, there are no appointments available until Monday." But I need to see someone now – I'm desperate. Only the thought of my responsibility for Max stops me from going under.

12th May – Friday

I receive a letter from Jamie today in which she writes:

> *"Since Angel's birth I'm a changed person. I feel as though I have eventually grown up. And, given the chance, I can get my life together. I know that I have said it before but I always knew that I'd end back up on the same. But this time NO WAY! I realised, when in the hospital looking at her, what I could have done taking all the drugs and how lucky she is to be 'normal'. It makes me wonder how I could have been so selfish."*

Jamie has said she doesn't want Angel to join Ben at Linda's. This means the baby will be moved as soon as possible, probably to a black family because this is social services' policy.

Jamie has 'rights' and what she says goes, even though this is her third child to be taken into care.

Surely it would be better for brother and sister to be together? It is crazy – there will be three siblings in three different places.

Social services are taking Angel up to visit Jamie in prison on Thursday this week and Tuesday next.

16th May – Tuesday

I receive a letter from Jamie, in reply to my letter in which I said she used her children as pawns:

> *"Don't ever write to me again, or visit me. Just stay away from me from now on. I never want to see you again as long as I live."*

I reply to Jamie saying,

> *"I realise you are rock bottom. It's up to you now"*

and I enclose a stamped addressed envelope, hoping she will reply.

20th May – Saturday

I don't regret writing to Jamie as I did.

I hope Jamie writes soon and that all will be forgiven. Joy has offered to go to court and support Jamie, while I try to keep in touch with her by letter. Instead of taking antidepressants, I shall relax with a glass wine for a change – it makes me feel so much better.

24th May – Wednesday

Dionne rings me. She has received a letter from Jamie, which reads:

> *"Dexter and I are still together. He has moved to another town. How I miss him to the max.*
> *I intend to stay off crack when I get out. I've had enough. Believe me, my junkie days are over. Me and my baby, and maybe Dexter, will one day come off the crack. It is the longest relationship I've ever had. He has three baby mothers who hate me.*
> *When I get out, I plan to get my head together, just settle and concentrate on being a good mother.*
> *Mum and me are not speaking anymore.*

25th May – Thursday

I can't believe the letter I receive from Jamie this morning: *"Dear mum,"* ending *"Love, Jamie."* It is quite chatty, and there is no hint of her awful recent letter. Her mind is so erratic.

27th May – Saturday

In the afternoon the phone rings, "Hi mum, it's me. I'll have to be quick because I'm using a friend's card...I'm in Holloway."
I am surprised because every prison has been mentioned in her expected move, except Holloway. Jamie seems happy. "It's really nice – much better than Risley. I've been here two days now."
She sounds really good and it has uplifted me no end.

4th June – Sunday

Unexpectedly, Jamie has been transferred to Drake Hall open prison in Staffordshire. I now feel strong enough to visit her.
We are pleased to see each other, and as we hug we wipe the tears from our cheeks. There is lots of news to catch up on after five weeks. After our embrace, Jamie apologises for the awful letter she sent me.
There is very little security in the large visiting room. We sit at a small table in a quiet corner. There would be every opportunity, if one wished, to pass drugs. No wonder there is a drug problem in prisons.

I show Jamie the photo of Angel and Ben. "When is Angel moving to Linda's?" asks Jamie.

"She's not," I reply, "because that's what you requested."

"I don't understand," says Jamie puzzled. "I definitely want Angel to go to Linda's," and scribbles on an envelope, 'To whom it may concern – I wish Angel to reside at Linda Davies' together with her brother Ben,' and hands it to me to give to social services.

Perhaps if the 'system' had not bowed to Jamie's wishes in the first place, we wouldn't now be faced with her changing her mind – and Ben and Angel would have always been together.

Jamie talks of her stay in Holloway prison. "It was great there mum. There was a swimming pool and good gym. We were with Jamaicans – the yardie women waiting to be deported – and I kept shouting at them about crack.

I've been doing maths at Drake Hall, but I'm hopeless," she giggles.

"Do you think I could get rehab when I leave here?" she asks.

"You'll probably have to wait until you get out to organise it," I tell her.

"I don't want to return back to my old haunts, otherwise I'll go back on drugs," she admits.

As we chat Jamie announces, "Oh, by the way mum, I'm having the five-year contraceptive patch in my arm when I come out."

"Good – something positive at long last." Then I stop to think...what Jamie says now she forgets five minutes later. I let it go in one ear and out the other.

19th June – Monday

Still nothing in the post: most strange! Jamie is becoming unreliable – is she getting drugs in prison I wonder?

The social worker informs me Jamie is due out on the 30th June. She will probably do a disappearing act as soon as she gets out, before her cheque fraud hearing.

Angel's foster mum takes her over to see Ben, at Linda's. Linda phones to let me know how things are going.

She tells me Angel appears to be affected by crack, crying all the time, is restless, and has a stare – just like Jamie's stare as a baby. Ben had the stare when he was young, but I haven't seen it in Max.

23rd June – Friday

Chris Lambrianou, who was a member of the infamous 'Kray' twins gang, called at my house to discuss our parent support group. He is involved in a drug rehabilitation centre near Oxford, after having spent many years in prison.

"Jamie would like to go for rehab.," I tell him, "but has been told there's no funding."

"The money is always there," says Chris, "but you've got to fight for it."

"But I'm worn out, Chris, and can't fight anymore," I tell him despondently.

25th June – Sunday

As Pat, Dionne and myself walk through the prison gate towards the guard's office, we can see Jamie basking in the hot sun on a bench in the prison gardens and she waves. We are escorted away from other visitors because Jamie's visiting order only permits half an hour visiting. At the prison canteen about a dozen prisoners sit at tables anxiously waiting for their visitors.

Jamie is bonny, and pink in the face from the sun. She has a moan about the weight she has put on.

"I've been a disaster working in the kitchens," she says laughing. "I dowsed the chef with the hosepipe; dropped a tub of margarine on the floor; and broke cups and saucers. The prison has docked my pay."

How on earth, I wonder, would she ever be able to cope with a baby?

"What are you going to do when you get out?" I ask.

"I've got a place in a housing association hostel – that's good because it means I will eventually get one of their flats. My social worker has organised it."

As we leave the prison I turn to Pat. "You know, I don't think Jamie has changed. I can't think why, or put my finger on it."

"No, she hasn't changed," agrees Pat.

Jamie seems a harder woman, and totally in a dream – not as bad as she was three weeks ago. But of course she was getting over having the baby then. We shall have to wait and see what happens to Jamie next – it will always be the unexpected.

I tell Pat, "I reckon within two weeks out of prison she will be back on crack."

29th June – Thursday

I receive the news that a foster mother, who is black, has been found for Angel – even though she hasn't looked after a baby for many years.

I am dumbfounded, and everyone involved in this case is astounded as well.

Originally Jamie asked that the baby be near her when she is released from prison; but her more recent request that they be placed together has been ignored and social services have steam-rollered ahead.

They are more bothered about placing with similar ethnic background, than the welfare of the children.

Brother and sister will soon be in different homes.

Only Taking Cannabis – 1995

3rd July – Monday

Out of the blue I hear from an excited Jamie, saying, "I'm coming out Wednesday." I dread it, knowing our crises will begin once more.

Jamie's drug counsellor has suggested that she sorts out Max's access with the social worker. I am flabbergasted and annoyed at her interference. Social services have not been involved regarding Max's access. This worker has only known Jamie twelve months and hasn't got a clue of her history or details of my court order.

It is my responsibility to arrange reasonable access. I have never denied Jamie this, although many times I have wanted to say, "Jamie, I've had enough." Consideration also has to be given to Max's emotional well being and stability.

If Agencies worked with parents instead of against them, there would be a far greater understanding of the situation. They rely on what the addict tells them – most of which is lies. But, of course, in their eyes the addict is always right.
"You can see Max once a month," I tell Jamie.
"Twice a month," she demands.
"Jamie, I can't look to the future because I feel too ill."

She changes the subject. "I'll come over to your house for my clothes."
"No, I'll bring them to you." I say.
I can't face Jamie coming here. This way, I can keep her at arm's length – away from my home, my haven of peace and sanity.

4th July – Tuesday

I call to see baby Angel and Ben. Running out to greet me Ben hugs me saying, "Hello grandma."
How my heart is touched – he is gorgeous.

253

Angel is staying temporarily with Linda while her foster mum is on holiday. She is beautiful, with a thick mass of silky straight hair; dark brown skin as soft as a peach; and big melting soft brown eyes. She lies contented, falling asleep in my arms.

A care worker calls after a short while to take her to visit Jamie in prison.

I don't know when I will see Angel next. She is off to the new foster mother this week. We all say it is ridiculous she should be moved but social services are adamant.

Angel is half-caste; has a white mother; her brother is quarter cast with white foster parents, and she is currently with white foster parents; her other brother is white; she has a white grandmother (me); and the only roots Angel will be sure about (her mother's) are white.

What on earth is going on is this country today? If I had the strength I would fight. In 1993, it was stated in Parliament that the child's welfare is of paramount importance, before political correctness. Surely, and everyone agrees with me including the foster mum, that political correctness should mean Angel and her brother Ben staying together?

5th July – Wednesday

8.45 a.m. "Mum. I'm out, and at the rail station."

My heart sinks and I feel sick. I can't believe it, so early in the morning.

"Mum, you sound down," Jamie says worried.

"I'm feeling desperately low," I tell her.

Jamie says she's off to buy some hair clips for Angel. She hasn't changed – with Ben at three months old it was sunglasses; Max had Reebok trainers at eight months, and hair slides for Angel at nine weeks. She treats them like dolls.

"Have you got any money?" I enquire.

"£50," she replies.

Jamie asks again, "Are you sure you're alright, mum?"

Where do we go from here I wonder? What will happen next?

Max keeps busy with rehearsals for the musical 'My One True Friend' in Stratford.

Jamie doesn't phone back as she said she would. This is the first indicator to me, being unreliable, that she has gone straight back to smoking crack.

6th July – Thursday

Jamie apologises for not phoning last night explaining, "I had two pints, was unconscious, and had to stay at a friend's house. I'll never drink again."

When I enquire if she is installed at the hostel, she says she hasn't gone there yet. Nothing has changed. I throw my arms up in despair. I thought something would happen by the end of her first week out – not within twenty four hours!

Max and I take Jamie's clothes over and I am pleased to see she looks as bonny as ever.
"Are you alright mum?" she asks.
Will she ever understand how she has devastated my life and how ill I feel as a result?
"Where did you stay last night?" I enquire.
"With my new friend, Tony. He bought me an Indian meal," she says, "and I was absolutely sloshed. Dexter has been around asking everyone where his woman is, meaning me."

Her mood suddenly changes. She becomes hard and snaps, "When I see social services tomorrow, I'm going to demand more access to Angel."
Jamie originally agreed access with them to see Angel for two hours, three mornings a week.
"I'm off clubbing tonight," she says with that devilish glint in her eyes.

"Have you got your glasses yet?" I ask.
"No, they were useless in prison, taking ages over everything," she replies. "The dentist said my teeth were excellent."
"You still have your brace in, which should have been removed five years ago," I remind her. She just shrugs her shoulders as if she doesn't really care.

We arrive at the women's hostel, a three-storey Victorian terraced house.
"It's really lovely," says Jamie as she unloads the three black sacks of clothes from my car.
"Mum, can I see you before court?" she asks, "In case I get sent down. Knowing my luck, I probably will."

8th July – Saturday

The police (CID) contact me. They have re-opened a past murder case. The detective says, "Someone has been in touch with the office and mentioned Jamie's name. Was it you Mrs. Harrison?" he asks. I assure him I didn't phone, which leaves us both puzzled.

9th July – Sunday

6.45 a.m: The phone rings – makes me jump. I have been conditioned to expect that early calls spell trouble. "Hi, Mum," Jamie says, light-heartedly. "It's me."
"What's the matter Jamie, so early in the morning?" I ask.
"I'm bored," she says, "so thought I'd ring for a chat...I've got a new pair of dungarees. Nothing fits after prison, and I have a grant from the social.
Mum, can I come to see Max in the musical?" I agree.
Jamie gives me her phone number at the hostel. "If you ring, make sure you say who you are. People, who know Dexter, keep knocking on the door asking for me," she says, annoyed.

11th July – Tuesday

We meet mid-morning near the foster-home. Jamie looks extremely well and very plump, about a size 16. She has been to see Angel, saying very little except, "She's so beautiful."
Immediately changing the subject she asks, "Do you like my new dungarees?" Not having had her grant through yet, it is my guess she has shoplifted them.
I enquire, "Are you using, Jamie?"
"No," she replies.

We drive over to meet her friend Tony, at his business premises. He is a well-spoken, intelligent guy, with a friendly smile, and appears okay. At long last, I think to myself, she is friendly with a decent hard-working black businessman.
Jamie appears disorientated – probably because she has been institutionalised in prison. However I suspect she is now drinking heavily, from what she says.

14th July – Friday

Jamie is due to come over for Max's school sports today. Halfway through she still hasn't arrived. Max wins his first race and his mummy isn't here to see him.
Suddenly Max glances up and sees Jamie, grins and runs across the field to greet her.
As we sit in the hot sun, Jamie asks, "Do you like Tony mum?"

"He seems okay," I say cautiously, remembering how many times I have been conned before. "Trouble is, everyone you have introduced me to has turned out to be a dangerous pimp or dealer."

Jamie says, "Tony is too good for me."

I detect, from her tone, that she is bored and missing the excitement she is used to.

20th July – Thursday

Jamie's cheque fraud hearing is today. I can't bear to hear the lies, so Pat has agreed to go into the courtroom while I wait outside, and let me know what happens. Jamie is late and her anxious solicitor chats to me. Eventually she arrives with her friends, Tony and Carla. The girls are similarly dressed in short dungarees, and Carla has a peak cap back to front on her head. Both look like very ordinary young kids, not the crack addicts and prostitutes they really are.

Jamie looks healthy, plump and bonny – so different from the $6^1/2$ stone she was last year. Her hair is slightly highlighted.

I become suspicious when I notice how orange her make-up is – a sign she is on crack.

While waiting to be called by the court, we sit on the grass verge outside in the baking sun. Tony quietly pulls me to one side: "I'm trying to control Jamie but can't understand her," he whispers. "She goes out for an hour and is gone twenty four."

Pat and I look at each other. "Oh no-- she's back on crack!" I exclaim.

Jamie is bubbly and says, "I feel great. Don't you think I look good mum? I'm only taking cannabis."

"You look marvellous, Jamie," I agree.

At the end of the hearing the magistrates commit Jamie's case to Crown Court at the end of the month.

Afterwards, Carla and Tony join us for a drink in a nearby cafe. We chat about the yardies and, as always with these people, I tread very carefully. Then, to my surprise Tony boldly announces, "I'm a Yardie." I want to crawl under the table and hide!

He explains, "I'm a true Yardie and came from the yards of Jamaica to Britain, at the age of seven."

Jamie asks me for the address of the crack rehab. at Bristol. 'Crack'? I think to myself – but Jamie says she is only using cannabis?

As we drive home Pat is excited suggesting, "This may be the one guy to sort Jamie out. She has grown up a lot recently and perhaps this time she will get herself sorted out."
Dubious, I turn to Pat saying, "I can't look ahead. I see before me a pair of weighing scales that could tip either way at any time. And they do...

Just one hour later, back at home, I receive a call from Dionne.
"Angela, I can't believe it," she says. "Did you know Jamie is working the streets and back on crack? When my brother Clinton, told me I didn't believe him, so he insisted driving me to find her. There was Jamie on the streets, walking up and down looking for business. "I wound down the window saying, 'Jamie I can't believe it'."
She giggled, 'I'll never change.'
I asked her, 'Are you back on crack?'
She replied, 'Yeah'."

Clinton told Dionne that Tony uses crack, is possibly a dealer, and takes all Jamie's earnings. I can't believe this intelligent guy is a pimp...the same as all the others, and I've been conned again.

I am dumbfounded and in a state of shock. My prediction, 'Jamie will be back on crack within a fortnight,' has come true – exactly to the day.

Constantly my predictions are right and it quite frightens me. Four years ago I predicted 'Jamie will be dead by the age of twenty-five'. Only two and a half years to go – I only hope I am proven wrong.
My mind is at bursting point and there is so much hurt and sadness deep within me.

24th July – Monday
7.30 p.m. Jamie phones saying, "I've seen Dexter and he wants to see Angel and get back with me. But he'll have to sort himself out first." Jamie speaks with a very rough accent, an indication she is using. "Our phone ain't working, init?" she says.
She confirms she will be coming to see Max in the musical.

26th July – Wednesday
The play commences...no sign of Jamie.

Eventually she arrives half an hour late, having missed Max's most important acting part. At least she saw him in later scenes.

Immediately, I notice her make-up is very orange and blotchy, from using crack. She proudly watches, smiling happily as Max appears on stage.

Jamie will have such lovely memories of this evening, I think to myself as I drive her back to her seedy haunts.

Determined to find out more about Tony I say, "He'll probably turn out to be as violent as all the others."

"That's what Hughie says," agrees Jamie. "Tony wanted me to marry him – but no way. He was too serious and got me worried."

"Marry? After knowing you for just a few days?" I say surprised.

I remind her of when I first met Clinton, my introduction to Steve Dred his brother, and Leroy who involved her in armed robbery: all charmers, but turning out to be heavily involved in pimping, crime and drugs.

Jamie says, "I'm returning to Hughie who is a real good friend, with no ties." As we drive to his house via the back streets we see girls working. It upsets me – they look so young and so vulnerable.

"Can you see the pimps, Mum," says Jamie, pointing out guys hanging around a row of terraced houses.

Jamie knocks on Hughie's door and he pops out and waves. He doesn't have the long black curly hair anymore – it makes me smile to see he is totally bald.

Jamie hugs me through the car window and as we part I say, "Take care."

28th July – Friday

The phone rings, "Mum? It's me," says Jamie, trying not to cry. She says a few words, then she sobs. After a after a few seconds calms down.

"Are you okay?" I ask.

"I am going for rehab," she says. "I've arranged it all myself with my drug worker. She says it could be next week..."

I interrupt. "Jamie, you're on crack again, aren't you?"

"Yes," she replies. "How I hate myself for what I'm doing – if I don't sort myself out I shall lose Angel – I shall lose everything."

"No one can sort out your life but you," I tell her.

Jamie agrees and says she'll have to go for detox first.

To boost Jamie up as she continues to sob I tell her, "I'm proud you are trying to sort yourself out.

By the way, who is the male I can hear in the background?"

"Tony," she replies. "He's really pleased I'm doing it."

Why has she left Hughie's place, and gone back with Tony after finishing with him, I wonder? Jamie never changes.

I receive a phone call this evening from a distraught Stratford mother, Ellie, whose daughter recently went off with a black guy in Birmingham. She is so relieved to find someone to speak to who really understands. Her daughter failed to return home three weeks ago.

Ian and Ellie are such a lovely couple – professional and middle class. They have loved and supported their daughter Lucy throughout life, and you would never have believed she could end up on crack. But then it can happen to anyone.

Ellie pops around this evening for a chat. This is where parents score over agencies – we can provide a listening ear, with first hand experience, out of hours, seven days a week.

29th July – Saturday

"Hi – this is Hughie. Is Jamie staying with you?" he asks. She left my house a couple of days ago with my washing and hasn't returned." He sounds worried because, apart from Jamie disappearing, he hasn't any clothes to wear!

I gasp, "Oh no, not again. No sorry, I haven't seen her. She phoned yesterday saying she is going for drug rehab. and was with Tony."

Hughie is concerned, "I last saw her for a short while, after you dropped her off here, and then she disappeared. I can't understand why she has gone back to Tony?

I'll go and look for her. I know where his flat is," he says. "I'll phone and let you know she's okay."

About 20 minutes later he rings, "Jamie's alright," and he hands her the phone. Jamie sounds very alert and bright.

"What about Hughie's washing?" I ask. "It's all safe," she says. "Why shouldn't it be, what's the worry?"

I arrange to meet Jamie before we go on holiday.

This evening Ellie phones excited, saying, "My daughter rang this morning to say she was sorry for everything and will be coming home tonight. So far she hasn't arrived and I'm out of my mind with worry."

I advise her, "Sit down and have another glass of wine. Addicts are unreliable. They really mean what they say, when they say it. But seconds later they forget everything they have said."

Later, Ellie phones to say her daughter has phoned to say she isn't coming home after all. "You were right Angela," she says. "Thanks for helping me be prepared."

31st July – Monday

I am very excited because we are seeing Jamie today. I must be feeling better in myself although I get an overwhelming feeling occasionally that something is wrong.

Max and I wait for her outside McDonald's in Coventry but she doesn't turn up. I am sad we won't see her before going away on holiday...but then we are probably the last people Jamie is thinking about tonight – she is likely to be stoned out of her mind.

Crackhead

Unreliability – 1995

2nd August – Wednesday

'Things are really bad', repeats over and over in my mind as we travel to Devon. When Max and I arrive, I tell my friends that I sense something has happened to Jamie.

An hour later, my lodger, Laura, rings me from Stratford. "Angela, there's a message on your answer phone from Jamie's hostel. They want you to ring urgently."

I call them straight away and my intuition was right. "Have you seen Jamie?" they enquire. "Everyone is extremely worried. She was last seen five days ago. We are reporting her missing to the police."

I decide not to panic and put them in the picture. "Jamie often goes missing when bad on crack."

"We will ring you if there is any news," they assure me.

3rd August – Thursday

No further news. The police aren't interested because Jamie is over eighteen. The community police officer says he will make enquiries to find out if Jamie has been seen.

She did not attend court yesterday for Angel's care order.

I ring Tony and ask, "Have you seen Jamie?"

"Not since she phoned you from my place last Friday," he says. "She was very bad then." I hear him ask someone in the room, "Have you seen Jamie?

They reply, "She was seen with Dexter on Tuesday."

I ring her solicitor, "Has Jamie been in touch? She's gone missing, and is back on crack." The solicitor gasps in disbelief, saying she hasn't heard from her. She is even more astounded when I tell her, "Jamie was on crack when she attended court the other day."

4th August – Friday

The hostel inform me that the community beat officer says Jamie was

Crackhead

seen on Wednesday. I decide to return home from Devon a few days early, not being able to rest, knowing something is very wrong.

5th August – Saturday

I phone Tony, "Any more news?"
"Yes, I saw her last night. She was in a hell of a state – so skinny and dirty," he says, disgusted. "I got her back and she stayed the night, but this morning she was gone again. Jamie hasn't been back to the hostel for a week now.

She's on the brown stuff," he informs me. "She's mad because the guy she's staying with is a dealer, surrounded by brown, and has it on tap. Jamie is really ill. She has lost so much weight and all the rubbish is coming out: she is covered in boils – her chest, legs, her whole body. She's also occasionally smoking crack. I can't believe Jamie is so skinny.
Only a week ago she was very plump, overweight if anything, and in just one week she has become skin and bone.

"Jamie said she is going to write to you, asking for help," says Tony. "She says you are the only one who can get her out of the situation, and perhaps you could collect her and bring her home."
"How can I Tony? I've done everything I possibly can. Over and over again she has let me down. There is nothing more I can do. I have to get on with my life and look after Max. It is no good me cracking up."

He tells me, "Last night I told Jamie to clean herself up, have a good night's sleep, and today I'd take her to the Leicester Carnival. But she disappeared. "I tried my best." he says. "Tonight, when I return from the carnival, I will see if I can find her."

I ask him, "Please tell Jamie she will lose her accommodation by today if she doesn't return."
Tony promises he will be in touch if there is any news. I am pleased I have contact with Jamie's associates. In the long run it pays off and gives me peace of mind knowing where she is and what is going on.

As I put the phone down, I am relieved. The news is bad but I know she is still alive. Unless Jamie seeks help, she will soon be dead.
What life does she have now, existing from one fix to another, with three

264

children in care, and two going for adoption? She has nothing left but pain. Please God help her find peace within herself.

6th August – Sunday

Afternoon. Jamie can hardly speak..."I'm sorry Mum, really sorry." She sounds so down and says, "I'm at the hostel."
"Can I pop over and see you?" I ask. She seems pleased and brightens up.
Pat and I drive over. We are greeted by a very pale-looking Jamie. She has big spots all over, is painfully thin, with hollow eyes that have lost their sparkle.
Poor Jamie, she looks so forlorn. We enter the tastefully furnished hostel accommodation. Pat takes one look at Jamie and announces, "Jamie, I think you've got chicken pox – don't pick the spots, for goodness sake."
"But I have," says Jamie. "I'm itching like mad."
Jamie explains she has been out of her mind on heroin. She stayed in a dirty, dingy flat, and has been working on the streets." "Serves the punters right if they catch chicken pox," I joke.
We sit for a while chatting. "Most of the girls in the hostel are gay," she tells us, screwing up her nose.
"What cooking facilities have you got here?" asks Pat.
"There's a kitchen, but I don't cook anyway," Jamie replies, with a giggle.

She tells us, "For the past eight days, I've been staying at an awful guy's flat. He gave me loads of heroin for free at the beginning, and then started to cut it down.
I realised he wanted to use me for buying drugs, or to go on the game. He was really horrible and wanted sex," she says, "but I wasn't having it. The heroin was very dirty – leaving loads of black stuff on the foil after smoking.
On Saturday night I had a clear moment in my head," she says. "I knew I just had to get out. Eventually, I ran away from the guy and returned to the hostel."

"Why did you leave Tony's flat?" I ask.
"There was a guy called Manny there and I didn't trust him. He appeared to have designs on me."

"How about coming along with us to Joy's?" I suggest and Jamie's eyes light up.

Joy is pleased to see us. During our conversation, she makes sure Jamie remembers her address, repeating it over and over again. "It's no good writing it down because you will only lose it," she says. Ring me if things get bad again?" she tells Jamie.

"Last week," says Jamie, "someone phoned the hostel saying I'd been beaten and dumped. It's awful they could do that, getting everyone worried."
When we drop her back at the hostel Jamie says with such gratitude, "Thanks mum for coming over."
As we drive back to Stratford, I unwind and become more relaxed. But will Jamie return to the hostel tonight after working, I wonder?

7th August – Monday

Jamie tells social services she intends to go for rehab., and wants Angel moved to be near her wherever she goes.
The social worker says it's impossible. Jamie isn't showing total commitment, and didn't see the baby at all last week.

Jamie phones from Tony's. I am surprised she has returned after saying things are so dangerous.
"Are you alright?" I enquire. "You sound very strange."
"I have a cold," she says.
I warn Jamie, "Keep a clear head otherwise you will be in a mess again. You don't want to lose your accommodation – you might not get another chance."
"At least I'm still there," she says, "even though the police found burnt foil in my room recently."

8th August – Tuesday

Lunchtime, Jamie rings, "I'm bored and phoning from Tony's while he is out."
She is very excited about clothes she has bought for Angel, which I suspect are shoplifted. "I feel dead proud of myself," she says.

As Max and I arrive at Linda's, Ben runs out to greet me with a big grin on his face, "Grandma, grandma," he says excitedly. Ben is as lovely as ever. He is extremely energetic – nothing like his mother and brother who were quiet and sensitive at the same age.
Angel arrives with her foster mother. She is such a beautiful bonny baby.

Her glowing dark brown skin is flawless; and her black silky straight hair is starting to flick and curl on top. She is beautiful. When I stroke her face she smiles and her big eyes look up at me, melting my heart.

Jamie didn't attend her access visit to Angel this morning. Yet she told me on the phone she bought clothes today for her. Priority of buying clothes before seeing her daughter just isn't on. She hasn't seen Angel for at least four visits now and, when she has been, she always arrives late.

Jamie is due to see probation today. They are annoyed she hasn't attended for court reports. She is getting so unreliable.

Dionne rings this evening and confirms she has heard Jamie is okay, but she has been involved in a fight.

11th August – Friday

I am surprised to receive a call so early. "Hi mum, are you okay?" Jamie sounds very cheerful.

"Are your spots any better?" I ask.

"They've almost disappeared," she replies.

"Where were you yesterday when I phoned?" I enquire. "There was no reply from your room."

"I was asleep and felt really poorly on a come-down," she says.

"Are you still using heroin?" I ask.

"Yes, only £20 per night, instead of £150 on crack," she says. "Trouble is, it's making me feel ill. There's loads of rubbish in it. It's an awful thought that the rubbish must be in my lungs."

"Are you with Tony?" I ask.

"No. He wanted money all the time," she said bitterly. "I've seen Dexter these past two days. We are just good friends and it's much better now we don't go out with each other."

"Have you seen the drug agency about methadone?" I enquire.

"No, but I will go when I'm in town this afternoon. I'm going to try on some clothes," she says excitedly.

Jamie hardly ever talks about Angel or Ben, and hasn't visited her baby for 2 weeks. It looks as if Angel will be abandoned, just like Ben.

14th August – Monday

A lively and excited Jamie greets me at the hostel door and rushes to the car to see Max.

Crackhead

I tell Jamie, "I've brought Ellie along, whose daughter recently went on crack. She wants to ask you some questions."
Jamie invites us into the hostel. She is bubbly, with bright blue eyes, and looks so well. The spots, which are clearing, are covered with heavy make-up. She is wearing a big 'T' shirt and denim frayed shorts, revealing her slim figure.

"Hey" says Jamie, "I was offered £1,000 cash, and crack worth £6000 this week. I turned the guy down because I don't like him. I should have accepted. He told me I would do well with him – fancy letting that amount go through my fingers. I must be mad," she says.
She puts on her new black leather ankle boots on, which enhance her slim legs. So different from the heavy trainers she wore when she attended court three weeks ago.

The five of us, including my Goddaughter Tamsin, set off for our picnic in the shade of the old oak tree at the Memorial Park, with the warm evening sun filtering through (the temperature is 90°).
While a starving Jamie tucks into the food, Ellie asks Jamie the one question she badly needs to be answered. "What is your fascination for these black guys, especially when they are so violent?"
"They're good in bed," jokes Jamie. "Apart from that, they're fascinating."

"Are you using crack Jamie?" I ask.
"Yes," she replies quite matter-of-fact.
"What about the drug agency? Have you seen them?"
She snaps, "I'm going tomorrow – okay," and doesn't want to discuss the matter further.
"What about the baby's father?" asks Ellie.
With a glint in her eye, Jamie giggles saying, "I spent four hours with Dexter the other night. I still think he's rather nice." "
Are you going to work tonight, Jamie?" Ellie enquires.
Jamie confirms she is.

We drop Jamie off at the hostel after a very happy relaxed couple of hours. As I drive back home, I turn to Ellie saying, "I never know if this will be the last time I will see her."
Ellie remarks she is surprised how open Jamie is.
I tell her, "I get a lot of happiness and memories from such a simple thing as a picnic."

"It's hard to believe my daughter is in the same situation as Jamie," she says, although I don't think she works on the streets."

How sorry I feel for Ellie. I know exactly what she is going through as the parent of a crack addict.

With all this stress, I have to live a very simple life. I have given up child minding, and have no energy for a social life. But I continue with the parents support group and school talks. I experience lots of happiness, warmth and love with my work – probably more than most people do in a lifetime. This must be what life is really about.

18th August – Friday

Jamie tells me, "I was out working last night until 4.00 a.m.
You'll never guess who I'm seeing today?" she asks. "Clinton – and he's rather good looking these days."

"Be careful, Jamie," I warn. "Remember how he treated you."

"Don't worry – we are just good friends." she replies. "Mum, can we meet before the court hearing in two weeks?"

I agree I will be in touch to arrange something, but two weeks in Jamie's life is a long, long time and anything can happen.

24th August – Thursday

10.00 a.m: I ring the hostel. Jamie isn't there and I leave a message.

I contact Angel's foster mum who tells me Jamie should have been there this morning, but hasn't turned up.

I feel so sad for her children. The longer Jamie messes about, the longer the delay in Angel and Ben being adopted, and the harder it will be to find adoptive parents.

How awful I feel today. Something is wrong. I feel I have a tight band around my head; my whole being aches. I have just have to sit and wait.

25th August – Friday

Still no word from Jamie – things must be bad. She is probably stoned and in hiding before the hearing.

I phone the hostel again. The staff have not seen her, they tell me, "If she doesn't turn up in the next couple of days she is likely to lose her accommodation."

Oh well, another day over. Hopefully, I'll get a good night's sleep to prepare me for whatever.

26th August – Saturday

7.00 a.m: I feel dreadful – butterflies in my stomach and on edge. I drive over to the hostel to see if there is any sign of Jamie. A young woman answers the door and tells me, "Jamie hasn't been seen for three days now."

It doesn't look as if she will return and chances are she will lose her accommodation. I am used to Jamie's disappearing acts but still I have this dreadful feeling something is wrong.

28th August – Monday

Morning: "Hello Mum, it's me."

"Are you okay?" I ask.

"Yes," she says, but sounds very subdued.

"Where have you been? What have you been doing?" I ask anxiously.

"Enjoying myself and having a good time," she says. "After all, I might as well if I'm going to jail."

"When did you return to the hostel?"

"Yesterday," she says.

"Jamie, have you seen Angel?"

"How could I?" she replies sharply. "My money was stolen from here last week when I fell asleep on the settee."

"Social services would have paid your travel expenses," I tell her.

"They've already given me the money," says Jamie.

I am very angry with her. "You are not showing full commitment to Angel, are you?"

After a pause she says, "What's the point if I'm going into prison? I think I will get two years."

"Will you be at court?" I ask.

"Probably not. I'll feign illness," she replies.

31st August – Thursday

Various agency representatives assemble around the table at the N.P.C.C. offices, for a meeting to discuss Angel's case. Jamie is late, and eventually arrives looking very rough, and on edge. She gives me a hug. I whisper, "We will go to Joy's after and you can see Max," and I can see she relaxes.

Jamie has visited Angel only seven out of twenty-four visits. The drug representative says, "It's not surprising...because Jamie takes drugs at night, and the after effects prevent her from seeing Angel early morning."

Jamie snaps, "I want to see my child at a reasonable time of the day. I'm not up until the afternoon." Jamie is rough and course and shouts across the table, accusing everyone, "You're preventing me seeing my baby."

They all agree, "We must start thinking what is best for Angel, not Jamie."

Jamie shouts, "I want to see my baby to suit me; I intend to have her back in the end." She storms out of the room shouting, "I'm not coming back." The meeting informs me, "It has been decided to permit Jamie to visit Angel in the afternoons, and arrange for her to see the drug agency to discuss rehab."

"May I speak?" I ask as I hold back the tears. "Jamie has been on drugs for seven years. The woman you see here today, the addict, is not my daughter. I have seen the neglect of her children.

For four weeks last year, when she took methadone, Jamie was beautiful. She was also off drugs for three months in prison.

But, every time, Jamie returns to drugs and her dangerous lifestyle. She can't survive without them and says this is what she wants."

I stress firmly, "Jamie has been given all the opportunities over, and over again."

With the exception of one or two representatives, everyone agrees with me.

The drug worker says irately, across the table, (trying to shock me I think), "Jamie is in a very violent situation – she hammered on the door of the agency recently, having been beaten black and blue."

My blood boils. "That's nothing new," I tell her. "I regularly get calls in the middle of the night when Jamie has been beaten. I have kept a diary for six years and, every time she is beaten, she returns to the guy."

I tell everyone, "Even if you change the times for Jamie to visit Angel, I don't believe Jamie will turn up." The meeting agrees with me.

"Where do we go from here if Jamie goes to prison?" they question.

I smile, "Anything could happen in the next few weeks. Live for today – as I do. Tomorrow may never come."

After the meeting I drive to Joy's to collect Max, only to be greeted by Jamie at Joy's front door. I half suspected she would go there after storming out of the meeting. She looks so thin and hard-faced, with heavy make-up; Jamie's horrendous lifestyle is starting to age that once pretty, dimpled, youthful face. She grabs her stomach complaining of pain.

1st September – Friday

I woke up this morning feeling very low.
If it wasn't for Max, I could quite happily give up. I have little help with him and, while I struggle, everyone gets on with their own busy lives. I don't think they appreciate how lonely and hard it is, bringing up a youngster as a fifty year old single parent; let alone having to cope with my ongoing crisis.

I am so very tired, and must sleep. I ring Joy for a chat and feel better. It is so much easier to cope with her support.

4th September – Monday

I sense something is wrong, so I phone the hostel. The woman I speak to is very helpful. "Things aren't looking good for Jamie. She hasn't paid her rent and, unless she gets her money and benefits sorted out, she will have to leave the hostel. I honestly don't know how you cope," she says.

The Guardian ad Litum from the court, acting on behalf of Jamie's children, informs me it is likely Angel will be adopted with Ben because of Jamie's non-commitment.

11th September – Monday

Jamie rings – sounds bright as a button.
"Where have you been and what have you been doing?" I ask.
She replies, "Oh, I've been around," not giving much away. "I've been to see Angel today.
Must go now, money's running out. I've got a bus to catch," she says hurriedly. "Will speak to you later."

Early evening Jamie rings back. "It's much better now I'm visiting Angel from two to four o'clock in the afternoon. Her hair is now very curly and the foster mum is putting coconut oil on.
Angel screamed for an hour while I was there and I couldn't stand it."
She signs off by saying "I'll phone you after visiting Angel tomorrow."
Jamie's bright voice puts my mind at rest.

12th September – Tuesday

I attend a meeting organised by our local social services, inviting other agencies to look at Parent Support Network in the area. I voice my worries about the need to support carers who look after their grandchildren, or who are in care due to drug abuse.

The senior social worker is annoyed and insinuates I am talking rubbish, stubbornly saying, "I don't know any children in care because of drugs," and ignores the issue – sticking her head in the sand like all the others! But I know she could well be faced with the problem before too long.

19th September – Tuesday

Jamie sounds very cheerful. "Are you okay?" I ask.

"Fine," she says but isn't forthcoming, as usual, as to what she has been up to.

"Have you seen Angel?" I enquire.

"Yes, yesterday" she replies.

"How is she?" I ask.

"Boring," she says in a long droning voice.

I can't believe my ears.

"I'm only joking," she laughs. "Angel was pretending to be sick."

"How on earth can a five-month-old baby pretend to be sick?" I ask.

"I haven't seen Angel today because I was too tired," says Jamie.

When I ask her if she has been to the drug agency she says, "I'm going tomorrow."

I am cross. "You say that every time we speak."

"I will meet up with you next week, perhaps for lunch?" I suggest.

"I'd rather have a home-cooked meal," says Jamie. "We've been talking about our mums' cooking at the hostel."

"Perhaps you can come over before you go to prison," I suggest.

21st September – Thursday

It has been a beautiful warm sunny day and I feel so good. The social worker contacts me to say Jamie hasn't been to see her baby for a week. So Jamie didn't go to see Angel this Monday, as she told me she had.

25th September – Monday

I call on Ellie and her husband. Their daughter Lucy is at home, totally out of her mind on a come-down from crack; very restless, sitting one minute, jumping up the next, heavy eyes, and in a daze. She is desperate to see her boyfriend who is on remand.

Her family are determined to seek help and they lock all the doors in the house. She is hysterical, threatening suicide, while two girl friends together with her father hold her down.

Eventually the doctor calls. He doesn't have a clue on the devastating effects of drugs on the abuser and their family. Feeling sorry for Lucy, he tells her not to listen to anyone and offers to get her away from the house. He gives no thought to the fact Lucy has nowhere to go, and is threatening to throw herself under a bus.

He proceeds to lead her out of the house but Lucy's father, furious with the doctor, prevents him taking his daughter. He shows the doctor out, "You are not wanted here," he shouts and slams the door.

We suspect Lucy may try to do a runner. Fortunately, with a lot of persuasion, she decides to remain at home with the security and love of her family; thus proving the doctor wrong. His actions could have proved disastrous, especially if Lucy had returned to Birmingham... homeless and suicidal.

I find most doctors I have encountered, particularly the older ones, are unable to comprehend addicts' and their families' problems. We have met many parents, through our support work, who have been let down by doctors. Every doctor should be educated on drug issues.

Lucy's family are prepared to move heaven and earth to get her off crack – they will handcuff her to the bed if necessary! There is such desperation of family and friends when they lose someone they love to drug addiction.

I suggest to her parents, "Take it one step at a time."

"Angela, we have been lucky and had help from Lucy's friends," says Ellie, "but you have had nobody to support you over the years."

26th September – Tuesday

Angel's care order hearing is at court, 10.00 a.m. but there is no sign of Jamie.

Her solicitor phones the hostel. Jamie says she is taking a shower, having forgotten about the hearing, and will be there shortly. She is also due in Magistrates court today after failing to appear yesterday.

By eleven o'clock still no sign of Jamie and she is already an hour late. An anxious court decide to proceed without her.

After hearing evidence from the social worker and solicitors, the magistrates are extremely concerned and say priority must be given to what is best for Angel. The social worker says they wish to see Angel adopted with Ben because Jamie has shown no commitment. After a break the magistrates return and, having considered Jamie's previous history, they state:

> "Jamie has had many violent partners, including one boyfriend who attempted murder by shooting.
> She has tried to commit suicide.
> Her friends are violent.
> Jamie is involved in criminal activity.
> We wish to see Angel adopted with Ben."

Jamie's solicitor states Jamie will not oppose the care order. The magistrates turn to me asking, "Have you anything to say?"
I tell them, "I agree totally with the way things have been handled."
The care order is granted to everyone's satisfaction.
It is now mid-day, over an hour since Jamie said, "I'm on my way," but there is no sign of her. I drive to the hostel and a warden tells me, "Jamie went to court." They are surprised she hasn't turned up.
"Jamie isn't looking well and is very thin," she says. "She has now paid her rent so will be allowed to stay for the time being."

27th September – Wednesday

The hostel phones during the day to say, "Jamie's okay – but there's a small problem. One of the girls has taken clothes and perfume from Jamie's room. Could you describe the perfume which Jamie says you gave her?" they ask. "The police want us to confirm Jamie is telling the truth. She says the perfume is very special."
After I describe the bottle they say, "It is obviously Jamie's," and pass the phone to her.

"Jamie, are you okay?" I ask. "Why didn't you turn up at court?"
Casually she replies, "I arrived at court at twelve but it was too late."
I know she wasn't there then. Jamie doesn't bother to enquire how Angel's hearing went.

"Would you like to come for lunch on Sunday and see Max before you go to prison?" I ask.

"I'd like that," she says excitedly, and enquires, "What are we going to have? I'd love roast lamb, roast potatoes, and veg. And Mum, can we have blackberry and apple crumble for pud?"

She sounds so bright and happy. I arrange to collect her at one o'clock on Sunday.

Putting the phone down, I feel so much better and am excited at the prospect of us having lunch together. When I have Jamie home for a roast dinner, it is always a very happy event. Of course, she has to come when it suits me and when I can cope emotionally. I now feel ready to invite her.

It is eight months since Jamie last came home, on Max's birthday.

Max and I go over to see Ben and Angel this afternoon. I am glowing with happiness. Ben is very affectionate towards me and he and Max get on so well together.

Bonny Angel, just five months old, arrives with the social worker. Having been in the hot summer sun, she looks very Jamaican. Ben has quite a different complexion and is pale and olive. Angel's hair is very long and curly on top. Her skin is perfect, just like Jamie's natural family who all have beautiful clear skin. She gives me a great big smile and seems very happy.

I will be glad when next week's court hearing is over. Hopefully Jamie will be in jail and we will all get some rest.

Testing Brown – 1995

1st October – Sunday

After an eight-month break Jamie is coming home, and I am excited but very tense at the prospect. We go over to collect her at one o'clock.

I ring the doorbell of the hostel and Jamie appears bleary-eyed and pale, in her silky pyjamas. "Sorry, I was in bed," she says and ushers Max and myself to her bedroom.

Her clothes have been sorted out into black bin liners.

"Do you like my pyjamas?" Jamie asks. "I acquired them – you know where."

I can't believe Jamie has the nerve to return to the department store, which has banned her nationally, but she seems to get away with it.

Jamie looks very unwell, her face pale and spotty, and she has put on weight.

"Mum, would you like my pipe for your drugs display case?" she asks and proceeds to hand me her crack pipe: made from a Sudacreme tub about $2^{1}/_{2}''$ high, the top covered with foil held by an elastic band. The foil is pierced with tiny holes, and is blackened from the crack that has been burnt on top. Pierced through the side of the tub is an empty plastic biro case, for drawing the smoke through the foil.

"Right, let's go," she says, popping a cardigan over her pyjamas.

"Dressed like that Jamie?"

"Why not," she replies as she gathers up her precious patchwork quilt, which she wants me to keep safe for her.

In the car Jamie puts on her make-up and is immediately transformed. She is bright and chatty but warns me, "I'll probably be ill later, on a come-down. But I'll be okay and can get more brown when I go back tonight. I sometimes have crack, but it's usually brown these days and I've managed to cut it down from 1 gram, to $^{1}/_{2}$ a gram."

Back at home Jamie, snuggles up in her quilt on the settee with the TV on, from 2.00 till 5.00 p.m., and then retires to bed for another hour.

She chats for a short while but there is no mention of her children in care.
I don't mention them for fear of aggravating her.
"Will you be at court tomorrow?" I ask.
"Probably not," she replies. "I'd rather die than go to prison."

"Bet you were surprised I was at the hostel this morning," Jamie laughs.
"I didn't get to bed until three this morning, but was determined to be
there when you arrived. There's no way I would have missed my meal –
I've been looking forward to it all week and telling me mates about it."

Jamie tells me she is going into hiding at Sindy's. At least I know she is
okay there. "I now work for a guy as a tester for brown," she tells me,
"and get my gear free or half price."
"You're mad – it could be lethal," I say alarmed. Whatever I say, Jamie is
more interested in talking about the northern Yardies and Ben's father,
than listening to me.
We unload the sacks of clothes. "I'll need the green sack for when I get
caught," she says.

As the hours pass, Jamie is on a comedown, getting agitated,
argumentative and feeling ill. She phones her dealer, ordering half a
gram, to pick up as soon as she gets back.
"At least I don't have to worry if I work or not tonight," she says, "I
haven't got any pressure now I'm not working for anyone."
After a bath, putting on her make-up and doing her hair, she is ready to
return to city night life.

2nd October – Monday

The barrister approaches as I walk through the entrance of Crown
Court.
"Is Jamie coming?" he enquires anxiously.
"I doubt it," I tell him.
He is annoyed but not surprised. "If she turns up, chances are we could
get her off," he says.
I proceed upstairs to the public gallery which encircles the first floor of
the oak panelled hexagonal, Georgian courtroom, graced by a high
domed ceiling. The judge peers sternly over his half-moon gold-rimmed
glasses and the clerk calls, "Jamie Harrison."
Dead silence...then the Barrister explains to the Judge, "Miss Harrison
saw her mother yesterday and it is unlikely she will appear. I understand

she has returned to drugs and prostitution, saying she would rather die than go to prison."

"Angela, If you see Jamie, could you ask her to hand herself in?" requests Jamie's solicitor. "This way, she may still get off."

3rd October – Tuesday

"Hi Mum." Jamie sounds really good.

"Are you okay?" I ask.

"Yes, I'm fine." Her mobile phone sounds rather distant. "How did it go yesterday?" she enquires.

"The barrister suggests you hand yourself in to get a lighter sentence," I tell her.

Very surprised, Jamie says positively, "Oh right. I'll probably do that then."

5th October – Thursday

Tonight, when Jamie phones, I can hear music in the background. "I've got a splitting headache," she complains and snaps at me aggressively, but apologises afterwards.

"Do you need your fix?" I ask. "No, I've just had one."

"I won't ask where you are Jamie. It's probably better if I don't know, with you being in hiding." She agrees, and assures me she will keep in touch.

7th October – Saturday

Jamie makes contact and sounds quite happy. "I've moved but can't say where. People here are only interested in money, and they will inform if they know where I am.

I'm not on the streets anymore but working at what I'm good at," she says. "Someone has put up money for me to share a newly furnished house with another girl. It has TV, video and stereo, and a new suite. It's fabulous. I'm making lots of money." Jamie seems very happy.

"What name are you using?" I ask.

Jamie giggles, "I'd rather not say – it's advertised everywhere."

10th October – Tuesday

"Mum, my hands and feet are swollen like balloons and itching like mad," cries Jamie on the phone, in a panic.

She sounds beside herself, so I offer to go straight over.

"Where are you?" I ask.

"Sindy's house," she replies. Jamie has lied and been staying with Sindy all the time!

I ring the hospital and they advise, "Get Jamie here straight away. There's lots of dirty heroin around."
Sindy sounds pretty scared. I advise, "Phone for an ambulance immediately and I'll be over." When I arrive, the ambulance is parked outside the house.
Sindy greets me saying, "Jamie's refusing to go to hospital."

Jamie appears at the front door in her short silky pyjamas. She looks painfully thin, her face is pale and spotty, and hair bedraggled. "I'm okay mum. The swelling has gone down now," she says, "and my hands and feet are only slightly swollen."
In her hand she holds a fork. "This is the only thing I can scratch myself with...I'm beside myself with itching."

Because Jamie refuses to go to hospital, the ambulance men arrange for a doctor to call and check her over. The doctor doesn't have a clue about drugs and advises Jamie to go to the drug agency – useless advice, because they are closed out of office hours. He gives her a prescription for cream to relieve the itching.
"The heroin leaves lots of rubbish after smoking," Jamie gasps, "If I'd injected, I could be dead by now."
"Why did you lie to me about being set up in business?" I ask.
"I didn't want you to worry."
"Where do you get your money for drugs?" I ask.
"I have my regular clients," she replies. As I leave, she turns to me saying, "Don't tell the police I'm here will you?"

During the evening I receive a distressed call. Jamie is very down and weepy. "Hi mum, I need someone to talk to."

13th October – Friday

These days, Max is very happy. He knows his mummy takes drugs, but isn't aware she is in hiding from the police and has been ill.
Max and I are very close. He often says, "I love you Mum. I don't want you to ever die." My age worries me. I hope I survive many years to come to be here for him.

14th October, Saturday

"Hi, it's me. Just to let you know I've remembered your birthday on Monday."

I'm excited, and think – this is a good day. The last two years Jamie has forgotten. Even if she gets caught this weekend, or is high as a kite on my birthday on Monday, she has remembered.

During the evening I hear from Jamie again. She is dying to tell me, "Mum, I'm in a national newspaper soon, under the name of Sophie. Don't take any notice 'cause they're bound to sensationalize."
"What is the article about?" I ask.
"Disappearing prostitutes over the past couple of years," she says.

16th October – Monday. My birthday

I drive over to see Jamie. As I arrive, she is peeping around the front door. An Asian guy of large stature drives up and parks outside, then makes his way over to speak to Jamie. In a panic, she runs to my car, "Mum, I won't be a minute," she says. "Can you wait here? This guy's brought me some money."

A drug deal, I wonder? I try to keep myself occupied in the car, while curiosity gets the better of me and I peep without making it obvious. Suddenly I realise that he is a punter as he enters the house. A couple of minutes later he leaves and drives off.

Jamie runs over to me, very embarrassed. "Oh, I'm really sorry mum. I didn't think he would arrive at the same time as you...I'm so sorry...and on your birthday as well."
"Jamie, nothing shocks me these days," I say.
She invites me in the house, and continues to apologise for the unfortunate incident. Into my hand she places a card, insisting I open it straight away. Such a very special car: I read out aloud the words on the front, 'For My Mum, My Best Friend'.
Inside, Jamie has written:

> "Dear mum, (my only mum).
> Thanks for being the best mum in the world,
> My Best Friend,
> Love Jamie."

"You are my one and only mum," says Jamie. My other mother tried to get me to call her mum, but you are my real mum."
What a wonderful birthday present – all the money in the world couldn't have bought anything more precious. I am really touched.

Once again, Jamie apologises about the punter who had called. "How much did you make then?" I ask. "£20," she replies.

"£20, for just a couple of minutes!" I exclaim.

"I wasn't going to hang about," she laughs.

Jamie looks attractive, her make-up beautifully done, enhancing her blue eyes. But I suspect, underneath the mask, she looks ill. Her hair is up in two tight buns on top which she says makes her hair curly. She is wearing a green/plum stripy velor jumper and jeans; making her look very respectable, nothing like a prostitute.

Jamie can't wait to see my latest photos of Ben and Angel. As she browses through and selects photos for herself, she fights back the tears.

What a birthday!

19th October – Thursday

"Everything is fine," says Jamie on the phone. "Dalton is here. Do you remember he came to your house, (December 1994) when I returned home for the film. I was on methadone then.

Linda, the foster mum, phones very excited. "Angel is being moved here to join Ben, because of Jamie's lack of commitment to her."

It has taken social services nearly six months to come to this decision. At long last brother and sister will be together.

24th October – Tuesday

8.30 a.m. I receive a call from a cheerful Jamie. "I'm off with Dalton and staying at his place now," she says.

"I will probably come and see you on Thursday, Jamie."

"Mum, I may not be good – I'm doing cold turkey."

"How long have you been off the brown?"

"About twelve hours," she says.

Later Jamie, frightened and weepy, phones me. What now, I wonder? Arrest, beating or is she on a comedown?

"Mum, I don't know what to do." Jamie sounds scared. "It's my hands and feet again. The itching is awful. Should I get to hospital? Dalton is with me."

"Go straight away," I tell her. "I will ring the hospital and warn them you are on your way over."

The staff nurse is very helpful and asks me for details.
Ten minutes later Dalton rings me, "We are waiting for an ambulance."

I tell Jamie I have spoken to the hospital.
She is annoyed. "Mum, did you give my real name?" she asks, worried because she is in hiding.
"Yes I did, Jamie. You can't use false names when your life is at stake."

Reluctantly she agrees. "It's a bit better now, Mum, but I shall go to hospital anyway. I took twenty DF118 tablets because of cold turkey. I couldn't stand the pain – I was going out of my mind."
I ring the drug agency asking, "Could it be the heroin or DF118's making Jamie ill?"
"Both, possibly. It could be her liver or kidneys, or possibly rubbish in the heroin. At least she should get a thorough check-over in hospital."

25th October – Wednesday
The nurse is most helpful when I phone, and tells me, "Jamie discharged herself last night at midnight, after waiting three hours. She looked very poorly. There was nothing more we could do, except put on the record card details of identification such as tattoos, just in case she is brought in another time under a false name."

I am annoyed with Jamie because she hasn't had the full check-up she needs. Later, she contacts me. "Why did you discharge yourself?" I ask. "Jamie, I don't want you dead."
"Mum, you don't know how ill I felt with cold turkey. I just couldn't stand it any longer and had to get out."
We arrange to meet tomorrow. I am looking forward to seeing her again but haven't told Max just in case she doesn't turn up.

Early evening: "Mrs. Harrison? This is Dalton." He sounds very subdued. "Jamie has been shoplifting. Why does she do it?"
"She can't help herself," I tell him, "I suppose it gives her a buzz. Has she been arrested?" I ask.
"Yes. She's at the police station and is due to appear in court tomorrow. The police have searched my flat," he says, stammering and in a state of shock.
I tell Dalton, "I want Jamie to go to prison. Her life is so much at risk and at least she will be safe there."

Mid-evening: Jamie rings from the police station, sounding quite cheerful. "Oh well," she says, "I don't suppose I'll be going far. Mum, please can you bring the green plastic bag of clothes to the station. I'm in court tomorrow and Saturday. Will you come on Saturday?"
"I will if I can."

It looks as if Jamie's game of hide and seek has come to an end. She may get crack or heroin in prison but hopefully it will be cleaner and in smaller quantities. Perhaps, at long last, Jamie will get the medical check-up, while in prison, that she desperately needs.

26th October – Thursday
I hold my breath until we know for definite Jamie has been sent down.

Dalton rings to let me know Jamie has appeared in court for shoplifting, and appears on the cheque fraud charge tomorrow. When I take the bag of clothes to the police station I am told, "Prison rules have been changed and we are unable to pass it to Jamie."

Later in the evening, I receive a call from the station, "Jamie is very unwell and a doctor has been called. She tells me you have her methadone?" says the officer.
I'm annoyed and tell him I haven't got any here.
"Well, I must admit she has been telling lots of different stories," he says. "The doctor has left tablets for her but we had to check about the methadone first."

27th October – Friday
Crown Court – 10.30 a.m. Jamie's barrister greets me.
Dalton joins me in the public gallery. Whispering, he reminds me that it is ten months since we met at my house.
We agree Jamie's only chance is to go to prison – otherwise she will soon be dead. With proper meals, a routine, and not working on the streets, her body will have a chance to recover.
The hearing is delayed and I have to leave in haste.

Max and I set off to visit Ben and Angel. We walk towards Linda's house and I hear a little voice shouting, "Grandma... Grandma." As Ben runs out to greet us, it suddenly dawns on me he won't be a Harrison much longer. Linda and I chat excitedly about the imminent arrival of Angel into their family.

Early evening, I contact Dalton for the latest news on Jamie. "She has got sixteen months for £15,000 cheque fraud," he says.

Jamie has admitted to me she has done £100,000 plus but her solicitor assures me, "Anything coming to light hereafter will be written off. We are taking it to appeal and Jamie may get her sentence reduced to three months."

My heart sinks and I feel sick. Surely not – she could get off with three months for £15,000 cheque fraud? Where's the justice in all this? Sixteen months is not long enough, and that will be automatically reduced by half.

JAMIE IS COSTING THE TAXPAYER A FORTUNE! There are the legal costs, non-attendance at court, and police constantly searching for her. The fraud department have spent many hours putting their case together; and she has not bothered to attend probation, a condition of her prison release.

Social Services are financing two children in long-term foster care. They have a social worker, link worker, arrange many meetings (including with NSPCC), and finance medical costs, advertising for adoption, and court attendance.

Jamie has received income support for herself and her baby (even though he is not with her); together with a grant of £600, and a loan for £900, which has not been repaid, plus many small grants. All this has been financed by the taxpayer, to the tune of thousands of pounds for just one drug addict.

And, most important of all, there has been the emotional cost to us all – myself, her father and brother, and her three children.

Jamie should pay for the crime she has committed. Society cannot tolerate this situation any longer. Government and authorities deny there is a problem. Alan Howarth, my MP is the only one who has listened at grass-roots level as to what is really going on. He understands and has tried to help.

Evening: Jamie makes a surprise call from H.M prison Pucklechurch, near Bristol, and sounds very low. She says, "I'm only here for a few days and think I may be transferred to Drake Hall."

"Dalton will be down to see you soon," I tell her. "I hope you appreciate what a good friend he is. None of your other so-called friends have ever been there for you."

29th October – Sunday

Yet another murder! Sindy rings, very distressed. "A guy called Manny was shot dead last night," she says. "Jamie wanted to bring him back to my house last week, and I refused."

Thank goodness she was in prison when he was shot. I am relieved that Jamie can't possibly be involved this time. The name Manny is familiar and I remember Jamie mentioning him after being released last July. He lived at Tony's place and had designs on her.

Dalton must be keen. He tells me he popped down to Pucklechurch yesterday.
I warn him, "Be careful, otherwise Jamie could hurt you."
"After Manny's murder," he says, "I'm very aware how dangerous Jamie's friends are and I could be putting myself at risk."
"There is little chance Jamie will ever change," I tell him.
Dalton openly admits to me, "There's nothing sexual in our relationship."
What is Dalton really about, I wonder? I can't trust anyone any more. He voices his concern that Jamie might be released early. "What chance does she have of ever getting on her feet?" he asks.
A letter arrives from Jamie today. It's a good thing I have been open about my daughter and hold no shame. On the outside of the envelope she has written:
"Yes, Mr. Postman, it's me again. I'm back in jail. 16 months this time!"

Plans Afoot – 1995

1st November – Wednesday

Early evening, Jamie unexpectedly phones. "I must be quick," she says. "The police are coming to interview me about Manny's murder."
I joke, "Oh well, at least you weren't involved this time. You were in prison when it happened."
"Yes, I was involved," she says with a giggle.
I can't believe it. "How on earth could you have been?" I ask.

"Last Monday, Dalton and I went out with Manny and his girlfriend," she says. "Manny tried to shoot his friend, but the pin in the gun got stuck. We were used as a get-away car.
He was a very good friend to me," says Jamie solemnly. "He tried to get me off the brown."
"Was he a pimp?" I ask.
"Yes."

"Jamie, please don't let Dalton down. He has been so good to you."
She laughs, "Don't worry. I'll probably marry him. He's really good for me."

2nd November – Thursday

Sindy rings to enquire if I am okay.
She tells me, "Last week Jamie and Dalton met Manny, the guy who was murdered. Jamie rang asking if she could bring him back to my house but I refused saying, I didn't want those sort of people here...they are too dangerous. Now look what's happened."

3rd November – Friday

As we chat on the phone, I ask, "Jamie, are you pregnant?"
Sounding happy, and relieved she says, "I'm not, Mum. They've tested me in prison and my period started as soon as they told me. It must have been the heroin affecting my body.

"I'm hoping to do a hairdressing course at Drake Hall and get a NVQ qualification," she says excitedly. "There's the possibility of me attending daily rehab when I come out."

"That doesn't sound a good idea," I say concerned. "Too much temptation with your friends around. You would be better going away."

"Yes, I suppose so," she agrees.

5th November – Sunday

This evening, Jamie rings from prison and has a long chat with her Dad. She tells him, "They've got nothing against me anymore."

"So you are sorted out, Jamie?" he asks.

"Well, I say that now," she replies laughing.

"What about the shoplifting?" he enquires.

"I do it when I'm bored," she says.

"But what happens when you get out of prison?" he asks, worried.

Dalton asks me to send him a copy of the documentary, 'Every Parent's Nightmare', in which Jamie says, "You can never trust a Crackhead." Perhaps he will understand her more after seeing it.

6th November – Monday

"What are you doing now, Jamie?" I enquire when she rings from Pucklechurch.

"I'm bored," she replies. "There's nothing to do."

"Jamie, please don't lead Dalton on."

"What do you mean?" she snaps. "Mum, I'm only twenty-two and have a lot of living to do."

Very excited she says, "I'm definitely going to Drake Hall. They have a place for me."

Although there has been such sadness over the years, there have been very happy moments too.

This afternoon Mikey, Max's father, collects him from school. There is such delight on their faces as their eyes meet. Mikey picks Max up, and swings him around as they hug.

Driving back home, I turn to Mikey saying, "Who would have thought, at our first meeting in 1989, that we would be where we are today?"

He pauses for a moment to reflect, then looks at me. "To be honest, Angela, I thought I'd be dead by now."

8th November

"Hi, it's me. Just a quick call to let you know I'm at Drake Hall," says Jamie. I'm so pleased. Pucklechurch was the worst place I've ever been to. Guess who's here, mum – Collette. She's doing twelve months for robbery." Collette is the youngster I helped, and who shared Jamie's flat.

Jamie tells me,"I've felt awful coming off the methadone. I have terrible 'flu symptoms and can't sleep. I wish they would let me come down as usual without methadone – it's not half as bad."

11th November – Saturday

Dalton rings this evening, after visiting Jamie. "How was Jamie?" I ask. "Just Jamie – the same Jamie," he replies, sounding disappointed, as if he had expected to see a change. But it wasn't to be.

"I've been approached by my tenants' association," he tells me. "They are aware Jamie has visited my flat, and they feel threatened by her." Jamie must have a widespread reputation, since his flat is in a very respectable part of the city and not where she normally hangs out. Later, when I tell Sindy of Dalton's problems, she says, "My neighbours don't talk to me because of Jamie. I don't know why I do it for her. I wouldn't do it for anyone else."

14th November – Tuesday

Jamie is crying saying, "I'm in hospital. Mum, can you get up this weekend?" she asks.
I confirm I can which brightens her up no end.

I attend a review meeting with social services regarding Ben and Angel, and it is recommended that the two children be adopted together. There is to be a resource panel meeting in November and adoption panel are to meet in February 1996. The link worker is most anxious, saying she thinks the meeting in February is leaving it too late. The older the children are, the more difficult it will be to place them.

17th November – Friday

On the envelope of her letter, Jamie has written another message to the postman:
> 'Yes, the owner of this house has a criminal for a daughter and she's in prison – but I swear I'm innocent. Please start a petition to get me out.'

Jamie is very keen to see me and I look forward to my visit.

Tonight I speak to Joy and tell her, "I am very frightened...everything I have predicted over the past few years has come true. Three years ago I predicted Jamie would be dead by twenty-five. I hope this is one prediction I have got wrong."

19th November – Sunday

Pat and Dalton come with me to visit Jamie. As we drive along, Dalton says, "Collette has written to me saying, 'Don't be surprised if Jamie turns up on your doorstep.'"
Thoughts buzz through my head. Oh no, here we go again. Jamie is contemplating doing a runner.

Dalton tells me the video has had a profound effect on him. He now realizes what the real Jamie is about. Over the five months of filming, he can see the change in Jamie's personality and looks as she gets deeper into crack.

At Drake Hall we proceed to the main building. Jamie looks wonderful, sitting at the table in the canteen waiting for us. She is blooming and her face is almost free of spots; she is no longer skinny, but looks bonny and very healthy once more.
Excited, and with a big smile on her face, Jamie gives me a hug, and greets Pat and Dalton. She is chatty and bubbly.
But I know, deep down, she is the same old Jamie, and nothing has changed. She giggles about her shoplifted clothes, lifestyle, and the people she mixes with on the outside. There is a glint of excitement in her eyes as she speaks.

"It's so boring in Drake," she says. "I'm working in textiles but hope to get a move. All we do all day is read magazines."
"Can't you do hairdressing or something else interesting?" I ask her.
"No," she says, "I'm not in long enough."
"What about books – do you have a good library?" I enquire, knowing she loves reading.
"It's okay," she says.

Jamie hasn't changed. She tells me, "I'm coming home for Christmas. I'm planning on it...you can definitely expect to see me."

Everyone laughs, thinking she is joking...but I know Jamie is serious. "After all," she says. "I only get an extra 21 days, halved, if I do a runner." We shake our heads in disbelief. No wonder she is planning to escape for a second time – ten days is no deterrent. It is all a big joke as far as Jamie is concerned. She needs a new challenge, danger and excitement. In disbelief, with eyes popping out of his head, Dalton is aghast as he listens in disbelief to Jamie speaking.

"Are there any drugs in this prison?" enquires Pat.
"Yes, they're rife," replies Jamie.
We press her, "Tell us more."
"They can be paid for with cigarettes and phone-cards, "she tells us. "Draw (cannabis) is mainly available. It's smoked in the cells."
"Why don't the authorities stop it when they smell the stuff?" I ask her. Jamie shrugs her shoulders. "There's absolutely nothing they can do about it. They will never be able to stop it."
Pat says, "It would be easy to put drugs in flowers and plants brought in by visitors."
Jamie laughs, "It is easy. We have a sniffer dog called Ozzy, but he hardly ever finds anything."
We talk about crack and she says, "I don't want it anymore."
"Time" is called by the prison warders. We part with a big hug, and as we wave farewell across the room, Jamie looks choked and near to tears.

Back in the car we all sigh, pondering for a moment on things Jamie has said. I speak first. "Jamie hasn't changed. She's still the same Jamie with that devilish glint in her eye. She revels in talking about her friends, the guns and violence, and escaping from prison."
Dalton is overcome with emotion. "I don't know whether it's best to visit Jamie again," he says. "Last week I felt suicidal after seeing her. I'm very disappointed Jamie doesn't appear to have changed."

24th November – Friday

Dalton enquires on the phone, "Angela, does Jamie go to church?"
"Why?" I ask him.
Again, he asks, "Does she usually go to church?"
"She did go as a child but not nowadays."

Dalton is puzzled. "It seems strange Jamie has asked me to see her at the Catholic church on Sunday at 10.00 o'clock, at Eccleshall, near the prison."

"Oh no. It sounds as if she is definitely planning to escape," I tell him. "Well, she did put in her last letter, 'Don't be surprised if I come home with you," he says, "but I thought she was joking."

"Don't get involved, Dalton," I warn him. "You could be arrested, lose your job – in fact lose everything."

"Oh I won't," he says.

"What shall we do at Christmas if she escapes?" I ask him. "I'll give her a dinner but she would have to return to Drake Hall. Neither of us can have her to stay. If she doesn't go back to prison, she will return to friends and drugs."

Dalton agrees, "We can't let Jamie do that. I would take her back to the prison."

"Did she say anything else in her letter?" I enquire.

"Yes, about Angel." Dalton sounds very down. "Jamie says it looks as if she has lost Angel...and she sounds quite suicidal."

"Jamie desperately needs psychiatric help," I tell him. "I'm worried she will try to commit suicide when she comes out."

Dalton insists he drives up to the church on Sunday, saying he will phone to keep me in the picture.

25th November – Saturday

I am very worried, having received a very depressed letter from Jamie:

> *"I know I've lost all my children.*
> *Simply I've got nothing left to live for.*
> *I have no purpose now.*
> *Why should I give up the drugs?*
> *At least I'll be able to forget everything.*
> *THE END.*
> *love Jamie.*

Immediately I write to Jamie and tell her of the positive things in her life.

Late afternoon, Dalton calls at my house after visiting her. "I can't make Jamie out," he says. "She seems fine, but did say some strange things; she can't understand why you are unable to look after all her children. She implied it's your duty and says you are colour prejudiced.

Jamie also implied you forced her to go to Art College, against her wishes."

"Such a load of rubbish," I tell him. "Jamie always wanted to be a dress designer."

"In her letter to me," he says, "she asked me to take in some heroin because she's so depressed. But obviously I didn't.

She isn't being allowed to church tomorrow and is planning to escape on Christmas Eve.

Jamie is out of her mind and there's nothing more I can do. She desperately needs psychiatric help."

As Dalton departs I joke, "Oh well, suppose we will have to be on standby at Christmas."

27th November – Monday

I pluck up courage to phone the Sister of the health wing at the prison. She is extremely kind and understanding, and listens as I explain Jamie appears suicidal in her letters, and says she desperately needs heroin. Sister says, "Don't worry, I'll speak to Jamie today."

I am relieved, and give her permission to tell Jamie I have phoned voicing my concern.

28th November – Tuesday

Jamie writes:

> "I am going to fight for Angel. My worker from the drug agency is visiting me about it."

I don't trust them. They shouldn't interfere without knowing the true story over the past six years. They haven't got a clue what Jamie is really like – her emotional instability and physical inability to be a mother to her children. Where and when is it all going to end?

Feeling awful, I ring the social worker. She reassures me, "Don't worry Angela. After all, Jamie hasn't bothered to contact the foster-mum, or myself, for a couple of months now. The courts will definitely take that into consideration."

I can't cope. I have given up child minding, socialising, and keep-fit; and also decided to step down as joint co-cordinator of our parent support group at Christmas...I am now at rock bottom.

Max needs me and I have to carry on for him. I believe he was sent as a guiding ray of light and hope.

Will it ever end? How can I put up with this for maybe another twenty years? I want to enjoy life. In the New Year will make a conscious effort to go forward with renewed enthusiasm. Currently, every minute of my life is living and breathing drugs.

Church of Freedom – 1995

2nd December – Saturday

"Jamie is planning to escape this weekend," Dalton informs me. I AM ANGRY AND EXASPERATED – THE SYSTEM HAS FAILED US AGAIN.
Jamie has passed security clearance at Drake Hall prison – even though she escaped from there last year, is constantly on the run from the police, and hardly ever turns up for court hearings.

She is going to church on Sunday and has asked Dalton, "Be there at 10.15 and leave your car opposite the church so I can make my escape."
"You are not getting involved Dalton, are you?" I ask.
"No, but I shall be there to try to persuade Jamie not to do it."
I tell him, "Jamie will escape if she gets the opportunity, even if you don't turn up."
He agrees with me. "I have given it some thought and promise I'll ring to let you know what happens."
"It's my guess she will return straight back to her friends," I tell him.
"I shouldn't think she will," he says. "The girls I've been speaking to tell me she owes a guy a lot of money."
I wait with baited breath to see what happens on Sunday. Jamie has escaped before and can easily do it again.

3rd December – Sunday

Mid-day. I phone Dalton on his mobile, thinking he is probably on the motorway returning from Staffordshire. "Dalton, is everything okay?" I enquire.
"It went as you predicted," he says.
"What? Has she done a runner?" I ask.
"She's here if you want to speak to her," he says calmly.
"Surely, I haven't heard right?"
There's a pause..."Hello mum. I've just been to Sindy's," says Jamie.
"She looks terrible and has lost so much weight."
"You mean she's using?" I ask. "Yes, more than likely," replies Jamie.

"Honestly, mum, it's enough to put me off drugs for life. I will never take drugs again."
"I've heard it all before, Jamie," I exclaim.

"Mum, it was awful in Drake Hall," she says. "I warned them, and said I'd leave, especially with the situation over Angel. I pleaded with probation and the prison to move me but they wouldn't listen. They said, in so many words, 'We will see you again when you get caught'."

Jamie recalls, "They strip-searched me after Dalton's last visit. It was disgusting."
She goes on to say, "We were given £2.50 a week pocket money. Soft drugs could be bought with a phone-card. When pay day arrived, the girls are in debt because they had to give double back for their drugs."

I remind Jamie, "In your first letter from Pucklechurch prison you said, "Although I am locked up, I feel free."
"Yes," she says. "If I had been locked up in a secure prison, I would be able to get on with my sentence, knowing I have no alternative. But it was terrible at Drake Hall – I couldn't hassle it any more," she says, "knowing how easy it is to get out."

"How did you manage to escape?" I enquire. "A taxi took three of us to church, dropped us off and left us there. I just walked in the church and out again."

Concerned at Dalton's involvement I warn, "He'll get into trouble, Jamie, if he gets caught."
"No he won't," she says. "He can't be done, because I was out on licence and therefore not absconding."

I am astounded. Jamie promises to keep in touch. A couple of hours later, Jamie leaves a message on the answer phone for me to ring her, sounding very happy and giggly. "I'm drinking Hooch alcoholic lemonade. I've had a meal; just a beefburger, but it was wonderful."

4th December – Monday
"I'm never going back to prison," says Jamie. "I'll never do it again – the cheques, I mean."

"Eight months is such a short sentence for your crimes. I think it's awful." I tell Jamie, "You never pay for your crime. I've had enough."

Jamie says excitedly, "Dalton has bought Christmas presents for the children. He let me choose them because I haven't got any money."
While I am in the bath, my doorbell rings and Max answers. Two police stand on the doorstep. Sitting at the top of the stairs, towel around me and dripping wet hair, I apologise for my state, and remain there as they speak. "Are you aware about Jamie?" one enquires.
"Yes," I reply. "I've written to the Chief Inspector to inform him she won't be coming here." Armed with this information, the officers leave quite happily.

8.30 p.m. Jamie phones, very weepy. "I've left Dalton because he was just getting too much."
"Jamie, you've had some brown," I tell her.
"No I haven't," she snaps aggressively – a sign she has. "I'm just very tired because I've had no sleep."
She can't hide the truth from me anymore. Yesterday Jamie was bubbly, today very weepy. Jamie is using. Her short-temper is proof enough for me.

5th December – Tuesday

I write to the governor at Drake Hall prison, Alan Howarth MP, and Michael Howard Home Office Minister, about the farce of Jamie's security check clearance and escape from prison. Dalton is pleased I have done so and agrees it can't be allowed to continue.

He tells me, "Jamie is at Sindy's. It was awful last night when I went to Sindy's house. She told me Jamie wasn't there but I saw her going into the place.
"Dalton, is she back on drugs?" I ask
"Yes, she's definitely smoking again," he tells me.
7.00 p.m: Jamie phones sounding much brighter. "Jamie, are you using again?" I ask.
"No," she snaps. She doesn't know that Dalton has told me the truth. "Jamie I know you are – you were weepy last night."
Still she denies it, saying, "I was just very tired."

6th December – Wednesday

Today there is an bitter north wind, with light snow showers. As arranged, Jamie and Dalton are waiting for us at 1.30 p.m. in Coventry town centre. Max runs up to Jamie and they embrace, pleased to see each other after such a long time.

Jamie looks good. Her make-up is lightly done, and her hair loose – now much longer, below the shoulders. She is wearing blue jeans and black short boots. A skimpy 'T' shirt emphasizes her big bust, over which she wears a man's light-weight blazer. She looks frozen and says, "I've left everything at Drake Hall and haven't even got a heavy winter coat with me."

We amble along to a cafe. While Jamie is preoccupied with Max, Dalton tells me, "On Monday, Sindy went mad when I called because she was in the middle of a deal for a large quantity of cocaine. She didn't want me to know what was going on."

He confirms, "Yes, Jamie smoked as soon as she returned to Sindy's on Sunday night.

"But I can't believe it," I exclaim. "Sunday lunchtime, she told me what a dreadful state Sindy was in and it put her off drugs for life."

We agree Jamie is in great danger. I whisper to Dalton, "I will contact the police immediately. Jamie must be put inside for her own safety."

"Leave it for 24 hours," he says, "because I want to take Jamie shopping for some clothes. I will always be there for Jamie."

As we sit having coffee Jamie giggles, "I worked in the laundry room for an NVQ (National Vocational Qualification)." Here is a very intelligent woman, and all they can offer her is training in laundry work. No wonder she was bored out of her mind.

7th December – Thursday

Early morning Jamie contacts me. "I'm not at Sindy's anymore. She was raided last night -- by police looking for me.

Dalton and I are off shopping."

Mid-morning Sindy phones. "Angela, do you know where Jamie is? Is she okay? Police raided my house 1.30 this morning, looking for her. It was awful. I was so worried they would wake up my daughter. They swarmed in neighbours' gardens, in the street, everywhere."

She tells me, "Jamie is now staying with a married guy called Richie."

Late afternoon: Jamie phones from Dalton's car, "Hi mum, we've had a fantastic time. Dalton has bought me a peach coloured cashmere coat which is fabulous, and a white chenille jumper." Jamie sounds so excited.

I don't agree with Jamie escaping from prison. If, however, the system is so lax, who can blame her wanting to be free for Christmas?

8th December – Friday

Dalton phones, early evening. "Angela, have you heard from Jamie?"
"I've heard nothing, which is strange because she promised to take Max to the cinema. She's so unreliable," I tell him.
"Jamie didn't have drugs yesterday," he says, "but she was very childlike, like a fifteen year old."
"I've been told a user stops maturing at the age they start taking drugs," I tell him, but warn that Jamie can also be a sophisticated, mature, and evil woman.

"Does Richie spell trouble? Is he involved in drugs?" I enquire.
"As far as I'm aware, he smokes lots of cannabis but that's about it," says Dalton.
I smile, saying, "Oh, I've heard that one before."

Joy phones distressed and depressed, having found a 14" meat knife in her son's bedroom, and a dealer has been constantly knocking on the door. What can she do? There is no easy answer.
She asks her son to leave the house but he refuses. She is scared for the safety of her little girls. "It's only with your support, Angela, that I have survived," she says.

9th December – Saturday

Dalton rings, sounding very worried. "Richie promised me he would get Jamie to phone last night, but she didn't. I am very concerned."
"Dalton, I sense something is very wrong," I tell him.

"Jamie brought a guy along on the train," says Dalton. "He's Jamaican and seems a nice enough guy."
"Do you know him?" I enquire.
"No. Jamie just asked if he could come along."
Alarm bells ring. In the past, the guys accompanying Jamie have proved to be minders. "I am concerned we might lose touch with Jamie," I tell him.

Dalton says with a tone of urgency, "I'll go and look for her."
Later he phones to say, "I've found Jamie and she's calling at my flat mid-day. I wonder whether I should call the police now?"
"Leave it to me," I tell him. "I will contact them immediately. We must get her to safety." Hopefully, Jamie will go to a more secure prison, which is what she wants.

I notify the police that Jamie will be at Dalton's flat, and they thank me for my help. Anxiously, I wait for news as mid-day passes. An hour or so later I notice the answer phone flashing.
"It's Jamie. Thanks for phoning the police," and slams the phone down. I feel dreadful for what I have done.
A second message from Jamie – "Mum, it's Jamie again. Would you be able to phone please? Don't worry, I'm not going to shout at you like I did at Dalton. He deserves it, okay. Speak to you later. Bye."
I am unable to speak to Jamie at the station. She sends a message via the officer, wanting writing paper, pen, clothes and food.

Dalton contacts me, sounding very worried. "Jamie was wild with me when I called at the station. She said she was enjoying herself and now I've ruined everything for her."
I assure him, "She always cools down after a while."

During the evening Jamie rings. I quite expect her to go berserk but she is unexpectedly friendly.
"I'm boiling mad with Dalton for informing the police," she says.
I put her straight, "Jamie, it was me who phoned them."
"It's okay for you to do it, because you're my mum," she says, "but not Dalton."
Once again, I stress it was my decision to inform. I try to explain, "Jamie, it was for your own safety. I knew things were bad for you, possibly dangerous."

"Mum, do you know who bought the brown, the day I came out of prison?" asks Jamie. "Yes, it was Dalton. He wanted me to be his little woman, to be supervised 24 hours a day. You know that's not me."

Calming down, Jamie says, "Mum, I've begun to realise my one true friend is you."

10th December – Sunday

Jamie has been using Dalton. When he dropped her off after the shopping trip after spending so much money, she returned to Richie and didn't bother to contact Dalton again.

Sindy phones me, "The police have warned I must not harbour Jamie, otherwise I could go to prison. I can't risk losing everything." She confirms Dalton bought drugs for Jamie as soon as she came out of prison.
"Why?" I ask, "Is he round the twist?"
"I wonder myself sometimes," she says.

12th December – Tuesday

A message on the answer phone, "Mum, I am off to Holloway prison today. Can you send me some money please? Will write."

This evening a friend takes me to a pub in town to listen to folk music. It is just the tonic I need, and I feel so relaxed when I return home.

14th December – Thursday

Today, I notify our parent support group that I intend to step down as joint co-cordinator. I am so unwell. Our group has grown beyond all recognition, and it is time to let them move forward without me. Over the next few months, I must recharge my batteries before Jamie is released from prison and our next crisis.

"Another prostitute has been found murdered," it states on the news. My heart misses a beat, but then it dawns on me – it can't be Jamie – she is safe in Holloway. For the time being, she is protected from the violent world she lives in. Tonight I can relax and sleep in peace.

15th December – Friday

I receive a letter from the governor of Drake Hall prison, replying to my letter concerning Jamie's security check. He states:

> "Jamie was assessed as suitable to go unescorted to Church after being at Drake Hall for about three weeks. She was allowed to attend Mass at the village church."

'Suitable' – they must be joking with her past history!

Jamie phones and is keen for me to visit Holloway.

"I'd like to see you before Christmas," I tell her, "I'll ring the prison to make an appointment." I am also looking forward to calling on Jamie's sister, Kate, who lives near Holloway."

18th December – Monday

I tell Dalton, "Jamie has written, asking if you can let her have money for phone-cards. Why do you help her?" I ask. "She only wants you for your money."
"I ask myself the same question," he replies. "Only two of the girls have ever bought me a meal and Jamie was one of them. I believe it showed she cared."

19th December – Tuesday

I travel up to London by train and meet Kate. She drives me to Holloway prison, a modern building, not as daunting as I had imagined.
There is confusion on my part at reception, and the officers assume I know the routine. I hand in my visiting order. The officer is abrupt and suspicious, treating me as if I'm the criminal.
By now I'm tired after my long journey and get cross.
An officer, behind a glass screen, pushes a button on a panel to let us through two sets of sliding glass doors. In the waiting area we leave our coats and bags in lockers. Only cash in hand is permitted, for the purchase of refreshments.

After being frisked, we are pointed in the direction of a flight of stairs, and enter a large room like a factory canteen. I count eleven officers, scattered around the perimeter and watching everyone's movements like hawks. So different from Newhall, Risley and Drakehall prisons.
High up on the walls at regular intervals, are large convex mirrors. A TV monitor in one corner is eagerly surveyed by three officers. As never before, I feel 'big brother' is watching.

Jamie's name is shouted out and an officer escorts her to a table.
She is very pleased to see me, and smiles as we hug. How well she looks. Her make-up is very pretty and she is wearing the white jumper Dalton bought for her.
Jamie, is her old bubbly self, and chats non-stop, as always on visits. We talk about Dalton and I express my concern saying, "You mustn't use him for his money."

Screwing up her face, she says, "Why not? He was awful. He should have warned me the police were coming to his flat."
She laughs, "Mum, you could have left it until after Christmas to tell them where I was."

"What about Richie?" I ask. "Have you had any contact with him? "
"Yes, I've written to him," she says. Jamie has that devilish look in her eyes again.
"Mum, I wasn't in danger as you thought. Richie is okay – he used to be one of the biggest importers of cocaine in the country, but gave it up when the police were on his tail."
I don't believe for a minute he has given it up, I think to myself.
"Richie is really nice," Jamie says, sounding rather keen. "I suppose you'd say I was his mistress. While I was on the run, he set me up with a flat and was really good to me."

"The girls in my cell think you're wonderful, Mum," she says. "They loved the felt tips you sent in." Jamie smiles cheekily, like a young mischievous child.
"We have had a wonderful time drawing on the cell walls. We weren't allowed the glitter glue you sent. Imagine what they'd have done with that.
There are five in my cell altogether, two of them are Yardies."

As I walk over to the serving hatch, Jamie jumps up from her seat shouting out, "Hey mum, can you get me some chocolate?"
Suddenly, there is an almighty bawl from a warder – "Sit down," he shouts across the room and everyone looks round. Jamie reluctantly returns to her seat.

"According to Dalton, there was a dealer at Sindy's house while you were in hiding?"
"Yes," she confirms, smiling. "Some guys brought along cocaine and we smoked with them for hours, staying up all night...it was wonder-ful."

Jamie looks up and shouts in a loud voice, so everyone hears, "Mum, can you arrange for our MP to come and visit me. I must tell him what is really going on in this prison."
I want to crawl under the table as everyone looks in our direction.

"By the way," says Jamie, "my article will be in the paper soon – about the murderer recently given life. He propositioned prostitutes in our area."
"Time please,"shouts a warder. We hug and say goodbye. The door is unlocked; every female visitor passing through has the palm of their hand stamped with invisible ink.

21st December – Thursday

Another day, another saga. National press headlines: 'The Kinky Wife Killer' to be quizzed by serial murder cops over vice girls' deaths. As I read on, the article says, "In the red light district haunted by this killer, a call-girl called Sophie says, 'He was a regular. There was nothing kinky about him when he was with me. But the girls talked about him and said he was weird. There was something cold about him that sent shivers up your spine'."
'Sophie', that name rings a bell. Of course...Sophie is Jamie. I remember Jamie telling me the article is about prostitutes and written under the name of Sophie.

23rd December – Saturday

I meet Dalton to collect his presents for my grandchildren. He says, "After having given a lot of thought over Jamie, I realise she's involved in another way of life and enjoys it. I shall remain a good friend, and visit her if she contacts me."
Looking at Max, Dalton says, "I just cannot understand why these girls abandon their children."
"Drugs become the first love of their life," I say sadly. "Often they are held to ransom by their pimps."

He tells me, "I get a buzz from seeing Jamie's face when she actually pays for presents rather than shoplifting them. I've done it for other girls and get pleasure from seeing their delight in handing cash over at the till."

24th December – Sunday. Christmas Eve

This morning I am very excited. Max and I visit Ben and Angel. I have bought a video camera to film them before they are adopted. Ben is so pleased to see me, and Angel crawls around the room with a permanent smile on her face.
It is wonderful to see their happy faces as they open their presents. It makes me realise how lucky we are that contact is being maintained.

25th December – Monday. Christmas Day

Today has been the most relaxing Christmas Day I can remember. For the first time in years, I don't have to worry about Jamie. Yes, today has been just perfect.

28th December – Thursday

Must write to Jamie. Maybe she will write soon and let us know how Holloway celebrated Christmas? I have had an excellent day today, feeling really well. Just what I need – Jamie is locked up safe inside and we can get on with our lives.

At the beginning of this year, 1995, I had hoped for a better and happier future. Instead it got worse day by day. I wonder what is in store for 1996? After my visit to Holloway I know Jamie hasn't changed and will continue the same as ever.

29th December – Friday

A letter drops through the letter box. Immediately I know it is from Jamie because of the messages and pictures she writes on the envelope. The postman must think she's crazy. Perhaps she is.

She starts her letter, "There are five girls in my dorm," writing like a kid at boarding school.

31st December – Sunday

I am so tired and just need to sleep. Today I step down as joint-coordinator of our support group.

Now I must wind down completely and catch up on myself. There are friends I haven't seen for months, jobs in the house, and letter writing. Most important of all, I shall have time for myself, Max, and my son and his family. Now, I must concentrate on healing my body and mind.

Crackhead

Celebrations – 1996

1st January – Monday

"Hi, It's Jamie. Happy New Year!" She sounds very jovial.
"We had a fabulous time last night in the prison," Jamie giggles. My mates, not me, set the trees alight outside."
"How on earth did they do that?" I ask.

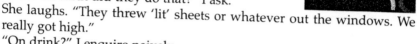

She laughs. "They threw 'lit' sheets or whatever out the windows. We really got high."
"On drink?" I enquire naively.
"No, can't say what," she replies, knowing someone might be listening.

She sounds like a kid at boarding school, full of tricks and pranks. As we speak an officer bawls, "Come off the phone and get back to your cell."

2nd January – Tuesday

Jamie phones requesting, "Mum, can you get Dalton to bring up a pretty duvet cover, pillow cases, towel, floor rug, and leggings. All these were burnt last night. I'm feeling wonderful," she says.
Jamie sounds high – which isn't surprising since she is on so much Valium and anti-depressants. She seems far happier at Holloway than at the other prisons and, at long last, she is getting medical attention.

I phone Dalton to arrange to let him have Jamie's things. He surprises me when he says, "If I was asked to help Jamie escape again, I would."
"Dalton, I can't understand why you risk everything – your career and family, knowing you could end up in prison?"
Dalton agrees, "Everything is at stake – but I would still do it again."

7th January – Sunday

"Get your House in order. Put yourself first, before channelling your energy into other people."

As I hear the medium's words, directed to the audience at church, I realise he is right and my life has to change. I must start living for *me* now.

8th January – Monday

Over one hundred videos of Jamie's BBC programme have gone into the community as part of the schools' drug education programme, and also to police, health authority and parents. I am so proud of Jamie for making this film.

When Jamie was fifteen, drugs were considered a taboo subject and not discussed in schools. Few teenagers were involved with drugs in 1989. Youngsters of today are very different. Drugs are everywhere and almost 50% of kids in rural towns are experimenting. At long last the subject is being brought into the open and both pupils and parents are becoming informed on drug issues.

Max is aware what drugs are, and sees the effects they have on his mother. I am doing my best to educate him, give him lots of love, and can do no more. If he chooses to take drugs in his teens it will be his decision. There is nothing I can do to stop him.

Jamie asks when I am taking Max to see her?
"I have no intention of taking him into the daunting atmosphere of Holloway," I tell her. "He shouldn't have to endure sliding glass doors, frisking, TV cameras, mirrors and so many aggressive looking guards."

Jo, an addict friend of mine, asks how Jamie is getting on in prison. She offers, "I'll send Jamie some silver loop earrings as a pressie. I understand how Jamie must feel because I've been there and I've got the 'T' shirt." I am very touched by her kind generosity.

11th January – Thursday

Surprise call, "Mum, I'm moving tomorrow to Brockhill prison at Redditch." I hope it is a secure prison this time.
There never seems to be a break, even when Jamie is in prison, and I am getting tense once more. She will only be half an hour journey from here.

"My elbow and arm hurt this morning," says Jamie. "Remember, I was hit by a taxi some time ago?"
There have been so many incidents but I can't recall this one.

16th January – Tuesday

Every day I wake up with flashbacks and my mind has been scarred forever. My life seems a dream, and every time my predictions prove right.

I ring Kate, to tell her that her sister is now at Brockhill. As we chat, Kate tells me she lived with foster parents after she was born, was due to be adopted, but at the last minute her mother changed her mind.

Kate says her mother put into care, as a toddler, and as she tells her story, I shake my head in disbelief. It all sounds so familiar. Jamie's story is history repeating itself.

Having listened to Kate, I now know that Jamie is the image of her mother in every way.

I heard a radio programme today, talking about people with tendencies to crime, addiction, heavy sexual activity, and personality-seeking excitement. It has been proven these people have different cells in the brain, which show up on a brain scan, and are believed to be hereditary.

20th January – Saturday

Alan Howarth, my MP, has sent me a letter he received from Anne Widdecombe, MP in charge of prisons at the Home Office. Reference Jamie's escape from prison, Ann Widdecombe states:

> "Jamie was considered suitable for temporary release from prison to attend church and on the 3rd December she returned to the prison promptly after the service. However on the 10th December she failed to return. In assessing Ms Harrison's application, they were aware that she had absconded last year during a previous sentence, but they also bore in mind that when she returned she finished her sentence without further incident."

I am very angry. Ann Widdecombe has got her facts wrong. Jamie did NOT attend church on the 3rd December – just the 10th when she escaped. She continues:

> "Drake Hall prison's suicide awareness policy has been highly commended, but at the time she absconded Ms. Harrison had not given any indication to staff that she was a suicide risk."

Again, Ann Widdecombe has been misinformed. I spoke to the Sister at the prison and made her aware of Jamie's suicidal tendencies. She was going to talk to Jamie about her problem.

21st January – Sunday

9.00 a.m. Jamie rings to wish Max a happy sixth birthday.
"Mum, guess what I'm doing in here? A hair and beauty course," she says.
Dalton rings and tells me he took some cannabis in for Jamie.
"Gosh, was that difficult?" I ask.
"No, it was very easy," he replies. "Jamie also asked me to take in some brown, but there was no way I'd do that."

25th January – Thursday

Jamie jokes in her letter and talks about her stay at "this health farm", and the hair and beauty course she is doing. Kate phones me and reads a letter Jamie has written to her. At the bottom Jamie writes,

> *"The guilt I feel now, even though I am only twenty-two, is killing me. Tina probably blocks things out of her mind, like I do.*
> *Kate, I have pictures of you at your wedding on my wall. Even though we have never been close, I have always thought about you.*
> *I'm looking forward to seeing you.*
> *All my love, Jamie.*

Kate says, "It says so much in this letter. The awful guilt makes Jamie feel worse, so she tries even more to hide it. The drugs block it all out for her."

28th January – Sunday

Brockhill prison is nestled in a small valley in the Worcestershire countryside, surrounded by a high wire fence. Immediately next-door is Blakenhurst, a high-walled secure male prison.
A thin layer of snow has turned to ice, and a bitter north wind blows as visitors wait for the gate to be locked. On the wall by the entrance is a board announcing heavy penalties for the smuggling of drugs into prison. Security is relaxed and the guard smiles – unlike Risley and

Holloway where the guards were so strict and humourless. We are ushered to a security check and frisked.

The visiting room is large and friendly, with comfortable armchairs, grouped around small coffee tables, providing a relaxed atmosphere. The three warders chat to each other. Only one sits keeping an eye on everyone. After being allotted a table, we sit and wait while the inmates enter one by one, both male and female.

Jamie comes bouncing over, looking absolutely fantastic. Fashionably dressed she wears thick black tights, denim fringed shorts over, and a denim sleeveless revered button-up blouse. A black sweatshirt with the word 'Armani' in white, is slung over her shoulders.
As we hug, I notice how well she looks – probably from the high dose of valium. Opposite me sits my healthy, bubbly, smiling, daughter. Her mousy colour, curly hair, falls well below her shoulders, and her make-up is beautiful.

I reflect on memories of my daughter on the run just before Christmas – thin, spotty, pale and ill, and being rushed to hospital.
A beautiful woman sits here before me today – the daughter I wish she could always be; but as we converse I realise, underneath, is the same old Jamie who will never change.
Jamie laughs, displaying the dimples in her cheeks. Excitedly, she tells me about her three day a week hair and beauty course, and proudly points at her painted nails.

We chat about Dalton. "He loves me, and wants to marry me," says Jamie. "But I won't of course."
"Why did Dalton buy you cocaine on the Sunday night you escaped from prison -- when you stayed at Sindy's?" I ask.
"I threatened to go to work, and he did it to stop me," she replies. "I had an ounce of pure cocaine and it was wonderful."
"Did you also take crack?" I ask. "Yes," she says with excitement in her voice.

Jamie tells me she had drugs in Holloway from one of her cell mates. From the look in her eyes, I know she is still an addict at heart.

My counsellor from the drug agency visited me in Holloway," says Jamie. "There is talk of me going immediately for rehab when I am released. After that, I want to get a job in hairdressing and beauty, and then have Angel back."

I voice my concern, "Jamie I won't say any more after this, because it will only cause argument, but I think things are best left as they are. You will never change. And what about Ben?"

"I was wondering if I could have him as well," she says.

Jamie changes the subject and talks about her hair, make-up and nails. She enquires after Max and I tell her, "He is fine. I've decided to bring him along next weekend, because this prison is so relaxed."

Jamie is pleased. "I told you it was okay here didn't I?" she says.

Over the other side of the room, children happily play in the toy corner. On the far side of the room young male inmates, wearing denim jeans and blue/white pinstriped shirts, chat to their families.

Three young men arrive. Jamie's eyes follow them to their seats. They are just her type – black, with dreadlocks, and smartly dressed.

Jamie has her usual large supply of chocolate and fizzy drinks from the refreshment hatch and chats non-stop.

"I had a lovely letter from Kate," says Jamie. "She told me about her childhood. I can't believe how alike Tina and I are.

By the way, mum, you'll be pleased to know I'm having my teeth done and getting new glasses,"

"Does this mean you will finally have that seven year brace removed? After all this time, Jamie, it's a miracle."

We hug and kiss warmly, and wave goodbye. I feel really positive. At long last Jamie, a very bright young woman, is getting what she needs; security, medication and education.

Education & Medication – 1996

1st February – Thursday

Jamie is excited when she rings. "Mum, have you noticed I can't talk properly? I've had the brace chains taken out of my mouth.
My glasses will be ready soon. They're wicked – small gold round ones. And free!"

4th February – Sunday

I drive Kate, her two children, and Max to the prison to see Jamie. We wait anxiously and then spy Jamie on the other side of the room searching for us. I wave and she comes bouncing over – not going around the chairs, but climbing over them like a monkey.
Immediately, I sense she is very different from last week – this time jittery, and tense.
Her sleeveless dress reveals she has put on a lot of weight.
She is very pleased to see Kate and they have so much news to catch up on, so I leave them and join the children in the play area.

From a distance I observe the sisters. They are wearing identical brown boots, and their hair is almost the same colour and length.
I return to sit by them.
"I've got the same dress as you," Kate informs Jamie.
Jamie tells Kate she is having gold-rimmed glasses soon. Kate looks up surprised. "I've got that style as well."

We are seated next to an officer who constantly watches us. Jamie tells us, "He's here because Dalton and his friends were rather rowdy on last Friday's visit.
The girls brought me in some brown," she whispers. "Only a little," she qualifies.
Maybe this explains her mood – totally different from Jamie I visited last week. She was beautiful then and now she is so hard and tense.
"They are doing random drug testing here," she says.
"How on earth do you get away with it?" I ask.

313

"Well, I've figured that one out. They don't test over the weekend, so if I take it Friday I should be okay by Monday. It takes three days to go through the system."
"Does Dalton still give you money?" I ask.
"Yes, £10 a week," she replies.
Jamie complains, "The prison doctor is reducing my valium, but if I don't get it I'll go out of my mind."
Kate warns, "Jamie, the drugs you take will have harmful long-term effects on your body."
"They already have," says Jamie. "I'm having tests on my kidneys because of the pain."
"Where's the pain?" I ask. She points to the bottom of her spine, not the kidney area.
"It's a known fact that crack and heroin affect the bones," I tell her.

Jamie tells us, "The prison is to become all female in September, and the men will be leaving."
"Do you prefer it here or in Holloway?" I ask.
After some thought, she says, "Holloway, I suppose. The girls in here aren't in my league – you know what I mean? This is a privilege prison, not normally for people experienced like me." Jamie is still the hardened criminal. What chance is there she will ever change?

Kate remarks, "Jamie, you are so much like mum. Even your mannerisms are the same; just now you shrugged your shoulders, laughing at the same time; and your eyes are those of mum looking at me. You look so alike," she says. "Mum also has a real temper."
Jamie smiles, "And I have."
Time up. Jamie shouts out loudly and defiantly, so everyone hears including the officer nearby, "Thanks for bringing in the drugs." I am annoyed with her, and poor Kate is embarrassed.

The sisters embrace each other with affection, and the children kiss Jamie goodbye. As we leave, the officers call for the inmates to stay in their seats. An officer winks at me – some of them are human after all.

Travelling back to Stratford, Kate says, "I wish Jamie would keep in touch more often. On the other hand the future doesn't look hopeful for her, so perhaps it's best this way."

Agreeing with Kate, I voice my fear that Jamie's lifestyle may well kill her in the end.

5th February – Monday. Jamie's 23rd Birthday

I reflect on Jamie's childhood birthdays – always happy, full of fun and love, parties and excitement. I remember the cards and presents she gave to others – always making her cards with tender loving care and written with affection.

Today Jamie is spending her birthday in jail. Years ago I never dreamed this would be Jamie's destiny. She was such a good little girl, quiet and well behaved. It just goes to prove that no one can predict how their children will turn out.

Jamie rings from prison. She laughs, "I nearly died this morning, in front of all me mates. There was a rose from Dalton on the dining room table. I was so pleased to see Kate, and I love her children," she says. "I'm wearing the gold earrings she bought me, they're great."

10th February – Saturday

I reply to Ann Widdecombe's letter, stating she has got her facts and dates wrong regarding Jamie's escape from Drake Hall.

Tonight I look through the albums of Jamie as a child and wonder why she has turned out like this? In her last junior school report it stated: "Jamie constantly gives of her best and takes pleasure in pleasing. She has been a cooperative and pleasant member of her class."

There was a hint things weren't quite right in some of her childhood photos – the hard look, and raised fists. Looking back, I remember she was a very determined and independent child. From her early teens Jamie started to change in character, becoming more troublesome and wayward. I wonder why?

11th February – Sunday

Today I visit my grandchildren. Ben is nearly three and due to go to nursery school soon. Nine-month-old Angel is climbing the stairs and walking around the furniture. My visit is very happy but I leave heavy-hearted, knowing their lives are to change drastically before long.

Tonight I phone Dalton, "How did you get on at prison yesterday?" "It's strange," he says, "I took a girl with me, and all she and Jamie talked about was drugs, dealers, and the people they knew. Jamie will never change," he says, sounding dejected.

13th February – Tuesday

The social worker phones to inform me, "Jamie is refusing to sign her medical papers and is opposing the adoption of Angel. This will hold everything up, although there is little chance she will get her back."

Jamie makes me very angry. How can she do this to her children? No way will she change, or be able to offer the baby a stable loving background.
I assure the social worker I shall act as a witness in court, if needs be. After all, I have evidence in my diaries of her inability to look after children.
My main concern is that the children be adopted as quickly as possible for their emotional stability and I tell the social worker, "I'm not frightened of Jamie any more."

I ring Linda, the foster mum. We discuss the possible damage to Jamie's children from her taking such large quantities of crack during their pregnancies. There were times when Jamie took as much as £2,000 of crack in a weekend. Both children appear to have survived, and are very healthy and bright, in view of their foetal abuse.

14th February – Wednesday St. Valentine's Day

I am over the moon when a letter and a beautiful hand-made Valentine's card, arrive from Jamie this morning. She writes:

"I love you.
Thank you mum for adopting me.
I'm sorry I have caused you so much trouble. I truly mean that.
Your daughter, Jamie."

This card is priceless and makes me very happy. I write back immediately saying,

"Although I have been through so much, I wouldn't have changed you for the world."

In the evening Jamie phones. "Mum, I've got some news for you," she says. "Are you sitting down? Take a deep breath"...
Panicking, I take a deep breath. Is she pregnant?
Silence...and then
"Mum...I've had my nose pierced again." she says.
I can't believe it. Having a nose pierced is quite insignificant these days.

When Jamie was fifteen and had her nose pierced, things were very different. We were mad – her dad, myself and teachers. Jamie was the only one in her school.
Eventually, she was forced to remove the stud, although we were unaware she continued to put it in at raves and parties – as her dad discovered to his horror when he collected her one night. Today it is acceptable for youngsters to pierce themselves all over the body, including in the tummy button.
We laugh about it, and there is relief on my part – I thank God we don't have another pregnancy on our hands. As I put the phone down, I feel a glow inside. This has been a really good day – with Jamie's letter, and the phone call which leaves me 'up' instead of 'down' for once.

15th February – Thursday

I attend a meeting at the foster mum's house this morning. Jamie is opposing adoption, refusing to sign papers, including medical records, or meet the social workers. If Jamie goes to court to fight, it will cause further delay. She has a new solicitor recommended by the drug agency and says he is good on child custody.
She hasn't bothered to ring the foster mum to enquire about the children, saying she doesn't have her number, even though I have sent it to her twice. Dalton is sending Jamie £10 a week for phone-cards, so she must be able to afford calls.

As the meeting progresses, Angel happily grins and walks around the furniture. She sits on my knee and I realise how much I love her. Her smooth silky brown skin touches my cheek; she is warm and relaxed as I run my hand through the short tight corkscrew curls covering her head. The link worker recommends, "Things must get moving on the adoption. There has been too much delay. Photos must be taken, and enquiries made into availability of interested families. Social services cannot go to court until they have prospective parents."

I hope they get things moving and that the children are adopted as soon as possible.

17th February – Saturday

After lunch Max, Pat, and I make our way to Brockhill.

As we walk over to our allotted table, Jamie makes us jump. "Boo," she says as she creeps up behind. The new glowing Jamie looks fantastic, her skin is so clear and weight just right at about 8 stone. Her highlighted hair is piled up on top. She looks very intellectual wearing gold-rimmed spectacles, has a gold stud in her nose, and wears the gold earrings given to her by her sister.

As usual, the clothes she wears have been borrowed from a fellow cell mate – denim designer dungarees, and underneath a similar colour bodysuit. Jamie looks just wonderful.

She sits down, cuddling Max saying, "I'm doing mainly art now. I prefer it – two days art and one day hair and beauty."

"You are much better off here in Brockhill than the other prisons," I suggest. "Better than spending 23 hours in a cell, as you have done in the past."

Jamie agrees. "They have a certain amount of freedom here, although sections are locked at times. We normally go to our rooms just to sleep and have our own key. Although I go to my room a lot because I like it there," she says.

The girls in my cell are crackheads although one says she's off now."

I chat to Jamie about her prison escape and she says, "I warned everyone, including probation and officers, that I was going to get out."

Jamie tells me that, after my phone call to the health unit Sister at the prison, she was given anti-depressants. The prison was fully aware Jamie had a problem and this contradicts Anne Widdecombe's letter.

18th February – Sunday

So many bad memories, pain and heartache are locked inside me. I have survived by putting events in the back of my mind and trying to forget – but they keep coming to the surface.

One of the hardest things to live with is denial by authorities, and failures in the system: the law, social services, probation, prison and doctors.

20th February – Tuesday

I cannot get away from Jamie for even a few days. She phones me saying, "I've been put on report again for shouting 'You lazy bastard' while my medication was being sorted.

My drug worker came to see me today about rehab and to talk about Angel," says Jamie. My heart drops. If only they knew the true story and the real Jamie. They give little thought to the needs of the child, only to the addict.

23rd February – Friday

Jamie's dad visits her in prison for the first time, looking very apprehensive as we wait to go through. "Do we speak through glass?" he asks nervously.
"Of course not," I laugh.
While he buys drinks at the hatch, Jamie comes bouncing over. She looks really good. Her hair is up and to one side. She has borrowed a sleeveless summer dress and is wearing her little brown Victorian style lace-up boots.
As Jamie chats to her dad she asks, "Do you like my nose stud?"
"No," he says abruptly.
"I did it myself with a pin," she says, winding him up. "It didn't hurt." I can see him reeling inside from the thought.

"Do you realise who is paying for all this?" he asks as he looks around the room at the other prisoners, "Me and my taxes." He gets restless, wanting to go; looking very relieved when "time up" is called.

On the way home he goes quiet and then comments, "Jamie will never change will she?"
Jamie is much happier now her dad has made the effort to visit. It means so much to her while she is in prison, knowing she hasn't been forgotten.

6th March – Wednesday

The governor of Brockhill walks towards me. Much to my surprise she introduces herself, sits by me, and chats while waiting for Jamie to be brought through to the visitors' area.

"Fortunately Jamie is still very young," she says. "There is always a chance."

"Jamie is quite a character," I tell her. "She appears to have a split personality. I have maintained for a long time she needs psychiatric help, but no one has ever bothered because Jamie doesn't ask for it herself."

Agreeing she says, "I did wonder this morning, when Jamie went mad in my office."

I tell her how pleased I am with Brockhill. Jamie's medical problems have been sorted out. At long last she has glasses, they have taken the brace out of her mouth, and given her Valium to calm her down.

I tell the governor, "This is the first time Jamie has not written home saying, 'I'm totally bored.' She is very happy doing art and hairdressing. At long last, after all this time, someone seems to be getting it right."

Jamie comes bouncing over to join us – she looks wonderful and is by far the prettiest woman in the room. Her skin is spotless and her dimples have returned, giving her that cheeky look once more. She is wearing her nose stud, and on her cheek by the outer corner of her eye, glitters a little gold star. She is dressed in short dungarees and sleeveless body suit.

"They found me guilty today mum," she says. Then glancing at the governor and myself, she asks in a happy and giggly mood, "What have you both been saying about me?"

I turn around to the governor, smiling, and I say, "I've done my best. It's not the way I have brought her up. I think her genes have a lot to answer for." Jamie laughs and agrees.

"I won't take up any more of your valuable time," says the governor, leaving us to chat.

"She found me guilty this morning for shouting at an officer," says Jamie. "I've got to pay £1.50 fine and stay behind the door for three nights."

"Behind the door?" I question.

"It means my movements will be restricted for a couple of hours each night but I don't really mind. I respect her for what she's done," says Jamie. I was sent to the office after being found guilty and went absolutely mad.

Do you remember the stare I had when I was little? The officers say my stare is intimidating and I don't even know I'm doing it."

I remind her, "When I tackled you about handing yourself in to the police, you stared right through me and looked as though you could stab me."

"Oh, I wouldn't do that to you mum.
They've increased my valium," she says with a smile. "I went berserk while hairdressing and they gave it to me to calm me down."

I ask, "Jamie, have you thought any more about what you are going to do when you get out of prison?"
"I've had details of four rehabs. today, but I'm not sure," she replies.
"I'd like you to come and stay with us for a week or so upon your release."
"Oh, thanks mum. I'd like that," she says smiling, really pleased.

"Jamie, your dad went to see a medium last week and she told him, "Your daughter is heavily into drugs. The spirits have tried to talk to her but she wouldn't listen."
Jamie's eyes stare in disbelief. She looks shocked.
"Mum, you are never going to believe this...when I was in the hostel, before Christmas, I hated my room. It was so scary and the lights kept flickering. I struggled as I felt my head being held down on the bed and I could hear voices – those of dad's girl friend, Vernon who was murdered, and grandma. I was very frightened because it was so real."

As we hug Jamie hands me a lovely hand made mother's day card of which she is very proud, and two small hand-made cards for Joy and Pat. There is also a card for Max in which she says, "To the love of my life, Max. All my love, hugs and tugs, Mommie."

Reflecting on my visit, I can't believe my meeting the governor and how good it felt to chat to her about Jamie's problems. I only wish it could be the same with probation and drug agencies. Everyone should work together for the benefit of the drug user, the criminal, and the family.

17th March – Sunday. Mother's Day
During my visit, the devil glints in Jamie's eyes and lurks in her wry smile. There seems to be no change in her whatsoever. As we speak, Jamie's mind wonders, either she gazes around the room or changes the subject. Valium, the legal drug, rules her brain as much as illegal drugs do. She is vague and unreliable – saying what she intends to do, but will never see it through.

On our way home from the prison, we call to see my son and his family.

My daughter-in-law reads the tarot cards and I ask, "Will Jamie go for rehab?" The answer is, "She will, but won't see it through."
Then I ask, "Will Jamie return to drugs soon after her release? The answer is a very positive, "Yes".

31st March – Sunday

I am horrified to learn from Dalton that Jamie has written asking, "Please arrange marriage upon my release from prison. I'm serious."
Exasperated I say, "She's out of her head and will let you down Dalton. Do you think she's doing it to try to get Angel back?" I ask.
"I did wonder," he replies.

Devil Eyes – 1996

2nd April – Tuesday

I receive a cheerful letter from Jamie but no mention of marriage. This afternoon the foster mum phones to say Jamie has sent Ben a card in which she writes:

> *"Dearest Ben,*
> *I will always love you.*
> *Be good and look after your sister.*
> *Always in my heart,*
> *love mommie."*

I know deep down Jamie loves them so much.

5th April – Friday

Ben's third birthday and I call to give him his present. He is quieter and not such a pickle. Angel is beautiful and I am so touched as she put her arms out for a cuddle.

How I wish social services would move urgently on their case.

A letter arrives in which Jamie writes 'I was trying Dalton out regarding marriage but have heard nothing from him.'

7th April – Easter Sunday

I smuggle some brown into prison this afternoon, at Jamie's request...not heroin but two Cadbury's chocolate cream eggs! Easter wouldn't be the same for Jamie without them. I tuck them inside my bra.

Dalton is waiting in the car park for us. He smiles as he also produces two cream eggs and Max puts them in his pocket. Officers frisk us but they find nothing.

Why on earth do they bother? It could have easily been drugs. Frisking perhaps prevents guns and weapons getting in – but where there's a will there's a way as far as drugs and cream eggs are concerned.

Crackhead

Jamie laughs as Max announces loudly, "Mummy, I've brought you some Easter Eggs," and proceeds to put them on the table. Quickly we hide them until we have an assortment of crisps, drinks, and chocolate before us. Jamie drools with delight as she takes her first bite, and I quietly slip my warm squidgy eggs onto the table.

I become aware of the presence of Jamie the user, and start to feel numb. The person talking is the criminal who was on the run just before Christmas.

Jamie tells me, I had a close shave last week. Some lads threw cannabis out of the window and I passed it to Annie to smoke.
I could have died – I was tested an hour later, and to think I could have had it in my system. It was a good thing my mate had it instead of me.

I'm on 'medium' at the moment and intend to try for 'enhance' soon," says Jamie. She explains, "This is the standard set for privileges – being drug free, or for good behaviour. Like, not shouting at the warders," she laughs. "On enhance we get six visiting orders a month and are allowed to spend private cash on tobacco."

She says the drug worker has been again to see her about Angel.
My blood boils. "What do they know of the situation?"I ask. "They've only known you twelve months whereas I've known you for twenty three years."
I warn Jamie, "If there's to be a fight, I'll be standing in the dock with social services, and have all the evidence I need. The facts were presented by the judge in court recently, but neither you nor the drug agency bothered to turn up."

Immediately Jamie snaps, "I'm not discussing it." She wells up and sounds choked. "Anyway, they are not interested in what has happened in the past." During the visit, Jamie doesn't ask once about her children's welfare. I am stunned by her lack of interest.

I feel so drained. Although Jamie tries to persuade me to stay, I leave fifteen minutes early. Enough is enough.
Sometimes, I wish the stranger Jamie would disappear off the face of the earth, so we can get on with our lives in peace. I am very angry with the agencies and solicitors who interfere. They are only interested in the mother's interests – *but what about the best interests of the child?*

10th April – Wednesday

Jamie's cellmate, Annie, has few visitors and I pop over to see her at Brockhill. She is very worried and tells me, "Jamie is getting three lots of laxatives a day and losing weight. I stormed into the room and threatened the woman supplying her. I said I would report her because Jamie isn't constipated."
I tell Annie that it concerns me Jamie is losing weight rapidly and appears very thin.
She says, "Our new cell mate and myself ban Jamie from the bathroom for two hours after a meal, to ensure she doesn't force herself to be sick by putting her fingers down her throat. I am sure she's bulimic."
Worried, I ask her to tell Jamie I intend to write to the prison.

Annie looks at me seriously, and her tone changes. "Jamie thinks you won't have Ben and Angel because of their colour."
I explain to Annie, "Race has nothing to do with it. I feel so ill and am unable to look after them. Jamie has also told Dalton the same thing."
Annie agrees with me it would be impossible to have them.

In the evening Jamie phones. "Mum, don't write to the prison, whatever you do," she says in a panic. She promises me she will eat properly and I know Annie is keeping a watchful eye over her.

11th April – Thursday

Jamie sounds bored when she rings, and I ask, "What are you doing?"
"Nothing," she replies. "Classes start again next week. I've been playing basketball and I like that because I can kill everyone in the other team."

I write to Jamie this evening explaining why I can't look after all her children. Dalton rings for a chat. "Jamie says she is only going for rehab to get the children back. She has asked me to take some brown in, but I won't."

15th April – Monday

Jamie writes to me:

> "I don't care what you say to me, but I know you'll always love me. I'll always love you 'cause you have always been there for me – even at 4.00 a.m. I couldn't have gotten a better mum than you. I've never thought of you as my 'adoptive mum'. You'll always be my mum, mother and mummy."

This letter makes me realise that everything has been worthwhile.

18th April – Thursday

Dalton shows me a letter from Jamie. She writes of her concern for my health, saying her priority must be, upon release from prison, to learn to drive so she can look after me. She states, "I'd always promised I would look after mum in her old age."

Old? I'm only fifty-one!

I tell Dalton, "Jamie really believes what she says at the time of writing. Tomorrow it will be something totally different."

He talks about the working girls he knows, saying, "They all have high hopes wanting rehab but eventually most of them return to drugs."

27th April – Saturday

Jamie is really awful today. Before us sits the criminal, prostitute, and crack and heroin addict, joking about her crimes. And those mischievous 'devil eyes' glint with excitement. During the one hour visit there is no let up, and no sign of my daughter.

Jamie's new below-the-shoulder hairstyle, highlighted, and permed in tight curls, gives her the aura of a prostitute. Her language is rough and course, normally a sign she has been using. Maybe the valium is affecting her? Jamie's concentration is virtually nil. As we speak her mind wonders and she changes topics of conversation mid-stream.

Dalton sits listening quietly as I chat to Jamie about rehabilitation upon release. She has no idea where she is going and is very vague about what is expected of her. I don't think she is interested anyway.

We discuss chapter titles for my book a. I suggest, 'Never Trust a Crackhead.' She laughs, "You mean, 'Never trust Jamie' – full stop!" As we chat about her past crimes, current prison sentence, and semi-automatic guns, I remark, "Jamie you could make a fortune with your life story."

"You're joking," she replies, "I'd get life for all the things I've done."

Throughout our visit, Jamie talks in criminal jargon. I am extremely cross, and when I ask her to stop she says, "What do you expect, Mum? I'm in prison.

I'm bored," she sighs. "I keep getting into trouble here. I've been chucked out of English – too easy, even for two year olds. I'm doing drama now," she says, uninspired.

As we prepare to depart, Jamie rises from her seat which is forbidden, and skips over to a officer at the desk.

"Tell me mum how good I am in here," she jokes.

"Oh wonderful," he replies.

I smile and say, "I'm sure you understand why I can't have her living at home?"

"I don't blame you," he laughs.

As we wave goodbye to Jamie, Dalton turns to me saying, "Isn't it depressing." I nod in agreement. On previous visits Jamie was super. But today we both know she hasn't changed and we feel very low. Finally we drive off knowing it will take a miracle for Jamie to change – but miracles can, and sometimes do, happen.

29th April – Monday

Angel's first Birthday: she greets me with such a warm smile, and looks so pretty with those huge brown eyes. It is sad that prospective adoptive parents have missed Angel's babyhood; the excitement of her first tooth, first words, and those precious first steps.

1st May – Wednesday

Jamie phones, "Mum, I'm bored and want to chat. Can I have the foster mum's telephone number? I'm not going to chicken out this time."

Ten minutes later Linda rings, "Jamie has phoned to enquire about the children."

At last, after two and a half years, Jamie has made contact to find out how they are.

3rd May – Friday

Jamie, oh Jamie, why can't you leave us alone to get on with our lives and give us some peace?

She phones excited, "Mum, I've had details of a college business studies course come through. But I don't think you'll approve of where it is...Stratford."

My heart sinks. "What about rehab?" I ask.

"Oh, I'm not sure what I'm doing yet," she replies.

Don't panic, I think as I put down the phone and remind myself that most of what Jamie says doesn't happen. The thought of having Jamie living in this town, further disrupting our lives, drives me to distraction – it is too painful to contemplate – and drugs are freely available here in Stratford, just as they are anywhere.

If Jamie goes for rehabilitation, and proves her commitment to come off drugs, I will give her my whole hearted support; but coming here straight from prison will never work.

5th May – Sunday

Bluebells in Bramble Wood. I start to unwind and relax as we picnic in the warm sunshine around the pond, entertained by musicians, readings of poetry and sonnets. Afterwards, we follow a track through the woods, reaching a sunny glade and watch Elizabethan dancing. Children excitedly play hide-and-seek amongst the trees. By the end of the day I feel wonderful, my batteries recharged ready to face the world...and Jamie.

Dalton rings to say he saw Jamie yesterday. "She seems fine and talks of doing a business course."
"I suppose she wants to set herself up as a 'madame' with her own call-girl business," I suggest.
"How do you know that?" he asks, surprised.
"Because, Dalton, I have heard it all before,"

10th May – Friday

Pat and I visit Jamie. She looks wonderful with her hair piled on top, and curls cascading down.
In her pierced nose is a silver' semi-automatic' gun stud. "Do you like it?" she asks. "Dalton bought it in for me. When he went to the jewellers he asked for a semi-automatic (meaning an earring) – but they thought he meant a real gun, and promptly gave him directions where to get one in Birmingham."
Pat and I are aghast.

"Do you like my new dungarees?" asks Jamie. "We're not allowed to swop clothes but I found a way around that. I went to reception and made a fuss, saying they had omitted the dungarees from my prop (property) card. They apologised and added them on to the rest of my property."
Bubbling with excitement she says, "Mum, we've made super Viennese curtains for our dorm."
"Where did you get material from, and how do you gather them up?" I enquire.
"White prison sheets," she giggles, "and we hold them up with pink towels, courtesy of the prison as well. We nick the fabric and materials from the art room and keep them under our beds."

Pointing to her large tattoo of an eagle with Leroy blazed across it, Jamie declares, "It's awful and I am going to get it removed by laser. It only costs £50 per session for six sessions."
"Why did you have it done in the first place?" Pat asks.
"Oh, suppose I was feeling clever at the time," she replies.
"Are you still on Valium, Jamie?"
"Yes, they've started to reduce it but I'm trying to get them to 'up' it," she replies.

Towards the end of our visit a black guy walks past Jamie. Eyeing him up and down she says, "He's rather gorgeous." Will Jamie ever ever change, I wonder? Jamie appears much more normal – not as rough and coarse as she was a fortnight ago.
As I leave, much happier and less depressed, I turn to Pat saying, "She's still the same old Jamie, isn't she?"
Pat sighs, "Yes, she's never going to change."

Dalton and I chat this evening about our concern that Jamie has no interest or direction for the future. He says he can offer her a room in his flat, just as a friend, until she decides what she wants to do.
I am relieved there is somewhere for her to go when she leaves me. But I warn Dalton: "A note of caution. Within a few days Jamie will return to crack and heroin."
In my heart I know she will get involved in crime and prostitution immediately to pay for her habit.

16th May – Thursday

I attend a review meeting on Angel and Ben. It is taking social services so long to get anything done. I am exasperated. There has been no advertising and the court has yet to be booked. They haven't even looked for families yet.
Administration is so slow. It all seems such a mess – with no thought for the children themselves. Time is ticking by and as they get older they will be harder to place. Social workers are leaving and not being replaced to save money. It doesn't help the work load of those left, particularly when they themselves are on holiday or sick.

18th May – Saturday

Out of the blue Max says, "I miss my Mummy." Will Jamie ever understand what she has done to her children?

Today, I meet a young woman, Kim, who lives in Stratford. Twelve months ago she was involved in the same lifestyle as Jamie. I would never have dreamed I could meet a crack/heroin addict, ex-criminal and ex-prostitute, living in this small market town. Kim tells me she was desperate for crack only yesterday – ready to give up everything, including her partner and methadone programme, to return to her former life.

Immediately we have an understanding, are on the same wavelength, and I tell her, "I'm here with a lending ear and understand."

Jamie phones and tells me, "I have taken my first level word processing and passed. I really enjoy it." Thank goodness she has found something she enjoys doing.

24th May – Friday

"Angela – I've found a gun down the side of the settee, and I'm petrified," says Joy. She sounds scared out of her wits. "I think it's just a pistol but I'm desperately worried about the girls safety." I try to reassure her, but unfortunately have little knowledge on guns.

"Jamie, what have you been doing with yourself?" I ask on my visit.
"Drama – boring," she replies. "I'm having a break from word processing," laughs Jamie, "because I keep deleting people in my sleep."
"Have you had any heroin recently?" I ask her, knowing a friend had taken some into prison.
"I had 3 to 4 lines but it made me ill," she says (heroin is burned in lines or rows on the foil).

25th May – Saturday

Dalton sounds shocked on the phone. He tells me he was strip-searched for drugs as he entered prison but fortunately didn't have anything.
"I'm concerned," I tell him. "If Jamie is using it proves things won't be easy when she comes out.

31st May – Friday

Jamie is wonderful on my visit and talks sense for once. She is pleased with herself saying, "I've taken myself off the valium, and don't want it any more. The screws were really annoyed because I made the decision – not them." For the first time in ages Jamie seems normal and concentrates on what I say. Is it because she isn't taking the valium, I wonder?

She tells me, "I have written to Dalton to thank him for everything he's done.
Probation can organise me a three-bed roomed house when I come out."
I recall we have been here so many times before. "What about rehab?" I ask.
"I will take it, if offered," says Jamie, "but the drug agency hasn't been in touch."
"I'll contact them if you want me to?" I say. She is pleased at my suggestion.

As I prepare to leave, Jamie says, "You know mum, it's awful really, but, when I go to bed at night, this place feels just like home."

Crackhead

Rehabilitation – 1996

7th June – Friday

I chat to a worker at Jamie's drug agency, about my worries for her future. I tell him I am concerned we can't work together, for the good of the addict. Parents and family members are always viewed with suspicion, even if the addict wishes us to be involved. I tell him my local drug family worker  says that latest statistics indicate better and quicker results are achieved if family members are involved in rehabilitation. Pat and I saw this working in practice at the combined addict and family meeting at the hospital in San Diego, California, last year, and it seems to work fine.

He tells me a letter has been sent to Jamie stating that no finance is available for rehabilitation, and his words hit me. For the first time in seven years, I feel I am ready to cry. I explain, "I have predicted Jamie will be dead by the age of twenty five, another two years. If she dies, I shall always wonder if she could have made it, given that one chance."
Feeling so down and dejected I say, "Where do we go from here? Jamie will come out of prison clean and can stay with me for two weeks-- and then what; back to her friends, working, and returning to crack.? The future looks very bleak."

In the past, the Home Office used to finance drug rehabilitation and it was relatively easy to get funding. However, today, agencies have to apply to a pool of money and, with so many others in need, drugs are not considered a priority.
"Whoever is in power, I don't believe it will make the slightest bit of difference," I tell him.
"I'll have another chat with Jamie's counsellor," he says, which leaves me a little bit more hopeful.

12th June – Wednesday

Jamie sounds elated. "Mum, someone has been to see me today and there's a chance of rehab. They say they will fight for funding."
I can't believe it. Maybe my visit helped to push the point home.

"I've got bad asthma," says Jamie, "and couldn't catch my breath the other night. I now have inhalers."

14th June – Friday

As I enter Brockhill, it seems unusually quiet. Most of the men have been moved out and it becomes an all women's prison within a fortnight.

Jamie is pleased to see Max and myself. She is very excited her drug worker has been to see her. I look her in the eyes. "It's up to you now Jamie. If you get funding this could be your one and only chance."
I notice marks on her chest. "What are those white patches?" I ask.
"Oh, haven't you seen those before? They are cigarette burns," she says.
"When did you get them?" I ask.
"Can't remember," she replies.

Jamie keeps asking me, "Mum, are you excited I'm coming home?"
"Yes, of course," I tell her, but try not to give away my feelings of apprehension.
As we chat, I watch in disbelief as I see one of the inmates pick up a crisp packet from the table, take something out and put it down her trousers. I have heard this is one way drugs are passed over by visitors. They can also be passed across mouths during kissing.

We talk of my book and the murders. "I didn't do any of them," she laughs, "but the police have queried why I am always involved when someone is shot"

18th June – Tuesday

Max and I are on holiday in the Costa del Sol: 'It's a beautiful life'...the song rings out throughout the grounds of our hotel on this hot balmy evening.
Yes, it's a beautiful life, but also very sad. I watch Max playing with other young children in the pool, just as I did with Jamie and her brother many years ago. Today, parents observe their little ones with the same hopes and ambitions we had for our children.
My nightmare could never happen to them – so they think – but they must be told, "We are all vulnerable – drugs are everywhere and it can happen to anyone, including *you*!"

Tonight I lie in bed relaxed, knowing I am thousands of miles away from Jamie, and all my problems.

23rd June – Sunday

Down to earth with a bump – as my plane lands, I am back in the world of reality. As soon as I walk through the front door, the phone rings.
"Mum, I'm out on the 10th July. I've had two weeks knocked off."
I panic – Jamie will be home in just two weeks!
There is a letter from her and I have to smile:

> *Hope you guys had a good holiday. It would have been a lot cheaper if you'd just booked into 'Brockhill holiday camp.' Sunbathing every day, and the food's not bad – menu choice of six things every meal.*
>
> *And it's not far from home. Forget the travelling. There's a bus leaving your local police station every day. All this is inclusive in the price. Only one condition – you have to be a criminal. Keep this in mind for next year's vacation.*

27th June – Friday

During my visit, Jamie talks of rehab. and what she will do if there is no finance available.
"Perhaps I could help towards the cost?" I say. "You must be given the one chance, if that is what you want."
"Mum, I can't accept any money from you. If I didn't see it through, I would feel I was letting you down."
I appreciate Jamie being honest and not taking me for granted. Most addicts would grab the opportunity.

She laughs, "The hostel I lived in last won't accept me this time, even though they were assured that I'm really good now. They refused saying, "We were told that last time."
Jamie is very excited about coming home although I can't say I feel likewise. I foresee lots of problems ahead.

3rd July – Wednesday

I discuss Jamie's future with Dalton and warn, "If Jamie has even the smallest bit of crack or brown we will lose her. Whatever happens, she must NOT be allowed to return to her friends. He agrees with me. "Dalton, you must come over to Stratford if you want to see her."

It is seven months since we last heard from Mikey, Max's father. Max keeps saying, "I miss my daddy." Mikey's mother says he has lost his job and has nowhere to live, which is bad news. I always worry Mikey will return to drugs.

Jamie phones, and is dying to tell me, "I'm wearing a dress I made in here. It's really good."
"Did you use a sewing machine?" I ask.
"No, I did it by hand," she replies. It reminds me of Jamie's mother, when she told me she made her clothes by hand when she was young.

10th July – Wednesday
Mikey at last contacts his son. Max grins with joy when he hears his daddy's voice on the phone. Although he assures me he's not using, I have been suspicious because of his unreliability.

I receive a letter from the HM Prison Service in London regarding my complaint that Jamie passed prison security checks. They state:

> "The prison carried out a thorough assessment before Jamie was allowed out to attend church. The governor concluded that she was suitable for temporary release."

I am angry. How on earth can anyone, especially a prison governor, consider Jamie should be allowed out to church on her own with a record such as hers?

Jamie is due to be released from Brockhill and collected by Dalton in half an hour.
8.00 a.m: I receive a call from Sindy, saying, "Jamie has written. She wants to collect her clothes from my house. Angela, whatever you do don't let Jamie come here. She will go straight back on drugs."
8.45 a.m: "Hi Mum, I'm out," says Jamie, on a high, and sounding dazed. "The warders played a joke and wouldn't let me out. It was awful."

Lunchtime she arrives home with Dalton, after having called at probation, and is elated, chatting non-stop.
Max and Jamie's eyes meet as he comes out of school and he is so thrilled to see her. He attracts his teacher's attention. "This is my mummy," he tells her proudly.

Jamie immediately phones her past boyfriends – so soon after being released. In the evening, she pops her head around the door announcing, "Mum, we are just going out for a drink." In my naivety, I believe she is popping just down the road. 11.30 p.m: Jamie phones, "Mum, I'll be home about one-thirty."

"Where are you?" I ask.

"At Dalton's flat," she replies.

Oh no, surely not. Jamie will be back on drugs tonight for sure.

11th July – Thursday

When I get up, I find a note from Jamie – "Mum, had a good night, had a drink and sorted a few things out."

Mid-morning she appears ashen at the kitchen door. "Mum, I feel so sorry for myself. I drank too much Vodka last night. How I hate myself," and she staggers to the bathroom to be sick.

"You'll never guess who I saw at the chip shop last night?" she says. "Dexter" (Angel's father). She screws up her nose. "He was so dirty, scruffy and thin. He looked dreadful, and I told him so."

"Jamie, why on earth did you go over there?"

"Mum," she replies, "We couldn't go into Stratford. I feel so out-of-place there, as if everyone's staring at me.

"Will Jamie ever feel comfortable in the presence of normal people?

Apart from being ill, she is very upset and near to tears. "We called at Dalton's flat and I talked to the girl who rents a room from him. Dalton says he's supporting her while she tries to come off drugs. But I think he might be having it off with her," she says. "I'm so hurt he could do this to me after having visited me every week in prison."

We pop along to a cheap clothes store. I offer to buy her some new clothes, giving her a chance to discard her scruffy prison clothes. The check out woman turns round saying, "Has your daughter just returned from college?"

"Oh yes," I reply, and smile to myself thinking, little does she know.

She turns to Jamie. "Just back from college, I understand? What have you been studying?"

Jamie quickly answers, "I've just finished a business course, including computers," and walks from the store giggling.

12th July – Friday

I remark, "Jamie, your make-up is very orange." Is this a sign she has had crack? Surely, not so soon after her release.
All day Jamie has been tired and says she isn't sleeping at night.
Dalton turns to me, "Angela, is she always like this?"
"Yes, especially when she's using. Also, I predicted she would sleep for days, after being on a high from the excitement of her release. Jamie has now hit a low."
This evening, she returns with Dalton back to his place.

13th July – Saturday

Max is playing his mummy and me against one another. When Jamie first came home she constantly handed £1 coins to him. He is now making demands all the time. Jamie informs me she is finishing with Dalton, which I quite expected.

14th July – Sunday

Jamie goes with Dalton and Max to visit her old cell mate at Brockhill. When they return home Jamie laughs, "Max did the dance he learned in Spain, with a wiggle and hands on hips. He performed for the governor, the inmates, and visitors, and they loved it." Max proudly shows me the £2.00 he earned from a spectator.

15th July – Monday.

"Mum, they've got funding for rehab," says Jamie excitedly. She has received a call from her drug counsellor. "I have an interview in London tomorrow."
As we hug each other, she says, "Mum, I'm really going to do it."

Jamie spends the whole day at the DSS offices. Later in the afternoon, Max enquires, "Where's my mummy?"
Time ticks by...no sign of Jamie. "I want my mummy," he cries. "Where's my mummy."
I phone Dalton at 7.30 p.m. "Yes, she's here," he says, "but she has popped to the shop."
"I'm livid. What on earth is she messing about at?" I ask.
I ring half an hour later. "Dalton, has she had anything?" I ask.
"Yes, on Wednesday," says Dalton.
I can't believe it, even though I suspected – the sleeping all day, headaches, aggression, and orange make-up. He took Jamie to buy heroin within

338

hours of her release, after agreeing with me she should not leave Stratford under any circumstances. What the hell is this man about? How can I trust any man Jamie gets involved with? How can I ever trust Jamie?

She phones, apologising to both myself and Max. "I'll be home soon," she assures us.

One hour later: there is still no sign of Jamie. It is getting late. Max is upset wanting to know why mummy hasn't come home.

I'm getting furious and ring Dalton again. Jamie is still there. After an argument she says, "Okay. I'm not coming back – I'll go and do something else," and hangs up on me. A few minutes later she rings back. "I'm sorry for what I said and I'll be home soon."

Half an hour later, Jamie and Dalton arrive. Dalton stands silent as Jamie cries hysterically, "Tell her Dalton. Tell her what's been going on. He sits down staring ahead, not saying a word. "I think you'd better leave," she tells him.

As he leaves, I ask him to phone. After all, he has been there for Jamie nearly every week for eight months – giving her support, friendship, money and presents.

Jamie appears depressed but eventually quietens down. At this point in the evening, I hand her my diary to read. Relaxing across the sofa, she slowly brightens up.

At one point in my book, Jamie talks of getting an awful bruise by walking into a lamp post – I thought she had been beaten. Jamie laughs. "You know, mum, I really did hit a lamp post."

As she turns over the pages she says giggling, "It's dead good, mum," and occasionally sighs, "Oh, isn't it awful. I can't believe I was so stupid. I wish the book was about someone else and not me – the only trouble is, I know what's coming next. I must have been hell to live with." She pauses for a moment, and then says, "It's good you kept details."

I remind her the drug counsellor is taking her to London for the rehab interview tomorrow. But Jamie has also said she will be visiting a friend in prison. "Sod rehab," she says angrily. "I'm going to visit him." Will she ever get to London I wonder?

17th July – Wednesday

Jamie returns home from London very excited. "I've been offered a place. And you'll never guess – the woman who interviewed me went out with Dexter," (Angel's father). Jamie is very happy and excited, saying she is really looking forward to starting in a few days time.

We chat about her time in prison and she tells me, "When I got three nights behind doors for punishment, Annie and I started making Venetian blinds for our cell. This led to an interior decoration business. The blinds were made with prison sheets or material out of the art room, where we also got dye, paint and tape. We dyed the fabric in buckets in the bathroom and then did hand sewing in the bedroom. We were paid in biscuits, chocolates, and tobacco. Eventually we made curtains, Viennese blinds, pillows and cushions."

Jamie jokes, "They used to chuck me out of classes because I was so disruptive. In fact one guy even said he would pay me to stay out – but I never saw any money. The teachers were scared of me and thought I was schizophrenic. One officer said, 'Jamie you spend half a day in bed, and the other half you cause trouble. Why can't you spend all day in bed'?"

Dalton rings to put me in the picture, and confirms he is going with another woman.

I tell him, "Jamie is going for rehab next week," and he seems surprised she is actually doing something about it.

"Why did you take Jamie back to the city, on the evening she was released?" I ask.

"She asked me to," he replies.

I tackle Jamie. "I didn't ask him," she says. "He just took me, and even gave me the money for the brown."

18th July – Thursday

1.00 p.m. Jamie pops into town, a 5 minute walk, to do a little shopping. It is scorching hot. She can't stand the heat, so I expect her home within an hour; I also know she wants to collect Max from school.

4.00 p.m: no sign of Jamie. Max is asking, "Where's my mummy?"

6.00 p.m. I am getting concerned. Max starts to cry, "Why doesn't my mummy phone. Do you think she has taken drugs?"

"I don't think so," I try to reassure him. Whatever she is doing, she is not giving him a thought.

Perhaps she has gone to Birmingham, Coventry or the Phoenix Music Festival in Stratford?

7.30 p.m: over six hours later – in walks Jamie as large as life, bubbly and chatty. "Sorry I've been so long mum. I was in town and decided to pop over to Blakenhurst Prison to visit my pen-pal. The traffic was awful because of the festival, so I had to come back on the train via Birmingham." I am exasperated. "Jamie, do you realise the worry you have caused? Max has been so upset. You could have phoned." Max is standing in the background telling his mummy off.

"Whoops, sorry," she says. She is just like a young child.

19th July – Friday

A letter arrives from Ann Widdecombe of the Home Office, sent via my MP. She states that she has written to point out an error in her previous letter, regarding Jamie's escape from Drake Hall.

> "The error occurred because computer records had been misinterpreted."

Jamie sleeps in until 11.30 a.m., and is pale and snappy.

At 4.00 p.m., she says, "I'm just popping to get some cigarettes while you take Max to his friend's party."

We return 5.30 p.m. No sign of Jamie. By now the shops are shut and it has taken Jamie two hours to purchase cigarettes.

Max asks, "Is mummy coming home?"

I try to console him. Jamie promised she would phone if going anywhere. How can she be so cruel to him? Max can see for himself the effects of his mother's addiction, especially her unreliability.

I go to bed, leaving the back door open and not knowing where she has been all evening. She only went to get cigarettes...six hours ago.

Tomorrow morning Jamie's sister is due to stay for a couple of days. I toss and turn worrying whether Jamie will be here tomorrow? Kate has said, "Jamie's life won't be worth living if she disappears."

At 3.00 a.m. I get up: to my relief Jamie is fast asleep in bed. She has often told her friends, "I'm just popping out for a short while," and doesn't return for hours or days. Nothing has changed.

It will be a miracle if she sticks at rehabilitation.

20th July – Saturday

Max is cross with Jamie for not coming home and hits her. He later tells me, "Mummy said she went to the Phoenix Festival."

Mikey, Max's father, phones and I am pleased contact has been revived. He now has a good job and flat.

Kate arrives, and after lunch the sisters go shopping, giving them a chance to get better acquainted. Although very similar in looks and dress, there is one noticeable difference – Kate speaks well, as Jamie used to. But Jamie sounds rough and coarse, and announces, "At least I'm speaking better than when I was in jail."

As I turn to say good night to the girls I smile to myself. They are settled, in their pyjamas, watching a video, tucking into popcorn, crisps and cola. Twenty years of their sisterhood has been lost. They look relaxed and happy together and yet lead such very different lives – one married, with two children, and a good job in London; the other a prostitute, drug addict, and criminal, with three children in care.

Jamie, as a little girl, often used to say, "Mummy, I wish I had a sister." Now one of her wildest dreams has come true.

21st July – Sunday

After a very happy weekend, Kate returns home to her family in London. News on the radio announces another guy has been shot.

I call to see Kim, the ex-addict and former prostitute, living nearby. She and her partner, Eddie, invite Jamie into their home. I worry Jamie might be a bad influence on Kim but, on the other hand, Kim has admitted she used crack and heroin recently. I am very worried about Kim because she is heavily pregnant.
Jamie and Kim are like peas in a pod, both being addicts, criminals, and prostitutes.
Eddie, of course, understands how horrendous it is to have a family member who is an addict. So very few people really know what it is like.

Shortly after we return home, Kim phones, desperate. "Ange, I've run out of methadone, and can't get my script till Tuesday." Jamie comes to her rescue and gives her some valium.

22nd July – Monday

Kim is in cold turkey and sounds awful on the phone. She calls round, looking dreadful, hunched up with terrible stomach pains. Her script has gone missing at the chemist. The drug agency says that they cannot help, even though she is suffering and frightened. Her doctor has warned, "Never go without medication – you could go into early labour."

Jamie offers, "Kim, I can get you methadone," and after a quick phone call we drive over to Jamie's dealer. Kim has gone with Eddie's blessing because he knows there is no alternative.

In the car park of the flats, I sit and observe Jamie and Kim waiting for delivery of the methadone. During the next 20 minutes a number of people appear; two lads sit on a wall; a girl chats to Jamie; a respectable-looking young woman gets out of a car and joins the others by the flats' entrance; in another car the occupants look out the windows in anticipation.

Eventually the dreadlocked guy arrives and hands out his deals, leaving Jamie until last. Everyone scurries away, or jumps into their cars and drive off, while Jamie and Kim chat to him.

Again, as an outsider looking in, I find it hard to believe what I am seeing. How on earth can this happen so blatantly in the open? Why don't the security cameras of the flats pick up the dealing? It is just as if everyone has been casually waiting for an ice cream van, purchase their ices, and then disappear to get on with their lives.

Kim runs back to my car. Desperate, she says, "Quick, Ange – I need the nearest loo. I must have my gear straight away." I drive them to the shopping centre.

"Did you get heroin instead?" I ask Kim.

"Yes, he didn't have any methadone."

"We've just learned the name of the guy shot a few days ago," says Jamie. "Mum, I can't believe it, he was one of my main suppliers."

I drop them off and we arrange to meet at a nearby shop in fifteen minutes. When the girls turn up, Kim looks bright eyed and happy. She openly announces, "I had four lines and feel so much better."

"Jamie, have you used as well?" I ask.

"No, of course not. In fact the smell made me feel sick," she says convincingly. But I don't trust her.

Next stop, the DSS offices. Kim and I wait inside, while Jamie's spends ages being passed from one department to another. I glance at Kim and start to panic; she is nodding off to sleep. I nudge to wake her, fearing she may fall out of her chair. Nearby on the floor is a guy zonked out to the world and I have visions of Kim doing likewise.

Back at home, during the evening, the girls swop clothes. Jamie gives Kim some maternity wear and Kim hands over to Jamie some of her smart clothes saying, "I won't need them for the time being and you'll find them more useful at rehab."
I observe and listen and they are identical in every way. Conversation leads to criminals they both know: prison, working, and using rocks and brown. Kim announces laughing, "We've adopted each other as sisters." But knowing how reliable addicts normally are, I doubt their friendship will last long.

23rd July – Tuesday

This evening Kim and Jamie announce they are going to walk into town for a drink. Jamie asks, "Mum, do I look okay?"
She looks dreadful, and I tell her, "With those clothes and long bleached hair, you look as if you are going to work."
Angrily she turns on me, "Are you saying I look like a hooker?"
"Yes," I say bluntly.

While they are out, I receive a call from Eddie. "Ange, can you check and see if the car's outside?"
My heart drops as I look out the window – the car has gone.
A couple of hours later the girls return home happy and giggly.
"We had a wonderful drink," they tell me.
"Where did you go with the car?" I ask.
Jamie pipes up, "Oh, we parked by the pub." They sound very convincing, even though the pub is only 5 minutes walk away.
Can I believe Jamie? I have my doubts and think they used the car to get drugs.

24th July – Wednesday

My good journalist friend, John, calls to meet Jamie before she goes to rehab tomorrow. Jamie tells him, "I want to come off drugs but will probably continue to work. I get £32 a week from social security, and can earn that in less than half an hour with a punter."
During her stay with me, Jamie has constantly talked about getting her children back – but never once has she mentioned seeing them or phoned to find out how they are.

This evening as Jamie prepares to go to rehab, she writes to me about her thoughts on my diaries which tell of her tragic life.

Dear Mom,

After reading your book 'Crackhead', it made me think about things and all the problems that I have caused.

I first started to take drugs to see what the big attraction was. I had seen my friends doing drugs and they all said the same thing 'how good they felt after having them.' So, clever me did what they did! And before I knew it, I was just another Junkie.

The past 7 years all seem like a blur now. It is like a bad dream and I feel I've wasted those years that could have been spent making a good life for me and my kids.

I don't think the system has been too lenient with me; but when I first got into trouble I wish I had been sent to a re-hab. Then maybe I could have sorted myself out. I realise it's also my own fault I've got myself into trouble.

Mum, you've been so good to me all the way through; picked up the pieces when I've messed up. You always let me be up front and honest with you.

I've always known that I have caused pain and hurt through my addiction. This may seem selfish – but I just took more and more drugs to blank out the thoughts and the guilt I've felt.

It has been hard staying away for long periods of time just so you wouldn't have to see the mess I was in.

I am going to London and rehab. tomorrow and I know I'll have to face a lot of things that I've kept inside. I will make the most of it that I can. I am determined to succeed and get my life in order and get my kids back, so I can be a good mum to them. And hopefully you'll be proud of me again.

I have got nothing to show for the past seven years apart from three lovely children.

I could never put a value on the money that I've spent on drugs. But put it like this – if I had saved it all, I would have a house, a car and everything.

If only I could go back 7 years and wipe out all the trouble I have put you through, but I know that'll never happen. My only wish now is to make a good future for myself so none of us have to relive this nightmare again.

I guess seeing all of this through your eyes has got to be scary and it's all the same through mine too! I'm sorry for everything I've put you through, but please believe me, if I could re-live this in a different way – I would make you proud.

After reading Crackhead I feel so ashamed of myself that it's made me all the more positive for the future. Knowing that you'll stick by my side after re-hab. is my strength.

I would just like to say that I do love you Mom, even though I haven't shown it a lot over the years. I just need you to see that the love is genuine from today onwards!

Love Jamie

25th July – Thursday

The big day has arrived at last – Jamie's one chance in life to prove herself, although I have my doubts she will stay at rehab more than a few days. She says she is looking forward to it but seems very nervous. The journey to London is tense. I turn to look at Jamie and see the hard, evil look on her face, that of the addict/criminal.

The rehabilitation centre is a large detached house set in a suburban area of London. Just inside the hallway, as we arrive, a guy turns to Jamie saying sharply, "Say your goodbyes and then we'll sort your things out," and disappears. We stand there astounded and Jamie is very upset. She is not feeling well and has almost lost her voice. We have travelled for three hours in heavy traffic and are desperate for loos and a cup of tea, and have been made to feel very unwelcome.

Jamie turns to Max. She wipes the tears from her eyes and gives him a big hug and kiss. As we turn to leave, I bump into Jamie's key worker. "Are you off?" she asks."Would you like a cup of tea before you go?" Someone is human in this place after all. We are ushered into a sparse room, with no pictures and just a few chairs. Just what Jamie needs to make her feel at home, I think to myself.

I ask the guy serving the tea, "Are there any house rules? Can Jamie go out or have visitors?" He turns to Jamie, saying, "You can go out, but with an escort for the first month. An application has to be put in to our weekly meeting." Jamie's face drops. The guy leaves the room and she pulls a face. "They'll be lucky if I stay here a week!" she exclaims. As we say our farewells and hug I ask, "Give it a try for a few days Jamie," but I know she has already made up her mind. Back at home I sigh, relieved that Jamie is a couple of hours away from us. We can now start to unwind. The past two weeks have been horrendous.

28th July – Sunday

Jamie rings. She doesn't sound well, and her voice is very hoarse. She rings again in the evening, very fed up. Things must be bad.
I tell her, "Jamie, try to stick it out just a few more days.
To which she replies, "One day, more likely."

31st July – Wednesday

Jamie sounds really low, "I'll be back home before long," she says. Horrified, I exclaim, "You mean you'll be back in this area – NOT BACK HOME!" Jamie laughs. She knows I mean it this time.

Crackhead

Miss Suburbia Cracks It? – 1996

3rd August – Saturday

"It's so pathetic here and I'm leaving tomorrow," says Jamie. "I want to be with people who live in the real world. Mum, I don't suppose you can come and get me?" she asks.
"No I can't. You'll have to get yourself back," I tell her.

4th August – Sunday

I wait anxiously for a call from Jamie.
Kim rings, very worried. "Ange, she's gone. I rang the rehab and spoke to her room mate. She said Jamie spent her time putting make-up on and crying. She woke up crying this morning, left two cases in the office, and walked out."
"I'm not too worried because I know she will phone sooner or later," I tell Kim.

A couple of hours later, Kim phones. "We want to help if we can and Jamie can stay with us."
Horrified at the suggestion I plead, "Don't have her to stay, please. She will let you down. Jamie always does. And what about Max and myself?" I ask. "There is no way I can have her living on my doorstep. I can't cope emotionally – my mind will just blow!"

Kim confers with Eddie and returns to the phone. "Whatever you say. We want to help you. Are you okay? Ange, you are our friend, you've helped and been good to us and we shall abide by your wishes."

It is such a relief to have someone to talk to, and unbelievable I have met someone who really understands the effects of crack, heroin and prostitution – so close to home. In this prosperous tourist town most people won't acknowledge there is a problem. I am more convinced there's a God up there, and fate has taken a hand.

Evening: Jamie rings, sounding as happy as a sand boy. "Mum, I'm okay. I hitched a lift to Newark," she says, "and I've got a job working for three days selling at the antique fair."

"What about your two cases at the rehab?" I ask.

"Did you arrange to collect them?"

"No," she says "They didn't know I was leaving. Perhaps I can get them soon." But chances are she won't.

I shall sleep well tonight because Jamie sounds okay and very happy. Although she says she is in Newark she may be lying. Perhaps she is elsewhere in the country working the streets. Everything Jamie says has to be taken at face value.

5th August – Monday

Ben is very excited. Linda says, "All afternoon he's been saying, 'Grandma's coming'." He looks and acts so grown up. Angel is happy, bonny, and walking. I feel so much pain in my heart. What of their future? Will they ever be able to settle with adoptive parents?

Linda assures me she will do everything possible to make the adoption run smoothly. I have complete faith in her years of adoption experience.

It is over a year since Jamie showed no commitment to Angel. Social Services are dragging their feet. At a meeting twelve months ago, those attending were horrified at the delay in adoption in view of the children's age. They said that the older the children become, the harder it will be to place them.

We are now nine months on and prospective parents have not been advertised for. Social services are due to apply for an adoption freeing order with the court in the Autumn; so we are looking to 1997 at the earliest for adoption. The foster mum says she sees it going on for a long time yet and will be booking Ben in to school.

It is evening and the phone rings. "Hi Mum. I'm back at Dalton's flat. Have you heard?" she asks. "I'm coming to stay in Stratford. Kim and Eddie have asked me to stay with them," she says excitedly.

"How long for?" I ask, feeling numb and my heart racing.

"Permanently," she replies. "I'm hoping to get a job in Stratford."

How could they do this to me, after their reassurances on Sunday that they wouldn't have Jamie to stay? How can I trust anyone ever again? This is the final straw.

Maybe I am not being fair to them, or Jamie. Perhaps, one day, I shall be grateful they gave her the chance. But deep down I know Jamie has had all the chances and blown every one. In my heart I don't believe she will ever settle into normal suburban life.

It is a lonely existence, trying to cope with crisis upon crisis. This past year has been particularly hard but Joy, Solace, and the drug family worker have been wonderful, ringing to ask, "How are you Angela?"

I have learned, through experience, that a person in crisis needs to know someone cares. Just a short call saying, "How are you?" is the greatest uplift one can receive. Many professionals and support agencies should take heed. They must realise it is very difficult mentally to pick up the phone for support when in crisis. It needs to be the reverse.

6th August – Tuesday

Kim and Eddie have gone against their word. I'm hopping mad. With adrenalin rushing, I storm round to see Kim. She is surprised and shocked at my attitude. I'm almost at the point of tears and tell her, "I can't cope with Jamie living a couple of roads away and calling around when she feels like it. And what about the effect on Max? In the end Jamie will only let him down."

Angry, I ask, "Kim, why on earth did you do it?"
"Eddie gave me the chance, and I must do the same for Jamie."
Exasperated, furious, and in tears, I storm out of the house saying, "I've had enough."
Jamie rings, hysterical, from Dalton's flat. "You don't want me anymore," she says.
"I can't understand why you don't want me to have this chance to sort out my life."
I try to reassure Jamie I still love her, but she slams down the phone. I am worried because she sounds suicidal.

I am so unhappy. Why can't Jamie leave us all alone? Max and I will stay with my son and his family for a few days. He lives nearby and the break should do us both good.

9th August – Friday

Tension mounts. Bill tells me, "Jamie phoned. She says she is sorting herself out and getting a job."

Eddie contacts me. "Kim just wanted to give Jamie a chance. The girls are learning to cook and Jamie is helping with the housework," he says with enthusiasm. "And she hasn't touched any drugs."
I have heard all this before, I think to myself. When Jamie came home December 1994, she took methadone and was wonderful for two weeks. But she soon got bored, returning back to her friends and crack within a month.
I begin to doubt myself. Perhaps I should be full of hope that Jamie will change? But in reality, I know she won't.

10th August – Saturday

Jamie appears smiling at my front door to see Max. I feel so sick and tense. She pops out for a short while, and I receive a call from Eddie. He apologises for letting Jamie stay, but says Kim insisted.
Shaking and upset I tell him, "Eddie, I'm very hurt. Professionals are horrified you have put me into this situation."
"But I wonder what they will say in a year's time?" he asks. "The girls are both really trying hard and seem to be very good for each other."
"At this rate I shall crack up altogether," I tell him, near to tears.
After a brief pause he says, "Ange, I hope we can still remain friends?"
"Of course," I reply.

After lunch, Jamie and I spend the afternoon in town. I can't relax. Before me is a stranger, not my Jamie. Max is unusually naughty, playing myself against his Mummy. How much longer can I stand this...but then everything could be very different in a couple of weeks.

14th August – Wednesday

I have decided to be firm over Jamie's contact with Max. He must have stability and is already showing signs of upset with her around. I tell Jamie she can have phone contact mid-week and see him for a few hours at weekends, thus giving him a routine – essential if she should do a disappearing act...which I predict.
On the phone Jamie sounds fine and has been to the DSS to sort out her money. I wonder if she is taking the opportunity, when she goes, to see her friends and get drugs?

16th August – Friday

Jamie is continually saying she is applying for a job at a local company. "Have you applied for that job yet?" I enquire.

"No, but I am going to," she replies. "I must get a job. It's boring sitting around here all day."

Alarm bells ring...whenever Jamie says, "I'm going to," she never does. And that word boring means trouble is brewing.

17th August – Saturday

I have invited Jamie for lunch and she turns up with Kim. The girls are looking good and very bubbly. But I feel threatened and tense with them both here and can't explain why.

"Mum, can I have my sewing machine?" asks Jamie – the machine she had for her eighteenth birthday, and which I rescued from Sheffield. I never thought I should see the day Jamie would use her treasured sewing machine once more."We're off to buy some material in town at the charity shops," she says.

While they are out, Eddie phones. As he talks I sense something is wrong...he then tells me he has problems with Jamie and Kim. "They've bought gear (heroin)," he tells me. "They are both bone idle and don't do anything for themselves. They are so much alike it's incredible and all they talk about is drugs and prostitution," he says, exasperated.

I told Jamie, 'No wonder your mother won't have you.' Also, I told her she must forget about her children in care, and I would certainly make sure she didn't have them back."

At long last I have support, with the interests of the children at heart. Someone has seen what Jamie is really like.

Numb, but not surprised, my prediction was right...Jamie is back on heroin and, as I feared, Kim is as well. With Kim so pregnant, I worry for the safety of her baby.

21st August – Wednesday

9.00 p.m. Jamie and Kim burst through my front door. There is a strange, inexplicable tense atmosphere. Kim waits in the sitting room while Jamie storms up to the bathroom, gets Max out of the bath, and gives him a cuddle.

I insist Max goes straight to bed because it is late. As he settles down for a story he cuddles into his mummy. Jamie announces, "Max, I'm going to give you £5 a week pocket money." I can't believe it. I am angry, knowing he will never see the money.

I suggest to Jamie, "Perhaps you could give him £1 and put the rest in the bank?"

"No," she says aggressively.

Why on earth did she have to come and disturb him just before he goes to sleep?

I join the girls downstairs as they giggle and joke. I feel so tense but can't explain why. "Look mum," says Jamie, waving a doctor's note before my eyes. "It says I'm an addict incapable of work, so I shall get over £70 a week income support, instead of £32."

What a waste of taxpayer's money. What better way to encourage drug addicts than to give them double the weekly allowance? It is about time the state gets its act together.

The girls are excited and chat non-stop. "Eddie took us to a golf range this afternoon." They laugh. "People there would have died in they knew the truth about us – two young respectable women playing golf in shorts and trainers – in reality drug addicts and prostitutes."

I am unable to sleep, tossing, turning, and heart pounding. This is ridiculous, I think to myself. Jamie can't do this to us. It must be stopped immediately.

22nd August – Thursday

During the afternoon I pop to see Kim and Jamie. "I'm exhausted from lack of sleep," I say annoyed. "Max didn't settle until long after you left last night. You can't come to the house again unless invited."

The atmosphere is tense. Jamie, the stranger, is sitting across the room. It suddenly dawns on me...of course – I have seen it so many times before – the awful inexplicable tension at my place last night. Jamie, and probably Kim, must have used yesterday before calling.

Taking a deep breath, I tackle Jamie about Max's pocket money. "He doesn't need you to buy love with big presents and money. He now thinks he can have whatever, whenever he wants. You are undermining my authority." Jamie, getting steamed up and agitated, shouts and storms out the room.

I depart in tears, feeling at my lowest ever. This cannot carry on any longer and I write to Jamie telling her so.

27th August – Tuesday

Eddie calls at my house. He tells me, "Jamie says she has decided to get on with her life without her children."
Maybe, at long last, she is making the conscious decision to let go.
He says they appreciate my difficulties, and have seen a change in Max's behaviour since Jamie came to stay with them.
Exasperated, Eddie turns to me, saying "I suppose I should have known better than to let Jamie come to stay."
What can I say?

28th August – Wednesday

Probation phone me to ask if I know where Jamie is? She hasn't attended while on licence from prison and an application has been made for a warrant for her arrest.
"Jamie is currently living in Stratford with a friend," I inform them. "I don't think it's going to last long because she is bored, and back on drugs."

Eddie rings, "Angela, when I returned home from your place last night I couldn't believe my eyes. In that hour or so, Jamie had run a dress up on the sewing machine. She has such talent – such wasted talent. In fact, it made me very angry," he says.

10.00 p.m: Eddie phones. "Jamie has returned home late...and she's had gear."

30th August – Friday

1.00 p.m: "Angela. Is Jamie there?" enquires Kim's young daughter in tears.
"No, I'm sorry, she isn't. Is everything okay?"
"Mummy's ill in bed," she says, and hands the phone to Kim.
"Hi Ange, have you heard from Jamie? She left here three hours ago to pop to to the supermarket, and hasn't come back. She took £20 off the kitchen work top to get bread, milk and potatoes." Kim sounds very distressed and in tears.
"Perhaps Jamie has gone to Leamington to get her brown," I suggest.
Kim agrees, "You're probably right."

During the evening I receive a call from Eddie telling me that Jamie hasn't returned.
"It's all too familiar," I tell him. "It follows the same pattern as when she stayed with me – popping out for a few minutes, then gone for hours."

"Ange, I shall keep Jamie's things in lieu of the £90 she owes me.
"It appears both Jamie and Kim have had hundreds of pounds worth of gear over the past week or so."

He hands the phone to Kim..."Jamie is working the streets, and that is what she wants," she says. "She's also been sleeping with Dexter and he is absolutely disgusting. He's so skinny and dirty.
Only yesterday Jamie said to me, 'How on earth can you stand it here – the washing, the cooking and ironing? It's so boring'."

31st August – Saturday

Jamie has disappeared, more than likely returning to her old haunts. There have been no goodbyes, absolutely nothing.
Max wanders around looking so sad. His mummy promised she would go with him for a picnic, but we hear nothing. As the children play happily in the wood, Max becomes clingy and subdued, taking a while to mix with the others. I sit on a log pondering and watching. It seems so unfair. What has Max done to deserve this?

1st September – Sunday

I attend a Christian spiritualist meeting and we have been asked to bring a flower in an unmarked envelope. Holding up my yellow gladioli the medium announces, "I can see lots and lots of notes, and writing – writing into the night. And wisdom being parted to others." How right she is. But there is no mention of Jamie.

After the meeting I tell her of my fears regarding my daughter. She looks up at me and says, "As a medium there is a lot I can't say. But what I can tell you is that I see your mother on the other side and a silver thread to your daughter. Your mother is there for her. Part of Jamie has already gone to her."
I leave the meeting comforted and much happier, for I know in my heart that we have lost part of Jamie.

5th September – Thursday

As days pass, I am experiencing terrible problems with Max. He is getting angry, and says 'no' to everything.

Eddie rings, "Ange, do you know where Jamie is? Kim has found jewellery and clothes missing and says Jamie has taken them."
"Are you sure?" I ask. "I can see a big question mark before me," I tell him.
"And we must remember Kim is also an addict...and addicts tell lies."
I phone Sindy, to ask if she has seen Jamie, but she hasn't. As we chat she tells me, "Jamie puts her life in jeopardy. Not only is she in danger from the guys, but from the girls who are jealous because she is good at her work."

6th September – Friday

8.00 a.m: Sindy rings, excited. "Someone saw Jamie on the beat after midnight yesterday, and she's okay."
"Thanks Sindy, I really appreciate you doing this," I tell her, and I can relax. We must go forward and live our lives, trying not to worry. Next time Jamie makes contact, she will be on a terrible downer or very ill.

For the past week, since Jamie left Stratford, Kim has been ill and has withdrawn into herself. She is frightened to step outside the front door. Lacking the company of young people, she admits to being very lonely, homesick – and is missing Jamie. "At least we could talk and understand each other," she says.
Kim phones me, sounding desperate, "Ange, I'm leaving Eddie. I feel stifled and can't take any more."

Concerned, I ring her health visitor who is sympathetic and understanding. I also call on the co-ordinator of a organisation supporting parents with young children. She says, "I must say, I haven't come across this problem over the years."

How I remember her saying those exact words to me a couple of years ago, when I had offered to be a volunteer, should an addict or prostitute require my support. She sharply made it clear no such problems had cropped up over the years, and are unlikely to.
At that time I turned away in tears, hurt at her ignorance. Professionals always consider they are qualified and know best. All the indications, a couple of years ago, were that we had a serious drug problem looming up in this area, and no one was prepared to acknowledge it.

Here today, I am faced with a crack and heroin addict, ex-prostitute, with children and another baby due in 5 weeks. Desperate, cold turkeying, depressed, and on the verge of becoming homeless, she has no-one to support her but me, and urgently needs help. But who is there? Everyone has buried their heads in the sand saying, "It's not likely to happen here in this quiet market town."

I ring the health visitor who is unconcerned. I tell her firmly of my experience with Jamie's pregnancies and my fears about Kim's condition, and say she must listen to me – things are very serious.

The health visitor and midwife finally agree to investigate and visit Kim. It becomes apparent, with only five weeks left to go, Kim has had no blood tests or hospital check-ups. She took heroin only two weeks ago, and is on methadone. The baby will have to go into the special care unit, in case it goes into withdrawal.

17th September – Tuesday

After three weeks' silence, Jamie finally makes contact and sounds very bright, much to my relief. "I'm fine," she tells me. "I'm working and staying with my friends, Suki and Lester."
"Are you still using?" I ask
"Yes. I've lost loads of weight. But I am pleased about that."
I agree to meet her at the weekend and she gives me her address.

21st September – Saturday

Joy and her daughters join Max and myself. As we pull up in the car park, Jamie comes bouncing over from the flats. Turning to me, Joy remarks, "This is the first time I've seen Jamie when she seems right and fits into her surroundings." She looks scruffy; her face is pale and spotty, with long blonde hair tangled and untidy. Her short-sleeved shirt, black slim jeans, and strappy high-heeled shoes, reveal a very skinny Jamie.

As I greet her with a kiss, her first words are, "Don't you think I look better now I've lost weight. I'm a size 8." Jamie was a size 14 three weeks ago when she left Stratford. It is a shock to see her so thin.
We drive to McDonald's and Jamie says, "I'm starving. I shall have a double cheeseburger, chips, apple pie, ice cream and sauce."
"How on earth do you keep so slim?" asks Joy who has a weight problem.
"Well," says Jamie, "I recommend working, taking loads of drugs, and three McDonald's a week. Guaranteed to lose a stone." Joy and I sit on

another table while Jamie eats with the little ones. "No-one would ever guess that Jamie used half a hour ago," says Joy, as we look over to Jamie laughing and playing with the children.

She gives Max a cuddle but the usual warmth isn't there any more. I see the stranger and become uneasy.
I tell Jamie, "Max has been so unhappy and aggressive since you lived in Stratford. Kim and Eddie will never know how they devastated our lives even more by their irresponsible actions. You disappeared from Stratford without saying goodbye to Max. It is vital you cuddle him and say goodbye properly now." I tell her.
Casually she mentions, "I've been with Clinton and see him nearly every day," (her violent ex-boyfriend, now out of prison). This is bad news, especially when she informs me he is now a heroin dealer.

Even though it is freezing hard outside tonight, Jamie says she will work. We drop her off at the flats and wait. Suddenly, five minutes later, a new-look Jamie comes prancing out of the flats. Jamie the prostitute makes her entrance, changed and ready for work. Her fair curly hair falls shoulder length, contrasting against the black jumper and mini-skirt, black tights and Doc Martin boots. She stands under the glow of a lamp post to light her cigarette. "Can you take me down the road?" she asks, and jumps into the car.
As we drop Jamie off, she quickly hugs Max saying, "Me love you."

He turns to her saying, "I'm going to miss you mummy and want you to stay." She seems in a hurry to get off, giving her son little attention. As I kiss and hug this cold, hard stranger, I realise there is little of the real Jamie present. I glance in my mirror as I drive off. She is already walking along the pavement looking for business.

"Have you ever experienced a 'silent sob'?" I ask Joy. "I've just had one. It's an uncontrollable movement of the lungs and rib cage, as in crying. I haven't cried properly for nearly eight years."
Joy nods, "Yes, I know what you mean."
We agree Jamie looks reasonably well. But, because she has lost so much weight in the past three weeks, I fear what is going to happen in the next three weeks? Today has been a good day for us all and we must enjoy it, not knowing what is around the corner. At least I have peace of mind that she has said goodbye to Max, and I am sure he will be much happier for it.

7th October – Monday

This morning I chat to a prison officer who worked in a couple of prisons with Jamie. "Yes, I knew Jamie well but we didn't get on."
He recalls, "In the morning she could be a lovely person but by afternoon she changed and was evil. Jamie was always talking about her son."
I tell him, "I am fed up with the media. The last interview I did they were trying to sensationalize, and get information from me, on drugs in Jamie's prison." "But there are plenty getting in," he says.

10th October – Thursday

11.00 p.m: I leave Joy's house and drive through the red light district to see if there is any sign of Jamie. It is three weeks since we last saw her. I need to know if she is well and how thin she is. The streets are deserted and there is no sign of her.

13th October – Sunday

3.40 a.m: The phone rings. "Mum it's Jamie." Things must be desperate, phoning at this time of night.
"Jamie, are you okay?"
"No," she replies weeping. Mum, can I come to stay tomorrow night? Just until Monday morning. I can then go for detox."
"No," I say firmly. It is so hard to go against my natural instinct but I have to be firm
"Why not?" she asks in tears.
"Because I can't cope emotionally, or with the effect it will have on Max.
"Why don't you contact Joy? She said only recently, 'Tell Jamie to ring if she ever needs a bed for the night'."
Jamie agrees to contact her in a few hours.
"Did you get my clothes from the rehab?" she asks.
"Yes, but there appears to very little – only two bags."
Jamie bursts out, "Oh no, I haven't got any clothes now. I've lost everything, absolutely everything."
My heart is unusually hard this time. "Jamie, you have lost your clothes so often," I remind her, but she takes no notice and continues to shout down the phone hysterically.

We talk for nearly an hour and conversation isn't easy. Jamie assures me she is okay, still using crack and brown and wants to get away from the area.
"I want to go for detox," she says.

But how can I take her seriously when she gave up rehab after a period of only eight days?

As we say goodbye, Jamie agrees to phone Joy.

It is odd – for the first time my adrenalin isn't rushing. I put off the light, turn over and go straight to sleep. In the past, after such a call, I would lie awake for hours. Something has changed within me and there is a distance between us as never before.

10.30 p.m: Jamie phones, much happier – she is staying at Joy's tonight.

14th October – Monday

I call over to Joy's. She tells me that Jamie can stay with her for a short while, just until she can organise council accommodation.

Jamie's body is covered in spots, which she tries to hide with make-up. She admits to having had heroin last night.

I drop her off at probation, and she stands at the bottom of the steps glancing at her watch. "I think I'll pop to the Benefits office first," she says. I know, for sure, this means Jamie won't get to probation today.

16th October – Wednesday.

I am fifty-two today. "Happy Birthday Mum," says Jamie. "I've got a present when I see you."

"Have you been to probation?" I ask.

"No, but I'm going to."

I tell Jamie, "Kim has had a beautiful daughter. The baby is small but fortunately she is showing no signs of withdrawal." We are all very relieved.

18th October – Friday

Jamie is still covered in spots and says, "I'm not touching drugs anymore. I'm on methadone."

She can't wait to give me my birthday present – a beautiful basket of bath oil and soap.

As Jamie parades around in new clothes, I enquire "Shoplifted?"

"Of course not," she laughs. "And I've got receipts to prove it. Ask Joy." Jamie's new attire, including a long skirt, gives her a sophisticated look.

"Have you been to probation?" I enquire.

"I'm going this afternoon," she says.

Crackhead

As I listen to Jamie, I realise all my feelings have gone. Guilt comes over me. I should not be feeling like this about my daughter. I have always said I will be there for her. Now, after nearly eight years of heartache and stress, I have changed and my heart is hard. I have learned to say, "No."

19th October – Saturday

"Mum, I haven't had any crack for ages," she proclaims excitedly. I last had crack on Sunday and brown on Tuesday. I'm really pleased with myself."
I smile. Jamie talks as if she hasn't used for months.
"Congratulations," I say, finding it very difficult to do so, knowing how often she has let herself and us down.

21st October – Monday

Jamie rings. She is bubbling with excitement and tells me of the new clothes she has bought. I can hear the same Jamie who was on TV, when she was adamant she wasn't using – but she was. We have a long way to go for me to be convinced she is now drug free.
Joy says Jamie is doing marvellously well but understands when I tell her I have no hope left.

22nd October – Tuesday

I hear from Jamie. She has bought more clothes.
"How can you afford them?" I ask.
"It's easy," she says. "I take a taxi from Joy's at eight in the evening, work for £60, which is all I need. And then, an hour later, I get one of the punters to drop me off home, saving me £5 in taxi fare.
"Don't you think that's dangerous?" I ask her.
"It's okay. I've told Joy that if I'm not home by midnight, to phone the police."

28th October – Monday

I speak to the probation officer. There is a warrant for Jamie's arrest with the police, for her non-attendance, but her licence runs out on the 23rd November.

Jamie phones. "Mum, the housing department have given me a flat. Very excited, she reads out a list of things she has bought for it. "I'm working very hard and it's nice to have these things rather than waste

my money on drugs. I went to see the flat today and it's lovely. There are two bedrooms and the decor isn't bad."
Jamie leaves me breathless.
"Where is she putting all the things she has bought?" I ask Joy.
"Under my bedroom window," she replies.
Jamie says she has been to see her drug counsellor. "She's very pleased with me and says I'm opening up, saying what I really feel."

30th October – Wednesday

"Because I've been on drugs so long, I've decided perhaps I could do a counselling course," Jamie tells me on the phone. It sounds good but how I wish I could be more enthusiastic. There have been so many promises, hopes and intentions over the past eight years, and many let downs. Maybe she will do it this time but I cannot look beyond today.
"Hopefully I get the keys in a few days," she says. "I will be getting a bed for the spare room so you can come and stay." Until it actually happens, I am conditioned to take everything with a pinch of salt.

I call to see Kim this afternoon. She looks so calm and serene cuddling her baby, and there is an aura of great happiness. After such drug abuse in the womb, it is a miracle her child has turned out so beautiful and perfect.
I have seen it all before, when Jamie was heavily addicted while expecting Angel. Yet her baby survived, healthy, beautiful, active and very bright. But, I wonder what unforeseen damage lies within those innocent little bodies, which may develop in years to come?

31st October – Thursday

I ring Joy and off load, voicing my feelings about Jamie. "I don't believe in her anymore. I have no hope left. Jamie lied to me, saying she saw probation a few days ago. She has had flats over and over again, but in the end it always go wrong."
Joy promises to have a word with Jamie; although I think she really believes Jamie will get her act together this time. In a few months, I am sure Joy will look at Jamie in a different light.

2nd November – Saturday

I voice my concerns, "Joy, I'm worried about Jamie going into a flat on her own. She's going to get very lonely and depressed. She hasn't any contact with many of her friends and doesn't know anyone in the area. There's a good chance we won't know if anything happens to her. She's in danger if she takes clients back, which she intends to do. I fear for Jamie's safety and feel something dreadful is going to happen."

4th November – Monday

Jamie chats excitedly about the things she has bought and is keen to show me the flat. I warn her of the dangers if she takes punters there. "Mum, every time I go with a punter, I put myself at risk. I have to do it for the money."
After putting the phone down, I reflect on what she said on TV...

"A step on the wrong toes, I could be dead. If I take the wrong sort of drug I could be dead. Or if I get into the wrong car if I was working the streets one night, I could end up dead. I think each day as I wake up, this could be my last day. Each time I go out on the streets, it could be the last time I go out there."

6th November – Wednesday

I arrive at Joy's, and Jamie talks endlessly about her new clothes and things for the flat. She looks brilliant, really healthy, and is dressed in a slinky black dress.
I feel really poorly today, and the tears well up, but Jamie doesn't notice. Joy holds my hand and gives me a hug. "I've never seen you like this before, Angela. Are you alright?" she asks.
Joy says, "I will have a word with Jamie. The way she is speaking to you is appalling."

Jamie can't wait for me to see her fourth floor flat. The rooms are spacious and decor reasonable; the sun shines through the large living room window, giving a warm, homely atmosphere to the place...I like it.

She is proud, having bought so much in less than two weeks, and stresses, "I've had to work very hard for it." Like most youngsters today, she has to have everything immediately regardless of any danger she puts herself in to get it.

Jamie is very hyper and tense at present, which is creating an atmosphere and putting a distance between us.

8th November – Friday

"I am frightened but can't explain why," I tell Joy. "What will happen when Jamie is in the flat? Every day now, you provide her with proper meals and you are there when she needs a listening ear. Once in the flat, she will be back to takeaways or, more than likely, will be eating nothing. She is getting very unreliable and you know what that means."

"I must admit," says Joy, "now Jamie has been with me a while, I can see what she's really like. She has only had toast and coffee all day."
"Do you think she's using?" I ask.
"Well, Jamie didn't come home until late this evening, after being out ages," says Joy. "I'm not happy. She didn't get to the social offices yesterday because she felt unwell."

Jamie seems to be feeling ill every day – I know she is using.

11th November – Monday

"Mum, I've had my hair cut into a bob and it's blonde now," says a bubbly Jamie. "I've got a new punter. He gave me £200." Jamie sounds very happy and excited. "He even gave me a gold bracelet."

Joy tells me Jamie is frightened to work her usual beat because some guy is after her, and has decided to work in a city close by.

15th November – Friday

Kim and Eddie call at Joy's this afternoon. Kim admits to Joy that she has found the items she thought Jamie had stolen.
I remember the big question mark I saw before me when Eddie told me of the theft. Thank goodness I have been proven right.
But I am annoyed with Jamie for losing a £250 suit, which she borrowed from Kim.

Over the past couple of days Jamie has been scared to leave the house and go to work. She must be in real trouble.

16th November – Saturday

I am exhausted from Jamie's constant talking – my head buzzes as we sit on the bare floor of her new living room, surrounded by boxes of flat-pack furniture, household items and her double bed.

"Something just clicked in my head," says Jamie. "I knew I had to get away from everyone and make something of my life. I've done all this myself in two weeks," she says, hardly pausing for breath. "I've worked so hard and have receipts for everything. I need people to believe in me after letting them down so often in the past. I want Max and my other children to be proud of me."

18th November – Monday

It is freezing tonight and I think about Jamie working the streets. She is desperate for money to do up her flat. But is it all worth it? She is surrounded by crack and heroin and I pray she has the strength to turn a blind eye.
She travels regularly by train to work and rings me at 10.15 p.m. She has made over £100 and is going home early.

21st November – Thursday

"How do you cope with the thought of your daughter out there, working as she does?" asks Joy. "I would find it very difficult if she was my daughter."
"I push it to the back of my mind," I tell her. "I suppose it's nature's way of surviving."
Jamie says, "Mum, I've now been off drugs for six weeks, and done it because I want to. I am so happy...the happiest I've ever been. Mum, are you proud of me? I know it has got to be me who does it."

26th November – Tuesday

I contact the social worker. "What's happening about the children?" I enquire.
"Not a lot," she replies. "There isn't any money available until April next year." I am furious and immediately write to the director of social services, with a copy to my M.P. – Ben has been in care three years this month!

27th November – Wednesday

I call at Joy's this evening. Jamie is preparing to go to work and tells me she has a nicer type of client, more up-market. Ready for work, she is dressed in a white silver glitter short-sleeved polo ribbed jumper and over-the-knee white socks. These are held up with ribbons tied in bows. I notice how bonny Jamie is looking.

As I drop her off at the station, I hug her and say, "Jamie, take care."
Jamie is getting unreliable again. She talks of going over to clean her flat
but hasn't bothered. She has made no effort to arrange for her second
hand cooker and fridge to be delivered, which I bought her for Christmas.

1st December – Sunday

Things have become impossible as far as my involvement with Kim and
Eddy is concerned. I write to say I will no longer be seeing them because
I cannot tolerate the lies and aggression – coping with one drug addict
is enough for me. I foresee many problems ahead for this couple in the
coming months.

While I decorate the flat Jamie tells me, "I don't like working any more.
Suppose it's because I'm not using." Jamie admits she took crack and
brown last week when she met another of her old associates. She seems
surprised I am not annoyed with her.
"What's the point of getting mad. No matter what I say, you will take it
if you want to."

"Mum, I want to prove myself a good mum to Max. "I wish I had got
my act together earlier then all this would never have happened with
Angel and Ben. When I'm settled I think I'll have another baby. I'll find
a guy, but there must be no ties."
I reflect over the past eight years during which time Jamie has had three
births, a miscarriage, and abortions. Will she ever stop to think of the
heartbreak and suffering she causes to the children she has borne? I pray
there will be no more.

She talks of the new patch she is working. "A black pimp tried to
pick me up on Saturday night. He asked who I was with and, when
I told him 'Dexter', the guy immediately left me alone. He didn't
know that Dexter is in prison. He thought I was seventeen and
inexperienced, but when I told him I am twenty four he soon changed
his attitude."

8th December – Sunday

"Mum, I made £275 last night," says Jamie very excited. I find it
surprising how much she makes in such a short time.

Almost Christmas – Joy is tripping over Jamie's things, as well as Christmas presents.

It is time for Jamie to move out. However, I can see Jamie is reluctant – it must be scary, the thought of moving into a large flat on her own and leaving the company of a large family.

We load her things into my car, and stay two nights at the flat while we work like Trojans. Jamie is very poorly with asthma, and struggles on as we go to town, in the Christmas rush, to collect flat-pack furniture and organise carpets.

I offer to buy £35 worth of fresh food and store cupboard items. Until Jamie has the cooker connected, I provide her with a single ring camping gas stove.

10th December – Tuesday

Jamie's phone is connected. She is thrilled to have a life line to the outside world and I feel happier I can contact her. While she assembles the furniture, I decorate. She has bought a second-hand suite today.

Towards evening Jamie gets very ratty and on edge. This happens every time I see her, and I am getting suspicious.

12th December – Thursday

I am worried because Jamie doesn't answer the phone. Eventually, when she does she says, "I'm sleeping all the time. Even the alarm and phone don't wake me up. I sleep all day, go to work, and then sleep again."

She tells me, "Mum, I've laid my carpet and it looks fabulous."

13th December – Friday

When I arrive at the flat, Jamie says she is short of money and prepares herself for work tonight.

First the perfect make-up: then she steps into a black flared underslip which comes just below her bottom, and puts on a black short sleeved polo jumper. Over-the-knee black socks, and black patent mid-calf heavily strapped boots complete her outfit. For warmth, on this bitterly cold night, she puts on a cashmere coat and white wool fur trimmed hat. A taxi calls to collect a very sophisticated and pretty woman.

16th December – Monday

"Angela, I have the police here looking for Jamie. They want a word with you," says Joy very worried.

The policewoman explains, "A punter has reported theft from his flat, by a prostitute calling herself Jamie. He says she was a skinny drug addict."

"But Jamie is very plump and on methadone," I tell her.

"We can't get a reply from her flat," says the officer. "She has seven days to report to the station otherwise we will arrest her." I explain it is difficult to get hold of Jamie because she sleeps so heavily.

Jamie rings me. She is very puzzled after speaking to Joy, claiming to know nothing of the incident and wonders if someone has set her up. An interview with the police has been arranged.

20th December – Friday

Jamie phones, weeping and in a terrible state. "Mum, they're keeping me in the cells overnight, because of the warrant for not attending probation." I try to quieten her down and point out, "Jamie, it's your own fault. How many times have Pat and I reminded you to attend and you ignored us? At least you haven't been arrested for the robbery."

"Thank goodness, they've dropped all charges for the robbery, because it was obvious it wasn't me," she says. "Mum, can you come to court tomorrow morning?"

21st December – Saturday

Jamie appears in court looking awful, colour drained from her worried face. She tells me she is scared she will be sent down. After a very quick hearing the case is adjourned. The solicitor assures us Jamie will be fined rather than sent to prison.

She appears in her beautiful cashmere coat, which now looks like a bundle of rags. "I slept on it in the cells overnight," she says. "The policewoman says I've changed. Usually I settle quietly in the cells, but this time I couldn't sleep and paced up and down. I was really scared I'd go to jail and lose my flat."

"Trouble is, more and more I don't want to go out at night," says Jamie. "My flat is cosy and I just want to stay by the fire."

24th December – Tuesday. Christmas Eve

During the morning Max and I take presents over to Ben and Angel.

Linda, the foster mum, is curled up in a chair very poorly. I feel sorry for her as the children run around, noisy and very excited with the prospect of Father Christmas's visit tonight.

Ben is nearly four, and gets on very well with Max.

Angel, nearly two, continually beams from ear to ear. She is a real character, with her tight black curly hair in three bunches.

As I drive home to Stratford, I wonder sadly, what 1997 will have in store for them?

Jamie is staying with us over the Christmas holiday. When we collect her she looks wonderful and is buzzing with excitement. She has bought Max loads of presents and is longing for Christmas Day. For the first time in five years she will watch him open his presents.

Before leaving the flat, I throw out much of the food from the fridge which is bad or out of date. It would appear, apart from malt loaf and biscuits, little else I bought three weeks ago has been touched. It doesn't surprise me because I have seen it all before – but I suppose this time I thought there was a glimmer of hope.

"I've got a craze for chocolate Maltesers," she says, "and even had to get up in the middle of the night craving for them." Empty packs are strewn everywhere around the flat.

We spend a happy Christmas Eve with Jamie's father, and visit my son and his family. They relax and chat, enjoying the Christmas atmosphere. Jamie is bright eyed, alert and looks very smart. Everyone meeting her over the past few hours says she looks brilliant. Upon our return home, Jamie plays draughts with Max and her dad late into the evening. She looks so pretty and acts very normal. I am happy at long last she is making such an effort and it is wonderful to have her company.

Jamie has gone over the top on the toys for Max. I tried to persuade her not to spoil him and tell her, "Showing your love, and being there for him, is more important," but she doesn't listen.

For the past few weeks, an excited Jamie has talked of going to church on Christmas Day, which I am really looking forward to.

25th December – Wednesday. Christmas Day

Max excitedly opens the presents in his stocking while Jamie watches, snuggled up in bed and yawning all the time. She falls back to sleep and eventually gets up at 3.00 p.m., after pressure from me.

There is no going to church in the end, no helping me to prepare the meal as promised, or spending time with her son...I am shattered.
Once downstairs, and on a high from methadone, she talks non-stop saying, "I'm so excited. This is the best Christmas I've ever had."

Shortly, after unwrapping the rest of the presents and eating her Christmas dinner, Jamie lies across the settee, sleeping on and off for the rest of the day and evening.

I am so disappointed. It has proved very quiet and lonely without her company, for Max and me. We could have made alternative arrangements to see family and not been on our own.

Max's father, Mikey, hasn't bothered to make contact with his son – no card, present or phone call. He is so unreliable. The same thing happened last year when he didn't make contact for a further eight months. Max asks why he hasn't heard from his daddy.

26th December – Thursday. Boxing Day

When Jamie gets up at lunchtime I encourage her to come for a walk up to the hills and woods nearby. She moans constantly and is very grumpy with Max, leaving him to run ahead through the woods.

Back at home, Jamie positions herself on the settee and sleeps or watches TV. She gets very snappy with Max. Her aggression continues into the evening, as it has done for weeks.

27th December – Friday

At one o'clock Jamie is still in bed and I persuade her to get up. Bleary eyed, she walks around like a zombie.
Max is disappointed and says, "All mummy has done is sleep in bed, sleep on the settee, and smoke."

There is a glimmer of the old Jamie late afternoon, when she decides to make a blouse from an old sheet and run it up on the sewing machine. She presents me with a card, thanking me for having her, and for helping her to move into the flat. It touches me because there is a glimmer of my daughter who, deep down, has a heart of gold.

It dawns on me – we have gone a full circle in eight years. Nothing has changed – her looks, make-up, clothes, T.V. and the sleeping--just as if she is stuck in a time warp. "You are just like a sixteen year old kid," I tell her, although she seems more like fourteen, acting like a big sister to Max.

"I feel like sixteen," she giggles.

I recall the first parents' support group I attended in 1993, when they stated, "A drug user stops maturing at the age he or she starts using." I now realise how right they were.

"Did you have a good Christmas?" someone asks Max on the phone. Stone silence, and then he replies, "No."

I feel so unhappy as I look at his sad face. I have worked so hard to make this a happy Christmas for us all.

28th December – Saturday

Linda, the foster mum, is suddenly rushed into hospital very seriously ill.

Ben and Angel are moved hurriedly to Linda's friends, also foster parents. The children are familiar with their new surroundings and I couldn't wish for a better replacement foster home.

With a sigh of relief, I drive Jamie back over to her flat. As Jamie surveys her cosy fully furnished flat, she beams with happiness saying, "When I was staying at a friend's, and things were really bad, I used to lie on the bed dreaming and planning out how I'd have my flat one day. But I never thought I would ever do it."

"I'm proud of what you've achieved in getting everything together," I tell her. "At long last you have possessions and a home to put them in."

Looking at a large picture on the wall of a country scene which her dad gave her for Christmas, she says, "I'm really pleased dad kept in touch." It has meant so much to her.

I put up the living room curtain poles. Jamie attaches the curtains, switches on the T.V. and lamp, and settles in for the night. She intended to work tonight, but with freezing temperatures outside she decides to remain in the comfort of her flat.

As she settles in for the night she talks about her past criminal activities. "I can't believe they haven't got anything against me anymore," says Jamie. "I still want to hide when I see police."

31st December – Tuesday. New Years Eve

The Director of Social Services has not replied to my letter of November, regarding Angel and Ben.

Over Christmas, John Major announces sweeping changes in adoption; he says children must be adopted more quickly, and without delays caused through political correctness. He proposes the setting up of adoption agencies. Unfortunately, it is probably too late for my grandchildren.

Joy and I have difficulty in contacting Jamie by phone. She says she is sleeping deeply all the time, and only gets up for work. I suggest her medication may need changing and she agrees to make an appointment to see someone – but I know she won't.

Jamie says she will be working tonight. The ground is covered with snow and there is a heavy frost. It is painful for me to think of her on the streets on this bitterly cold night. I try to blank it out.

I leave the old year behind, knowing my crisis will continue.

Midnight

"Happy New Year Mum."
"Thanks Jamie. A Happy New Year to you. Let's hope 1997 won't be as bad as last year."
Jamie laughs, "No, it can't possibly be...

Crackhead

Retaliation – 1997

1st January - midnight

Jamie phones, desperate and sobbing, "Mum, I've been robbed by a punter in my flat – he's taken all my money. The police don't want to know."
Some weeks ago, I had warned Jamie this would happen, but she didn't listen.

During the first few days of the New Year, the weather continues to be exceptionally cold at minus 10°. Jamie makes me smile when she tells me, "I put plastic carrier bags on my feet inside my boots when I'm working."

On the 3rd January, Linda, the foster mum, dies from cancer. Ben and Angel have lost the only person they have ever known as their mummy. I am so grateful to Linda and John for the wonderful start in life they have given the children – lots of love and stability.

But what will happen to my grandchildren now? This unexpected trauma in their little lives has thrown everything into disarray. The new foster parents will be equally as good, I am sure. It is the thought of Ben and Angel having to move soon to yet another family which really upsets me. If I had health and youth on my side I would move heaven and earth to keep them.

Joy and I are worried about Jamie's state of mind and the fact she sleeps all the time. Joy tells me, "She brought a guy around here and while we were chatting he said, 'Jamie has her heart in the right place – but where's her head?' We all know exactly what he means."
Now the flat is fully furnished, Jamie is getting restless and bored. She says she needs to do something, perhaps go to college, and asks if I will go with her to a college open day. But she doesn't mention it again.

One morning I receive a call from Jamie, very upset because she has dropped her methadone and smashed the bottle. There is no means of replacement until her next script, which is due in four days time. Over the next few days Jamie does cold turkey. She rings distressed, "Mum, I'm climbing up the wall and out of my mind."

I offer that she can come and stay for a few days, providing she doesn't zonk out all the time. When I arrive at the flat to collect Jamie, she looks dreadful, thin, pale, and very poorly.

A dealer knocks on her door with a bag of brown. Jamie wants me to watch her smoking, something I have never done before. First, she rolls foil to make a tube about the size of a cigarette. The heroin, £30 worth, looks like the amount of pepper one would liberally shake onto a meal. Jamie sprinkles it on a square of foil and holds a lighter under. Fumes rise as the heroin melts, turning black; she tips the foil back and forwards and the black sticky residue runs in lines.

At every inhalation of fumes (chasing the dragon), Jamie heaves almost to the point of being sick. Pulling a face, she says, "It's horrible." After about ten minutes the smoking ends, and she starts to look and feel much better.

She assures me she hasn't been using before, but I find three pieces of screwed up burnt foil in her waste bin.

Jamie comes back home and sleeps all weekend. She eventually admits to Joy and me that she needs psychiatric help. But when it comes to the crunch, a couple of days later, she decides she doesn't need help.

After a couple of days I take her back to her flat. In the past fortnight, since Christmas, Jamie hasn't touched the food in her store-cupboard. On the top of the fridge sits a pan of my homemade chicken soup, which has been there for two weeks. The cooker still hasn't been connected.

I receive a reply from social services regarding the delay in the children's adoption. As I expected, they have an answer for everything. But I know the truth because I have attended the adoption meetings – there has been a lack of finance and the children's files have been stuck in the middle of the pile.

At a recent meeting I learn things are now moving. Social services are due to advertise Ben and Angel towards the end of March, once money is available.

My suspicions are aroused when Jamie claims she went to court last week. I ring the courts, only to be informed Jamie didn't attend a hearing. There is now a warrant out for her arrest. Jamie continually courts trouble.

A few days later her flat door is kicked in by a so-called 'friend'. The council replace the broken door with a supposed secure heavy metal one.

On Max's seventh birthday, the 21st January, Jamie forgets to turn up here as promised. Max runs to the window looking for his mummy and is very disappointed when she doesn't show up. She promises to come the following day at lunchtime, and meet him from school, but arrives at 6.30 p.m. for just one hour. Again she has let him down.

Max's father doesn't bother to acknowledge his birthday either. How can he be so heartless?

Jamie is no longer bubbly and shows little emotion. She finally admits she is back on crack and heroin. When we call to see her at the flat she looks so ill, her face is pale and puffy. Her diet consists mainly of yoghurt, malt loaf and chocolate biscuits. She assures me she has an appointment with the doctor at the drug agency, but I discover she hasn't.

Very excited, Jamie rings to tell me a young lad has moved into her flat. I am wary, but she assures me, "Mum, it's okay and with no ties. His mother lives in a flat below. He has reorganised my living room and is cooking my meals." But I suspect if he is eating Jamie's food?

On Jamie's twenty-fourth birthday, the 5th February, I receive a phone call at midnight from the police station. They are keeping Jamie in custody overnight on the warrant for not attending probation once again.

Later in the day, once she is released, Max and I call over to her flat. Jamie is feeling very sick, restless and aggressive, and looks awful...she is definitely using. At her request, for her birthday present, I take over an assortment of food. As I carefully choose food in the supermarket, suitable for cooking on a single ring, I have a feeling her lodger will eat most of it.

The following day, at 6.30 a.m., I receive a call from Jamie in custody. She is totally off her head swearing. Babbling on, she tells me, "I was arrested for soliciting. The policewoman grabbed me by the wrists and hurt me, so I dug my elbows in her ribs. I'm suing the police for rough treatment and have got two witness statements." She does nothing more about taking up the case.

Jamie's lodger is causing her big problems. He turns out to be a heroin addict, and sold the birthday food I gave her for drugs. He has informed Jamie that his brother, just out of jail, is also moving into the flat. Jamie has had enough and arranges for some guys to call at midnight and evict the two lads.

I tell her, "Jamie, I'm worried they will retaliate, possibly by harming you or fire bombing the place." "Mum, don't worry," she says. "They won't dare do anything. They're scared and know they will be beaten to pulp if they touch me or the flat."

Over the next few days Jamie stays with friends because she is unwell. I am getting worried and tell Joy, "Jamie has no purpose in life except drugs. My biggest fear is that she may try to commit suicide."

19th February – Wednesday

4.00 a.m: The phone rings. "M...u...m. I'm going to kill myself," sobs Jamie uncontrollably, hardly able to talk. She's hysterical.
"They've taken everything...everything has gone from the flat.
I have nothing left...I'm going to kill myself...then you won't have to worry about me any more."

I try to keep calm. I have never been faced with threatened suicide before. While I get my thoughts together, I listen. "I can't go on anymore," she sobs..."I want to be dead."

A guy comes to the phone, says he is a neighbour, and the police are on their way.
"Mum, can you come over?" Jamie pleads.
I am reluctant, but wonder if I could ever forgive myself if she tries to commit suicide?
"Yes, I'll come over but in a couple of hours," I reassure her.
Jamie is relieved but continues to cry. She is so alone and desperate. Chances are she has been using tonight which makes things worse.

Trying to keep calm, I prepare for the unpredictable day ahead. I shower, eat a substantial breakfast, and take my medication – vital if I am to have the strength to keep going. As dawn breaks I wake up Max, tell him his mummy isn't feeling well, and we set off along the deserted roads. I am scared. What will I find? Where will Jamie go? I can't have her to live with me.

As I drive along the by-pass I pray, "Please God give me strength to get through this day." After dropping Max off at Joy's, I collect Jamie's friend and take her over with me to the flat. Warily we climb up the three flights of stairs. The heavy metal security door to the flat is ajar, the locks bent from the force of the break-in.

Jamie is now much calmer, huddled up in the corner of the settee. I give her a hug and she breaks down sobbing..."Mum, I've lost everything I so hard for."

As I look around, I see everything has gone: carpets, furniture, T.V., curtain poles, curtains, tables, bed and bedroom furniture, and Max's toys. In the kitchen the cutlery, china, and saucepans have gone; the cupboards are totally bare. Even the washing up liquid and loo rolls have gone. It is heartbreaking. The only things remaining are the cooker and fridge, her clothes, and the three piece suite.

A pile of heroin burned foil, cigarette ends and discarded lighters lie in the middle of the bare living room floor. Photos of Ben, Max and Angel have been flung into a corner, together with Jamie's personal papers.

"They've taken the picture dad gave me for Christmas", she sobs, "and the clown doll he bought me when I was little." She breaks down, "...and they've taken my sewing machine." After six years, Jamie has lost her precious sewing machine. Over the years it has been rescued from all over the country, but there is *no* chance of retrieval this time.

As I sit on the settee I notice the patchwork quilt, which she bought with the T.V. programme money, has also gone. She loved that quilt, and many a time she gave it to me to take back to my house, so she wouldn't lose it.

I take Jamie's friend back home and am horrified when she tells me the lies Jamie has told her – that she sees Ben and Angel regularly, and visited them with me last week; Jamie's father and myself didn't want her and sent her to boarding school at the age of four; I had snatched Max from her; and I have loads of money and recently bought a £3000 leather suite. This proves to me Jamie has a huge mental problem.

When I return, Jamie says Joy has phoned and offered accommodation until she can get another flat. I refuse to take her to Joy's until she has been to the hospital's psychiatric clinic for help. She agrees. The hospital doctor says she is surprised Jamie has been prescribed such a high dose of anti-depressants with methadone. The two are conflicting in Jamie's body and brain, resulting in deep sleep and suicidal tendencies. Jamie is pleased someone has understood and listened. The doctor tells Jamie she is welcome to go back at any time to talk through the pain and suffering in her life, once she has ..got stabilised on the methadone.

We rush to the doctor's surgery, situated amongst the high-rise flats, to organise Jamie's methadone. As we sit in the smoke-filled waiting room, she chats to girls she knows and seems so much at home. They talk of their children in care, drug use, being robbed, and going out working.

Jamie thanks me for everything and apologises for getting grumpy. "I am so tired and haven't eaten for weeks," she says yawning, and drops off to sleep in the car. I observe her pale, thin, spotty, scabby face and skinny hands. Once installed at Joy's, she zonks out on the sofa. I believe sleep is a great healer, and Jamie is in a great state of shock. Joy will cook her good wholesome meals and provide her with the warmth and companionship she desperately needs.

I arrange to meet my friend back at Jamie's flat in the evening, who is interested in purchasing the cooker. We agree £30, which enables Jamie to purchase tobacco and pay Joy for food for a couple of days.

Before closing the door of the flat for the last time, I sweep up the burned foil and stub ends. Otherwise it would be a bad reflection on Jamie if she applies for another flat. As I stand in the empty echoing room, I remember that same empty room in December before she moved in, when she was so full of hope. We are back to square one – Jamie has returned to live with Joy, with no possessions whatsoever except her clothes.

Jamie is out to the world and probably won't wake until mid-day tomorrow. How lucky she is to have Joy's support, without which I am sure things would be far worse. Now, at least for a few days, I shall be able to rest my body and mind...but what next? Jamie has already been looking this afternoon at furniture in catalogues for her next flat.

The following day I am surprised to see Jamie looks fantastic, bouncing back, and returning to her friends and working the streets once more. I am worried it is all happening too soon. She is in a state of shock and won't talk about the burglary.

I tell Jamie I can't face the thought of travelling over to see her anymore. From now on, she must come to see us. The robbery has had a devastating effect on me, as well as Jamie – particularly with the loss of her childhood possessions which were also so dear to me; and, of course, her precious sewing machine.

As the days pass, Jamie becomes unreliable and returns to crack and heroin. There is no sign of her making the effort to get another flat. For two days she hasn't returned home to Joy's – she has got herself into serious trouble with her drug associates.

Joy has been a tower of strength having Jamie back into her home. She is concerned, however, after some weeks, that Jamie shows no interest in getting new accommodation. Reluctantly, Joy tells Jamie she must show commitment to finding a place of her own as soon as possible.

The council give Jamie another flat. She is very excited, saying it is very cosy, has stairs, and is just like a little house.

With Joy's support, and that of the drug worker, Jamie goes back onto a methadone programme. She continues to work the streets to finance the furnishing of her new home, but states she hates doing it and hopes to give it up as soon as possible. Jamie is very scared of moving into the flat for fear of returning to drugs or having another robbery. There is no pressure on her to move out of Joy's home, now that she has shown commitment in getting another place. Joy is quite willing for Jamie to move out in her own time, thus giving her added confidence.

Crackhead

Reflections – 1997

Without Joy's support, I wonder if Jamie would still here today? I can't thank her enough for what she has done, giving Jamie a roof over her head, good food, companionship, encouragement and love. Joy's health is failing; life isn't easy for her with little girls to look after and sons who continue to use drugs. On top of all this Joy runs a drug help line for parents totally on her own.

The other day, I listened to Jamie talking to a youngster about her life. She said, "The trouble is, at the end of the day it all boils down to money. And I need money." As long as this is Jamie's philosophy in life, nothing will change. The only way she can get the large sums of money she needs is to work the streets, surrounded by drugs and danger.

As I look back over the years, I know I have done my best for Jamie. At the age of thirteen, she wrote an autobiography at school, in which she stated:

"I am small. I have to get people to notice me so I like to be outrageous.
I love adventure and challenge, and have a very vivid imagination.
I blow up at people easily and my close friends have learned to cope with my moods.
I love to be part of a group and lead things.
Whatever I plan never works out.
I am mischievous and like to wind people round my little finger.
I like to have clothes so I need lots of money.
Usually I am a nice person but can be nasty.
I can be silly and childish – and enjoy it!

This sums up my daughter Jamie today, eleven years later.

When Jamie was sixteen, she was paranoid; constantly looking over her shoulder, convinced she was going to be stabbed in the back. She made an appointment to see a doctor but didn't attend. This was in the very early days of her drug use. Maybe if she had sought help then, we wouldn't be where we are today. It is my opinion, and that of others, that Jamie is in desperate need of psychiatric help. But without her seeking that help, we cannot do any more for her.

I am lucky to have found Jamie's natural family and so many questions have been answered. I am convinced her genetic make-up has played an important part in how she turned out. No matter how hard I tried, Jamie says there is nothing more I could have done for her.

Although we have been through so much, I wouldn't have wanted things to be different. Jamie has always shown respect to me. She has never sworn at me personally, physically abused me, or stolen from me (apart from a few papers); and accepts the boundaries I draw between us. Many parents with children on drugs encounter problems which I have managed to escape.. I am very lucky. When things are good we are very close. Sadly those times are few and far between today.

I am sure Jamie knows in her heart that I have protected her children the best I can, from the perils of drugs. They will hopefully grow up to be decent living citizens, having had a secure and loving background... but then that is what Jamie had.

Through my experience with Jamie, I believe I am a better person, although it has been a long and very painful lesson. I have learned to accept people for what they are, not what I would like them to be. This applies in particular to Jamie and her friends.

Secondly, an addict's drug will always be their first love, before their family and friends. It is very difficult to understand why Jamie has abandoned such beautiful children. Deep down I know she loves them so much, but her drugs come first.

I have learned to put myself before Jamie. She must get on with her life and leave us alone. She has had all the love and support possible and if anything happens to her now, I must not reproach myself.

As a result of my being open and speaking out about my problem, other parents can discuss their fears and crises with me – they know I understand. I haven't got qualifications, nor am I a counsellor, but I can provide a unique understanding and knowledge from having been there and done it.

A parent has approached me recently – one of the mums who was standing in the playground of the junior school (end of February 1994), when I wanted to shout out about the 'real world'. Today her child, aged thirteen, is heavily into drugs and I am able to support her.

Many authorities at long last recognise there is a drug problem and now listen to us, the families of users. For too long we have been looked down upon, regarded with suspicion, and treated with the same contempt as the Drug abuser and criminal. Always, the abuser is given priority, before family, or what is best for the child. And yet it is us, the family and children, who are the victims. They take the drugs by choice. We have no choice.

I have seen improvements in the drug service; out-of-hours numbers are now quoted on the phone – after all, most crises happen during the night or weekends when drug agencies are closed.

Support for parents didn't exist years ago, and was something desperately needed by Joy, Pat and myself. There is now help; and support groups are recognised by agencies, the police, education, health departments and many more in this area.

Eight years on, my health has been badly affected and I merely exist from day to day – as most parents do whose children use drugs. It is difficult for me to take on board academic learning – my mind is blank. I love modern music but find it too painful to listen to. Wherever I go, whatever I do, I am reminded of Jamie.

It has been very lonely at times, even when there was support. In the end, it is only the parent who can make the final decision on what to do, when and how.

And what of Jamie and the future? When I read Joy's poem I know there must always be hope. She wrote it the first time she met Jamie...

An Oyster for Jamie

Deep below the ocean,
Warmed gently by the sun,
Things started into motion,
A life had just begun.

Enclosed inside its shell,
The sweet oyster slowly grew,
It seemed all was going well,
But no one really knew.

One day at first unnoticed,
In crept a piece of grit,
It was only small to start with,
And only hurt a bit.

The grit began to irritate,
The pain it got severe,
Drugs helped to stop the torture,
We couldn't see it from out here.

But please believe me Jamie,
You precious darling girl,
That one day if you wish it,
The grit could be a pearl.

JOY PALMER

End Piece – May 1997

At the beginning of May, as Jamie continues her methadone programme, she looks to the future with nervous enthusiasm, saying

At the moment I am finishing off my second flat, decorating and furnishing it. I found it all very hard at the beginning, after the burglary. It could either make or break me. I am too strong to be broken, so I've worked really hard and got there.

In the past three weeks I have had three cars; the first was a cheap car, but I had an accident; the second I returned to the person I bought it from – it was a load of rubbish; my third cheap car broke down. I am now saving for a better car now and am getting it 'all legal' with tax and insurance. Next week I start driving lessons.

I don't want to do anything illegal because I am trying to improve my life. I hardly work anymore, and hope to give it up in the future. I only go out when I need to.

In September I am changing my name and going to college, to do an access course in Arts, Humanities, and Business Studies, together with a counselling course. With this, I shall then go on to do a degree.

I cannot forget what has happened to me. I have had a very hard life. Reading this book, one might think I brought it upon myself. I don't think so. It was a series of events that happened, some good and some bad, but I would not have changed a thing. I have learnt about life the hard way – I've been there and done it.

I feel that I am very qualified to do what I want to do right now. But to be taken seriously I must get these qualifications. I am aiming to be a counsellor for drug addicts and working girls who want to 'get out'.

I was lucky. I had that support, and wish to say "thank you" to all those who have helped me to get where I am today.

Only time will tell if Jamie's ambitions will be fulfiled, but three weeks after she told me of her intentions, she still has not started those driving lessons.

Over the past few weeks I have been very lucky to meet two other grandmothers in a similar situation to myself, bringing up their grandchildren due to drug addiction. We can now support one another. I knew I was not on my own with the problem, but it has taken me six years to find others who have been what I have been through.

Recently, I have received support from a local social worker – something I have never had before. He has worked in large cities, dealing with families affected by crack and heroin. At long last here is someone working for authority who is on the same wavelength as myself. He understands the problems I face – a grandmother with a residence order for one grandchild, and two other grandchildren in care awaiting adoption.

Ben and Angel continue in foster care while social services try to find them a family. Recent advertisements for adoptive parents, placed in papers throughout the Midland's, had no response. Max and I continue to visit these two beautiful children, and the bond grows stronger between us every time we meet.

These days Max is a very well adjusted young lad, and feels secure with the routine of seeing his mother once a fortnight and, on the whole, his contact with her is happy and memorable.

On 27th May, Joy phones, sounding very subdued. "Jamie didn't come home last night," she says. After a second night has passed, without any sign or contact from Jamie, our fears grow for her safety. With every knock on the door and phone call, we anticipate the police.

After missing for two nights, Jamie eventually returns to Joy's. She phones me, saying "How I hate myself for what I have done." She tells me she went to Sindy's house, where she a cocktail of drugs, consisting of crack, heroin, Nitrazepam, Temazepam, DF118's, and injected speed ...all this within a period of 48 hours. When I tell her I am surprised she didn't overdose, Jamie says she has a high tolerance level. She assures me, "Mum, it was a one off, and I won't do it again." But the next night she fails to return to Joy's until dawn breaks, having used again.

On the 31st May, with blue skies and blazing sunshine, we relax under the shade of our favourite oak tree in the Memorial Park. As Max runs around playing on the grass, I ask Jamie about her relapse last week. She explains, "It is like two people inside me. One says 'I shan't take any drugs today,' ...and I do really well. But then, right at the last minute, the other person inside says, "Go on – just a little won't hurt, and it won't cost much,' ...and then I have some."

Jamie chats about the flat she moves into next week and her intentions to go to college in September. It would be wonderful for me to believe and hope she will achieve her ambitions. But I have been conditioned over the years not to look to the future, and to live each day as it comes. However, deep inside I am very scared.

Today is a good day ...really good. After all we have been through, Jamie and I are still friends and as we picnic with Max, there is lots of laughter and giggles. There is also sadness, as I look at Jamie's face and listen to her talk, for I see and hear the user once more.

But we are the lucky ones. I recently met the mother of a young prostitute who was murdered in 1993; and it makes me appreciate that I still have my daughter, and Max has his mother. I know that I have done everything possible for Jamie, and now she must get on with her life and leave us to get on with ours. She says there is nothing whatsoever I could have done to change the course of events.

There are so many parents out there who believe their children would *never* touch drugs. But how do they know? I didn't think this could possibly happen to my daughter, who had all the love, security and support, any child could wish for ...BUT IT DID!

I pinch myself – is this a dream I have been living? But then I come down to earth. In reality, I have been made aware that drugs, prostitution, and crime continue to increase, in cities and country areas alike. The government, authorities, parents and their children must be educated to cope with the ever-increasing effects drugs are having on our society. If not, we shall have failed future generations to come.

Crackhead

Acknowledgment

I should like to thank all those who have given their support to Jamie, her children, and myself over the years – especially the foster parents, Joy and Pat. Also, a big thank you to Gareth and Rosie, without whose help this book would still be just a diary.

My special gratitude goes to those no longer with us to read Crackhead:

AN ANONYMOUS KIDNEY DONOR

A young person, whose gift of life has given me the strength and health to be there for my family and other families affected by drugs – deceased 3.3.87

LINDA

A wonderful foster-mum who gave so much love to Ben and Angel while they were in her care – deceased 3.1.97, aged 47 years

LIZ

My good friend and neighbour who instigated my search for Jamie's natural mother – deceased 15.2.96, aged 41 years.

JO

A good friend, a drug user with a heart of gold – deceased 20.3.97, aged 36 years

Without their involvement in our lives, a very different story would be told. These people, and their influence on us as a family, will never be forgotten.

Crackhead

Glossary

Acid LSD –   Class A drug.

Acquired –   Shoplifted.

Brown –   Heroin. Class A drug.

Cannabis –   Class B drug. Also known as grass, draw, weed,
marajuana, etc.
Cannabis resin – Class A drug.

Chasing the –   Inhaling the burning fumes from heroin.
Dragon

Class of drug –   Legal classification under the Misuse of Drugs Act –
most severe penalty A, then B & C used for
determining penalties for possesion and supply.
Reflects perceived harm of drug.

Clean –   No longer using drugs.

Cocaine –   Class A drug derived from the coca leaf.

Coke –   Cocaine

Cold Turkey –   Physical withdrawal symptoms when coming off
Crack or Heroin.

Crack –   Class A drug made from cocaine which is treated with
chemicals to form small pieces of white waxy 'rocks'.
Crack is smoked. It can cause psychological
dependence and paranoid violent behaviour. Large
doses cause sleeplessness and convulsions. The effects
can be over in 12 minutes, leaving the user with
depression and anxiety. Heroin is often taken
afterwards to ... relieve the symptoms of 'coming down'?

Crackhead –   Person who smokes large quantities of Crack.

Crackhouse –   Main centre for dealing and smoking Crack.

Detox –   Detoxification. Period of becoming drug free.

DF118's –   Strong codeine based pain killers.

Draw –   Cannabis

Freebasing –   Smoking crack.

Front line –   Main street area for the supply of drugs.

Gear –   Heroin and other drugs.

Grass –   Cannabis.

High –   The effect of drugs on the user.

Methadone –   Prescribed heroin substitute.

Minder –   A person ordered by a pimp or dealer to follow, and watch, someone under their control i.e. prostitute.

Pipe –   Used for smoking mainly crack.

Rehab. –   Rehabilitation for drug dependency, usually residential

Rock –   Small pieces of crack cocaine, white and waxy.

Script –   Methadone prescription.

Smack –   Heroin.

Smackhead –   A person who uses large quantities of heroin.

Smoking –   Smoking drugs.

Stoned –   High on drugs.

Temazepam –   Tranquilliser (sleeping tablet)

Tripping –   Experience from taking LSD and other mind altering drugs.

Using –   The taking of drugs.

White –   Crack.

Withdrawal –   The effects of coming off the drugs.

Working –   Working as a prostitute

Yardies -   Drug dealers (men and women) mainly from Tivoli Gardens, Kingston, Jamaica.

V.O. -   Visiting order for prison.

THE NATIONAL DRUGS HELP LINE

0800 77 66 00

Crackhead